Dharmaśāstra
and
Social Awareness

Sri Garib Das Oriental Series No.—196

Dharmaśāstra and Social Awareness

Edited by

V.N. Jha

Sri Satguru Publications
A Division of
Indian Books Centre
Delhi - India

Published by:
Sri Satguru Publications
Indological and Oriental Publishers
A Division of
Indian Books Centre
40/5, Shakti Nagar,
Delhi-110007
(INDIA)

First Edition: Delhi, 1996

ISBN 81-7030-476-8

Printed at : Mehra Offset Press, New Delhi.

Printed in India.

Foreword

It is a matter of great pleasure to place in the hands of scholars, the present Volume which contains thirty research papers which were presented and discussed in the National Seminar on *"Dharmaśāstra and Social Awareness"*, at the Centre of Advanced Study in Sanskrit, University of Poona in 1994.

These articles are the best examples to show how the Dharmaśāstra literature pervades various aspects of Indian Social and Cultural Life. The Dharmaśāstra literature attempts to bring discipline in individual and social life in terms of values in which they believed in those days. Some values have been universal while others kept on changing in accordance with time. The impact of Vedic Culture can never be denied in the process of the Dharmaśāstra's attempt to bring order to the society.

Of all the types of literature in Sanskrit the Dharmaśāstra literature is very close to Indian Society. The present Volume is an attempt to highlight the social awareness reflected in the Dharmaśāstra literature. After late Mahāmahopadhyāya P.V. Kane, hardly there has been any serious attempt to project the contribution of Dharmaśāstra to Indian social and Cultural Life. It is hoped that the present Volume will inspire serious scholars to initiate serious research of Dharmaśāstra so that the best and relevant can be given to the modern society.

Indian Books Centre deserves our appreciation for bringing out this Volume. I hope the scholars in the field will welcome it.

V.N. Jha
Director,
Centre of Advanced Study
in Sanskrit,
University of Pune,
Pune - 411007.

Contents

1

Relevance of the study of *Dharmaśāstra*

Heramba Chatterjee Śāstri

At a stage of society where morality or spiritual values are dwindling at very fast pace (of. Manu, 1.81-82), presentation of arguments in favour of a *Śāstra* that is supposed to plead for the importance of *Dharma*, becomes rather difficult. It is deemed convenient to quote the introductory observations made by Professor J.D.M. Derrett, in his '*Dharmaśāstra and Jurudical Literature*' Otto Harrassowitz: Wiesbaden, 1973) where he looks at the question from the standpoint of law. In his own words:

"*Dharmaśāstra* means the science of righteousness and includes what the modern European understands by `law', without, however, exhausting that topic. The Asian idiom of norm-expression can easily be mistaken for law-teaching. The elaborate Indian texts dealing with legal procedure, no insignificant part of the dharmaśāstra could well mislead the readers into assuming that the śāstrīs were laying down rules analogous to the iura, or even the leges of the Romans. India, in reality, shares with Islam and with Judaism the belief that righteousness is an independent science of greater importance than mere day-to-day administration, and that the teacher's duty is to exhort, and to set standards of conduct based overtly upon transcendental considerations, recognising that decisions will be reached by judges, arbitrators or others, upon principles of ethics, or policy, but hoping that they would, if properly educated in righteousness, tend or endeavour to give just decision. . . The Indian teacher of the techniques of dispute-settlement would indeed be a specialist in a branch of the *Śāstra*; but unless he projected his study as a facet of the attainment of truth and enhancement of a supernatural order (not the mere quietening of complaints or enforcement of a royal policy) he would not be a dharmaśāstri". p.2.

In his *Some aspects of the Hindu view of Life According to Dharmaśāstra* (Oriental Institute, Baroda, 1952), p. 62, K.V.R. Aiyangar has attempted to present a comprehensive picture of what is to be understood by *Dharmaśāstra*. According to him:

"*Dharmaśāstra* is a comprehensive code to regular human conduct in accordance with the unalterable scheme of Creation, and to enable everyone to fulfill the purpose of his birth. The whole life of Man, considered both as an individual and as a member of groups as well as man's relation to his fellow men, to the rest of animated creation, to superhuman beings, to cosmos, generally and ultimately to God come within the purview of *Dharmaśāstra*. Among the duties that it lays down are both self-regarding and altruistic, those to the living and to the dead, to those who are alive and those who are yet to be born".

Dharmaśāstra has rightly been described as the queen of the sciences for the simple fact that it embodies in it several matters that inspire appropriately experts of different disciplines with its rich materials. Thus in its spiritual aspect this *Śāstra* in a systematic manner deals with the matters that are concerned with *Dharma* (spirituality). In the texts principally of Manu and Yājñavalkya, attempts have been made to define the nature of *Dharma* and its sources (see specially,*Manu*, II, 1-13; *Yāj*. 1.3, 6-8; interpretations of the verses by Medhātithi and Kullūkabhaṭṭa; as also by Vijñāneśvara. The *Dharmasūtras* of Gautama, Āpastamba, Baudhāyana, Vasiṣṭha in their introductory portions have the same topic of discussions. The commentators have not lost sight of the fact that the precepts of the Dharmaśāstra should be interpreted in adjustment with the exhaustive treatments of *Dharma* in the *Mīmāṃsā-Śāstra*. The duty-oriented aspect of *Dharma* has been stressed by Manu in his text. 1.107; 118).

The *Vyavahāra* section in the texts of Manu (chap. VIII; Yāj. II.), as also in the *Nāradasmṛti*, in the texts of Kātyāyana and Bṛhaspati are the wonderful gems that are counted as of enormous value for the legal experts to enquire into field of ancient Indian law.

For the sociologists and the anthropologists, the texts of *Dharmaśāstra* contain masses of materials and in this respect the text of Manu in different chapters are the best source-books.

The science of statecraft (*arthaśāstra*) is also to look for its source and support to the *Dharmaśāstra* (specially Manu, chap. VII).

In this way it may rightly be pointed out that the study of *Dharmaśāstra* is essential for a clear comprehension of all the stages and purposes of human life, namely, *Dharma, Artha, Kāma* and *Mokṣa*.

The designation *Dharmaśāstra* is appropriate and apposite in the sense that whatever may be the subject matter of the *Śāstra*, it is *Dharma*-oriented and because it is *Śruti*-based it may rightly claim to have unchallengable authority in the same form as the *Vedas* have, as pointed out by Manu:

Śrutis tu vedo vijñeyo dharmasāstraṃ tu vai smṛtiḥ/
Te sarvārteṣv amīmāṃsye tābhyāṃ dharmo hi nirvabhau/
II. 10

Yo 'vamanyeta te mūle hetuśāstrāsrayād dvijaḥ/
Sa sādhubhir bahiṣkāryo nāstiko vedanindakaḥ//II. 11

It is in this background that the importance of the *Dharmaśāstra* is to be understood.

For a clear understanding of the topic under discussion it is desirable to take note of the fact that the term *Dharmaśāstra*, presupposes a correct knowledge of the term *Dharma* which unfortunately has not yet attained a settled meaning that may really be counted. Relying on the different uses of the word *Dharma* in the *Ṛgveda*, which for any purpose is to be relied on as the oldest source of our knowledge on any topic relating to the Aryan culture, it may be stated with reservation that conveniently the term may be accepted as having a stereotyped meaning, without however abandoning the derivative one. There is no doubt about the fact that the word *Dharma* in its primary stage was derived out of √*Dhṛ* in the sense of holding or retaining or nourishing (√ *dhṛ dhāraṇa-poṣaṇayoḥ*). The meaning as ordinance of religious nature may be traced in *ṚV*., 1.22.18; V.26.6; VIII.43.24; IX.64.1 etc. When we have the expressions as: *tāni dharmāṇi* prathamāny āsan (1.164.43) the commentators in their own way explain as acts religious in nature (*Sāyaṇa:dharmāṇi anuṣṭthānāni*) when we have the same expression in the context of sacrifice:

Yajñena yajñam ayajanta devāḥ.
tani dharmāṇi prathanāny āsan, ṚV. 1.164

(Sāyaṇa explains: *dharmāṇi agnisādhyāni karmāṇi*)

We should also refer to identical expressions as: '*prathamaḥ dharmaḥ*' (the primeval or first ordinances) (R.V.III. 17.1: Sāyaṇa: Dharmaḥ dhāraṇāt. *Agneḥ yajñanirvāhakatayā taddhārakatatvāt dharmoagniḥ. Tathā ca mantraḥ: dharmānam agnim vidathasya sadhanam.* *ṚV* X. 92.2.

We have the expressions as: *Sanatā dharmāṇi:* (ancient ordinances) *ṚV.* III. 3.1; which also has reference to the sacrificial acts (Sāyaṇa explains: *sanata sanātanānixi yajñaṁ. . .*).

There are certain uses of the word which may be interpreted to mean spiritual power:

> *Dharmaṇā mitrāvaruṇa vipaścita vrata rakṣethe asurasya mayayā*
> *R.V.*, V. 63.7.
> Sāyaṇa explains: *dharmaṇā jagaddhārakeṇa vṛṣṭyādilakṣaṇena akarman...*
> In the *R.V.*, VI. 70.1x/
> *Dyāvāpṛthivī varuṇasya dharmaṇā viṣkabhite ajare bhuriretasa.*
> Sāyaṇa: . . *Varuṇasya sarvasya niyāmakasya dharmaṇā dhāraṇena* . .

we may be permitted to accept the aforesaid meaning. Reference may be made to the expressions like: dhruveṇa dharmaṇā (explained in the commentary as *acalena; dharmaṇā dhārakeṇa*); (for the same expression in the same text we find: Maruto minatu mitrāvaruṇau dhruvena dharmaṇā . . . *Vaj. Sam.* II. 3 and V. 27.

All these may refer to the fact that the seers themselves in one stage had no clear concept of *Dharma*. Subsequently however, more and more developments tended to follow. We may incidentally refer to the tendency of laying special emphasis on truth which in a *Ṛgvedic* mantra has been eulogised as superior to falsehood:

> *Tayor yat satyaṃ yot ard ṛjīyas tad*
> . . . *R.V.*, VII. 104.12

We find clear statement to the effect that one indulging in falsehood brings incompetence to perform sacrifice even:

> Amedhyo vai puruṣo yad anṛtam vadati.
> *Śat. Br.* 1. 1. 1. 1.

The teacher accordingly in his admonition to the new student insists on truth first in preference to *Dharma* even, as we gather from the *Taittirīya Upaniṣad*,. . . vedam anūcyācāryontevāsinam anuśāsti - 'satyaṃ vada'. 1.11.1. The *Bṛhadāraṇyaka Upaniṣat*, interestingly and quite relevantly equates the two - *satya* and *Dharma*:

Tasmāt satyaṃ vadantam āhur dharmaṃ vadatīti, dharmaṃ vā vadantaṃ *satyaṃ vadatīty* etad hy evaitad ubhayaṃ bhavati. 1.14.4.

Dharma assumes a more sublime and refiner form in the Vedic term *ṛta*, which occurs several times in the *Ṛgveda* itself, specially in the fourth Maṇḍala (IV. 23. 8-10). Here we become acquainted with the all-pervading influence of *ṛta*. It has been held that through this the bad acts are destroyed. For its sake the earth and waters are wide and deep. That Mitra and Varuṇa exercise lordship over the universe is because of *ṛta* (ṛtena viśvaṃ bhuvanaṃ virājathaḥ R.V. V. 63.7). They are protectors or *ṛta* (ṛtasya gopāv adhi tiṣṭhatho rathaṃ satyadharmāṇā parame vyomani: *R.V.* V.63.1). The epithets of Āditya are interesting: ṛtavān ṛtajātā ṛtāvṛdho ghorāso anṛtadviṣaḥ (*R.V.*, VII. 66.13). The moral aspect of *ṛta* finds expression in the statement of Yama, in his attempts to persuade her (yami) to desist from the acts of passion and sensuality:

na yat purā cakramā kaddhā nūnaṃ ṛtā vadanto anṛtaṃ rapema. R.V, X. 10.4

Because of the special, importance, the seers have gone far as to deify *ṛta*, mentioning side by side with other Vedic deities:

aditir dyāvāpṛthivī ṛtaṃ mahad indrāviṣṇu marutaḥ savar bṛhat. X. 66.4

(compare in this reference the statement of Manu:
Vṛṣo hi bhagavān dharmaḥ. VIII. 16).

Ṛta and *Satya* have been both equated arising as they are out or *tapas*: *ṛtaṃ ca satyaṃ cābhīddhāt tapaso ' dhy ajāyata.* R.V., X. 190.1.

One may construe a similarity between the three, *ṛta*, *vrata* and *dharma* and one mantra of the *Ṛgveda* makes mention of three side by side:

dharmaṇā mitrāvaruṇā vipaścitā vratā rakṣethe asurasya māyayā
ṛtena viśvaṃ bhuvanaṃ vīrājathaḥ sūryamā dhattho divi citrayaṃ ratham /

In the light of the discussion made above, we may interpret that *ṛta* represents the moral aspect, *dharma*, the spiritual aspect and *vrata*, the aspect of observances and performances of śāstric rites, rituals and duties.[1]

In the background of the Vedic concept of *Dharma*, which, as we have seen, was yet to assume a distinct and definable characteristic appeared in the field a significantly good number of *Śāstrakāras,* whose works have the appellations of science of righteousness - *Dharmaśutra* and *Dharmaśāstra* (defined by Manu as *Smṛti*:

Dharmaśāstraṃ tu vai smṛtiḥ. II. 10)

We may interestingly refer here to a discourse attempted on by Madhātithi, the great *Bhāṣyakāra* on the *Manusmṛti,* wherein it has been interpreted that by *Dharmaśāstra* we are to understand text where merely there is directive regarding acts leading to spirituality, more or less in a general way; but in the texts entitled *Smṛti* we are to expect specific directives regarding acts which are to be performed in Śāstric manner:

Yat kār yaṃ dharma-śāstyarthaṃ tad dharmaśāstram.

Yatra dharmaḥ śiṣyate, kartavyatayā pratīyate sā smṛtiḥ.

Medhātithi is in favour of accepting the derivative meaning of the word *Smṛti* declaring thereby that while in the *Śruti* the Dharmic prescriptions are directly available, the Smṛti texts present the same by a secondary method in the form of remembering (by the sages by Manu and the like):

Yatra śrūyate dharmānuśāsana-śabdaḥ sā śrutiḥ.

Yatra ca smaryate sā smṛtiḥ.

What we have to add is that the subtle distinction made between *Dharmaśāstra* and *Smṛti* is not convincing.

Whatever that may be, some eminent Dharma-sūtra-writers composed *Śāstra* in aphoristic style (They are are Gautama, Āpastamba, Baudhāyana Vaṣiṣṭha etc.). while others utilised the traditional method of composing the texts in metrical form, utilising the *anuṣṭup* metre principally, generally having the designations as *Saṃhitās* (such as *Manusaṃhitā, Yājñavalkya-saṃhitā* etc.). The purpose in general, may be stated to be re-stating and interpreting the *śruti* text in the proper context, evidently for effecting welfare of the society. Bṛhaspati gives expression to this concept while eulogising the speciality of Manu:

Vedārthopanibandhṛtvāt prādhānyaṃ hi manoḥ smṛtam.

Manu, while making reference to the purpose for composing his Śāstra, states that specifically such texts were intended for prescribing the specific duties of the members of the society (without which the social order cannot be maintained. It thus may rightly be claimed to be the *social science*):

Tasya *Karma-vivekārtham* śeṣāṇāṃ cānupūrvaśaḥ/

Svāyambhuvo Manur dhīmān idaṃ Śāstraṃ akalpayat /
1.102

In this capacity as *Smṛti* texts, these books embody, as far as mempry permits to do, the Vedic materials, whereas they are *Dharmaśāstra* since the writers here in adjustment with the Vedic texts formulate specific rules for guiding the lives and activities of the members of the society from birth to death, as we gather from the statement of Manu:

Niṣekādi-śmaśānānta mantrair yasyodito vidhiḥ /
Tasya śāstre ' dhikāro ' smin jñeyo nānyasya kasyacit / / II.16

The topics deals with in the *Dharmasūstras* (such as those by Gautama, Baudhā yana and Āpastamba) and the *Dharmasaṃhitās* (such thoseby Manu and Yājñavalkya), may in short, be stated to be three, namely, *ācāra, vyavahāra* and *prāyaścitta* (as classified by Yājñavalkya). More methodically, in twelve chapters, Manu present them as: theory of creation (chap. 1. verses, 119: his statement of summary: verses: 111-117). He asserts that he has made it his point to delineate the duties (*dharma*) of the respective territories (*deśa*); of the castes (*jātidharma*); of the families (*kuladharma*), as also of the persons outside the pale of the Aryan culture (*pāṣaṇḍa*) and of the guilds (*gaṇadharma*):

Deśadharmām jātidharmān kuladharmāṃś ca Śāśvatān /
Pāṣaṇḍa-gaṇa-dharmāṃś ca Śāstre ' sminn uktavān Manuḥ / /
1.119

This has been followed by the mention of the nature and sources of *Dharma* (Chap. II, 1.20; *saṃskāras,*[1] periods and procedures of pupilage: 66-249); Chap. III. dealing with marriage;[2] restrictions on marriage: *asapiṇḍā* etc. verse, 5; forms of marriage, verses, 21-34; highest estimation about women: '*yatra nāryas tu pūjyante ramante tatra devatāḥ*' verse, 56; five daily essential duties for each householder (*pañsa-mahāyajñā*) and other related information (comprising of 286 verses); the fourth chapter in 260 verses discusses the planned means of livelihood, the dos and donts, of the householders (*gṛhastha*); the fifth comprising of 169 verses, deals with food, purification (*śuddhi*). It is here that women's dependence at all the stages of life is stated:

Bālye pitur vaṣe tiṣthet pāṇigrāhasya yauvane /
Putrāṇāṃ bhartari prete na bhajet strī svatantratān / / V.148,

Other duties of the wife, vow of *Brahmacarya* during widowhood (mṛte bhartariv.160): '*Na dvitīyaś ca sādhavīnāṃ kvacid bhartopadiśyate'*. v. 162; For the VIth chapter we have 97 verses containing information relating to the life in the forest:

Gṛhasthas tu yadā paśyed valīpalitam ātmanaḥ/
Apatyasyaiva cāpatyaṃ tadāraṇyaṃ samāśrayet// VI.2

Discharging of the obligations:

ṛṇāni[3] *trīn apākṛtya mano mokṣe niveśayet/*
anapākṛtya mokṣas tu sevamāno vrajaty adhaḥ// VI.35;

eulogy for the house-holder's stage of life:[4]

sarveṣām api caiteṣāṃ vedasmṛtividhānataḥ/
gṛhastha ucyate śreṣṭhaḥ, sa trīn etān bibharti hi// VI.89

Dharma has been shoken of as of ten types where the moral aspect of life has been insisted on:

Dhṛtiḥ kṣamā damo' steyaṃ śaucam indriyanigrahaḥ/
Dhir vidyā satyan akro-deho daśakaṃ dharmalakṣaṇam//
VI.92

The seventh chapter with 226 verses is dedicated to delineate the specific duties of the king or head of the state and it is of interest to note that the term *dharma* has been used here to indicate duty (Medhātithi: dharmaśabdaḥ kartavyatāvacanaḥ. VII.1). While in the previous chapter insistence has been made on the duties of the Brahmins, where special stress has been made on the culture of moral and academic qualities, here in this chapter and F.n: 1 in p.5.

The purificatory acts, rightly having the appellation of *Saṃskāra*, have their importance in the sense that they regulate the life and activities of the Aryans throughout the life-career of the members of the caste, including the Sūdras in certain cases. Accordingly Manu in the strongest possible terms has gone to the extent of declaring that those who like to remain within the fold of the *Dharmaśāstra*, must pass through the rites and rituals as prescribed inthe *Dharmaśāstra*:

Niṣekādi-śmaśānānyo mantrair yasyodito vidhiḥ/
Tasya śādtre'dhikāro'smin jñeyo nānyasya kasyacit// II.16

Samskāra may be stated to be one of the cases where the *Smṛti* texts prescribe provisions that are directly enshrined in the *Śrutis* and in fact though finally the *Śruti* is the supreme source of Dharma (Dharmaṃ jijñāsanānānāṃ pramāṇaṃ paramaṃ śrutiḥ. Manu, II.13), the next rank is earmarked for the *Smṛtis* (tābhyāṃ dharmo hi nirbabhau, Manu, II.10). The *Ṛgveda* itself has the use of the term on different occasions and the idea of purification, perfection and protection thereof was associated with it for which see specially, R.V, V. 76.2:

'na saṃskṛtaṃ pra mimīto gamiṣṭhā onti nūnam aśvinā pastuteha.;
VIII. 33.9:

Saṃskārasya tadarthatvadvidyāyāṃ puruṣaśrutiḥ. VI. 1.35

The clarification of the meaning of the term as also the purpose of the same comes from Sabara:

Saṃskāro nāma sa bhavati yasmin jāte padārtho bhavati yogyaḥ kasyacid arthasya. On *Mīmāṃsāsūtra,* III. 1.3.

Kumārila in his *Tantravārtika*: Yogyatāṃ cādahānāḥ kriyāḥ saṃsjārā ity ucyante. p. 1078.; and Saṃkāra: Saṃskāro nāma guṇādhānena va sayād doṣāpana yanena vā. On *Vedānta*
sūtra, 1.1.4.

Rudraskanda on the *Khādiragṛhyasūtra,* II. 3.33 is more clear and specific:

See specially: Manu, II. 26-28; for women specially in respect of marriage: Manu, II. 66, 67; Yāj. 1.13

Ete garbhādhānādayaḥ saṃskārāḥ sarīraṃ saṃskurvantaḥ sarveṣu adṛṣṭārtheṣu karmasu yogyatatiśayaṃ kurvanti, phalātiṣaye yogyatātiśaye ca.

The best approach, however, is from Devala as contained in the verse:

Citrakarma yathānekair aṅgair unmīlyate śaniḥ/
Brāhmaṇyam api tadvat syāt saṃskārair vidhipūrvakaiḥ //
Quoted in the *Samṣkāratattva* of Raghunandana.

The numbers of such Saṃskāras, as is quite natural, must vary. Thus in *Gautama-dharma-sutra,* we have mention of forty Saṃskāras and eight *ātmaguna* (XII. 14-24), while in the text of Hārita only two such *Saṃskāras* has been enumerated as *Brāhma* and *Daiva* (Dvividhaḥ saṃskāro bhavati, *brāhmo daivaś* ca . . . referred to the *Smṛticandrikā,* i, p.13)

For detailed information relating toe Saṃskāra, see specially: P.V. Kane, History of Dharmaśāstra, Vol. II, Part. i, Second edition, Poona, 1974, pp. 188-267;
R.B. Pandey, Hindu Saṃskāras,
H.N. Chatterjee, Studies in some aspects of Hindu Saṃskāras in ancient India, Calcutta, 1965.

Of all the recognised *Saṃskāras,* marriage may rightly be regarded as the most important as it covers all the four castes including the Śūdras and is treated as compulsory for all except however for those who opt for a life of avowed celibacy. It is rite that has the sacred stamp of the *Ṣrutis,* where on different occasions this

Saṃskāra has been mentioned, defining the purpose, seriousness and other connected problem. An entire *Sūkta* has been included in the tenth Maṇḍala of the *Ṛgveda* which has as many 47 ṛks (almost an uncommon feature), where the marriage of Sūryā with Soma has been delineated almost with the minutest details and ritualistic parapharnalia, which in later ages have turned to be the source-materials for the *Gṛhyasūtras* on marriage.
Special reference may be made of the *mantras* that are pronounced even in modern days:

Gṛhān gaccha gṛhapatnī yathāso vaśinī tvaṃ vidatham ā vadāsi.
X. 85. 26

Iha priyaṃ prajayā te samṛdhyatām asmin gṛhe gārhapatyāya jāgṛhi
Enā patyā tanvaṃ saṃsṛjasvā 'dhā jivrī vidatham ā vadāthaḥ.
X. 85. 27

Sumangalīr iyaṃ vadhūr imāṃ sameta paśyata
Saubhāgyam asyai dattvāyā ' thāstaṃ vi paretana. X. 85.33

Gṛbhnāmi te saubhagatvāya hastaṃ mayā patyā jaradaṣṭir yathāsaḥ /
Bhago aryamā savitā puraṃdhir mahyaṃ tvād ur gārhapatyāya devāḥ // X. 85.36

This mantra forms the basis for the ritual called *Pāṇigrahaṇa*, which because of its importance has been regarded as the most essential of the rites of marriage and digest-writers have gone even to the extent of declaring it as marriage proper.

The *mantra*, noted below has its importance even this day, since it contains the affectionate blessings of the parents to the bride on her marriage:

Samrājñī śvaśure bhava samrājñī śvaśrvāṃ bhava /
Nanāndari samrājñī bhava samrājñī adhi devṛṣu //
X. 85.46

There are several important social problems connected with marriage and on the different aspects of the same several contributions have been made, for special reference of which the following may be referred to:

P.V. Kane, History of Dharmaśāstra, II-1, Second edition, 1974, Poona, chap. IX, pp. 427-598

H. Chatterjee Śāstri, Studies in the social background of the Forms of Marriage in ancient India, Vols, I and II, Calcutta, 1972

Chanchak Kumar Chatterjee, Studies in the rites and rituals of Hindu marriage in ancient India, Calcutta, 1978.

The concept of debt, spiritual and secular, is as old as the *Śrutis*. In ancient India, since birth a Brāmaṇa was under the obligation of discharging at least three debts (*ṛṇas*). The *Rgveda* (II. 28.9) we find a prayer to Varuṇa so that the worshiper may be relieved of the debts. Sāyaṇa interprets the *mantra* in terms of debts. The Atharvaveda (VI. 117) suggests that non-payment of debts brings the debtor under the fetters of Yama. (See Keśava in his *Paddhati* on the *Kauśikasūtra* (46.36). The *Kauśikasūtra*, (46.36-39) speaks about the obligation of the sons or Sagotras to discharge the debt creditor. The *Ṣatapatha-brāhmaṇa* is more clear in the statement that *ṛṇa* is associated with the very birth, from which one should make oneself free:

Ṛṇam ha vai jāyate yo ' sti, sa jāyamāna eva devebhyaḥ ṛṣibhyaḥ pirṭbhyo mānuṣebhyaḥ. 1.7.2.1. This obligation of discharging debtgets more serious consideration in the texts of *Dharmaśāstra*. Thus Manu goes to the extent of declaring non-payment of debt as one of the *Upapātakas* (XI. 64-65). He declares that one may think in terms of *mokṣa* only after the three debts are discharged:

ṛṇāni trīṇy apākṛtya mano mokṣe niveśayet. VI. 35

This concept is closely associated with another concept of offering the ball of rice called *piṇḍa*

(for detailed study of the same, consult:
Mitākssrā on Yāj. 1.52; Kane, Hisotry of Dharmaśāstra, II-1, 472ff; III. 558;
Sarvadhikari, The principles of Hindu Law of inheritance, 52ff;
D. Shastri, Origin and development of the rituals of ancestor worship in India), Manu accords special importance to the title if law (*Vyavahārapada*)

(teṣām adyam ṛṇādānam . . . VIII. 4) and Medhātithi rightly points out that even persons who have renounced the secular mode of life stand affected by this law (anena vanavāsino'pi spṛśyante).

Nārada has carefully analysed the principal aspects under which this title of law may be discussed in the verse:

Ṛṇaṃ deyam adeyaṃ ca yathā yatra yena ca yat/
Dānagrahaṇa-dharmāś ca ṛṇādānam iti smṛtam// (Nārada,)

All these points have been systematically discussed by H. Chatterjee Śāstri, in his, The Law of debt in ancient India, Calcutta, 1971.

The concept about the *āśramas* is interesting.

Derived from ā + śram, the word *Āśrama* is supposed to convey the sense of a stage where one exerts oneself (āśrāmyanti asmin iti āśramāḥ). The passage in the *Chāndogya Upaniṣad*, II. 23.1 has reference to three branches of *Dharma* and they may be indicative of the Āśramas, but the arrangement is not perfectly clear as we find in the later Dharmaśāstra:

Trayo dharmaskandhā (branches of dharma) yajño ' dhyayanaṃ dānam iti
prathamaḥ (stage of householder); tapa eva dvitīyo (vānaprastha) brahmacāryācāryakulavāsī tṛtīyo (brahmacarya), ' tyantam ācāryakule ' va
sādayan, sarva ete puṇyalokā bhavanti brahmasaṃstho ' mṛtatvam eti.

The *Jābālopaniṣad*[4] appears to present a more clear picture thus:

Brahmacaryāṃ parisamāpya gṛhī bhavet, gṛhī bhūtvā vanī bhavet, vanī
bhūtvā pravrajet . . .

See the observations of Śaṃkara on the *Vedāntasūtra*, III. 4.20

In the later stage of the *Dharmasūtras*, āpastamba categorically mentions them as four thus:

Catvāra āśramā gārhasthyam ācāryakulaṃ maunaṃ vānaprasthyam iti. II. 9.21.1.

Because of the importance of the first stage of life, the other three have often been accorded minor status. Some one goes to the extent of declaring the house-holder's status as the only one. Thus we have from Gautama first the rule that this stage should be treated as the *yoni* (source) of all the other *aśramas* (*Teṣāṃ gṛhastho yonir aprajananatvād itareṣāṃ*. 1.3.3.; thereafter the final rule, 1.3.35 declares it to be the only āśrama since in the Vedic texts there is direct mention of the same:

Aikāśramyaṃ tv ācaryāḥ pratyakṣavidhānād gārhā-sthasya.

Baudhāyana shares with Gautama the same view and refers to the fact that this classification of the *āsramas* was made by one Asura called Kapila, which need not be given important as such:

Aikāśramyaṃ tv ācāryā aprajananatvād itareṣām. II. 6.29
Tatrodāharanti-prāhlādir vai kapilo nāmāsura āsa. Sa tān etān bhedāṃś
cakāra devais saha spardhamānaḥ, tān manīṣī nādriyeta. II. 6.30

In respect of the Āśranas, three views have come into picture, namely, *samuccaya* (orderly co-ordination),; *vikalpa* (option) and bādha (annulment or contradiction). Vijñāneśvara has a long discussion on the point (on Yāj. III. 56-57):

Eteṣāṃ ca samuccaya-vikalpa-badha-pakṣāṇāṃ sarveṣāṃ srutimūlatvād icchayā vikalpaḥ.

For detailed discussion on the points relating to the *Āsramas* reference may be made specially to:
P.V. Kane, History of Dharmaśāstra, II-1, (Second edition), Poona, 1974, pp. 416-426
onwards the duties for the castes next in order, specially engaged in administration, special stress has been laid on the aspect of clean administration and obligation to protect and preserve the interest of the subjects:

Sarvasyāsya yathānyāyaṃ kartavyam parirakṣaṇam. VII.2
Raksārtham asya sarvasya rājānam asrjat prabhuḥ. 3
Varṇānām āśramāṇāṃ ca rājā sṛṣṭo' bhirakṣitā. VII.35

We have eulogy here for the proper and judicious application of *Daṇḍa*:

Yadi na praṇayed rājā daṇḍaṃ dandyeṣv atandritaḥ/
Śūle matsyān ivāpakṣyan durbalān balavattarāḥ// VII.20

The entire chapter is nothing but a wonderful mosaic of *arthaśāstra* material and morality since the king has been directed to follow certain rules in warfare (na kūṭair āyudhair hanyāt etc. VII.90-93) in accordance with the moral laws of high order (*satāṃ dharmam anusmaran*. 93).+ In adjustment with the ideal principles of justice and equity, the principles of taxation has been formulated here wherein the directive is:

Nocchinduād ātmano mūlaṃ pareṣāṃ cātotṛṣṇayā /
of. *Puṣpaṃ puṣpaṃ vicinvīta mūlacchedaṃ na kārayet*. Mahā, Udyo.3418 V. 139;

We should in this context refer to the Arthaśāstra: Kośamūlāḥ *kośapūrvāś ca sarvārambhāḥ*. II.2

The obligation of king as protector has been idealised when in the clearest possible terms it has been stated that indifference of the king to offer ready remedy when the citizen in distress seeks help, tantamounts to his death in living form:

Vikrośantyo yasya rāṣṭrād dhriyante dasyubhiḥ prajāḥ /
Saṃpaśyataḥ sabhṛtyasya mṛtaḥ sa na tu jivati / / VII. 143

Manu very prudently has instructed the king to avoid war as far as possible:

Na yuddhena kadācana. 198

The seventh chapter of this text represents the very developed concept of the science of statecraft and it has become a practice of all these texts on *Dharmasūtras* and *Dharmaśāstras* to include substantial portion of *Rājadharma* in their texts, the most developed form of which however has been traced in the *Arthaśāstra* of Kauṭilya.

Besides being deemed as the science of righteousness, morality and spirituality; or as a social science; the Dharmaśāstras have the fairest claim to be regarded as the most advanced legal science, so much so that in its structure and design and richness of contents, the *Dharmaśāstras* rightly may be regarded as presenting before the world a highly developed judicial system, the like of which is rarely to be traced even in the advanced civilised countries of the West, as rightly pointed out by Mayne (in the preface to the first edition of his Treatise on Hindu Law and Usage, 1878): Hindu Law has the oldest pedigree of any known system of jurisprudence, and even now it shows no signs of decreptitude[8].

Dr. Rash Behary Ghosh in his Tagore Law Lecture on the *Law of mortgage* states in continuation:

'The law which moved the admiration of Sir William Jones has ceased in one sense, to be the living law, and must be sought at the present day, not in our books of report, but in the texts of our sages and in the writings of the successive jurisconsults by whom Hindu Law was gradually moulded into system'.

In his Tagore Law Lecture for the year 1883, delivered before the University of Calcutta, on the Outlines of an History of the Hindu Law, Julius Jolly, states about the importance of the Hindu Law in the following lines:

". . . The Indian soil has not only been productive in deep thinkers, eminent founders of world religions and gifted poets, but it has brought forth a system of law which after having spread over the whole of the vast continent of India, has penetrated at an early period into Burma and Siam and has become the foundation of written law in these two countries".[1]

In continuation it has been held that in spite of its generally archaic character, Indian legislation in some respects has early reached degree of perfection equal or superior to anything to be met with in the contemporaneous law codes of Europe. p.3

Nārada interestingly records that in the contemplation of the writers of legal treatises there was a period where there was no necessity of legal treatises and subsequently such necessity was felt at a stage when the good qualities and virtues of the people dwindled:

Dharmaikatānāḥ puruṣā yadāsan satyavādinaḥ/
Tadā na vyavahāro ' bhūn na dveṣo nāpi matsaraḥ//. 1.1
Naṣṭe dharme manuṣyāṇāṃ vyvahāraḥ pravartate//. 1.2

In fact the entire text of Nārada is dedicated to the study of the *Vyavahāra* section and detailed study of the eighteen titles of law as also a *prakīrṇaka*. The verses of Kātyāyana have not yet been unearthed in its totality, and the verses attributed to Kātyāyana in the commentaries and the digests, have been collected and published under the title: *Kātyāyanasmṛtisāroddhāra* (Bombay, 1933) by Mm. P.V. Kane and a glance at the collected text will convince any one that the provisions contained therein in respect of the titles of law are of very high order. He is more elaborate and critical in his analysis of the treatment of *Vyavahāra* in respect of reply (uttara) v.165, and has a substantially developed contribution to the delineation of the question relating to the personal property of women having the technical appellation as *Strīdhāna* in as many as 38 verse (numbering 894-932). Thus Kātyāyana's treatment of *Vyavahāra* are far more developed and scientific than those of Manu and Yājñavalkya.

Unfortunately for us Bṛhaspati shares the same fate as that of Kātyāyana in the sense that his text in original form has not yet been traced and what we have this day is an excellent reconstruction of the text by K.V. Rangaswami Aiyangar, published in the G.O.S. (Baroda, 1941). The Vyavahāra section covers 228 pages in printed form while the topics relating to *Saṃskāra, Ācāra, Śrāddha, Āśauca, Āpaddharma*

(e.g: *Vṛddhau ca mātāpitarau sādhvī bhāryā sutaḥ śiśuḥ/*
Apy akāryaśataṃ kṛtvā bhartavyā Manur abravīt// 5.1

and *Prāyaścittakāṇḍa* have been recorded in pp. 231-386.
He categorically classifies the titles of law under two broad heads: civil and criminal: Hiṇsāṃ vā kurute kaś cit deyaṃ vā na prayacchati/

Dve hi sthāne vivādasys tayor bahutarā gatiḥ// 1.3

It is he who insists in a rational way:

Kevalaṃ śāstram āśritya na kartavyo vinirṇayaḥ/
Yuktihīne vicāre tu dharmahāniḥ prajāyate// 1.113

Though in the texts of Gautama, Baudhāyana and Āpastamba we meet with bare references to different aspects of *Vyavahāra*, it is in the text of Manu that principally in chapter VIII, comprising of 420 verses, the eighteen titles of law have been treated (*teṣām ādyam ṛṇādānāṃ* niḥṣepo ' svāmivikrayaḥ/ verse, 4-7). In his treatment of *ṛṇādāna*, Manu very interestingly refers to modern method of '*gherāu*' for the purposes of realising the money invested:

Dharmeṇa vyavahāreṇa cchalenācaritena ca/
Prayuktaṃ sādhayed arthaṃ pañcamena balena ca// VIII.49

Medhātithi explains: *ācaritam abhojana-gṛhapa-dvāropaveśanādi*

How much stress was laid on the importance of *Dharma* will be evident from the directive Manu that the members of the twice-born castes, if necessary, may take to arms, when there is apprehension of crisis in *Dharma*:

Śastraṃ dvijātibhir grāhyaṃ dharma yaroparudhyate/
Dvijātīnāñ ca varṇānām viplave kālakārite// VIII. 348
Ātmanaś ca paritrāṇe dakṣiṇānāṃ ca saṅgare/
Strīviprābhyupapattau ca dharmeṇa ghnan na dūṣyati// 349
Guruṃ vā bālavṛddhaù vā brāhmaṇnaṃ vā bahuśrutaṃ/
Ātatāyinam āyāntaṃ hanyād evāvicārayan// 350

About women the strict directive is:

Na mātā na pitā na strī na putras tyāgam arhati. 389

Several problems, social in nature, have been raised, specially in respect of the position of women regarding their right to wealth:

Bhāryā putraś ca dāsaś ca traya evādhanāḥ smṛtāḥ/
Yat te samadhigacchanti yasya te tasya taddhanam// 416

The ninth chapter with 336 verses has its importance for the simple reason that herein we have detailed discussion regarding the rights and obligations of women. The much talked for dependence of women in all stages of life (Pitā rakṣati kaumāre . . . IX. 3) is here. Persuasive good dealings have been recommended by Manu and his other statement is to be reckoned as indicatory of his view:

Prajanārthaṃ mahābhāgāḥ pūjārhā gṛhadīptayaḥ/
Striyaḥ śriyaś ca geheṣu na viśeṣo 'sti kaś cana// IX.26

Voicing the import of the śruti text, Manu is emphatic in his statement that there is no division or difference between the husband and the wife:

Ardho ha vā eṣa ātmanaḥ yaj Jāyā.
Manu: *Etāvān eva puruṣo yaj jāyātmā prajeti ha/*
Viprāḥ prāhus tathā caitat yo bhartā sā smṛtāṅganā// IX.45

Thus: *Na niṣkraya-visargābhyāṃ bhartur bhāryā vimucyate.* IX. 46. This proceeds upto verse IX.103. From IX.104 discussion centres round *Dāya* (laws of inheritance) and the discussion is most scientific and herein we notice modernity of thought sponsoring equalness of son and daughter:

Yathaivātmā tathā putraḥ putreṇa duhitā samā. 130

For recording of several types of sons, *Manusmṛti* opens before the sociologists wider gates for research in modern sociology and anthropology (verses: 159-181).

He presents for the first time picture of *Strīdhana*, personal property of women (verses, 194-200), which has received most developed shape in the text of *Kātyāyana*, as already discussed. His conception of private and personal property even living within the family is unique in character (*Vidyādhana* and *Śauryadhana*) (Verses, 206ff). On the duty of the king, a provision made by Manu be deemed ultra-modern:

Brhu-amaghāte hitābhange pathi moṣābhidraśane/
Śaktito nābhidhāvanto nirvāsyāḥ saparicchadāḥ// 274.

The tenth chapter may be regarded as the most important one in the sense that the most disputed question relating to the caste system has been dealt with here. This chapter in 131 verses contains wonderful source-materials for the anthropologists and sociologists specially on the point of inter-caste relationship. We meet here with the very interesting question of *Jātyutkarṣa* (upgradation of caste) and *Jātyapakarṣa* downgrading of castes. Here we find Manu's attempt to mention certain simplified *dharmas* general for all the castes:

Ahiṃsā satyam asteyaṃ śaucam indriyanigrahaḥ/
Etaṃ sāmāsikaṃ dharmaṃ cāturvarṇye ' bravīn Manuḥ//

X. 63

His analysis of the means of livelihood in normal times and in distress, is quite methodical and scientific and several illustrations have been cited. For the special categories of *Śūdras* there has been made provision for performance of religious activities, of course, without pronunciation of Mantras (*mantravarjaṃ na duṣyanti* . . . X. 127). The eleventh chapter with 266 verses deals with the expiatory measures in one of which there is provision for the Brahmins to approach the king personally by expressing frankly the offence committed (XI. 100). Interestingly there is provision for expiation in causing injury to the tree with fruits and flowers:

Phaladānāṃ tu vṛkṣāṇāṃ chedane japyam ṛkśatam. IX. 143.

The last chapter (12th) in 126 verses deals with topics of general nature concerning moral principles.

So much stress has been laid on the *Dharmaśāstra* of Manu because of the fact that his text is supposed to represent he very best standard that a *Dharmaśāstra* should reach for providing information relating to the members of all the castes of the society.

This ancient legislator was wise and prudent to realise that if the law is to invite obedience of the citizens it must have provision for adjustment with the changing circumstance of the society. Thus he ceclarez:

Anye kṛtayuge dharmās tretāyāṃ dvāpare pare /
*Anye kaliyuge nṛṇāṃ yugahrāsānurūpataḥ / /*1.85

This point later on has been elaborated by Parāśara in his *Smṛti* text, recording in addition that the law formulated by him is intended for the people of the present Kali age (Kalau parāśaraḥ smṛtaḥ . . .)

Actually this legislator has been bold enough to prescribe:

Deśabhaṅge pravāse vā vyādhiṣu vyasanes api /
Rakṣede eva svadehādi paścād dharmaṃ samācaret / /
Āpatkāle tu samprāpte śaucācāraṃ na cintayet / /
*Svayaṃ samuddharet paścāt savastho dharmaṃ samācaret / /*VII. last verses

Parāśara shares with *Nārada* the bold and modern directive empowering the women to take to a second husband during calamitious state:

Naṣṭe mṛte pravrajite klībe ca patite patau /
Pañcasv āpatsu nārīṇāṃ patir anyo vidhīyate / /
Nār. Strīpuṃ, 97);

This occurs also in the *Agnipurāṇa*.

Passing reference in short is to be made to the *Yājñavalkyasmṛti* with 1010 verses, coming next in importance to the text of Manu and in the text of *Agnipurāṇa* chap. 256 specially we find a good case whereby the text of Yāj. may be checked and verified in respect of the readings. Similar assistance may be available from the *Garuḍapurāṇa*, chap. 93. He in his section on *Ācāra* shows the same attitude towards women in respect of dependence (1.85); and showing of honour to them on different pretexts (1.82);

He like Manu, speaks of general *dharma* for all the castes:

Ahiṃsā satyam asteyam śaucam indriyanigraḥ /
dānaṃ damo dayā kṣāntiḥ sarveṣām dharmasādhanam / / 1.222

His direction regarding king is unique and rational:

Arakṣyamāṇāḥ kurvanti yat kiñcit kilbiṣaṃ prajāḥ /

Tasmāt tu nṛpater ardhaṃ yasmāt gṛhṇaty asau karān//1.337
His section on *Vyavahāra* is more methodical than that of Manu, comprising as it is of 307 verses and what is interesting is the concept of *Dāya* which through the very scholastic interpretation by Vijñāneśvara has changed the whole structure of the society, advocating specially the right of the sons to the ancestral estate by birth.

The interpretations offered by different digest-writers by elaborating the doctrine advocated by Vij. has led to the formation of different schools of law:

Benares school accepting the *Vīramitrodaya* as authoritative;
Mithilā school: . . . *Vivādaratnākara, Vivādacandra, Vivādacintāmaṇi;*
Mahārāstra or Bombay school: . . . *Vyavahāranirṇaya, Smṛticandrikā, Parāśarimāhavīya* and *Sarasvatīvilāsa.*

The Smṛti-directive are not always pleasant to the parties for whom they are intended. This may be one of the reasons as to why the *Bhaviṣyapurāṇa* has classified the *Smṛtis* under five categories:

Dṛṣṭārthā tu smṛtiḥ kācit adṛṣṭārthā tathāparā/
Dṛṣṭādṛṣṭārtharūpānyā nyāyamūlā tathāparā//
Anuvādsmṛtis tv anyā śiṣṭair dṛṣṭā tu pañcamī/
Sarvā etā vedamūlā dṛṣṭārthaṃ parihṛtya tu//181.22-23

They have been explained there with illustration:

(1. = *daṇḍa*; 2. = *sandhyā-vandanam*; 3. = *Brahmacārī* to carry a *Palāśa* tree; 4. = reasoning is to be applied, as in Manu, II.15: *Udite nudite caiva*; 5. = restatement of what is stated in the Vedas: Manus direction for a wandering ascetic (VI.38) is restatement of *Bṛhadāraṇyaka Upaniṣad*: III. 5.1: ***Vyutthāyātha bhikṣācaryaṃ***)

On this point there is long discussion in the *Mīmāṃsā* texts and the final conclusion comes from the *Śāstradīpikā* on the rule: *Hetudarśanāc ca*:

Ato śrutiviruddhaṃ dṛṣṭakāraṇaṃ ca smaraṇam apramāṇam, tato 'nyat pramāṇam.

Concluding observation

Within the very span of discussion it is absolutely impossible to present a clear picture of what *Dharmaśāstra* stands for. While the *Mīmāṃsā-śāstra* has dedicated itself to the sacred task of defending the spiritual and ritualistic aspect of the *Śrutis*; while the *Vedāntaśāstra* has made its point to develop the analytical and spiritual aspect of knowledge relating to the Spirit, justifying principally the *Upaniṣadic* way of attitude to the life and the Upaniṣads are important constituent of the *Śrutis*; the *Dharmaśāstras* have the most important role in the form of presenting before the society a norm of life for all the members, including those that do not belong exactly to their class, because they have other affiliations (i.e. the *pāṣaṇḍas*); thereby moulding the society for securing the ultimate end of life (niḥśreyasa). It may be stated that these texts are practical applications of spiritual doctrines for the betterment of the society. For each and every moment of life since birth, throughout the life and also thereafter the *Dharmaśāstra* is a ready guideline, a useful associate, a friend and philosopher, a right representative of the moral deity, Varuṇa, from whose *pāsa* it is almost impossible to escape. This *Śāstra* is the most voluminous in shape and contents and covers not only the directives of the regional writers of law (*dharmaśāstra-pryojaka*) (major such writers have been enumerated by Yājñavalkya (1.4-), but their numbers were more (for which See, Kane, History of Dharmaśāstra, 1-1); but also the *Bhāṣyakāras* and *Ṭīkākāras*; the *Nibandhakāras* as also their commentators and such Śāstra are being written even in recent times. This has a long evolution and social history is inseparably connected with it. Its study is essential and days are not far off when the society will have to find our Manus and Yājñvalkyas for formulating newer and newer rules in adjustment with the needs of the society.

Comments regarding the future of *Dharmaśāstra*:

Indian society at the hands of the political personalities and present legislators trained up in anglicised pattern of life and outlook, and necessarily retaining less affiliation for the past heritage of India, do not have any tendency of utilising the *Dharmaśāstra* materials for the betterment of the society. Thus after the constitution of 1950 and statutory changes in Indian law, *Dharmaśāstra* has practically been consigned to intellectual museum. Judges even hesitate not to declare that the days of Manu are over, but surprisingly we notice that as early as in 1970 in a sensational murder (Meera Tandon's Honeymoon, 13) at the Delhi Court, the learned judge in the judgment referred to the verse of Manu:

> ***Yathā nayaty asṛkpātair mṛgasya mṛgayuḥ padam /***
> ***Nayet tathānumānena dharmasya nṛpatiḥ padam /***
>
> VIII.44.

In Sankar Dome v Kalidasi Dasi (A.I.R, 1970, Cal, 461) it has been decided that S.B. Judges are not to question the correctness of Jīmūtavāhana's interpretation of the law.

Society even in this stage has an undercurrent of thought in favour of *Dharmaśāstra* and the Dharmaśāstrins should have a pious obligation to propagate what is there in such *Śāstra*, by following which the society may turn to be a better place to live in.

Notes

1. For the conception of *Rta* in its connection with sin in the Veda, see, M. Bloomfield, The Religion of the Veda and Upanishad, pp.12, 125;
   Keith, Religion and Philosophy of the the Veda and Upanishad, pp.83-85
   H. Lefever, The Vedic idea of sin,
   P.V. Kane, History of Dharmaśāstra, Vol. IV, pp.2-5.
2. Śāstrakāras hardly permit exaction of taxes (additional). Patañjali interestingly refers to the Mauryas as greedy of gold and thereby making arrangement of images: Mauryair hiraṇyārthibhir arcāḥ prakalpitāḥ. on Pā. V.3.99. *Rājatarangini* (V.166-177) makes mention of Śaṃkaravarman of Kasmir (883-902 A.D) as plundering 64 temples for money and imposing takes on *gṛhakṛtya*. In the 11th cen. king Harṣa of Kasmir plundered most of the temples (RajṬar. VII.1090) Kātyāyana gives expression to the principle that the taxes are realised more or less as thair fee for protecting the subjects:
   Prajāpālana-vitanana.
3. Yaj. rightly stresses that it is one of the duties of the king to bring the erring subjects morally in the right course:
   Kulāni Jātiḥ śreṇiś ca gaṇān jānapadān api /
   Vinīya svadharmāc calitā rājā sthāpayet pathi // 1.361.
4. Among the Buddhist people outside India, particularly in Burma, remarkable traces of Indian legal views and expressions are traced. Dr. Richardson in 1847 (2nd ed, Rangoon) edited the `*Damathat*' or the laws of Manu in Burmese and English and R. Rost wrote about the *Manusāra* composed in Pāli and about its relation with Manu (Indian Studies, 1, 315-320). In 1881 Fuhrer copied six palm-leaf manuscripts of the *Manusāra* and in 1882 published in the J.B.B.R.A.S along with parallel passages from Manu and other Indian law-books.
   R.C. Majumdar in his *Champī* records that in inscription no: 65 of Jaya Indravarman II, dated Śake, 1010, it has been stated that he followed eighteen titles of law prescribed by Manu (*manumārga*). See also Himansu Bhusan Sarkar, `The influence of the Indian, Dharmaśāstras on the evolution of the juridical literature of South-East Asia, in the Monthly Bulletin of the Asiatic Society, Bengal, Vol. VI, No: 5, May, 1977.

2

The Term Dharma: Its Scope

Hukam Chand Patyal

1.0. An attempt is made in this paper to discuss the semantic range and scope of the term *dharma (n)* in Vedic and Classical Sanskrit literatures. The discussion of the term *dharma* (Pali *dhamma*) in Buddhist literature lies outside the scope of this paper, yet we shall make very brief remarks.

1.1. The term *dharman (n.)* (early Vedic form) is derived from *dhṛ-* in the following way:

dhṛ-+-man-I-N(*-manIN* by P. 3.2.75)
*dhṛ-+-man-*ϕ [ϕ I (by P. 1.3.2 and 9)] [N (ϕ by P. 1.3.3 and 9)]
dhar-+-man (root *guṇated* by P. 7.3.84)
dhár-man (NIT-accent by P. 6.1.197)
dhárman n. barytonic form (see Balasubrahmanyam 1993: 106).[1]

In *ṚV.* we also get oxytonic form *dharmán(m.)* 'bearer, supporter, arranger' (see e.g. *ṚV.* 1.187.1; 9.97.23; 10.21.3; 10.92.2)[2]. In late Vedic we find both forms *dharmán* (see e.g. Śat Br. 5.1.4.4; 10.2.2.4 etc.), and *dhárma* (see e.g. Vāja S. 20.9; Tai Br. 3.2.7.3; Śat Br. 14.2.2.29 etc.). The consonantal one is earlier form whereas *-a* cending one is attested outside ṚV[3]. The word in Classical literature is *dharma (m.)* only. Etymologically the word is derived from *dhṛ-* 'to hold, 'to maintain, to restrain' etc¦ Mahā Bhā. 5.80.66; 8.49.50 proclaims; *dharmo dhārayati prajāḥ* 'Dharma restrains creatures'.

1.2. Dharma is a very difficult concept which cannot be very precisely defined or explained. This word is varioulsy rendered as "statute, ordinance, law; usage, customary observance, duty; (one's own) obligation, duty or self-initiated action (ethical, social, spiritual); right, justice, righteousness, good conduct; virtue, morality, religion, religious merit, good; attribute, quality, feature (both concrete and abstract); also personification of many human beings, deities, abstract pehnomena etc.". (See lexicons like PW., pw., MW., Apte, s.v. *dharma* and *dharman*; also EDS. III.i.1506-9, and 1512 (entries *adharma* and *adharman*). The term signifies "truth" (traditional or ceremonial), "moral obligation". This term in the descriptive sense signifies "correctness" (`the way things are') and in the prescriptive sense (`the way things ought to be)'. In the religious thought of ancient India the term reflects the connection between ontology, ritual ideology, social philosophy, ethics and canon law, and socio-ethico-religious duties for maintaining society. The root meaning of *dhṛ-*`to sustain, to maintain, to support, to uphold' [(cf. Lat. *fretus*)] (<*fre-*) `depending upon, daring to'), and *firmus* (<*fir-*) `strong in physical and moral senses, whence solid, hard, durable' (see Lingat 1973:3); Gk. *dikē* `justice'. *Dikē* `goddess Justice', referring to convention, morality and law (see Thieme 1973:346).

2.0. In the early Vedic (especially Ṛgveda) *dharman* `cosmic ordinance' is closely connected with *ṛta* `universal harmony or order'. In fact *ṛta* is an impersonal last, whereas *dharman* characterises those individual or personal actions that engender or maintain ontological cosmic order. In early Vedic *dharma* carries ontological sense or weight (cf. Mahony in Eliade (ed.) 1987: 329). In ṚV. there are a number of places where *dharman* would denote `cosmic ordinances' (but HDS. I.1 `religious ordinances or rites') (see e.g. ṚV. 1.22.18; 5.26.6; 8.43.24; 9.64.1 etc.). We come across refrains like *tāni dharmāṇi prathamāny āsan* (ṚV. 1.164.43d = 1.164.50b = 10.90.16b = Ait Br. 1.16 (3.5); also *dharmāṇi sanatā* (HDS. I.1 erroneously *sanatā dharmāṇi*) `ancient ordinances' (ṚV. 3.3.1). In some places *dharman* may also mean `stabilising power' (Gonda 1971: 128 (=1991:9), but HDS. I.1 `fixed principles' or `rules of conduct' (see e.g. ṚV. 4.53.3; 6.70.1; 7.89.5). In AV. (6.132.1-5) this power (which is Varuṇa's *dharman*) is employed in a magical rite. In the Veda we find a number of references where Varuṇa alone or Varuṇa-Mitra, is/are, entursted with duties of maintaining the *dharman*. Varuṇa is the personification of cosmic force. Varuṇa is identified by some scholar as "god Law/Order" (see e.g. Thieme 1973: 336). In ṚV. 5.63.7, the terms *dharman* and *ṛta* occur together in association with *vrata* `vow, religious rite'. Herein the seer says that Varuṇa and Mitra by means of their *dharman* and *māyā* watch over the *vratas* and rule the whole world with *ṛta*. At ṚV. 5.63.1 Varuṇa and Mitra are characterized as *sátyadharmāṇā* 'those (du.) whose ordinances are true'. Both these deities are entrusted with the maintenance of *dharma* of the gods (*devānāṁ dharmadhārayau*, Mai S. 3.8.9: 108.4). The stabilising power is ascribed to Mitra which is inherent in the universal order (ṚV. 5.81.4). In Śat Br. 5.3.3.9 Varuṇa appears as Dharmapati 'Lord of Dharma' (for other details see Gonda 1972: 129 ff. (=1991: 10ff.). [For many other Vedic references one may refer to Macdonell and Keith 1912 (=1958): 390-7; Hazra 1959:15 ff., and 1960:7 ff.; also Derrett 1973:2 ff.]

2.1. The writers of the Dharma- and Smṛti-texts meant by the *dharma* not merely a concept of religion but a mode of life or code of conduct, which regulated man's entire activities as a member of the society and also as an individual, and was a means of the goal of human existence (see HDS. II.i.2). In the Smṛti literature the term means an act of *vyavahāra*. The activities of *dharma* are classified into three groups, viz. *ācāra, vyavahāra* and *prāyaścitta*. Hindus contrast with *dharma* (what is good), both *artha* (the useful) and *kāma* (the pleasurable), all this triad motivates human behaviour and activity (on the triad see HDS. II.i.8-9). "A rule founded on *dharma* has an authority superior to that founded on *artha*, just as the latter has an authority superior to one motivated by *kāma*" (Lingat 1973:5). Manu Sm. 2.224 declares that wisdom is to be found in a harmonious combination of the trial which motivates human behaviour.

2.2. The source of *dharma* is to be found mainly in the Śruti (revelation, i.e. Veda). We get many cases where Dharma- and Smṛti-texts invariably depend upon the śruti for their authority.

Gaut DS. 1(1). 1-2; Vāsi DS. 1. 4-7 (cf. Āpa DS. 1(1). 1.2) enumerate three sources (*mūlas*) of *dharma*, viz. the Veda, Tradition, 'Good Custom or Practice of the *śiṣṭas*'. Manu Sm. 2.6 and Yājña Sm. 1.7 add one more source, viz. self-satisfaction or inner contentment (*ātmatuṣṭi*). Manu Sm. 2.12 also enumerates these four sources of *dharma*. As a matter of fact every rule of *dharma* must find its foundation in the Veda. "But in reality, it seems that when a Hindu affirms that *dharma* rests entirely upon the Veda, the word Veda does not mean in that connection the Vedic texts, but rather the totality of knowledge, the sum of all understanding of all religious and moral truths, whether revealed or not". (Lingat 1973:8; cf. HDS. I.4).

According to Mīmā Sū. 1.1.2 *codanālakṣaṇo'rtho dharmaḥ* 'Dharma is that which is indicated by the Vedic injunctions as conducive to highest good or goal (i.e. attaining the heaven etc.).' Mīmā Nyā Pra. 193.11 (sec.3)[4] also defines this concept in the same way 'Here *dharma* (duty) means any matter enjoined by the Veda with a view to attaining a useful purpose'.

2.3. In this subsection we shall be discussing various classificatory criteria or subgroups of the concept of *dharma*. Chāndo U. 2.23.1 says about three modes of virtuous life (*yajñaskandhas*). 'Sacrifice, study (of the Vedas), alms-giving, that is the first. Austerity, indeed, is the second. A student of sacred knowledge (*brahmacārin*) dwelling in the house of a teacher, absolutely controlling his body in the house of the teacher, is the third. All these attain meritorious words. He who stands firm in Brahman attains immortality'. Manu Bh. 82.7-8 (*on* 2.25) says about fivefold *dharma*, viz. *varṇadharma, āśramadharma, varṇāśramadharma, naimittikadharma,* and *guṇadharma*. Mitā. 2.1 (*on* 1.1.) adds *sādhāraṇadharma*, and makes the *dharma* sixfold. The term *dharma* stands for the duties of *āśrama*.

2.31. From the normative point of view the term *dharma* would mean 'the sum total of obligations or duties by which one 'fits in' the natural and social world'. Bhag Gi. 3.35 (cf. 2.31; 18.47) assents the concept of *svadharma*. 'It is better to perform one's own obligations or duties poorly than to do another's wel'. It is better to die while performing one's own obligations or duties, another's duty or obligation is dangerous'[5]. Performance of one's task or duty is indeed *dharma* (Mahā Bhā. 3.199.15). 'Duty determined by emergency or allowable in distress' is known as *āpaddharma* (see e.g. Mahā Bhā. 1.2.198; 1.97.21; 5.28.3; Viṣṇu P. 3.8.38 etc.). "Dharma certainly comprehends crises such as in road accidents, and the compensating of persons who have been injured and the deterring of individuals who would otherwise be criminally negligent". (Derrett 1973: 4; see Manu Sm. 8.290-6).

2.32. There are some definitions of *dharma* which recognise it as a sure means of happiness. Vaiśe Sū. 1.1.2 says: '*Dharma* is what leads to happiness and final beautitude' (*yato'bhyudaya-niḥśreyarasiddhiḥ sa dharmaḥ*). (Also see some similar references in Hazra 1959:15-16, fns. 3-6.)

Manu Sm. 2.9 emphatically says: "Those who support *dharma*, as it is presented in *smṛti* (sacred tradition) and *śruti*)revelation), gain happiness in this world and acquire happiness after death".

2.4. The great epic Mahā Bhā. is a veritable mine of many *śāstras* and ideas. The king is solely responsible for the maintenance of the moral order or *dharma*; he is *dharma* incarnate (Mahā Bhā. 3.183.22). The king's deed is the norm and all *dharma* is subsumed in *rājadharma* (Mahā Bhā. 12.63.25). Manu Sm. 11.83 openly declares: 'The Brāhmaṇa is declared (to be) the root of the sacred law and the Kṣatriya its tip' (*dharmasya brāhmaṇo mūlam agraṁ rājanya ucyate*). In Mahā Bhā. 1.1.66 (cf.5.29.46) Yudhiṣṭhira is metaphorically speaking a big tree: 'Yudhiṣṭhira is a big tree of righteousness; Arjuna is its trunk; Bhīma is its branches; the sons of Mādrī are its abundant flowers and fruits; and Kṛṣṇa, Brahman and Brāhmaṇas are its root[6]'. It is further said in Mahā Bhā. 5.40.12 (cf. 18.5.50) that *dharma* and *jīva* are eternal, but pleasure and misery are not. In Mahā Bhā. 12.59.14-5 it is said that in the very perfection of *dharma's* governance people protected each other with the help of the *dharma* alone (see Heesterman 1985: 198, also 156f.).

2.41. In Mahā Bhā. (and also in many other texts) Dharma is personified, and is identified with various deities, human beings, abstract concepts etc. Dumézil (1968:146; 151 f.; 170 ff.; see Gonda 1971: 120 (=1991:1) see continuation of Vedic Mitra in Dharma so far as Mahā Bhā. is concerned. Gonda (*loc. cit.* 126 (=7)) argues against Dumézil's hypothesis on the ground that Dharma is not associated with the figures with which Vedic Mitra is associated. Dumézil (p. 152 ff.) argues that the reign of Dharma's son Yudhiṣṭhira is entirely 'mitraic' in character (Mahā Bhā. 4.27.12 ff.). Gonda (131 (=12)) finds absence of 'mitraic' features (such as 'friendship', *śānti*, *satya*, redress). In ṚV. 10.14.7 we find certain relation between Varuṇa and Yama; and in Mahā Bhā. too Yama is known as Dharmarāja ('King of Dharma', cf. Mahā Bhā. 1.9.12f.; 1.50.11; 3.42.10). In post-epic texts, however, at times Dharma and Yama are identical. In Mahā Bhā. 1.121.22 Yama is Dharma. But in Mahā Bhā. 9.44.15; 12.192.6 the deities Dharma, Kāla, Mṛtyu, Yama are distinct. Yudhiṣṭhira is *Dharmarāja*, as he is just and truthful, patient and peaceful, though a *kṣatriya* yet he is a *brahman* ('rooted in *brahman*'; cf. Mahā Bhā. 2.60.31; 2.62.26). "Yudhiṣṭhira's kingship, in the epic myth, is the symbol that expresses the sovereignty of *dharma* on this earth". (Biardeau cited in Gonda 1971: 13 (=1991:13)). Dharma was created by Brahmā from his right breast in the human form for the sake of production of human beings (Mahā Bhā. 1.60.30; 12.91.16). Lord Kṛṣṇa as the Highest Being is identified with Dharma and other gods (Mahā Bhā. 3.13.19). Nārāyaṇa is said to have taken the birth as Dharma's son (Mahā Bhā. 7.172.51). In Mahā Bhā. 14.53.11 Dharma is Kṛṣṇa's eldest son, compassionate towards all beings. Dharma has three sons, viz. Śama "Peace", Kāma "Pleasure", Harṣa "Happiness" (Mahā Bhā. 1.60.31). Dharma when worshipped, or *dharma* when duly observed, manifests himself (itself) in peace, pleasure and happiness. [For a detailed mythological account of Dharma in Mahā Bhā. one may refer to Hopkins 1915: 58 ff.]

2..42. In Sanskrit we have compound expression *sanātanadharma* 'the primeval or ancient norm or ideal or religion'. The refrain *eṣa dharmaḥ sanātanaḥ* (cf. Pali *esa dhammo sanatano, Dhammapada* 1.5) is repeated quite often in Mahā Bhā. (see e.g. 1.113.13d; 3.13.6d; 3.30.50b etc.; see *Pratīka Index* I. 592a on Critical Ed.; also cf. Rāmā. 2.27.30; Manu Sm. 7.98; 9.64 etc.). Mahā Bhā. 3.92.16d reads *eṣa panthāḥ sanātanaḥ*. [On Etemal Dharma, see O'Flaherty (1976:94 ff.)]

There are many more one-sided definitions of *dharma*. Some of these are: *ahiṁsā paramo dharmaḥ* 'non-violence is transcendent *dharma* (Mahā Bhā. 1.11.12a; 13.116.1a; 13.116.25a; 13.117.37a etc.); *anṛśaṁsyaṁ paro dharmaḥ* 'compassion is transcendent *dharma*' (Mahā Bhā. 3.67.15c; 3.203.41a; 3.297.55a; 12.220.109c; 12.316.12a; 13.47.20a; 13.59.6a etc.); *ācāraḥ paramo dharmaḥ śrutyuktaḥ smārta eva ca*. 'The rule of conduct is transcendent law, whether mentioned (i.e. taught) in the revealed texts or in the sacred tradition'. (Manu Sm. 1.108). There are many more expressions of the type in vast Sanskrit literature.

2.43. 'Truth' (*satya*) and 'Justice or Righteousness' (*dharma*) are mutually associated. In Tai Ā. 7.11.1-4 Vedic teacher gives valuable instruction to the student: *satyaṁ vada dharmaṁ cara. . . satyān na pramaditavyaṁ dharmān na pramaditavyam* 'Speak the truth, practice *dharma*,. . . be not averse to truth, be not averse to *dharma*'. Sāyaṇa renders it as 'Agnihotra and other rites etc.' Hazra (1959:19) supports Sāyaṇa, but I would like to take the term to mean 'righteousness'. Both *satya* and *dharma* are organically related to each other. The kings acting out of truth uphold *dharma* (AV. 5.17.10). Dharma is associated with Satya, and both of them being complete and four-footed in Kṛtayuga (Manu Sm. 1.81). BṛĀraU. 1.4.14 says that nothing is higher (*param*) than *dharma*, and *dharma* and *satya* are identical. Dharma himself says that 'know that *ahiṁsā* 'non-violence, consideration for life', *samatā* 'equilibrium, impartiality', *śānti* 'tranquility', *tapas* 'asceticism', *śauca* 'purity' *amatsara* 'absence of jealousy', are the doors (through which I am accessible) (Mahā Bhā. 3.298.8; Nīla. *dvārāṇi dharmaprāptimukhāni*).

2.5. The concept of *dharma* in India (or even in South Asia) is closely associated with that of *karman*. The idea that one's actions in this world determine the conditions of one's life in the future. An act (*karman*), performed with a desire, creates what is known as *karmāśaya 'karmic* residue, accumulation for receptacle of *karman*', either meritorious (*dharma*) or unmeritorious (*adharma*), depending upon the quality of the act (see Mahony, in Eliade (ed.) 1987:263; Potter in O'Flaherty (ed.) 1983:243f.). In classical Vaiśeṣika, as represented by Praśastapāda, *adṛṣṭa* is a comprehensive term for *dharma* 'merit' and *adharma* 'demerit', two of the twenty-four qualities (*guṇas*) enumerated in the list of categories (*padārthas*) of the system. Vāiśe Sū. of Kaṇāda has only list of seventeen *guṇas* which excludes *dharma* and *adharma*. "The integration of *dharma* and *adharma* into the list of *guṇas* is a symptomatic step in the process of final systematization of Vaiśeṣika and of its attempted merger of soteriology and "physics". (Halbfass in O'Flaherty (ed.) 1983:285). Vaiśe Sū. 6.2.1. ff. uses *adṛṣṭa* and *dharma/adharma* in a more or less religious and ethical perspective, referring to 'invisible' results of ritual and ethical activities, to their 'merit' and 'demerit'. Nyāy Bh. *on* 3.2.63 ff. (cf. also *on* 4.1.44 ff.) accepts the concept of *dharma/adharma* as being inherent in the soul; and the connection between the retributive efficacy of deeds stored as "dispositions" (*saṁskāras*) of the soul and certain physical process has been made more explicit. The term *adṛṣṭa* in the Nyāya system is not used as synonym of *dharma/adharma* (for further discussion see Halbfass, *loc. cit.*, 286 ff.). In most of the other philosophical systems *dharma/adharma* is called *karman*. In the Sāṅkhya system "meritorious behaviour or virtue" (*dharma*), "unmeritorious behaviour or vice" (*adharma*) appear among *bhāvas* "projecting set of predispositions" (cf. Sāṅkhya Kā. 23,44 and 67; see Larson in O' Flaherty 1983: 312).

2.51. The term *dharma* is usually taken to designate 'duty of a class (*varṇa*) or stage of a class' (*āśrama*), and hence *varṇāśramadharma*. Classical Hinduism in general emphasises *svadharma*, while *bhakti* cults emphasise absolute *dharma*.

2.52. In Hinduistic belief 'good' in the universe is valuable because it exists together with 'evil'. Goodness cannot exist without evil. According to Manu Sm. 1.26 and 29 '. . .the creator created *dharma* and *adharma* and made the pairs of opposites such as happiness and misery. And whatever he assigned to each at first creation, truth or falsehood, that quality clung spontaneously to it'. These creatures carried the *karman* of former creation and they carried this *karman* with them; they were created full of *dharma* ('truthful') or *adharma* ('false') (Viṣṇu P. 1.5.59-65, cited in O'Flaherty 1976: 48).

2.6. Rana (1990: 87-99) discusses the term *dharma* as found in ancient Indian inscriptions. Dharma in the Aśokan inscriptions appears to be used in the sense of Buddha's doctrine, though some scholars understand the term in the range of moral and other virtue (Rana 1990: 94). In the Gupta period the term was related to *dāna-dharma*, such as gifts of land, gold, money etc. to the learned Brāhmaṇas, construction of temples etc. King was the sole guardian of the *varṇadharma*. In the later inscriptions the term stands for 'duty of caste', viz. *kṣātra-dharma* etc. *Nirvāṇa* is regarded as the fruit of *dharma* ('pious deed').

3.0. As I have already said in section 1.0. of this paper that the term *dharma* as occurring in Buddhistic literature lies basically outside the scope of the paper, yet the concept will be discussed in a very brief manner. Buddhistic ideas of the term has lot of comparative value with the ideas of classical Hinduism.

3.1. In Buddhism the term *dharma* denotes truth, knowledge, morality, and duty. After acquiring knowledge one becomes aware of *dharma*, and thereby one becomes free from bonds of phenomenal existence. The ceaseless effort to strive for *nirvāṇa* is the ultimate duty in Buddhism (cf. Skorupski in Eliade (ed.) 1987: 332-8). The compound expression *dharmakāya* signified transcendental reality of all beings and appearances. The word *dharma* is also used in the technical sense. There is no substance or person but there are *dharmas* (psycho-physical elements) which flow according to the law of dependent origination that is set in motion by the law of *karman*. These *dharmas* have many divisions and subdivisions.

3.11. In Pali *dhamma* signifies 'natural law, world order'; which regulates the principles of existence. The natural law is revealed in the Teaching of Buddha, which connotes *sīla* ('morality-good conduct'), truth and good. "The nearest to "good" in a general sense, would be, I think, Dharma". (Horner 1950: 10). Balasubrahmanyam (1993: 110) provides a semantic chart of the sense of *dhamma*: world order, natural law; factors of existence, material ideas, morality; principles of existence; teaching of the Buddha's doctrine; conditioning phenomena. In Pali canons the word *dhammatā* denotes 'higher or cosmic law, a general rule, practice, phenomenon, etc.' (see *Saṁyutta Nikāya* 1.90; *Dīgha Nikāya* 2.12; *Aṅguttara Nikāya* 2.36 etc.; see Balasubrahmanyam 1993: 113, n.11). Buddhists maintain that all *dhammas* are impermanent (but Mahā Bhā. 5.40.12 (cf. 18.5.50) expresses the opposite view that *dharma* and *jīva* are eternal, see section 2.4. of the this paper). Hazra (1960:34) remarks that in Buddhist literature (Sanskrit and Pali) *dharma* (*dhamma*) as a simplex or in compounds is employed in the sense of duty, justice, religion, religious doctrine but never in the sense of 'municipal or secular law'.

4.0. Tai Ā. 10.62.1 praises twelve virtues or qualities, one of them is *dharma* ('duty'). The *dharma* is said to be very base or foundation of the entire universe:

> *dharmo viśvasya jagataḥ pratiṣṭhā loke dharmiṣṭhaṁ prajā upasarpanti dharmeṇa pāpam apanudanti dharme sarvaṁ pratiṣṭhitaṁ tasmād dharmaṁ paramaṁ vadanti* // (Tai. Ā. 10.63.1)

'Dharma is the foundation of the whole universe; in world people approach the most ardent follower of *dharma*; by *dharma* they remove sin or evil; everything rests on *dharma*; so (people) declare *dharma* to be the most excellent'.

In Rāmā. 3.8.26 also significance of *dharma* is shown:

dharmād arthaḥ prabhavati dharmāt prabhavate sukham /
dharmeṇa labhate sarvaṁ dharmasāram idaṁ jagat / /

'From *dharma* accrues *artha* (the pleasure); from *dharma* accrues *sukha* (happiness); through *dharma* one attains everything; *dharma* is the very essence of this world'.

The *Suttanipāta* (1.10.1) says: *dharmo suciṇṇo sukhaṁ āvahati* 'Well-purified action brings forth pleasure or happiness'.

4.1. Recapitulation

By way of recapitulation we can make some of these observations. The term *dhárman (n.)* or *dharmán (m.)* is attested in early Vedic and in late Vedic, whereas in Classical Sanskrit we have *dharma (m.)*. The term is derived from *dhṛ*-'to hold, to maintain, to sustain, to preserve' etc. In ṚV. *dharman* is 'cosmic ordinance' as against *ṛta* 'universal harmony or order'. In the ancient Indian Culture *dharma* represents "correctness", both in a descriptive sense ("the way things are"), and also in a prescriptive sense ("the way things should be"). It reflects the inextricable connection in the religious thought of India between ontology, ritual ideology, social philosophy, ethics and canon law, and socio-ethic-religious duties for maintaining society. The concept of *dharma* cannot precisely be defined. It is indeed, the very basis or foundation of everything in the universe. Through *dharma* one can attain happiness in this world and also in future. The concept of *dharma* is closely connected with the concept of *karman*. In the typical Indian or Hindustic hierarchy *dharma* appears first and it is followed by *artha, kāma* and *mokṣa*. According to the ancient adage *satya* and *dharma* ought to be observed very meticulously. Typologically there exist many classificatory criteria or divisions. The *dharma* can be individual, common, caste or profession based etc. In Buddhism the term does not appear to be in the sense of *vyavahāra* (juridical law). In many philosophical systems the term *dharma* stands for 'merit' or 'meritorious results', as against *adharma* 'demerit' or 'demeritorious result', etc.; and roughly corresponds to what we call *adṛṣṭa* (*dharma/adharma*) in the Nyāya-Vaiśeṣika systems. The *dharma* is also a personification of various deities, human beings, abstract concepts etc.

I hope that I have explained with sufficient clarity the very wide semantic range and scope of the term *dharma(n)* in the diachronic and comparative manner.

Notes

1. Balasubrahmanyam (1993: 106) is right in saying that ṚV. has retained barytonic accentuation.
2. Oxytonic form *dharmán (m.)* is an agent noun; whereas barytonic form *dhárman (n.)* is an action noun. It must be noted here that some agent nouns have acute accent on the suffix, see e.g. *brahmán (m.)* 'priest' as against *bráhman (n.)* 'prayer'; *sadmán (m.)* 'sitter' as against *sádman (n.)* 'seat'. For some such cases of action and agent nouns, see Whitely, *Skt. Gr.*, sec. 1168c; Macdonell, *Ved. Gr.*., sec. 165, p. 128. Of course there are some agent nouns with acute accent on the root portion.
3. For *dhárman, dharmán*, and *dhárma* forms one may refer to *Alt Gr*.. II.i, sec. 43a, p. 142; II.ii, sec. 80b, p. 178; sec. 500c; p. 675; sec. 596, p. 749; sec. 602b, p. 756; sec. 602-3, p. 758; sec. 604b and 605a, p. 760f.; sec. 608b, p. 765; sec. 609b, p. 767; III, sec. 144d, p. 265. Also see Mayr. II. 94-5.
4. Mīmā Nyā Pra. 193.11 (sec. 3) *tatra vedena prayojanam uddiśya vidhīyamāno 'rtho dharmaḥ/*
5. Bhag Gi. 3.35 *śreyān svadharmo viguṇaḥ paradharmāt svanuṣṭhitāt/svadharme nidhanaṁ śreyaḥ paradharmo bhayāvahaḥ//*
6. Mahā Bhā. 1.1.66 *yudhiṣṭhiro dharmamayo mahādrumaḥ skando 'rjuno bhīmaseno ' sya śākhāḥ/ mādrīsutau puṣpaphale smṛddhe mūlaṁ kṛṣṇo brahma ca brāhmaṇā ca//*

References

Alt Gr. = Wackernagel, J. et al.

Balasubrahmanyam, M.D. 1993. 'Sanskrit *dharma* and Pali *dhammo*'. BDCRI 51-52.105-14 = Prof S.M. Katre Ftel. Vol., Pune: Deccan College.

Derrett, J. Duncan M. 1973. *Dharmaśāstra* and *Juridical Literature* (*A History of Indian Literature*, Vol. IV, Ed. J. Gonda). Wiesbaden: Otto Harrassowitz.

Dumézil, G. 1988. *Mythe et épopée*. Paris.

EDS. = *An Encyclopaedic Dictionary of Sanskrit on Historical Principles*, Vol. III, Pt. i. 1982. Poona: Deccan College.

Eliade Mircea (ed.). 1987. *The Encyclopedia of Religion*. Vol.4 (see Dharma entry). New York: Macmillan Publishing Company. London: Collier Macmillan Publishers.

Gonda, J. 1971. 'The Vedic Mitra and the Epic Dharma' *JRAS*. 1971. 120-33 (=1991. *Selected Studies*, Vol. VI.i 1-14. Leiden: E.J. Brill).

Halbfass, Wilhelm. 1983. 'Karma, *Apūrva*, and "Natural" Causes: Observations on the Growth and Limits of the Theory of Saṁsāra', pp. 269-302. In: O'Flaherty, Wendy Doniger (ed.), 1983.

Hazra, R.C. 1959 and 1960. 'Dharma-Its Early Meaning and Scope', Pts. I-II. *Our Heritage* (Calcutta) 7:1.15-35 and 8:1.7-34.

HDS. = Kane, P.V.

Heesterman, J.C. 1985. *The Inner Conflict of Tradition* (*Essays in Indian Ritual, Kingship and Society*). Chicago and London: The University of Chicago Press.

Hopkins, E.W. 1915. *Epic Mythology*. Strassburg (Grundriss Series).

Horner, I.B. 1950. *The Basic Position of Sila*. Colombo: The Buddha Sahitya Sabha.

Kane, P.V. 1930 and 1941. *History of Dharmaśāstra*, Vol. I. and Vol. II.i. Poona: Bhandarkar Oriental Research Institute.

Larson, Gerald James. 1983. 'Karma as a "Sociology of Knowledge" or "Social Psychology" of Process/Praxis', pp. 303-16. In O'Flaherty, Wendy Doniger (ed.). 1983.

Lingat, Robert. 1973 (Eng. Tr. J. Duncan M. Derrett). *The Classical Law of India*. Berkeley, Los Angeles, London: University of California Press.

Macdonell, A.A. 1910 (Indian reprint 1968). *Vedic Grammar*. Varanasi, Delhi: Indological Book House.

Macdonell, A.A.; Keith, A.B. 1912 (Indian reprint 1958). *Vedic Index of Names and Subjects*. Vol. I. 390-7. London: John Murray (Indian reprint. Varanasi: Motilal Banarsidass).

Mahony, William K. 1987. "Hindu Dharma", pp. 329-32. In: Eliade, Mircea (ed.), 1987.

Mayr. = Mayrhofer, M. 1963. *Kurzgefaβtes etymologisches Wörterbuch des Altindischen* II. Heidelberg: Carl Winter Universitätsverlag.

O'Flaherty, Wendy Doniger. 1976 (reprint 1988). *The Origins of Evil in Hindu Mythology*. Delhi etc. : Motilal Banarsidass.

——(ed.). 1983. *Karma and Rebirth in Classical Indian Tradition*. Delhi etc.: Motilal Benarsidass.

Potter, Karl H. 1983. 'The Karma Theory and its Interpretation in some Indian Philosophical Systems', pp. 241-67. In: O'Flaherty, Wendy Doniger (ed.), 1983.

Rana, R.S. 1990. 'Dharma as depicted in Ancient Indian Inscriptions'. *Bhāratīya Vidyā* 50: 1-4. 87-99.

Skorupski, Tadeusz. 1987. 'Buddhist Dharma and Dharmas', pp. 332-8. In: Eliade, Mircea (ed.), 1987.

Thieme, P. 1973. 'King Varuṇa'. In: *German Scholars on India*, Vol. I. 333-49. Varanasi: The Chowkhamba Sanskrit Series Office.

Wackernagel, Jacob; Debrunner, Albert. 1896-1957. *Altindische Grammatik* I-III. Göttingen: Vandenhoeck und Ruprecht.

Whitney, W.D. 1962 (Indian reprint). *Sanskrit Grammar*. Delhi etc.: Motilal Banarsidass.

3

Concept of Dharma and Dharmaśāstra

D.N. Shanbhag

Literature called as 'Dharmaśāstra' forms an important part of Sanskrit Literature. Both the terms Dharma and Śāstra have significant meanings connoted by them. First we take the term Dharma.

Generally in common parlance the term Dharma is rendered into English as 'Religion' (which deals with the relation of man with God comprising of worship, rituals etc.) and Śāstra as 'sacred literature' or 'canonical work' to be obeyed implicitly. But as P.V. Kane[1] rightly observes, "Dharma is one of those Sanskrit words that defy all attempts at an exact rendering in English or any other tongue. That word has passed through several vicissitudes". In the words of B. Kuppuswamy,[2] "Dharma has been one of the most powerful and influential terms in Indian thought and society for several millenia, right from Vedic times upto to-day. However, there are diverse ways in which it has been used. It stands for religious observance, righteousness, justice, conformity to law, conformity to custom, obedience to the social order, sense of duty, etc. and thus has religious, moral, ethical as well as legal significance. This is one important reason why it is impossible to translate the word into any other non-Indian language". It is also true that this word Dharma has been often misunderstood and as a result it is more disliked or condemned than subjected to correct understanding.

What is this Dharma? And what did our ancestors achieve by following Dharma? In this connection, I wish to point at a verse[3] which tells us about Kṛtayuga which is considered to be the most happiest state of any civilized society. It states that "in the Kṛtayuga, there was no Kingdom, no King, no punishment and no punisher.

People were protecting mutually by Dharma itself". It means that they were all living happily by performing their respective Dharma. They were not committing any crimes nor were they tormenting one another and as such there was no need to have a 'King' or any type of government to maintain law and order, or to protect people from any type of injustice or exploitation. Thus the entire society was living happily, the basis of individual and social happiness being Dharma.

There is also another verse[4] stating Dharma to be the cause of happiness: "All activities of living beings are for the sake of securing happiness and happiness is impossible without Dharma. Hence one must be engaged in Dharma".

It is well known that Indians believed in four goals of human existence. They are: *Dharma, Artha, Kāma* and *Mokṣa*. Materialists may believe in only two goals viz. *Artha* or worldly prosperity and *Kāma* or worldly happiness. Sage Vyāsa at the end of the *Mahābhārata* proclaims[5] that even *Artha* and *Kāma* do result from *Dharma*. Āpastamba approves.[6] So it means that a knowledge of Dharma is necessary even for those who are seekers of only worldly pleasures.

The *Rāmāyaṇa* rightly sums up "One obtains everything through Dharma. Whole world has Dharma as its essence or basis".[7]

Hence we can conclude: (1) Dharma did establish a happy society without misery or exploitation and free from crime and punishment. (2) Dharma causes happiness. (3) Dharma brings about material benefits and physical pleasures. And (4) Dharma is the root cause of all.

Now the question is, what is this Dharma? Many attempts have been made to give an idea of Dharma. Some are based on the meaning of its root viz. *Dhṛ* meaning to uphold, to support, or to nourish. Dharma is (1) that which upholds the worlds (*Dharati lokān iti dharmaḥ*); (2) that by which every thing is supported. (Dhriyate anena iti) (3) that which supports (the worlds and human society) (*Dhārayati iti*)[8] and (4) that which supports the universe (*Dharati viśvam iti*). (5) Dharma is so called because of *Dhāraṇa* or of its nature of supporting. Dharma upholds people at large. The decision is that Dharma is that which is possessed of *Dhāraṇa*.[9] (6) Dharma is so called because it upholds one who has fallen, one who is falling and one who would fall in future.[10] (7) Dharma is that due to which there is the gain of happiness both worldly and other worldly.[11]. (8) That which causes well-being is stated by the term 'Dharma'. (9) Performance of Dharma means the performance of ordained actions as a means to gain extra-ordinary well-being or bliss.[13] (10) One rises high by Dharma and slips down by Adharma.[14] (11) Dharma is the strong foundation of the universe and the world.[15] (12) That which is the direct cause of the worldly prosperity and other-worldly bliss of living beings is Dharma.[16] (13) The rule of Dharma was laid down for the smooth functioning of the life of beings.[17] (14) A verse [18] sings the omnipotence of Dharma: "Dharma bestows everlasting and Supreme bliss; it secures eternal feet of the Lord; it imports perfect intellect and inner bliss; and it provides rich progeny and reputation".

The *Smṛticandrikā* states that, that action which is approved and lauded by Āryas or duty-conscious people who are well versed in sacred literature is Dharma and that which is censured by them is Adharma.[19]

All these references to Dharma mean that Dharma gives us whatever we desire to possess. viz. Worldly progress, material prosperity and all-round pleasure and also other-worldly and everlasting happiness and bliss. Hence one can secure everything through the performance of Dharma.

Now, to know what is Dharma, we must know that which is the cause of our pleasure and happiness both here worldly and here after other-worldly. So what is the cause of our happiness or misery, pleasure or pain, success or failure, and so on?

Sage Vyāsa has given the answer to this question in the *Mahābhārata*. He says[20] "Happiness is by good deed and misery by a bad one; everywhere one gets fruits as per his deeds. No deed, no fruit". In other words one's own deeds are the cause of one's happiness or misery.[21] Hence, the *Gītā* declares-[22] "Man is his own architect of himself. He can make or mar himself". There are also other statements which bring out the same thought: (1) Sacred treatises show `As you sow, so you reap'.[23] (2) In this world one's own deeds raise one high or fell one down.[24] (3) Just as one who digs a well goes down slowly and just as one who builds a wall gradually climbs up, so too a man descends or ascends by his own deeds.[25] (4) One becomes meritorious by good or meritorious deeds and becomes sinful by bad or sinful deeds.[26] (5) Just as light and shade do always co-exist so too are the deed and the doer joined together.[27] (6) One creates one's own misery; one causes one's own happiness.[28] (7) Whatever deed one performs whether auspicious or dreadful, its fruits are experienced by the same one only.[29]

So it is well said "Man is lonely in his birth, lonely in his death and again lonely in reaping the fruits of his actions".[30]

Thus we can observe that one's happiness is due to Dharma and that good deeds cause happiness. And misery is due to Adharma and that bad deeds cause misery. Hence, *Dharma* means *Satkarma* or *Puṇyakarma* all meaning good deeds, meritorious actions; these are the same as 'ordained duties' or 'prescribed actions'. Accordingly, at many places the terms *Dharma* and *Karma* have been used as synonyms,[31] Where the meaning of the term *Karma* is contracted as *satkarma* or 'good deed'. Hence Dharma means one's own *duties* (*Dharmaśabdaḥ Kartavyatāvacana ityuktam*) as by performing one's own duties one gets happiness here and hereafter. P.V. Kane sums up Dharma as, "the privileges, duties and obligations of a man, his standard of conduct as a member of the Āryan community, as a member of one of the castes, as a person in a particular stage of life".[32]

Now, we can turn to the assertion about the Kṛtayuga which informed that people were protecting mutually by performing their respective Dharma or duties. Accordingly we can create an atmosphere of perfect social good and happiness by becoming completely duty-conscious and performing our duties to the satisfaction of the concerned. Because, man is a social animal and his happiness or misery is invariably connected with the happiness or misery of his society. He has to live in the midst of the society following the dictum "Live and let live". Society consists of innumerable individuals who must function as parts of a big machine which functions smoothly only when its parts, small and big, function according to their place and role in the machine. No trouble arises if all parts function properly. So too is the case of men and women forming parts of their society. Social good and happiness are proportionate to their performing their duties properly and diligently. Problem of social disorder and the resultant chaos and confusion arise only when one neglects one's duty or when one interferes in the duty of others. Hence it is declared. `*Dharmo rakṣati rakṣitah* (Dharma protected, protects). It is like following meticulously the traffic rules, which when followed by one and all protect one and all.

So Dharma means Duty; performing Dharma means performing one's own individual and social duties. It is also true that Dharma is that duty which on its performance leads one to the good and well-being both of one as an individual member of the society and of the society as a whole. And so the ancient seers exhort emphatically to perform one's own duty in the Convocation Address, "*Satyam vada; Dharmam cara*" (*Taittirīyopaniṣad*). At this stage the question arises "How to know one's duties leading to individual and social welfare?" And here enter the Dharmaśāstra to instruct about such duties.

Now, coming to the term Śāstra, the term does not denote any one work or treatise. It is derived from the root '*śās*' to teach, to instruct, or to advise. Hence, *śāstra* means that which instructs or an instruction or injunction. The term *śāstra* is interpreted as *śāsti trāyate iti* which means that which instructs and also saves or protects. Hence it stands for that treatise which imparts instruction to human beings about their duties and thus protects their interests. It is well said, "*Śāstra* is that which regulates and declares 'do's and don't's of human beings through eternal Vedas or through works composed by learned men".[33] It is also laid down that a *Śāstra*-work should not cause any disorder or confusion,[34] because any disorder or confusion harms the individual and social interests and well-being. Only therefore, Arjuna is advised in the *Gītā* to follow the authority of *śāstra* whenever he gets any doubt about what is to be done and what is not to be done.[35] And a verse distinguishes human beings from other animals on the basis of following or not following the *Śāstras*. It says, "Animals act as per instinct; men act as per *Śāstra*".[36]

Further to know how the Dharmaśāstras are authoritative and why they should be obeyed, we must know the sources of the Dharmaśāstras. Their authors were intent upon social and individual good of the humanity as a whole. The concern of the ancient Indians towards humanity as a whole is reflected in their age-old prayer[37] to the Lord where they pray for the happiness, sound health and the noble thinking of one and all and note of any particular group of people limited by any region, time, caste, class, creed or any such extraneous restrictions. There are also other beliefs of Indians which clarify their nobility and liberality of thinking having always the well-being of the entire human society in their mind and heart. These are[38] (1) Let noble thoughts come to us from all sides. (2)

Earth is the mother; I am her son. (3) One must live for one's salvation and for the welfare of the world. (4) Let us make the entire humanity noble and duty-minded. (5) The whole world is one family.

Hence one can find that Indians laid great stress on renunciation, rather than on personal enjoyment so much so, that Indian culture has been characterised as *Tyāgamayī* or full or renunciation. It appears that Indians taught the lesson of 'first give and then eat' to make people at large to be ever-conscious of their duties more towards others than to themselves. They declared:[39] (1) One who eats alone is a worst sinner. (2) Collect with hundred hands; distribute with thousand hands. (3) Enjoy after giving; do not cover anybody's wealth. (4) Some secured salvation with renunciation. (5) Those who cook only for their own sake experience only sin. (6) He who enjoys without giving to others is only a thief. (7) Only that much which fills one's stomach is one's wealth; if anybody thinks more to be his wealth, he is a thief fit for punishment. (8) They collected wealth only for charity. (9) The good, like clouds, receive only to pour out.

Ancient Indians also laid down simple formulas to practise successfully the dictum of 'Live and let live'. They declared:[40] (1) There are only two statement of Vyāsa pervading his eighteen *purāṇas* and they are: (a) Obliging others leads to blissful merit: and (b) harming others makes one a sorrowful sinner. (2) I state in only a half verse what has been stated by crores of scriptures: Oblige others for gaining merit; harm others and incur sin. (3) Treat others as you wish to be treated by others.

All this has been elaborated only to point out that our ancestors had in their heart utmost concern for the welfare of the entire humanity and such noble and largehearted persons had been assigned the significant work of laying down Dharma or individual and social duties of men and women through their compositions called 'Dharmaśāstra's. Such great persons who devoted their lives for the good of the society, some times even at the cost of their own personal pleasures and comforts, were revered by one and all and their words were obeyed implicitly. It is well said by P.V. Kane: "The conception of Dharma was a far-reaching one and it embraced the whole life of man. The writers on Dharmaśāstra meant by dharma not a creed or religion, but a mode of life or a code of conduct, which regulated a man's work and activities as a member of society and as an individual and was intended to bring about the gradual development of a man and to enable him to reach what was deemed to be the goal of human existence".[41]

Hence we can conclude that Dharma is Duty and Dharmaśāstra means Instruction regarding Duty by Universal Well-wisher.

Footnotes

1. *History of Dharmaśāstra*, Vol, p.1.
2. *Dharma and Society*, Macmillan, Delhi, 1977, p.16.
3. न राज्यं न च राजासीन्न दण्डो न च दाण्डिकः।
   धर्मेणैव प्रजाः सर्वा रक्षन्ति स्म परस्परम्।। महाभारत.
4. सुखार्थाः सर्वलोकानां मताः सर्वाः प्रवृत्तयः।
   सुखं च विना धर्मात्तस्माद्धर्मपरो भवेत्।।
5. ऊर्ध्वबाहुर्विरौम्येष न च कश्चित् श्रृणोति मे।
   धर्मादर्थश्च कामश्च स किमर्थं न सेव्यते।।
   [अर्थसिद्धिं परामिच्छन् धर्ममेवादौ चरेत्।
   न हि धर्मादपैत्यर्थः स्वर्गलोकादिवामृतम्।। – महाभारत]
6. तद्यथा आम्रे फलार्थे निर्मिते छाया गन्ध इति अनूत्पद्येते एवं धर्म चर्यमाणं अर्था अनूत्पद्यन्ते। –आपस्तम्बधर्मसूत्र.
7. धर्माद्वि लभते सर्वं धर्मसारमिदं जगत्।।
8. यो लोकान् धारयति, येन मानवसमाजो धृतः स धर्मः।
9. धारणाद् धर्ममित्याहुः धर्मो धारयते प्रजाः।
   यः स्यादधारणसंयुक्तः स धर्म इति निश्चयः।।
10. पतितं पतन्तं पतिष्यन्तं धरतीति धर्मः।
11. यतोऽभ्युदयनिःश्रेयससिद्धिः स धर्मः।
12. य एव श्रेयस्करः स एव धर्मशब्देनोच्यते।
13. अलौकिकश्रेयः साधनत्वेन विहितक्रियात्वं हि धर्मत्वम्।
14. धर्मेण गमनमूर्ध्वं गमनमधस्ताद्भ्वत्यधर्मेण।
15. धर्मो विश्वस्य जगतः प्रतिष्ठा।
16. प्राणिनां साक्षादभ्युदयनिःश्रेयसहेतुर्यः स धर्मः।

17. लोकयात्रार्थमेवेह धर्मस्य नियमः कृतः।
18. धर्मो ददाति धनमक्षयमुत्तमं तु
धर्मो ददाति पदमक्षयमच्युतस्य।
धर्मो ददाति विमलां धियमात्मसौख्यं
धर्मो ददाति बहुपुत्रयशांसि नृणाम्।।
19. यमार्याः क्रियमाणं तु शंसन्त्यागमवेदिनः।
स धर्मो यं विगर्हन्ति तमधर्मं प्रचक्षते।।
[कर्तव्यमाचरन्कार्यमकर्तव्यमनाचरन्।
तिष्ठति प्रकृताचारे स वै आर्य इति स्मृतः।।]
20. शुभेन कर्मणा सौख्यं दुःखं पापेन कर्मणा।
कृतं भवति सर्वत्र नाकृतं विद्यते क्वचित्।।
21. सुखस्य दुःखस्य न कोऽपि दाता।
परो ददातीति कुबुद्धिरेषा।।
22. उद्धरेदात्मनात्मानं नात्मानमवसादयेत्।
आत्मैव ह्यात्मनो बन्धुरात्मैव रिपुरात्मनः।।
23. यथा कर्म तथा लाभ इति शास्त्रनिदर्शनम्।
24. लोके गुरुत्वं विपरीततां वा स्वचेष्टितान्येव नरं नयन्ति।
25. यात्यधोऽधः व्रजन्युच्चैर्नरः स्वैरेव कर्मभिः।
कूपस्य खनिता यद्वत्प्राकारस्येव कारकः।।
26. पुण्यो वै पुण्येन कर्मण भवति, पापो वै पापेन।
27. यथा छायातपौ नित्यं सुसम्बद्धौ परस्परम्।
एवं कर्म च कर्ता च संश्लिष्टावितरेतरम्।।
28. आत्मना विहितं दुःखमात्मना विहितं सुखम्।
29. यत्करोति शुभं कर्म तथा कर्म सुदारुणम्।
तत्कर्तैव समश्नाति।
30. एकः प्रजायते जन्तुरेक एव प्रलीयते। उकोऽनुभुङ्क्ते सुकृतमेक एव च
दुष्कृतम्।।

31.(i) अग्नौ प्रास्तं तु पुरुषं कर्मान्वेति स्वयं कृतम्।
तस्मात्तु पुरुषो यत्नाद् धर्मं संचिनुयाच्छनैः।।

(ii) धनानि भूमौ पशवश्च गोष्ठे भार्या गृहद्वारि बन्धवः श्मशाने।
देहश्चितायां परलोकमार्गे कर्मानुगो गच्छति जीव एकः।।

(iii) दारा ह्यपत्यं भृत्यश्च बान्धवाः प्रियवादिनः।
गच्छन्तं नानुगच्छन्ति धर्म एवानुगच्छति।।

(iv) को हि जानाति कस्याद्य मृत्युकालो भविष्यति।
युवैव धर्मशीलः स्यादनित्यं खलु जीवितम्।।

(v) आयुर्न सुलभं लब्ध्वा नावकर्षेद् विशांपते।
उत्कर्षार्थं प्रयतेतनरः पुण्येन कर्मणा।।

(vi) स्वे स्वे कर्मण्याभिरतः संसिद्धिं लभते नरः।।

(vii) स्वधर्मे निधनं श्रेयः।।

32. Op. cit. Vol. I., p.2

33. प्रवृत्तिर्वा निवृत्तिर्वा नित्येन कृतकेन वा।
शासनाच्छंसनाच्चैव शास्त्रमित्यभिधीयते।। भामती, I.i.3.

34. न ह्यव्यवस्थाकारिणा शास्त्रेण भवितव्यम्। शास्त्रतो नाम व्यवस्था।।
–महाभाष्य on वार्तिक 4 on पाणिनि VI. i.135.

35. (i) तस्माच्छास्त्रं प्रमाणं ते कार्याकार्यव्यवस्थितौ।।

(ii) यः शास्त्रविधिमुत्सृज्य वर्तति कामकारतः।
न स सिद्धिमवाप्नोति न सुखं न परां गतिम्।।

(iii) येषां शास्त्रानुगा बुद्धिर्न ते मुह्यन्ति भारत।। महाभारत

36. मतयो यत्र गच्छन्ति तत्र गच्छन्ति वानराः।
शास्त्राणि यत्र गच्छन्ति तत्र गच्छन्ति वै नराः।।

37. सर्वेऽत्र सुखिनः सन्तु सर्वे सन्तु निरामयाः। सर्वे भद्राणि पश्यन्तु मा कश्चिदद्दुःखभाग्भवेत्।।

38. (i) आ नो भद्रा क्रतवो यन्तु विश्वतः।।

(ii) माता भूमिः पुत्रोऽहं पृथिव्याः।।

(iii) आत्मनो मोक्षार्थं जगद्धिताय च।।

(iv) कृण्वन्तो विश्वमार्यम्।।

(v) (a) वसुधैव कुटुम्बकम्।।

(b) यत्र विश्वं भवत्येकनीडम्।।

(39) (i) केवलाघो भवति केवलादी।।

(ii) शतहस्त समाहर सहस्रहस्त संकिर।।

(iii) तेन त्यक्तेन भुञ्जीथाः मा गृधः कस्यस्विद्धनम्।।

(iv) त्यागेनैऽकेमृतत्वमानशुः।।

(v) भुञ्जते ते त्वघं पापं ये पचन्त्यात्मकारणात्।।

(vi) तैर्दत्तानप्रदायेभ्यो यो भुङ्क्ते स्तेन एव सः।।

(vii) यावदाभ्रियेत जठरं तावस्वत्वं हि देहिनाम्।

अधिकं योऽभिमन्येत स स्तेते दण्डमर्हति।।

(viii) त्यगाय संभृतार्थानाम्।।

(ix) आदानं हि विसर्गाय सतां वारिमुचामिव।।

40 (i) अष्टादशपुराणेषु व्यासस्य वचनद्वयम्।

परोपकारः पुण्याय पापाय परपीडनम्।।

(ii) श्लोकार्धेन प्रवक्ष्यामि यदुक्तं शास्त्रकोटिभिः।

परोपकारः पुण्याय पापाय परपीडनम्।।

(iii) श्रूयतां धर्मसर्वस्वं श्रुत्वा चाप्यवधार्यताम्।

आत्मनः प्रतिकूलानि परेषां न समाचरेत्।।

(41) Op. cit. Vol. II. p.2.

4

Woman and Dharmaśāstra

Ujjwala Panse

Status of women in the society has remained all through an important and interesting point for those who care to think just because a woman really offers whatever she has to make her family happy. Her family is her first concern even in these modern times. It is also true that in most of the cases whatever sacrifices she makes go without taking any notice of them by other family members. Still the fact remains that a woman—be it a mother or a wife or a sister or a daughter plays the role of the backbone of the household life of the family—and in modern times if the woman is well educated she is the main partner even in the intellectual endeavours of the family members. But one has to accept with regret that even under these circumstances the main outlook of men and even of women to look at a woman has not changed much—for which our Dharmaśāstra is mainly responsible.

While reading Dharmaśāstra (DŚ) texts we come accross (i) some rules that talk of the duties of women and (ii) some that talk of the rights. These are the two main tools to judge their opinions about the issue. This is one thing. The other point is that one often finds that there are some rules which contradict either the same author or some other author on DŚ. To explain, there are two types of contradiction: (1) A text contradicts some other text by some other author and (2) there are contradictory rules in the same text. For the later a popular answer may be that of interpolation which may not be convincing at many a time.

My contention is: the first type of contradiction i.e. the later person contradicting or rather differing from the earlier author is nothing but an instance of changing outlook or of the development of thought in case of the particular issue. Whereas if one looks a bit more carefully at the contradictory rules in the same text one becomes aware that even in these texts there are two types of rules as in any other *Śāstra* namely, general rules and exceptional rules (*utsarga* and *apavāda*). General rules are to be applied generally and exceptional ones exceptionally. What I mean is, general rules are meant for the people at large who lead very normal life and do not have any type of an exceptional i.e. extra-normal or difficult fase of life to pass through. But the exceptional type of rules are meant for those who for one reason or the other are not in a position to have all the things in order or just say goody goody type of life if one may say so.

My contention is, both these types do reflect the author's social awareness but the second type does more so as the situations in which this type of rules are applicable are really the crusial ones that need a bit more careful handling. And the way a Dśkāra prescribes the rule for such times in life of a person speaks very much of general frame of his mind, his over all vision of life and his view on a particular issue. If a *śāstrakāra* fails to handle such a situation, the result would be detrimental to the person concerned and this will certainly be very much undesirable and disappointing to the society.

Thus, the rules which seem to be contrary to general rules are mostly of the type of exceptional rules.

The aim of this paper is, thus, to look into some of the exceptional type of statements which may reveal some deeper layers of the minds of some of the prominent Dśkāras like Gautama, Baudhīyana, Viṣṇu, Manu and Yājñavalkya that thought of women who had to face some uncommon situations in their lives. After examining these statements we shall try to draw some conclusion regarding their opinion about women.

While stating the *strīdharmas* i.e. duties of a woman the Dśkīras normally begin with the proper time of marriage of a girl, and then prescribe the duties of a married woman, the duties of a wife whose husband is away on journey and the duties of a widow. That is why, the paper is divided into the following parts:

(1) Rules concerning marriage of girls
(2) Rules concerning the *proṣitabhartṛkās*
(3) Rules concerning the widows, and
(4) Observations.

Rules concerning the marriage of girls

While stating the proper time of marriage of girls right from Baudhīyana, Gautama upto Manu we see that generally they have stated: A girl should be given in marriage before she attains puberty because, otherwise her father will be a sinner.

Baudhīyana (4.1.12) says,

दद्यादगुणवते कन्यां नाग्निकां ब्रह्मचारिणे । which means:

A girl (daughter) should be given in marriage to a deserving *brahmacīrin* when she is a *nagnikā*. This word is explained by the commentator as, 'नग्निका वस्त्रपरिधानाभावेऽपि लज्जाशून्या' which amounts to saying, 'when she is very young and small in age'.

Gautama states: गृहस्थः सदृशीं भार्यां विन्देतानन्यपूर्वां यवीयसीम् (*Gautama Dharmasūtra* (Gau Dhasū) 4.2). Tr.: A *gṛhastha* should obtain a wife who is similar to him (in many respects) and who is not given to any one else before and who is younger in age. And then prescribes the time of giving a daughter in marriage in Gau Dhasū (18.22) as: प्रदानं प्रागृतोः ।

Tr.: The giving (should take place) before (she attains) puberty. And then adds, अप्रयच्छन् दोषी । (one) who does not give (his daughter in marriage at proper time) is at fault.

Manu says

प्रयच्छेत् नग्निकां कन्यां ऋतुकालभयान्वितः ।
ऋतुमत्यां हि तिष्ठन्त्यामेनो दातारमृच्छति ।। 9.88 ।।

Tr.: (A father) being afraid of the time of (her attaining) puberty should give his daughter (in marriage when she is) a *nagnikā*. If she remains (at her father's house) when she has (already) attained puberty then to the giver (of such a girl who has attained puberty) goes the sin.

He also says:

उत्कृष्टायाभिरूपाय वराय सदृशाय च ।
अप्राप्तामपि तां तस्मै कन्यां दद्याद्यथाविधि ।।

(Manu 9. 73)

Tr.: (A father) should give his daughter to him who is excellent match for her and who is similar to her, even if she is very small.

These are general rules in this matter. But it is quite understandable that all people do not have same circumstances i.e. same facilities or same amount of favourable conditions and so on. To explain; there is every possibility that in some case there would be some difficulty in following these above mentioned rules due to the lack of certain favourable conditions. What does it mean? Let us think of a situation where a father, in spite of his willing to give his daughter in marriage is unable to get a proper match for his daughter. In such a case a question arises, whether he should bear that sin of not giving his daughter in marriage at a proper time or he should give his daughter to any Dick, Tom or Harry to avoid that sin.

Baudhāyana 4.1.12 answers this question as follows:

दद्यादगुणवते कन्यां नग्निकां ब्रहमचारिणे।
अपि वा गुणहीनाय नोपरून्ध्याद्रजस्वलाम्।।

Tr.: One should give his daughter to a deserving bachelor or even to an undeserving one (but should) not retain her (upto the time) when she attains puberty.

Manu's answer to this question, however, is:

काममा मरणात्तिष्ठेत् गृ हे कन्यार्तुमत्यपि।
न चैवेनां प्रयच्छेत्तु गुणहीनाय कर्हिचित्।।

Tr.: Certainly, let the girl stay at her (father's) house after attaining puberty also, even upto her death but he should never give her to an unworthy (match).

This opinion of Manu, according to me, is very important. Here, clearly differing from Baudhāyana and setting aside his own principle and all so-called social bindings, Manu straightforwardly states that in such a situation there is no harm even if the daughter stays at her father's house until her death. But in no case should he give his daughter to an unworthy person.

Let us think of some other situations. Suppose, there is nobody to look after a girl or to search a husband for her. Here again the question arises: what should the girl do? Is she given freedom to seek a husband for herself or she has to remain unmarried the whole life?

In answer to this question almost all the authors of *Dś* have unequivocally granted the freedom of *svayaṁvaraṇa* i.e. choosing a husband by the girl herself.

There is a difference of opinion concerning the period of time that the girl has to wait for. Some like Gautama, and Viṣṇu have stated that she should wait for three *ṛtus* after she attains puberty and then should choose a husband for herself. *Gau Dhasū* (18.21) says:

त्रीन् कुमार्यृतूनतीत्य स्वयं युज्येतानिन्दितेन
उत्सृज्य पित्र्यानलङ्कारान् ।

Tr.: A virgin should unite with a good (person as her husband) after crossing three *ṛtus*—(she should be) leaving the ornaments from her father.

Viṣṇu states: (*Viṣṇu Smṛti*) (*VS*) 24.40)

ऋतुत्रयमुपास्यैव कन्या कुर्यात्स्वयंवरम् ।
ऋतुत्रये व्यतीते तु प्रभवत्यात्मनः सदा ।।

Tr.: A girl should choose her husband herself after crossing three *ṛtus* as when the three *ṛtus* are over she has the right over herself.

Whereas, Baudhāyana, Manu etc. have said that she should wait for three years.

Baudhāyana Dharmasūtra (Bau Dhasū) 4.1.15 runs as follows:

त्रीणि वर्षाण्यृतुमती काङ्क्षेत पितृशासनम् ।
ततश्चतुर्थे वर्षे तु विन्देत सदृशं पतिम् ।।

Tr.: A girl who has attained puberty should desire to follow the discipline of her father for three years and then in the fourth year she should obtain a husband who matches her.

Manu says: (Manu 9.90)

त्रीणि वर्षाण्युदीक्षेत कुमारी ऋतुमती सती ।
ऊर्ध्वं तु कालादेतस्मात् विन्देत सद्दशं पतिम् ।

Tr.: A virgin after attaining puberty should wait for three years but after the lapse of this period (of three years) should obtain a match (for herself).

The commentator of *manvarthavivṛti* adds here, *vindeta svaprayatnenaiva*. She should herself search our a husband. There is nothing wrong in it.

It is clear that in case of a girl whose parents or relatives do not search a match for her even after she attains puberty the same rule is applicable. Manu 9.91 says it clearly:

अदीयमाना भर्तारमधिगच्छेद्यदि स्वयम्।
नैनः किञ्चिदवाप्नोति न च यं साऽधिगच्छति।।

And then adds:

अङ्कारं नाददीत पित्र्यं कन्या स्वयंवरा।
मातृकं भ्रातृदत्तं वा स्तेना स्याद्यदि तं हरेत्।। Manu 9.92//

A girl who so chooses her husband herself should not accept any ornaments* from her father or from her brother and so on.

Thus, it is obvious that Manu has incorporated both the sound opinions, one that of Baudhāyana that she should wait for three years and not for three *ṛtus* and also one that of Gautama that she should not accept any ornaments from her father or mother etc.

Nārada Saṁhitā 13.21 also favours the *svayamvaraṇa* practice while saying:

यदा तु नैव कश्चित्स्यात् कन्या राजानमाव्रजेत्।
अनुज्ञया वरं तस्य प्रतीत्य वरयेत् स्वयम्।।

Tr.: When there is nobody (to seek a husband for her) the girl should go to the king and should choose her husband herself with his (the king's) permission.

Yājñavalkya 3.64 also opines:

अप्रयच्छन्समाप्नोति भ्रूणहत्यामृतावृतौ।
गम्यं त्वभावे दातॄणां कन्या कुर्यात्स्वयंवरम्।।

Tr.: (A father) not giving (his daughter in marriage) obtains the sin of killing an infant in each *ṛtu*, It is however to be understood that when there is absence of the persons who give her in marriage, she should choose her own husband.

Now think of a situation where a proposed husband of a girl passes away. The custom of paying some money (śulka) to the girl's father by the proposed match was prevalent in those days. Suppose, that money has been paid i.e. marriage is fixed and meanwhile the proposed husband passes away. Manu 9.69 states that in such a situation the brother-in-law i.e. 'would be brother-in-law' of that girl should marry her.

यस्या म्रियेत कन्यायाः वाचासत्ये कृते पतिः।
तामनेन विधानेन निजो विन्देत देवरः।। Manu 9.69 ।।

Naturally, looking at it from a modern point of view or say humaniterian point the question of the opinion of the girl concerned arises in our mind. Is there any importance to it? Or the girl has to simply obey the commands of the Dś?

Manu 9.97 says:

कन्यायां दत्तशुकायां म्रियेत यदि शुल्कदः ।
देवराय प्रदातव्या यदि कन्याऽनुमन्यते ।।

If a proposed husband i.e. one who has paid the money (to the father of the girl) passes away, then she is to be given to the younger brother of the deceased, if the girl so agrees.

The significance of the condition laid down by Manu is also duly noted by the commentators. We may look into them one by one as they are self-evident of the fact that changes and gradual sophistication of the issues did take place.

Medhātithibhāṣya while commenting upon the above verse says: यस्याः पित्रादिभिः गृहीतं शुल्कं न च दत्ता, केवलवचनेन देयत्वेन व्यवस्थिता, अत्रान्तरे स चेन्म्रीयेत .....देवराय प्रदातव्येति ...... तत्रापि कन्याया अनुमतौ सत्याम् । अथासत्यां कन्यायाः शुल्कस्य च का प्रतिपत्तिः? यदि कन्यायै रोचते ब्रह्मचर्यं तदा शुल्कं कन्यापितृपक्षाणामेव। अथ पत्यन्तरमर्थयते तदा प्राग्गृहीतं शुल्कं त्यक्त्वा अन्यस्मादादाय दीयते।

Manvarthavivṛti opines: पुरुषार्थं यदि अनुमन्यते। अननुमते तु नान्यस्मै देया किन्तु कन्यैव तिष्ठेदिति फलिष्यति।

Manvarthamuktīvalī states: यस्या म्रियेत इति प्रागुक्तं नियोगरूपम् इदन्तु शुल्कग्रहणविषयम्।

Manvarthacandrikā comments: 'यस्या म्रियेत कन्याया' इत्यस्माद्विशेषं वक्तुमाह कन्यायामिति। वाग्दानशुल्कग्रहणाभ्यां वा भेदः। तथा च तस्याः स्वत्वनिवृत्तेरननुमतौ स्वयंवरा स्यान्नतु बलाद्दातुं शक्येत्याह यदीति।

Nandinī interprets the verse as follows: अनुमत्यभावेऽन्यस्मै देया, 'सकृत्कन्या प्रदीयते' इत्यस्यायम् अपवादः।

As I stated before, we can feel how one of the old commentators namely *Manvarthavivṛtikāra* opined that the girl should remain *Kanyā* for the whole life and how the later commentators show broader side of their mind. The latest commentator i.e. of *Nandinī* clearly accepts that this is an exception to the rule, 'सकृत्कन्या प्रदीयते' and that the girl should marry with someone else.

Rules concerning the *proșitabhartṛkās*

Now let us turn to the statements in connection with a woman whose husband is away on journey. If we look into the *Visnu-smrti* to begin with, Visṇu states: भर्तरि प्रवसितेऽप्रतिकर्मक्रिया । परगृहेष्वनभिगमनम् । द्वारदेशगवाक्षेष्वनवस्थानम् । (*Viṣṇu smṛti* 25.9—11).

When the husband is on journey (the wife) should not decorate herself, should not go to others houses and should not stay (longer) in the doorway or at windows.

The general and basic rule by Manu in this context is meant for men. Manu 9.74 says:

विधाय वृत्तिं भार्यायाः प्रवसेत् कार्यवान्नरः ।
अवृत्तिकर्षिता हि स्त्री प्रदुष्येत् स्थितिमत्यपि ।

meaning: A man should go on journey for any work after providing his wife with sufficient amount of money for her necessities. Because, otherwise there is a possibility of her falling to an error. Manu (9.75) further states: विधाय प्रोषिते वृत्तिं जीवेन्नियमम् आस्थिता । i.e. when the husband is on journey and he has provided his wife with the necessary amount his wife should lead a regulated life i.e. should remain faithful to him.

Now there is very possibility that some man may go on journey without giving the sufficient money to his wife. In such a case what should the woman do? What is her duty? Manu says: प्रोषिते त्वविधायैव जीवेच्छिल्पैरगर्हितैः । (Manu 9.75) This means that she should sustain her life with honourable means of livelihood.

The general rule of Manu himself for all women in general is that a woman is always dependent on a man. He clearly opines that either her father or her husband or her sons protect her (Manu 9.3). But still when an uncommon situation of the type mentioned above arises he directs the woman to live with self-respect.

Now let us look at this:

प्रोषितो धर्मकार्यार्थं प्रतीक्ष्योऽष्टौ नरः समाः।
विद्यार्थं षट् यशोऽर्थं वा कामार्थं त्रींस्तु वत्सरान्।

(Manu 9.76)

Tr.: A woman should wait eight years for her husband who is on journey for some religions purpose, six years if he is away for learning or to acquire fame and three years if he has gone to marry another girl.

This statement of Manu implies that a woman may not wait after this stipulated time i.e. if she goes to some other person after the above mentioned period, she is not at fault. The commentator of *Nandinī* observes: ऊर्ध्वं भर्त्रन्तरपरिग्रहे न दोषोऽस्तीत्यभिप्रायः।

Thus, though it is a general rule laid down by Manu that under all circumstances a woman has to serve, honour and be faithful to her husband (विशीलः कामवृत्तो वा गुणैर्वा परिवर्जितः। उपचर्यः स्त्रिया साध्वया सततं देववत्पतिः। Manu 5.154); still in the cases mentioned above Manu clearly allows a woman to have another partner.

Rules concerning the widows

Viṣṇu says: मृते भर्तरि ब्रह्मचर्यं तदन्वारोहणं वा। (*Viṣṇusmṛti* 25.14) i.e. when the husband dies the wife should observe *brahmacarya* or she should accompany him on the funeral pyre.

Now let us look at the statements of Manu pertaining to the widows. General rule in this connection says that a woman should not betray her husband after his death. She should not even utter any other man's name (vide Manu 5.157:). न तु नामापि गृह्णयात् पत्यौ प्रेते परस्य तु।) She should not go to any other man either to acquire her livelihood or for the purpose of having a child.

Manu further says if she observes *brahmacarya* after her husband's death then she will attain heaven even if she has no son.

मृते भर्तरि साध्वी स्त्री ब्रह्मचर्ये व्यवस्थिता।
स्वर्गं गच्छत्यपुत्राऽपि यथा ते ब्रह्मचारिणः।।

(Manu 5.160)

These are general rules in this context. Manu condemns the

tendency of woman's going to some other man after her husband's death.

But let us imagine the following situation: A woman becomes widow in the prime of her youth. She is left without a son and she does not want to die (i.e. to accompany her husband on the funeral pyre). Here who is going to support her? What should she do? Here Manu speaks about the *niyogavidhi*. What is a *niyogavidhi*? If a woman desires a child, as a support to her, she may have if from her brother-in-law or from a relative, if allowed by the elderly persons.

देवराद्वा सपिण्डाद्वा स्त्रिया सम्ङ्नियुक्तया ।
प्रजेप्सिताधिगन्तव्या सन्तानस्य परिक्षये ।।

(Manu 9.59)

Thus, it is clear from this that eventhough Manu condemned *niyoga* in normal circumstances, he himself allowed it to be observed in some particular situation (in Manu's words:

अत: परं प्रवक्ष्यामि
योषितां धर्ममापदि । Manu 9.56)

It is quite evident from this that he does not want to bar women's fundamental right to life.

Conclusion

The following are my observations on whatever we have discussed so far:

If we compare Manu with other Dśkāras we are in a position to say that Manu is more elaborate in his dealing with any issue. Not only elaborate but also practical and considerate as he did not deny the fact that there could be some complicated or extra-normal circumstances where all his general rules could not be applied in toto. Or if applied they will not prove to be meaningful but they might prove detrimental to women's welfare. And so, he made some exceptional type of rules which could be employed in those extra-ordinary situations.

We can clearly see from the verse काममा मरणात्तिष्ठेत् etc. i.e. Manu 9.89 that Manu did not want to do any injustice to women by prescribing some rigid and harsh rules, though this was done by his predecessors like Baudhāyana.

About the issue of *svayaṁvaraṇa*, we can say that this issue has been considered practically by almost all the Dśkāras and they have granted certain amount of freedom to women to choose their husband when they are well grown up and have to find their own way out. Right from Baudhāyana, Gautama everybody has sanctioned it which might be very much in vogue in the then society.

Looking at the rules that Manu states about the *proṣitabhartṛkās* we can easily feel that he has taken into account all the possible situations that might have arisen in those days. This was neither done by Viṣṇu nor by anybody else. No one but him has said that a husband should go on journey only after making arrangements of money for his wife. And has also given the solution if this does not work.

In the modern times these rules may seem to be insignificant but they definitely bore much importance at the time they were laid down.

In case of widows we have seen that Viṣṇu is very very brief on this issue when he states: मृते भर्तरि ब्रह्मचर्यं तदन्वारोहणं वा । Manu also agrees with him when he opines that the ideal position of the widows is to observe *brahmacarya* after their husbands' death, still he thinks of some adverse situation and lays down the *niyogavidhi*—eventhough it is not appreciated by himself under normal circumstances.

In short, the verse पिता रक्षति कौमारे etc. (Manu 9.3) reflects the actual status of women in general in the then society. But it can be observed from what we have discussed so far that nowhere the humanitarian outlook is sacrificed by Manu. The exceptional rules bear testimony to this fact. There is no doubt that Manu wants women to have protector in the form of father or husband or son all through in all stages of their life, but at the same time he wants that a woman should not be put to any disgraceful state of life.

One may find apparent contradictions in his statements, but if all the contradictions are read together with the conditions in which those appear, it will not be difficult always to find grounds for those apparent contradictions. As I said before, mostly, those cases of contradictions may appear to be exceptions to the general rules.

5

Madhva's Concept of Dharma

K.B. Archak

Madhva who flourished from 1238-1317 A.D. was the foremost propounder of the Dvaita System of Vedānta and shone as a pole-star in the field of Indian Philosophical systems. He has been famous for his realistic thoughts. No doubt, unlike others, Madhva being a celebrated realist, fought for upliftment of the society which was puffed up with ignorance, and established a new mode of *Dharma*. *Dharma* is the divine gift of rules of conduct for the well-being of individuals and society. And this *Dharma* is called *Parama Dharma*.[1] Thus the *Rāmāyana* advocates 'to follow the rule of law and not the rule of power'.[2] This rule is never harmless but is positively ennobling.

An introductory part of the *Gītā-tātparya-nirnaya* of Madhva throws much light on the concept of *Dharma*. Therein, Madhva applies a prefix of *Parama* to *Dharma* and considers it with exalted meaning. He states that 'worship of Lord Nārāyaṇa through the performance of *Nitya-naimittika-karmas* in accordance with one's fitness (*Svavihita-vrtti*), and through devotion (*Bhakti*) - is alone *Paramadharma*; and that which is contrary to this, is all *Adharma*.[3]

Madhva's view of performance of the *karmas* in the form of worshipping the Supreme Brahman, is very significant. For, this kind of performance gives rise to the detachment from the fruits of the respective action.[4] Thus *karmas* should be God-centered. It is the way of becoming free from the taint of sin.

The seminal principle of dedicating one's *karma* to the Lord is clearly stated in the *Bhāgavata Purāṇa*:[5] Whatever he does with his body, speech, mind or senses, reason or intellect, or by the force of his inherited nature, he should consecrate all as an offering to Lord Nārāyaṇa.

In his commentary on the *Īśāvāsya Upaniṣad* Madhva emphasizes that the necessity of the performance of *karmas* for a knower of Brahman too. If he fails to do so, verily the bliss of his self-realization is diminished. Therefore, let all work always.[6] The *Brhamasūtra*: "*Nīyamācca*" (III.iv. 7) says that the *karmas* of *jñānins* do not make any difference to or cause any excellence in the content and power of their knowledge as such; but have a bearing only on the fruits thereof by way of intensifying the bliss derived from those fruits. Further he sets forth: `the devas are born *jñānins*. Still there is appreceiable enrishment in the fruits of their knowledge through *karmas* such as Rājasūya or Aśvamedha as in the case of Pāṇḍavas. Such *karmas* have the power to enrich only the fruits of their *jñāna*.[7]

Thus Madhva's aphoristic word "*Svavihitavṛtti*" Suggests that *Paramadharma* primarily consists in the performance of daily and occasional duties in accordance with one's *varṇa* and *āśrama*, in a spirit of detachment and with the notion that all these are to be surrendered unto Brahman. In this connection the *Gītā* declares "He who performs his duties by abandoning the attachment of the fruits thereof, and dedicates his deeds to Brahman is untainted by sin as a lotus leaf by water".[8] This cleanses the mind, which further brings spiritual stability leading safely on the path of meditation. This preparation takes man to the state of *Bhakti*, the means of liberation through the grace of Lord.

Bhakti or devotion to the Lord is another cardinal aspect of *Dharma*. Madhva has shown that the path of devotion is sure path to secure liberation by God's grace. He defines *Bhakti*:[9] "That firm and intense love to the Supreme Lord surpassing all objects of desires, based upon and adequate knowledge and conviction of God's glory and magnitude, is called *Bhakti*." And from this *Bhakti* alone results release. Thus, the supreme love following the wake of previous knowledge and lasting for ever is designated as *Bhakti*. The *Bhagavadgītā* agrees with this idea:[10] "Of these, the man of wisdom ever steadfast and possesses firm devotion to me, excels; for, I am supremely dear to the wise and he is dear to Me". The question follows here that how to secure the knowledge of God's majesty, without which *Bhakti* is impossible? For this, Madhva says that there are premiet instruments of securing knowledge of Brahman, viz., *Śravaṇa*, *Manana*, *Nididhyāsana* and *Bhakti*.[11]

Bhakti is the basic qualification of the seeker which should continue even after securing liberation. As such, Madhva distinguishes three stages of devotion: (1) which precedes knowledge of Brahman, (2) which that follows the knowledge, (3) a third that comes after direct realization. It is thus effectively said by Madhva in his *Anuvyākhyāna*:[12] "The seeker gets the knowledge of Brahman by devotion; the devotion increases by that knowledge, and by the increase of devotion he comes to have direct vision of Brahman, by this direct vision of Brahman, the devotion intensifies, and by such intensified devotion he attains liberation, and by still more intensified devotion in the state of liberation, he, experiences his absolute bliss".

In the Dvaita Vedānta, this *Bhakti* is regarded as consisting of nine types: hearing Lord's greatness, eulogizing Him, recollecting him, serving his feet, worshipping, paying homage, attending on, loving, and self-surrendering.[13] These activities must be undertaken sincerely and consciously for the sake of cultivating Bhakti. These activities provide not only the variety but also exercise for *Bhakti*. If this type of *Bhakti* is wanting, all deeds are null and void.[13]

Madhva lays stress on another aspect of devotion i.e. *Virodhabhakti*. On the one hand the wording *virodhabhakti* itself is self-contradictory. Because it generally is admitted fact that any kind of love disagrees with hatred. Madhva does not deny this fact. Yet on the other hand, while speaking of Śiśupāla in his *Gītābhāṣya*[14] Madhva takes care to point out that Śiśupāla was not an ordinary sinner. In Śiśupāla's case, the hatred was specially chosen because of intense love; hence it is only a form of love. What brought liberation to him was the submerged love, and not the hatred. Such passages should be treated as *Arthavāda*.

Madhva in a pursuit plane of Indian tradition, persistently lays an emphasis of moral conduct in the seeker which however is quite essential in the cultivation of *Bhakti*. He makes an assertive statement that the moral purity of the aspirant is pre-requisite means to acquire the knowledge of Brahman, without which there cannot arise firm devotion.[15] He specifically mentions requisite aspects of morality, such as (1) speaking truth, (2) worshipping always the elderly ones, (3) not disclosing the secrets of others, (4) being impartial to both friend and enemy. He has to cultivate the sense of detachment from the worldly pleasures. He should be contented with what has been given by God. He should keep himself always away from evil habits. Thus, he should bring such *Vairāgya* into practice; then only his pure devotion, otherwise that devotion would become mere deceit and hypocricy.[16] In the *Gītābhāṣya*, Madhva quotes with the approval of *Viṣṇupurāṇa* which declares that an amoral person is a cheat and cannot possess any amount of devotion.[17] Hence, it is clear that a real devotee is an ideal human fit to be followed by others.

Though the action of a virtuous person appears to be unworthy, it is worthy in its true sense. The criterion of righteous (*Dharma*) and unrighteous (*adharma*) depends on the person performing that particular action. That is, if a person not possessing the qualities of a devotee above said, performs even good action, his action becomes *Adharma* or harmful, as such fit to be condemned. The society would not regard him to be a virtuous, as he does not basically possess the moral fitness.[18] Thus, in the frame of *Dharma* Madhva has given much importance to *Sadācāra* or moral purity which potentializes the knowledge and firm devotion leading to liberation.

Thus Madhva's idea of *Dharma* is the integration of three essential Yogas - i.e. *Karmayoga*, *Jñānayoga* and *Bhaktiyoga*, which mark the different stages in the progressive realization of Mokṣa.[19] In fine, the concept of *Dharma* according to Madhva embraces all necessary aspects which are beneficial to both the aspirant and society. Therefore, Madhva befits place of social reformer besides his being saint-philosopher.

Notes

1.. धर्मो हि परमो लोके धर्मे सत्यं प्रतिष्ठितम् ।।

Rāmāyaṇa. II.21.41.

2. धर्ममाश्रय मा तैक्ष्ण्यम् ।। *Ibid*., II.21.44

3. स्वविहितवृत्त्या भक्त्या भगवदाराधनमेव परमो धर्मः
तद्विरुद्धः सर्वोऽपि अधर्मः ।। *Gītātātparya*, p.6

4. यान्यनवद्यानि कर्माणि तानि सेवितव्यानि नो इतराणि ।।

Taittirīya Upaniṣad. I.II.I

तस्मादसक्तः सततं कार्यं कर्म समाचर।
असक्तो हि आचरन् कर्म परमाप्नोति पूरूषः।।
Bhagavadgītā, III.19

5. कायेन वाचा मनसेन्द्रियैर्वा बुद्ध्यात्मना वाऽनुसृतस्वभावात्।
करोति यद्यत्सकलं परस्मै नारायणायेति समर्पयितत्।। *Bhag*. XI. 2.36

6. ज्ञानिनोऽपि यतो हास आनन्दस्य भवेद्ध्रुवम्।
अतोऽलेपेऽपि लेपः स्यादतः कार्यैव सा सदा।।
Īśa.Up.bh. (Mantra.2)

7. ज्ञानिनामपि देवानां विशेषः कर्मभिर्भवेत्।
चीर्णेऽकृते वा ज्ञानस्य न विशेषोऽस्ति कर्मणि।।
M. Brahmasūtrabhāṣya, III.4.9

8. ब्रह्मण्याधाय कर्माणि सङ्गंत्यक्त्वा करोति यः।
लिप्यते न स पापेन पद्मपत्रमिवाम्भसा।। *Gītā*. V.10

9. माहात्म्यज्ञानपूर्वस्तु सुदृढः सर्वतोऽधिकः।।
स्नेहो भक्तिरिति प्रोक्तस्तया मुक्तिर्न चान्यथा।।
Mahābhārata-tāātparya-nirṇaya I.86.
cf. *Bhāgavata*., III. 29.11-12

10. तेषां ज्ञानी नित्ययुक्त एकभक्तिर्विशिष्यते।
प्रियो हि ज्ञानिनोऽत्यर्थमहं स च मम प्रियः।। *Gitā. VIII.17*

11. श्रवणं मननं चैव ध्यानं भक्तिस्तथैव च।
साधनं ज्ञानसम्पत्तौ प्रधानं नान्यदिष्यते।।
न चैतानि विना कश्चिज्ज्ञानमाप कुतश्चन।।
Brahmasūtrabhāṣya, I.1.I

12. भक्त्या ज्ञानं ततो भक्तिः ततो दृष्टिस्ततश्च सा।
ततो मुक्तिस्ततो भक्तिः सैव स्यात् सुखरूपिणी।।
अनुव्याख्यानम्, p.41

13. श्रवणं कीर्तनं विष्णोः स्मरणं पादसेवनम्।
अर्चनं वन्दनं दास्यं सख्यमात्मनिवेदनम्।। भागवत–VII.5.23
भक्तिहीनेन यत् किञ्चित् कृतं सर्वं असत्समम्।।
आध्यात्मरामायण. VI.7.66

14. द्वैषाच्चैद्यादयो नृपाः....इति भक्तिप्रियत्वज्ञापनार्थं
नित्यध्यानस्तुत्यर्थं च स्वभक्तस्य कदाचित् शापबलात्
द्वेषिणोऽपि भक्तिफलमेव भगवान् ददाति। भक्ता एव हि ते
पूर्वं शिशुपालादयः शापबलात् द्वेषिणः।। गीताभाष्य- IX.12

15. वेदास्त्वधीता मम लोकनाथ तप्तं तपो नानृतमुक्तपूर्वम्।
पूजां गुरुणां सततं करोमि परस्य गुह्यं न च भिन्नपूर्वम्।।
गुप्तानि चत्वारि यथागमं मे शत्रौ च मित्रे च समोऽस्मि नित्यम्।।
आचारस्य ज्ञानसाधनत्वोक्तेश्च। ज्ञानाभावे सम्यग् भक्त्यभावात्।।
Ibid., IX. 31

16. न भवत्येव प्रायः तद्भक्तः सुदुराचारः।----अतोऽन्यः
कश्चिद्भवति चेत् दाम्भिकत्वेन स अनुमेयः।। *Ibid.*, IX. 30-31

17. स शठमतिरुपधाति योऽर्थतृष्णां तमधमचेष्टमवैहि नास्य भक्तिः।।
Ibid., IX.31

18. धर्मो भवत्यधर्मोऽपि कृतो भक्तैस्तवाच्युत।
पापं भवति धर्मोऽपि यो न भक्तैः कृतो हरेः।।
सदाचारस्मृतिः - २९

19. योगस्त्रयो मया प्रोक्ता नृणां श्रेयो विधित्सया।
ज्ञानं कर्म च भक्तिश्च नोपायोऽस्ति कर्हिचित्।।
Bhāgavata. xi.20.6

6

Human Rights and Dharmaśāstra

Vinayaka P. Bhatta

Introduction

Fundamental human rights were conferred upon all the citizens by the constitution of many civilized free (post-war) countries of the world. The law-makers realised the importance of peoples' rights to protest and safeguard against federal and state interference with the basic human rights. The preservation of human rights and providing of equal opportunities to all sections of people irrespective of their caste, creed or religion, in all walks of life, is the most essential and indispensable condition of a free society. While the conferring and protecting of human rights have helped the people to accomplish all round development and reach great heights, violation and denial of human rights has invariably led to the lack of development of people and eventually to the destruction and downfall of the society as such. History is replete with the examples of societies/countries flourishing where the human rights were protected, and the same perishing where the rights were violated.

Thus, the amendment I in the Article VII of the U.S. Constitution on Bill of Rights (Edward S. Corwin 1947) proclaims that Congress shall make no law respecting an establishment of religion or prohibiting the free exercise thereof; or abridging the freedom of speech or the press; or the right of the people peacefully to assemble, and to petition the government for a redress of grievances. Also, amendment XIV of the same article proclaims that no state shall make or enforce any law which shall abridge the privileges or immunities of citizens of the United States, nor shall any State deprive any person of life, liberty or property without due process of law; nor deny to any person within its jurisdiction the equal protection of the laws. And similarly, the constitution of India on the Indian Bill of Rights (M. Ramaswamy, 1946) grants Indian citizens right and freedom of speech and expression, freedom to assemble peacefully without arms, freedom to move freely throughout the country, freedom to acquire, hold and dispose off property, and rights to petition the government for redress of grievances.

Problem

However, in ancient India, people belonging to different castes, creed and sex, cannot be said to have had (enjoyed) the same rights and privileges that the citizens of present free India enjoy today. They were not conferred upon the fundamental human rights and the equal opportunities by the writers of Hindu law and polity. The very concept of human rights and equal rights as defined and understood today seems to have been quite unknown and socially irrelevant to the people of ancient India; and hence not paid sufficient attention to by the writers of Hindu Law (Dharmaśāstra) and writers of Hindu Polity (Arthaśāstra).

Even satisfactory terms which mean human rights or equal opportunities are not found in Dharmaśāstra and Arthaśāstra works; and hence cannot be cited from these works as corresponding to the ideals of human rights and equal opportunities. The only term that comes somewhat close to the human rights is *'adhikāra'*, which actually means entitlement, qualification or privilege to do or undertake certain works and religious action (Gobhi Sm. 2.93, Laghvāśva Sm. 20.45, Smṛti Can. i.10.19). Also another term that may come somewhat close to the equal opportunities is *'svātantrya'*, which is used actually to mean freedom or independence in doing or performing certain duties (Nītivākyāmṛta. 24.39).

However, both these terms were used in Dharmaśāstra and Mīmāṁsā etc., only in connection with certain privileges (entitlement, qualification) and freedom of three higher castes or *varṇas* (Śāstra Dīpikā.6.7. on i.1.1) and male members of the society (Manu Sm. 9.3), and thereby limit and restrict the rights and freedom of different sections of people on the basis of their caste and sex. Thus, they are used negatively in the way of violating and denying the human rights and equal opportunities for the different sections of people, rather than positively in the way of conferring the rights and the opportunities upon all the citizens of India.

However, we know authoritatively from epics and other sources of history (Brahmāṇḍ P. i.29.56) that people led an orderly, peaceful and happy life, and were content to a large extent within the limits of their social and political life. Now, the question is what in ancient Hindu law books, Dharmaśāstra, and also in Hindu Polity, Arthaśāstra, makers of Hindu law and Polity had stated or observed exactly regarding the human rights and privileges, and how their statements were relevant to the well being of people of that time. Also, significant from the view point of human rights is the rights, rather the lack of rights and privileges of Śūdras in ancient India. In this article, I propose to examine the views of ancient Indian law makers, with respect to human rights of the Śūdras.

The reason for the violation of human rights

The reason for the violation of human rights and yet an orderly, peaceful and happy social life of the people in ancient India, is mainly two fold: (i)*The nature or form of society with its social hierarchy of class or caste structure (*varṇas*), and (ii)*psychology, belief, socio-religious customs and practices of people. The law-makers of Dharmaśāstra were mainly concerned with the enforcement of laws on duties of four different *varṇas* and *āśramas*, and the preservation of the purity and the social hierarchy of such *varṇas*; however, they were not concerned with the conferring of the human rights and privileges upon individuals. For instance, Gautama, Baudhāyana, Āpastamba, Vasiṣṭha, Manu, Yājñavalkya etc. dealt with different aspects of class structure of people (*varṇas*), their duties (*dharmas*), privileges (*adhikāras*) or disadvantages, different stages of life (*āśramas*), their obligations and responsibilities, Saṁskāras, daily purification of body (*śauca*), daily rituals (*nityakarmas*), impurity of birth and death (*āśauca*), judicial procedure and law (*vyavahāra*), expiatory rites (*prāyaścitta*) etc. Thus, it is clear that the writers of Dharmaśāstra attached far more importance to the duties, privileges, or disadvantages of *varṇas* and *āśramas*, and hence dealt primarily with the duties and the privileges (or disadvantages) of the people belonging to different classes (*varṇas*) and (*āśramas*), rather than to the conferring of the human rights and equal opportunities upon the people of all classes.

Varṇas or classes of people and their position

The term *'varṇa'* originally means colour or light (RV. I.73.7); however, in some verses of Ṛgveda, it is associated with the groups of people having a skin of fair or dark colour (RV. II.12.4) and thus with the two antagonist camps of people, namely *āryas* and *dāsas* (or *dasyus*) who differed in their colour of their skin and also worship. However, the same *varṇa* was extended in later times to cover the four different classes of people such as *Brāhmaṇa, Kṣatriya, Vaiśya* and *Śūdra* and the Puruṣasūkta, a later hymn of the Ṛgveda, records clearly all the four terms as signifying four different classes of people, though it is doubtful whether these four terms had acquired the denotation or the sense of the four different castes of people by birth at the time. It should be noted here that in later literature (Manu Sm. 8. 413), the term *'ārya'* had come to signify the first three *varṇas*, namely, the *Brāmaṇas*, the *Kṣatriyas* and the *Vaiśyas*, whereas the term *'dāsa'* or *'dasyu'* came to signify the fourth *varṇa*, namely the Śūdras, who were conquered by the Āryas and hence were slaves (*dāsas* or *dasyus*).

In the Samhitas (Tai S. VII. 1.1.6) and Dharmasūstras, (Āpa D.S. I.9.27.11) the *śūdra* is spoken of as 'dark *varṇa*' and not fit for sacrifices; although Tai S. (V.7.6.3) places the Śūdras on the same level as that of the Āryas and fit for receiving light; and thus the position assigned to the Śūdras was very low in the hierarchy of society. Also the Samhitas show that the Āryas or the three classes of Brāhmaṇas, Kṣatriyas and Vaiśyas had been differentiated and their privileges, duties, and liabilities had been fixed; and the Tai S. (I.7.3.1) states that the Brāhmaṇas are gods that are directly seen, and the Ṛgveda (IV.50.8) declares that the king alone, who places *brahma* first dwells happy; and also the TAi S. (II.5.10.2) states that the Vaiśya indeed sacrifices, being desirous of cattle; and thus the position of the three classes of Āryas had become much higher than that of the *dāsas* (or *dasyus*), i.e. Śūdras. However, as P.V. Kane (Vol.II.1941) states, in later times, owing to the cultural advance, division of labour arose, and numerous arts and crafts had been developed and created many sub classes based upon occupations; and the position of them was not that low.

The duties, the privileges and the abilities of the varṇas

The works on Dharma śāstra do not discuss the human rights

or fundamental rights of people as such; rather they discuss (Gaut D.S. X. 1-3, 7.50) the duties, the privileges of the first three *varṇas*, and the disadvantages of the last *varṇa* elaborately. While teaching of the Vedas, officiating at sacrifices, and receiving gifts had become the privileges of the Brāhmaṇas, the profession of arms and protection of the people became the peculiar privileges of the Kṣatriyas; and agriculture, rearing cattle, trade became the privileges of the Vaiśyas. On the contrary, according to the Dharmaśāstras (Āpa D.S. I.1.1.7) the special duty of the Śūdras was to render services to the Brāhmaṇas and others (serving the Brāhmaṇa conferred greater happiness to the Śūdras), and to obtain livelihood from them. Āpa D.S. (II. 2.4.25) lays down that the Brāhmaṇa alone can be the teacher of the Vedas, but in distress a Brāhmaṇa may learn from a Kṣatriya. The profession of teaching the Vedas could not have brought much money to the Brāhmaṇas, and thus it was the privilege of the Brāhmaṇas to officiate as priests. Jaimini (VI.6.18) says that it is a privilege of the Brāhmaṇas alone to officiate as priests as the Kṣatriyas and the Vaiśyas cannot be the priests. The third means of livelihood to the Brāhmaṇas was receiving gifts (*pratigraha*) from worthy persons.

The Brāhmaṇas were the *gurus* to all the *varṇas* by the mere fact of their birth (Āpa D.S.I. i.1.5); the king was the ruler of all except the Brāhmaṇas (Gautama, xi.1.); the king should exonerate the Brāhmaṇas in the matters of capital punishments (Gautama, viii 12); the Brāhmaṇas were free from taxes (Manu Sm. vii. 133); the Brāhmaṇas should not be killed by anyone (Manu Sm. xi. 89); and thus the Brāhmaṇas had all the privileges in the society.

The disadvantages of the Śūdras or denial of human rights

As the position of the Śūdras was the lowest in the society, the Śūdras were deprived of may privileges, i.e. fundamental human rights, and had many disadvantages and disabilities. The Śūdras were not allowed to study the Vedas. Writers of Smṛtis (Vasiṣṭha iv.3) state that the Śūdras are unfit for the *saṁskāras*, and hence cannot study the Vedas. It should be noted however, that there were traces that in ancient India, the prohibition of the study of the Vedas was not so absolute as the latter Smṛtis made it out to be. Chāndogya Upaniṣad (IV. 1.2) states that Raikva addresses and imparts Vedic *Saṁvarga vidyā* to Jānaśruti Pautrāyaṇa, a Śūdra.

Also, the Śūdras were not debarred from hearing epics such as Mahābhārata (xii.328). The Śūdras were not to consecrete sacred fires and to perform the Vedic sacrifices (Jaimini. 1.3.25-28). However, the Śūdras were entitled to perform *pūrta-dharma* and five daily sacrifices (Atri.6). According to Kane (Vol.2, 1941), there is some controversy regarding the eligibility (*adhikāra*) of the Śūdras for *saṁkāras*. Manu (X. 126) states that the Śūdras incur no sin by eating forbidden articles like onion etc. and they have no *adhikāra* for *saṁkāras*. Also, Manu (iv. 80) states that the Śūdras should not be asked to perform *vratas*. Aparārka comments on the verse that the Śūdras cannot perform the *vratas* in person, but only through a Brāhmaṇa. However, Manu (II. 32) prescribes that the Śūdras could perform the *nāmakaraṇa*-ceremony, and thus they were debarred from only the *saṁskāras* with Vedic *mantras*. The Śūdras were liable for higher punishment. Gautama (xii. 1-2) states that if a Śūdra commits adultry with a woman of three higher castes, his penis should be cut of, but, if a Brāhmaṇa commits adultery with a Brāhmaṇa women he was fined only a five hundred.

A Śūdra is impure for a month on death, while a Brāhmaṇa is impure for only ten days (Gautama xiv 1-4). A Śūdra could not be a judge on matters of litigation, whereas a Brāhmaṇa can be appointed as a judge, when king had other business. A Brāhmaṇa could take food at the houses of the members of three higher classes, but not at the houses of the Śūdras except in *āpad* (Gautama. xvii. 6, Manu Sm. iv. 253). However, a Brāhmaṇa can take food in the house of a Śūdra if the same is his cowherd or a peasant (Gautama xvii. 1-6).

The Śūdras came to be looked down upon so much that they could not touch a Brāhmaṇa or wait upon him, while the Kṣatriyas or the Vaiśyas could touch and wait upon them (Mahā Bhā. Anuśāsana, 59.33). However, Gṛhyasūtras (Hiraṇyakeśi i. 12.18-20) state that when Madhuparka is to be offered for a *snātaka*, the feet of the guest were washed by a Śūdra male or a female by touching him. Thus, there could not have been any ban against touching the Brāhmaṇas in earlier times. Since the Śūdra was not initiated into Vedic studies, the only *āśrama* out of the four *āśamas* that he was entitled for was that of a house-holder (*gṛhastha*). Mahā Bhā. (xiii. 165.10) reads that I am a Śūdra and so I have no right to resort to four *āśramas*. The value of a Śūdra and that of a woman were not much. The killing of a woman and that of a Śūdra were regarded as *upapātakas* (*Manu* xi. 66), and the *prāyaścittas* prescribed for were only *brahmacarya* for one year and gifts of ten cows and a bull; whereas the *prāyaścittas* prescribed for killing of a *kṣatriya were brahmacarya* for six years, and gifts of 1000 cows and a bull.

However, as P.V. Kane (Vol. 2. 1941) observes, if the Śūdras laboured under certain grave conditions and had disabilities, they had certain advantages as well. They would follow almost any profession except the few reserved for the Brāhmaṇas, the Kṣatriyas and the Vaiśyas. Even that many Śūdras became kings (Arthaśāstra, ix. 2), the Śūdras were free from many daily rites. They were not compelled to undergo any *saṁskāra* except marriage, they could partake any food, they need not practice any penances for lapses from the rules of Śāstras. Thus, despite being deprived of human rights, to some extent, they had ample time and freedom in undertaking any action and persuing the profession they liked to.

Untouchability

There is no denying that untouchability was practised in ancient India and certain subdivisions of the Śūdras were regarded as untouchables. In Vedic literature, several names occur which are considered in later Smṛtis to mean untouchables or *antyajas*. Ṛgveda (viii. 5.38) mentions *carmara* (tanner of hides) and Vājasaneyi Saṁhitā (30.17) mentions *cāndāla* and *paulkasa*. Also Chāndogya Upaniṣad (V. 10.7) states that those who did praiseworthy actions, acquire a birth in a good condition such as a Brāhmaṇa, and those who did low actions acquire a birth in a low condition such as a boar or a *cāṇḍāla*, and this has caused much apprehension regarding the low conditions and untouchability of certain divisions of the Śūdras among the modern writers, on Indian caste systems and human rights. However, it should be noted that in early literature mention is made of the fact that the Śūdras were allowed to be cooks for Brāhmaṇas (Gautama, 17.1-6), and hence there is no reason to suppose that untouchability was dominant in early times. Also, while in the modern times, the so-called untouchables are called *pañcamas*, the Mahābhārata (xiii. 47.18) states that there are only four *varṇas*. Untouchability did not arise merely by birth alone. Manu (ix. 235-239) prescribes that those guilty of murder of a Brāhmaṇa and theft of gold should be excommunicated, and when they perform *prāyaścitta*, they are resorted back to the caste and become touchables. Medhātithi on Manu (V. 133) states that shadow of a cāṇḍāla and the like should not be crossed; and Brāhmaṇa required a bath for coming under the shadow of a *cāṇḍāla*; however, Atri (249) makes an exception that when a person is touched by an untouchable in a temple etc., there is no taint of untouchability.

Also, the so-called untouchables were not entirely excluded from all sorts of worship; Yājñavalkya (1.93) states that *cāṇḍālas* were outside the Vedic rites such as *upanayana* but could worship images of *avatāras*; and the Bhāgavata (X.70) says that even the *antyāvasāyins* were purified by listening to the names of Hari.

Thus, the untouchability though deplorable as practised in ancient times in India was not as harsh as the discrimination against the Negroes taking the form of residential segregation in U.S.A. (Encyclopaedia of Social Sciences Vol. xi).

Slavery

Now as regards slavery. Like in many parts of the world, slavery existed in ancient India. The term generally used for slaves is *dāsa*, and the Ṛgveda (VIII. 56.3) mentions that *dāsas* can be given as gifts. However, the term in the Ṛgveda stands originally for the opponents of the *āryas*, and not for the slaves, but when the *dāsas* were vanquished in battle and taken as prisoners, they were treated as slaves and thus the term came to be used for the slaves. Though Manu (1.91) ordains that the Śūdras were for the service of the Brāhmaṇas, they were not to be gifted as slaves. This is clear from the fact that Jaimini (VI. 7.6) states that the Śūdra, who waits upon, cannot be gifted as a slave. Also, absolute slavery was not much in evidence in India in the 4th century, BC; and the treatment of slaves was generally very good. Kauṭilya (III. 13) says that Mlechas are not punishable if they sell their children, but an *ārya* cannot be reduced to slavery. Kauṭilya (V. 723) further declares that if a master has sexual intercourse with a female slave, and she is delivered a child, both the slave and the child should be given freedom.

Reśume

Now, it may be observed as follows: Against the overwhelming evidences of the rules depriving the people, especially the Śūdras and the women, of fundamental human rights, no positive and favourable conclusion regarding the conferring of the human rights on all the people in ancient India can be possible. The fundamental human rights and the equal opportunities as conferred upon the citizens in free India were certainly lacking in the ancient India. However, we can only make an attempt to understand and analyse as to why they were deprived of the rights and privileges, and also as to how much the Śūdras and the women were actually affected by the lack of the rights.

The very concepts of human rights and freedom or equal opportunities were not known or recognized as essential conditions required for the well being of people in ancient India as the individual human rights, apart from the rights of society, were not considered as important. Even the terms such as '*adhikāra*' and '*svātantrya*', which came very close to the concept of rights and equal opportunities, were used negatively by restricting and limiting rights and equal opportunities, rather than positively by conferring the same upon the people. Thus the law-makers ignored and neglected the human rights by being constrained by prevailing Vedic culture and social conditions which were highly partial towards Brahmins and other higher castes; and greatly baised against the Śūdras and the women.

The primary reason for the denial and the neglect of human rights must be held to be the propagation of the caste system, or the impositions of the duties related to the castes and to the different stages of life (*varṇāśrama dharma*) by the law makers of Dharmaśāstra. The law-makers were chiefly concerned with the preservation of the caste system and the ensuing social hierarchy as they thought and believed that the same would ultimately lead to the orderly development of the society. Also another reason is that the majority of people, excepting a few, like Karṇa (Mahā Bhā VIII.12.), did not revolt against the discrimination and violation of human rights as they too believed that adherence to the *varṇāśrama dharmas* and persuing the professions ordained by the Dharma śāstra are conducive to their good. The higher three castes, namely, the Brāhmaṇas the Kṣatriyas and the Vaiśyas had obviously greater advantages and privileges and were allowed to persue the professions of Vedic studies, ruling, agriculture and trade, whereas the Śūdras had many disadvantages and disabilities, and were not allowed to pursue any one of these professions; also they were treated as untouchables and slaves to some extent.

However, we shall be erring in our judgement if we do not appreciate and recognize the fact that despite violation of human rights, the Śūdras were not prevented from undertaking any profession except a few reserved for the higher three castes; and thus people on the whole were free to pursue a vast number of professions and prosper.

Also, it should be noted that the Śūdras, as stated earlier, were appointed as cooks in Brahmin households and used to wait upon the Brahmin guests; and therefore, untouchability was not practised so much; and even while being practised was not very harsh; also the Brahmins and others were not allowed to be treated as slaves and the slaves in general were prohibited from being traded of; or were treated very kindly; and so absolute slavery was not much in evidence in ancient India. Thus, finally it should be observed that non-conferring of human rights on the people in Dharmaśāstra did not affect the Śūdras and the women very badly; and so did not lead to the disorder or discontent among the citizens of ancient India.

References

Atri Smṛti (Atri): ASS, 48, 1905, Sm Sam, pp. 28-34.

Āpastambiya Dharmasūtra (Āpa D.S.): Ed. by George Buhler, Bombay, 1868, 1894.

Brahmāṇḍa Purāṇa (Brahmāṇḍ P.): VP. 1935.

Chāṇḍogya Upaniṣad: Ed. by V.P. Limaye and R.D. Vadekar, VSM 1958, Aṣṭād U. pp. 68-173.

Edward S. Corwin: The Constitution and what it means today. Princeton University Press, 1947.

Gautamapraṇita Dharma sūtra (Gautama): Ed. by G.S. Gokhale, ASS. 61, 1910.

Gobhila Smṛti (Gobhi Sm.): ASS. 48. 1905, Sm Sam, pp. 49-71.

Hiraṇyakeśī Gṛhyasūtra : Ed. by Kirste, Vienna, 1889.

Jaimini:Mīmāṁsāsūtra, ASS. 97, 1929.

Kauṭilya: Arthaśāstra, TSS. 82, 1924-25.

Kane, P.V.: History of Dharmaśāstra Vol. II, Part I, BORI Pune, 1941.

Laghvāśvalāyana Smṛti (Laghvāśva Sm.): ASS, 48, 1905, Sm Sam pp. 142-81.

Mahā Bhārata (Mahā Bhā.): Ed. by V.S. Suktankar and others, BORI, 1927-1961.

Manusmṛti (Manu Sm.): Ed. by V.L. Panshikar, NSP. 1933.

Pārthasārathi Miśra: Śāstradipikā, Ed. by G. Jha, NSP. 1915.

Ramaswamy, M: Fundamental Rights, Oxford University Press, New Delhi, 1946.

Ṛgveda (R.V.): Ed. by Max Muller, London, 1849-74.

Taittarīya Samhitā (Tai S.): E. Roer, and E.B. Cowell, BI 1860-99.

Vasiṣṭha Dharmaśāstra: A.A. Fuhrer, BSPS, 23, 1883.

Yājñavalkya Smṛti: Ed. by N.R. Acharya, N.S. 1949.

7

Social Relevance of Dharmaśāstra In the Present context of Fundamentalism v. Secularism

J.V. Joshi

I wish to draw attention to some of the following events:

1. The Fatava issued for the head of Salman Rushdie for writing Satanic Verses shocked the moral concience of the civilised the world today, which values the value of freedom of thought, expression and judgement.
2. The demolition of Babari Masjid created the earthquake-like tremers in India.
3. Terrorism in Kashmir, Punjab, and the politics of guns and bomb-blasts have shooked the foundation of national unity and integrity.

These and such similar events are happening all over the world today. They are taking place in the name of religion; and those who indulge in them call themselves as the protectors of religion and God. In fact, instead of Heaven, we have Hell on the earth now.

The present situation of religious politics, politicization of religion, religious fundamentalism, fanaticism has disturbed peace within the nation and has posed a problem for peaceful coexistence among the nations. A Second Look at Religion and serious rethinking about its role, utility and importance have become urgent, so that, personal, organizational and social life can survive, prosper and can make progress. To what extent and in what sense, Dharma and Dharmaśāstra are now relevant? Should religion be treated as thing of the past and be forgotten? Should there be a ban on the age-old traditions, and practices; forms of worship and prayer; that are advocated by the Dharmaśāstra of this or that religion? How to run the administration of a multi-religious country without the interference of religion? How to administer Law and Justice? Is it by accommodating conflicting religions or by remaining neutral to all religions or by eliminating religion from public life? The answers to these and such questions are difficult. They have become more difficult due to our vested interests, short-sightedness and ambiguities in our thoughts and actions. We raise the dust and complain that we cannot see. Our deafness to human cry and our blindness to the hard facts, to the heart of true religion and to misery and suffering, of which we are the authors, have led to present degeneration and decadence. Are there hopes for philosophical enlightenment? Are there any practical ways and means to amend the situation? How can we overcome the present crisis, where the cultural survival is at stake? What are the Roads to Human freedom, cooperation and coexistence; so that instead of Hell, we can hope for the Heaven on the earth?

I wish to limit the analysis and discussion to Hinduism.

A careful study of its origin and development shows, that it is not 'religion' in the Western sense of the term. The Western notion as developed in that historical context, is applicable to what may be called 'Prophetic Religions' viz. Judaism, Christianity, Islam Zorostrianism etc.. There the following features are noticed:

1. The Founder
2. The Sacred Text
3. Religious Organisation
4. A Set of Religious Beliefs
5. A Code of Conduct for the Followers.

Hinduism on the other hand is a process of events, movement of ideas, a stream of principles, doctrines, faiths and practices. It is really 'A Culture of the People' with different texts, views and perspectives, developed by seers and saints, interpreted by the Philosophers and poets, followed by the people with different historical settings, regional contexts, periods of time, with varied interests and orientations, with manifold life-styles and attitudes towards life. As such, Hinduism is 'Dharma' as understood as 'Sanskrit', much wider in scope and rich in its content than the Religions as understood in the West or in the Prophetic traditions. Buddhism, Jainism, Sikhism etc. arose as the creative expressions in Indian history, and have enriched its culture.

Moreover, there are Three elements in this cultural life.

1. Religious Core, which finds its expression in spiritual experiences of the seers and saints. This is Mokṣa-Vidyā or Sākṣātkāra-Darśana.
2. Religious Theory, which finds expression in the Philosophical Systems, as well as in the reflections of the thinkers.
3. Religious Rituals, which find its expression in the Smṛtis or Dharmaśāstra, which have tried to codify the *Ācāra*, *Vyavahāra* and *Prāyaścitta*, aspects of personal and social life.

Hinduism is an admixture of Revelation, Reason and Action. The paramount importance is given to Experience, while Reason and Action are supposed to be instrumental to Spiritual Realisation or Mokṣa; Reason or Philosophy explicating the essence or meaning of the Wisdom of the Śruti or Seers, while Action or Ritual serving as training in purification for perfection. The present-day Hinduism seems to be an outcome of the Śruti, Smṛti and Purāṇas, in which the core of spiritual experience, which is really fundamental to Dharma of seers and saints lagged behind, remained neglected, and was forgotten. It is replaced by Smṛti-Dharma of Do's and Do'nts (*Vidhi-Niṣedha*), Ritualism, and Brahmanic domination, along with the Paurāṇik-Dharma of Myths and Mythologies. The result is, instead of the Mokṣa-Vidyā of Seers and Saints, the religion of the Purohitas, Pandits and Purāṇikas became the dominent force ruling the religious masses. This led to one-sided other-worldly outlook, social stratification in the name of the *Varṇāśrama Dharma* blind faith and superstition and Closed Society. The Divine Inspiration and Vision were lost, even the saints suffered the agonies of persecution. Dogmatism killed the spirit the free inquiry and religion became the story of human bondage instead of Path-Way towards Perfection.

This is the story of every religious faith in the world.

What is the way through this Age of Darkness to the Light-Divine?

With the advent of Science and Technology, discovery of nature through experiment, understanding of the Natural Laws, man entered in the New Age. It is now the era of computers, space-exploration, world communication networks. It is the age of human confidence in the conquest of nature for human development and prosperity. The Worship of God is replaced by the Study of Nature. But man, in the course of this success become more self-centered, pleasure-seeking. Man entered in the age of Wars, Pollutions and human civilization came under the shadow of self-destruction. We now live in the period of power politics, exploitation, lust for affluence and alienation, where the beauty of life is lost and the values are vanishing, making life helpless and with no hopes. That means, Dogmatic Religion of Dharmaśāstra, as well as Destructive Science have led to the situation of blind-alley with no way out. The ideological situation in India is more precarious. We are sandwiched between Scientific Materialism and Religious Dogmatism. Our personal life is governed by the same religious beliefs, rites rituals; social life by the temple-worships and festivals. On the other hand we profess in our professional life to be non-religious, and we claim to be secular in our political games and gamblings.

To counter Religious Dogmatism or orthodox Dharmaśāstra, we need proper, reliable and useful Policy and Perspective. What is the picture now?

The term Secularism in its original sense refers to this worldly, material, non-religious outlook towards life. Such positivistic philosophy would be consistent with the implications of science and technology. But we do not dare to be scientific enough, in all its meanings and implication. We fear, it would shatter the religic-spiritual foundations of our national heritage and culture. Moreover, it is true that such attitude would do justice only to the '*Abhyudaya*' aspect of human life or to the *Pravṛtti-Dharma*.

We accordingly invented other two meanings of secularism, viz. State remaining neutral to the private religious affairs of the people. This has not been actually achieved, due to the vested political interests of the political pressure-groups, who play the game of majority or minority politics. This is reflected in our political decisions and voting behaviour at elections, as well as the visits of the VIPs and VVIPs to the religious shrines and activities, festivals, gatherings etc.

We, therefore invented yet another meaning of secularism, i.e. Religious Tolerence or *Sarva-Dharma-Samabhāva*. But this creates difficulties in public administration of Law and Justice. Respect for and tolerence towards the religion of others requires maturity of mind on the part of the citizens. Freedom of Worship, mentioned in Indian Constitution assumes that, religion would not hinder but help in ensuring harmony among various social communities. But when there is situation of group conflict because of the differences on the forms and ways of worship, we need 'Common Civil Code'.

Such a common civil code is necessary to ensure protection of security, maintaining peace and harmony, administration of Law and Justice, without which national unity and integrity cannot be safeguarded. Freedom of speech and expression, freedom of movement and organisation is possible, when the citizen feels confident that there is rule of law, there is equality of opportunity and equality before law, irrespective of one's personal cast, creed, sect or set of beliefs.

Our failure in this direction has resulted in a situation of anarchy and chaos, confusion and conflict; that too in the name of religion, which is supposed to be the source of universal harmony, love and sympathy, of devotion and wisdom.

The natural outcome has been, the rise and rule of the fundamentalist and terrorists, who use religion as a weapon to achieve their political objectives; as instrument to fulfill their selfish ends, using millions of people and their lives as means. The Dharmaśāstra, or codified religion, instead of teaching self discipline, becomes a gateway towards destruction and death. It is the death of Human Culture itself.

If we want to overcome this situation, some hard decisions would be necessary. These may include:

1. Ban on Fatavas for political objectives.
2. Ban on communal organizations creating mistrust among the members of different communities, and misleading the people.
3. Ban on misuse of religious property, literature.
4. Ban on religious politics, and religious discrimination in the name of minority or majority politics.
5. Ban on any activity, which promoted fundamentalism and terrorism.

Along with such negative measures, few positive and constructive steps would also be desirable. These may include:

1. To Treat Indian Constitution as New Dharmaśāstra, meant for all citizens. Instead of Manu, Parāśara or Yājñyavalkya, this would provide social and moral motivation, relevant today.

2. Common Civil Code for smooth administration of law and justice.
3. Peoples Education in the moral and spiritual teachings of seers and saints, which is true religion.
4. To consider India as Culture, rather than as land of religions.
5. To create social awareness about Universal Religion, to safeguard national unity and human survival.

Perhaps, this may save us from the dooms day and would lead to the Life Divine.

8

Śūdras and the Vedic Sacrifice

T.N. Dharmadhikari

It is generally held that the Śūdras had no role to play directly or indirectly in the Vedic rituals. They were not involved in it. On the other hand they were prohibited.[1]

On the investigation into the vedic rituals, it appears that the above belief cannot be totally accepted.

The very nature of the vedic rituals necessitated, at least indirect and in few cases, even direct participation of all the stratas of the society. The performance of a sacrifice required a large number of wooden utensils, clay utensils, clay bricks, the bamboo fencings and roof covers and baskets, the metal articles like *svadhiti, Paraśu*, the razor of iron, the *Rukmas* of Silver, golden chains, the piece of lead, the *kāṁsya* vessels, the cotton and linen clothes, the hides of antelope and tiger, the drums, foot-wears of leather, the carts and choriots, the bow and arrows etc., etc., which were manufactured by the craftsmen like carpenters, weavers, smiths, shoe-makers, hunters etc. Even barbers, plough-men etc. had some work in sacrifice. It may be noted that the craftsmanship-'śilpopajīvittva' as Śabara tells us, was prohibited for the three varṇas[2]. The soma shrubs were also purchased from a Soma-seller, living in valleys, who could bring the soma from the hilly mountains.

In the Rājasūya Sacrifice, the king had to perform the rite called, 'ratnināṁ havīṁṣi', in which the king had to go to the houses of the 'Jewels' of his kingdom and perform in their houses certain iṣtis. Thus he was required to perform the iṣṭi at the house of a Kṣattā and also of Akṣāvāpa, who were also regarded as jewels. Kṣattā is regarded as a son of a śūdra-man and a kṣatriya woman. Cp. Kullūka-śūdrāt kṣatriyāyāṁ kṣattā (on Mn X. 13).

Akṣāvāpa, otherwise called kitava, also appears on the dias of the sacrifice in Agnyādhāna rite[3] and in the dice-play at Rājasūya also. He also probably did not belong to the either of the three varṇas.

It may be noted that even a puṁścalī,[4] an harolt was not avoided by the vedic ritual, since she appears in the Mahāvrata-rite.

Thus it appears that, though all the above mentioned, probably did not belong to the three varṇas, were accepted, not only by the then society, but also by the sacred vedic rituals.

Even the Śruti texts directly prescribed the setting of three fires for a Rathakāra[5] and a certain iṣṭi for a Niṣāda - Sthapati[6].

Āpastamba attempted to include this Rathakāra in the fold of three varṇas[7]. But according to Śabara, Rathakāra neither belonged to the three varṇas, nor to the śūdra-class. This is really strange. Probably such interpretations were not intended by the Śruti texts, which enjoined the Ādhāna rite also for a Rathakāra, not belonging to three varṇas[8]. If Śabara's interpretation is accepted, it must be deemed as a remarkable mark in the development of sacrifice, since it extends the fold of sacrifice irrespective of varṇas.

Further, as the iṣṭi of the Niṣāda-sthapati is concerned, Śabara plainly accepted him as a non-āryan and even then deemed him fit for offering the iṣṭi on the basis of the vedic authority[9].

Śabara dissolves the compound, viz. 'niṣāda-sthapati' as a karmadhāraya and not a Ṣaṣṭhītatpuruṣa. Cp also Jaiminīya-nyāyamālā which naturally follows Śabara, in other context observes that a karmadhāraya has to be preferred to a ṣaṣṭhisamāsa[10]. Thus niṣāda-sthapati is an architect or a town-chief belonging to the Niṣāda community.

Kūṭa probably meaning the horns, is given away as Dakṣiṇā in this sacrifice. Śabara stated - that kūṭa is a suitable requisite for Niṣādas and not for Āryans and confirms thereby that Niṣādas were non-āryans[11]. Thus it is beyond doubt that the performance of this vedic iṣṭi was allowed to non-āryans also.

For setting up the Dakṣiṇa-fire, the Maitrāyaṇi Saṁhitā enjoins, alternatively, to bring the fire from the frying-pan (grid-iron) where meat or grain are roasted. The preparer of fried meat or grains, as the MS refers to, was a Vṛṣala pulkaka[12].

Āpśs also recommends to bring the fire from a house of a wealthy Śūdra; for setting up the Dakṣiṇa-fire.

The Kśs prescribes to construct a mound in śmaśāna, as high as knee,[13] for the pitṛmedha to be performed of a Śūdra. It may be noted that Pitṛmedha is prescribed for one who has set up the sacred fires[14].

The MS prescribing the *sapta-sthāvīrya* rite recommends that a sacrificer should include in his cow-pen, a young uncastrated bull brought from a cow-pen of a rich Vaiśya or from that of a rich Śūdra[15].

MS also prescribes that, one desiring cattle should bring twenty-one pieces of dried cow-dung from the cow-pen of a rich Vaiśya of from that of a rich Śūdra, enkindle them and offer twenty-one libations on that fire[16].

In the iṣṭi, the Adhvaryu gives a call to the oblation-preparer (haviṣkṛt), for threshing the paddy-(the husky-corn) in the mortor. In the sacrifice of a Brahmin, he gives a call with the words 'haviṣkṛd ehi', in the sacrifice of a Rājanya, with 'haviṣkṛd āgahi', in that of a Vaiśya, with 'haviṣkṛd ādrava' and in that of a Śūdra with 'haviṣkṛd ādhāva'. This has been prescribed by Apśs[17]. Rudradatta restricts this call viz. haviṣkṛd ādhāva in the sacrifice performed by a niṣāda-sthapati.

Allowing alternatives for threshing the paddy and pounding the grains, Āpśs states that a lady attendant (dāsī) or the Sacrificer's wife, pounds the grains. Or the wife threshes the paddy and a Śūdrā dāsī pounds the grains into flour. Rudradatta regulates this alternative and comments that the grinding of the corn be done by a[18] Śūdrā dāsī only. Thus a Śūdrā dāsī was unhesitatingly allowed in the sacrificial place for pounding grains of which the oblations were to be prepared.

Āpśs on the basis of Vedic authority, alternatively allows a Śūdra[19] to milk the cow, for the milk-oblation to be offered in Agnihotra or Sāṁnāyya oblation in iṣṭi. Rudradatta clearly states that a Śūdra milk-man has to recite the vedic formulas when he milks the cows[20]. Āpśs also prescribes the Vedic formulas to be recited by a śūdra milk-man as follows:-

The milk-man should hold the cords for tying cows and recite 'adityai rāsnā 'si' (TS 1.2.12). He should tie a calf with 'Pūṣā 'si' (T Br 3.7.4). The milk-man intimates the Adhvaryu that he is bringing the calf near its mother - cow, with a half verse - viz. 'ayakṣmā vaḥ prajayā saṁsṛjāmi rāyaspoṣeṇa bahulā bhavantiḥ' (T Br. 3.7.4.15; KS 1.3; 31.2). The milk-man then informs the Adhvaryu that, he is now sitting for milking the cow - with a full verse - viz. - ayakṣmā vaḥ prajayā saṁsṛjāmi rāyaspoṣeṇa bahulā bhavantiḥ / ūrjam payaḥ pinvamānā ghṛtam ca jivo jivantīḥ upa vaḥ sadeyam// (T Br 3.7.4.15)

Further, after milking each cow, the Adhvaryu asks the milk-man, 'which cow have you milked?' The milk-man replies-'amūm, yasyām devānām manuṣyāṇām payo hitam' (T Br. 3.7.4).

Thus a śūdra milk-man was required to recite the vedic formulas in the vedic rituals.

In the Varuṇa-praghāśa parvan of the Cāturmāsya sacrifice, at the offering of the karambha-pots, not the Hotṛ, but the Sacrificer and wife jointly recite a yājyā-verse - viz. 'yad grāme, yad araṇye, yat sabhāyāṁ, yad indriye / yac śūdre, yad arya enaś cakṛmā vayam- /yad ekasyādhidharmaṇi/tasya, avayajanam asi svāhā' - (TS 1.8.3) meaning-'the wrong we may have done in villages or in forests; in the assemblies or in case of speech, the wrong to the Śūdra or to the Ārya, the wrong, contrary to the law, either of that, O oblation, you are the expiation.

This verse (VS 20.17) is also utilised by Ks's (19.5.13) at the concluding bath of the Sautrāmaṇi Sacrifice.

This makes very clear that the sacrificer had no evil intention to do wrong against any member of the society and if he has unknowingly done any wrong he is undergoing the expiation.

In the important ritual of Agniciti, the Śatarudrīya offering is offered with the formulas collected in TS 4.5.1-11, which pay homage to many of the then existing communities, which include, Sūta, Sthapati, Vrātas. Kṣattā, Rathakāra, Kulāla, Mṛgayu, Śvani etc. and many more; According to Śruti, they also are the manifested forms of Rudra.

In Agniciti, while placing the *ruc* bricks on the pile, the Adhvaryu recites three verses—the last of which is as follows:-

rucam no dhehi brāhmaṇeṣu
rucam rājasu naḥ kṛdhi/
rucam viśyeṣu śūdreṣu
mayi dhehi rucā ṛucam// (TS 5.7.6.10)

which means—

Grant brilliance in our Brahmins,
place brilliance in our Princes,
deposit brilliance in our Vaiśyas
and also in our Śūdras,
With thy flame grant me brilliance.

Thus the sacrificer prays to deposit the brilliance, the *Ruc* in the Śūdras also, while placing the *ruc*-bricks in the pile.

One of the formulas collected in VS Chapter 26 runs as follows:

'yathemāṁ vācam kalyāṇīm
āvadāni janebhyaḥ/
brahma-rājanyābhyām
śūdrāya ca āryāya ca//
priyo devānām
dakṣiṇāyai dātuḥ iha bhūyāsam'//

meaning—Let me speak this auspicious speech to the people.
to the Brahmins, to the princes
to the Śūdra and also to the Āryas
So that I may be dear to gods
and also I may be dear to one who
offers the Dakṣiṇā—etc.

In Puruṣa-medha, one may see a very wide picture of the society and an attempt to bring them together on the sacrificial dias. The persons of all the classes are tied to the Yūpas, the sacrificial posts, and after upākaraṇa i.e. worshipping them, all are released. The puruṣas tied to the Yūpa include—Brāhmaṇa, Rājanya, Vaiśya and Śūdra—and also puṁścalū, Kaulāla, Karmāra, maṇikāra, iṣukāra, dhanuṣkāra, jyākāra, rajjusarja, mṛgayu, śvani, pauñjiṣṭha, naiṣāda, vrātya etc. etc. (VS 30.9 onwards). The intention behind this may be to celebrate the gathering of all the stratas of the society, under one roof of the sacrifice; and to imbibe that they are all the forms of the Virāṭ-puruṣa.

It should be remembered that the Purūṣa-medha was to be performed by one who desires to become *'Sarvam'*, the all, which is identified with the Universal Puruṣa.

From the above references, which are only illustrative, it appears that, even the so-called Śūdras and so-called Atiśūdras were directly or indirectly made involved in the fold of sacrifice from the Vedic times. They were allowed even to recite the vedic formulas.

In this state of facts, the references that Śūdras were not entitled for being involved in sacrifice, because they were born of the feet of the great Puruṣa, or they were not associated with any deity at their creation by Prajāpati should be looked upon as mere mythological, with very less historical value.

Unfortunately the quarter of the verse from the Puruṣa-sūkta of the Ṛgveda (10.90.12 or TĀ 3.12.6) viz. 'padbhyāṁ śūdro ajāyata' has been wrongly interpreted from the ancient times.

Āpśs 6.3.12 also stated[21]—that śūdra has been born of the contemptible part—viz. the feet of the Universal Puruṣa. In fact, the feet of the Universal Puruṣa can never be contemplated as contemptible. This interpretation of the Āpastamba appears to be quite contrary to the earlier Brahmanical thinking. Thus Śatapatha Brāhmaṇa states 'the foot is a foundation'[22]

Secondly the śūdras are not the only unit created form the foot of the Universal Puruṣa. Even [23] mother-earth, ekaviṁśa stoma, anuṣṭubh metre, the horse etc., are created from the feet of the Universal Puruṣa, the Prajāpati and they are never regarded as contemptible.

In the context of the Puruṣa-medha, Śūdra is indentified by the Ś Br. with Tapas[24] which means '*austerity*' and not only '*toiling*'..

Notes

1. Apaśūdrādhikaraṇa—Jaiminiya Śūtra 6.1.7 and Śabara on it. Taittiriya Saṁhitā 7.1.1 tasmāt śūdro yajñeṣu anavakḷptaḥ.
2. Śabara on—JS. 6.1.46-'Pratiṣiddham hi tasya śilpopajīvitvam' and on JS. 6.1.48-'pratiṣiddhatvāt śilpopajīvitvasyeti'.
3. Āpśs 5.19.2-4—Rudradatta-'akṣān prayacchan saṁpreṣyati kitavān.
4. Āpśs 2.1.15-19—Kūrceṣu hotrakā upagātāraḥ patnaya ity āsate/nikalpante patnayo ' pāghāṭikās-tambala-vīnāḥ piccholāh iti/nikalpante vīṇāvādāḥ śaṅkhān nāḷis tūṇavān iti/nikalpete brahmacāri puṁścali . . . etc. Cp also Āpśs 21.19.5-6.
5. TBr. 1.1.4.8—Varṣāsu rathakāra ādadhīta, Cp. Āpśs 5.3.18-Varṣā rathakārasya / Āpśs 5.11.7-ṛbhūṇām tvā devānām-iti rathakārasya /
6. MS 2.2.4—Vāstumadhye raudram carum nirvapet yatra rudraḥ paśūn śamāyeta/etayā niṣāda-sthapatiṁ yājayet/Śā hi tasyeṣṭiḥ/Kūṭam dakṣiṇā akarṇo vā garda bhaḥ/ Cp Āpśs 9.14.14.
7. Āpśs 5.3.19—Ye trayāṇāṁ varṇānām etat karma kuryuḥ teṣām eṣa kālaḥ/-Rudradatta-triṣu varṇeṣu antarbhūtā eva svavṛtti-karṣitā ye ratham kurvanti teṣām eṣa kālaḥ . . . etc.
8. Śabara on JS 6.1.50—hīnās tu kiñcit traivarṇikebhyo jātyantaram, na tu śudrāḥ no vaiśyḥ na kṣatriyāḥ/ — teṣām idam ādhānam/tasmāt atraivarṇikānām aśūdrāṇām etat ādhānam
9. MS 2.2.4—etayā niṣādasthapatim yājayet.
10. Jaiminiya-nyāya-mālā-3.3.24-31—Ṣaṣṭhi-samāsāt karmadhārayo balīyān/ 6.2.51-52-niṣādaś cāsau sthapatiś ca iti karmadhāraya-samāsasya mukhyatvāt.

11. Śabara on JS 6.1.52—kūṭaṁ hi niṣādānām eva upakārakam na āryāṇām. -kullūka-'niṣādaḥ śūdra-kanyāyām' (Mn 10.8).
12. MS 1.6.11—bhraṣṭrāt dakṣiṇāgnim āhareyuḥ/eṣa vā agnīnām annādaḥ annakaraṇam bhraṣṭram-tadāhur yathā vṛṣalo nija pulkakaś cikitset evam sa iti//
Cp Āpśs 5.14.3-ambarīṣāt annakāmasya/ Cp.Āpśs-tasya tredhā mahimānam vyaucchat iti/viṭkulāt vittavato vā ekayonaya ity eke//
13. Kātyāyana-Śrauta-Sūtra 21.4.16—kānu śūdrasya.
14. Bhāradvāja Paitṛmedhika Sūtra 1.1.2—athātaḥ paitṛmedhikam dahanam.../*āhitāgner* maraṇa-saṁśaye ... etc.
Cp. Sāyaṇa on TĀ 3.21, āhitāgner yo dahanādi-saṁskāraḥ so ' yam pitrmedhaḥ.
15. MS 4.2.7—yo vaiśyaḥ śūdro vā bahupuṣṭaḥ tasya gavām sāṇḍam vatsataram apagamayeta—... etc.
16. MS 4.2.10—yo vaiśyaḥ śūdro vā bahupuṣṭaḥ syāt tasya gavām goṣṭhāt ekaviṁśatim śakān āhṛtya ekaviṁśatim āhutīr juhuyāt//
17. Āpśs-1.19.9—haviṣkṛd ādhāva iti śūdrasya.
18. Āpśs 1.21.8-9—dāsī pinaṣṭi patnī vā/api vā patnī avahanti śūdrā pinaṣṭi// Rudradatta-patnī avaghātam eva karoti/ na peṣaṇam, tat tu śūdrā dāsī eva karoti//
19. Āpśs 1.13.15; 6.4.11.13—na śūdro duhyāt/duhyāt vā.
20. Rudradatta-on Āpśs 1.13.15—sūdrasyāpi dogdhuḥ mantrā bhavantīti vacanāt//
21. Āpśs 6.3.12—asato vā eṣa saṁbhūto yac śūdraḥ-(Rudradatta-asataḥ, ati kṛṣṭāt aṅgāt pādād iti/yāvat padbhyām śūdro ajayata iti śruteḥ)-etc.
22. Ś Br. 13.6.3.8—pratiṣṭhā vai pādaḥ/pratiṣṭhām evāsmai karoti/; also 8.7.3.19; 8.3.1.10-pratiṣṭhā caritram (=foot), also 10.3.2.11-pratiṣṭhe pādau. J Br. 3.295-dvipād yajamānaḥ pratiṣṭhityai/ etc.
23. TĀ 3.12.6—ṚS 10.90.14-padbhyāṁ bhumiḥ TS 7.1.1-pat-taḥ ekaviṁśam niramimīta-tam anuṣṭup chando ... vairājam sāma, śūdro manuṣyāṇām aśvaḥ ... etc.
24. Ś Br. 13.6.2.10—tapase śūdram/tapo vai śūdraḥ/ ... etc.

Abbreviations

Āpśs	—	Āpastamba Śrauta Sūtra
KS	—	Kāṇva Saṁhitā
Kśs	—	Kātyāyana Śrauta Sūtra
Mn	—	Manu Samṛti
Ms	—	Maitrāyaṇī Saṁhitā
ṚS	—	Ṛgveda Saṁhitā
ŚBr.	—	Śatapatha Brāhmaṇa
TĀ	—	Taittirīya Āraṇyaka

TBr — Taittirīya Brāhmaṇa
TS — Taittirīya Saṁhitā
VS — Vājasaneyi Saṁhitā
JS — Jaiminiya-sūtra

9

Historical Importance of the Devala Smṛti

Bhagyalata Pataskar

Purifying rites form an important and essential chapter in almost all the literature on the Dharmaśāstra. The word used for the same is *śuddhi*. The expiation rites also occupy the foremost position in the Dharmaśāstra. All what we can say about these two words is that the expiations are for the sake of purification. The idea behind it is once the expiation is over, the concerned person being pure, can be restored to social interaction as usual. However we do find the overlapping of the usages of two words.

I would like to clarify that I am not at all concerned with the details and the authenticity of the purifying rites but more interested in the social awareness shown by these purifying rites in case of those spoiled by the *mlecchas*. This awareness is shown by Devala smṛti as a need of a time. Hence I want to find out the social fact which motivated this Smṛtikāra to prescribe purifying rites particularly on contact of the *mlecchas* in great detail.

Something about Devala Smṛti

Devala Smṛti is not included in 18 main traditional smṛtis. The name Devala as that of a sage frequently occurs in the Mahabhārata[1]. Śaṅkaracharya refers to Devala as a writer of Dharmasūtra[2]. All these quotations deal with *Ācāra* (duty), *vyavahāra* (law), *Śrāddha* (offering oblations to the departed souls), *prāyaścitta* (expiations) etc. Hence Devala Dharmasūtra seems to be an independent work which is lost now, that is how justice P.V. Kane remarks[3]. The existent text entitled as Devala Smṛti and published in the collection of Smṛtis[4] appears to be a late compilation. There are 90 verses which specially deal with purification and expiation on contact with the mlecchas. Devala himself is referred to in two verses.

It is very difficult to arrive at the fixed time of Devala. All what we can say at this stage is Devala as a writer of Dharmasūtra must be different than Devala as a writer of the smṛti. The compilation of the Devala Smṛti may be late one, but the text must be existing earlier since it is referred to by Aparaka (1125 A.D), Smṛticandrikā (1200-1225 A.D). Śūlapāṇi (1375-1460), the mejor portion of the text must be existing before 12th century. i.e. in about 11th century A.D.

About the Word Mleccha

The word *mleccha* really bears a spectrum of meaning. There are references to the word right from the ancient literature. In all those meanings in various texts a common denominator is 'a foreigner', 'a stranger', 'an outsider'. Considering the time factor we can fix the meaning of the word mleccha as 'foreign inveders' i.e. Arabṣ Turks etc.

The other texts dealing with the subject i.e. *sparśane śuddhi* use the words *caṇḍāla, patita, śūdra* whereas the Devala Smṛti consistantly uses the word *mleccha*. Thus *mlecchanītasya śuddhi* seems to be the unique feature of this smṛti. As far as aims and objects of this paper are concerned I am least interested in the ritualistic details of the *śuddhi* rites.

Devala prescribes four types of Cāndrāyaṇa vow for the persons of four classes respectively[5] when they are spoiled due to the close association of the *mlecchas*. He had provided purifying rite for a person under the captivity of the *mlecchas* for more than one year[6].

Further he has prescribed the *prājāpatya* vow for comparatively more severe deeds which otherwise would have caused sin[7]. The act of killing the cow, eating the left over of a lower person, drinking the milk of a donkey, camel, boar, having sexual intercourse with a mleccha woman are regarded as very sever sins. But Devala seems to be liberal enough when he says[8] if a person under the captivity of the *mlecchas* is forcibly made to commit these deeds, then these do not effect as a sin but just cause physical impurities which can be removed by the prājāpatya vow.

He further states that two prājāpatyas or two *cāndrāyaṇas* will purify a person who is made to stay with the *mlecchas* for maximum 20 years[9]. However there is no *śuddhi* as such for one who is made to stay there more than 20 years.

He has discussed the issue with all its possible aspects. Suppose a person due to his close association of mlecchas becomes mleccha it means that he denies the purification and admits to be so. In such cases after the death of such person, his son need not offer funeral oblations to him[10]. This further signifies that Devala has sanctioned that if a person admits to be a mleccha his son can never be regarded as a *mleccha*.

When most of the Smṛtis prescribe abandonment of the kidnapped or the raped women[11] (of course other than one's own mother), Devala and Atri only show foresightedness and consideration in prescribing purifying rites for such a woman.

Devala says if a woman from Brahmin class falls in a hands of a mleccha and is forced to eat prohibited food, then she deserves purification by parāka vow[12]. Same provision is open for the women from the other classes.

If she is not enjoyed carnally and if she has not eaten the food from the mlecchas, then she gets purified with three rights[13]. Devala has gone one step father in considering a case of a woman who is raped by mlecchas and conceives. He says such woman gets purified by performing a vow called *kṛcchra sāntapana*[14]. It matters least to which class she belongs. He explains that as long as she bears an embryo she is regarded as an impure. However after delivering a child or after miscarriage she becomes as pure as the gold[15]. The implications are quite clear. Such women should be accepted by the family and by the society without any hesitation. It is surprising that the same sage Devala seems to be harsher to that innocent infant. He says, that child, if born should not be brought up by the same woman herself. Of course it should not be thrown away but should be given to some other woman, so to avoid the intercaste mixture in the society[16].

The idea of greater insistance on sacredness of marriage tie, of a stricter morality and a demand for greater decency might have provoked him to say so.

All what Devala means is such persons who are forcibly kidnapped, made to violate the rules, raped by the mlecchas should not be expelled out of the society. But they should be restored to social interractions after undergoing some purifying rites.

To esteem the historical importance of this thought, we must see the social and political situation then, i.e. before and in 11th century A.D.

The Arabs had conquered the Sindh in 712 A.D. and had established their control over there. The rest of the India was split into various small independent kingdoms then. Obviously the political structure of India was very weak and instable.

In 712 A.D. the king Dahir was conquared by Muhammad-bin-Qasim. A large number of Hindus and Buddhists were massacred. Only those were spared who converted to Islam. Muhammad-bin-Qasim himself wrote to Hajjaj "several infidels are converted or destroyed"[17].

Then started 17 expeditions of Mahammad Ghazni (997-1030 A.D). During these expeditions a large number of Hindus were slaughtered. Only those were shown mercy who became converts to Islam.

These invasions were followed by the same by Mohammad Ghori and the history went on repeating. The first invasion of Ghori was directed towards multan in 1175 A.D.

Thus forcible conversion, kidnapping of women, captivity of men was a burning problem then. Devala seems to have recognized the danger that in keeping such people away from the society begets a gap, which getting widen and widen gradually turns into rivalry. To add the situation there is every possibility of such people joining the enemy i.e. becoming treacher and taking revenge over the society.

The present smṛtikāra or the compilar of the present text understood the need of the time. If any provision on ground of Dharma is not made to assimilate such unlucky people to society, then such people would turn to be a diseased limb of a body that can neither be cut out nor can it be kept with. So he prescribed such purifying rite for such people. This is exactly what can be called social awareness of the smṛtikāra. He understood that unless such socialization of Dharma is made, Dharma would loose its very fundamental characteristics[18] "dhārakatva i.e. capacity to sustain, uphold the society".

The reference to the place at the beginning of this *smṛti* is also very significant. The *smṛti* commences with *sindhutīre sukhāsīnaṁ devalam munisattamam/sametya munayaḥ sarve idaṁ vacanam abruvan*[19]. The area which was first and most affected by this muslim inveders is the remote north west corner of India then, which belongs to Pakistan at present.

Unfortunately this liberal as well as revolutionary idea of re-conversion was not at all tolerated by the contemporary authorities on Dharma, and Devala failed to get any followers. Neither the Devala smṛti nor the purifying rites were given even due importance and recognition by the other concerning texts on Dharmaśāstra then. And the *mlecchanīta* or *mlecchaspṛṣt* who were the part and the parcel of our society once got discarded from us for ever and became the rival of the same society later on.

Thus the time had proved now that we had to pay a lot for this connivance towards Devala Smṛti.

Notes

1. Sabhāparvan. 59.7—*evam āhāyam asito devalo munisattamaḥ*. Śalyaparva 50. story of Asita Devala. Śabhāparvan 72.5. *triṇi jyotīmṣi puruṣa iti vai devalo ' bravīt apatyam karma vidyā ca yataś sṛṣṭāś prajās tataś*
   Tr. There are three lights in the human beings viz. an offspring, deed, knowledge; because the living beings originates from them.
   Even in Bhagavadgītā there is reference to Asita Devala. According to Mahabhārata account Asita Devala seems to be one character.
2. *Sa ca kāryakāraṇatvānanyatvābhyupagamāt pratyāsanno vedāntavādasya devalaprabhṛibhiś ca kaiścid dharma-sūtrakāraiḥ svagrantheṣu āśritas tena tatpratiṣedhe yatno ' tīva kṛto nāṇvādi-kāraṇavādapratiṣedhe.*
   That (i.e. *pradhānakāraṇavāda*—theory of *Pradhāna* as the cause of the universe) appears to be very nearer to the vedantic theory because it admits the non-difference between the cause and effect, and it is resorted to in their own texts by Devala etc., the writer on Dharmasūtra. For this a great effort was made to refute it and not so for the repudiation of the theories of a atom etc.
3. "That seems to have been an independent work. . .The Dharmasūtra of Devala to judge from the quotations in Kṛtyakalpataru, Aparārka, Smṛticandrikā and other early digests appears to have been an extensive one and to have dealt with most of the topics that are discussed in the Dharmasūtras of Gautama, Āpastamba, Baudhāyana, Hārita and others and also some matters in detail such as sāṅkhya and yoga".
   History of Dharmaśāstra, Vol. 1. part 1. P. 283. By P.V. Kane.
4. *Smṛtīnām Samuccayaḥ* pub by Anandashram, Pune. *ānandā-śramasaṁskṛtagranthāali* No. 48. *Bīs smṛtiyaṁ* along with Hindi translation parts I and II ed. by Shriram Sharma Acarya. Samskriti samsthan Bareli 1966.
5. *balānmlecchais tu yo nītas tasya śuddhis tu kīdṛśi*

saṁvatsaroṣite śudre śuddhiś cāndrāyaṇena tu.
parākaṁ vatsarārdhe ca parākārdhaṁ trimāsike.
māsike pādakṛcchraś ca nakharomavivarjitaḥ.
pādonaṁ kṣatriyasyoktam ardhaṁ vaiśyasya dāpayet.
prāyaścittaṁ dvijasyoktaṁ pādaṁ śudrasya dāpayet. Devala Smṛti 26-28. Tr. What sort of purification is (available) for one who is forcibly kidnapped by the mlecchas? In case of a Śūdra, staying for one year the purification is with *cāndrayaṇa* vow. In case of staying for half an year the *Paraka* vow purifies and in case of staying for three months the *Parākārdha* vow purifies. In case of month, the *Pādakṛcchra* in which nails and hair are removed. Threeforth of this is prescribed for the kṣatriya and half of it is prescribed for the Vaiśya, and one forth of that prescribed for Śūdra is an expiation for a brāhmin.

6. *mlecchannaṁ mlecchasaṁsparśo mlecchena saha saṁsthitiḥ. vatsaraṁ vatsarādūrdhvaṁ trirātreṇa viśudhyati.*

Tr. one who had eaten the food from the mleccha who had contact/touch with the mlecchas and who had stayed with the mlecchas for one year or more than one year gets purified with a period of three nights.

7,8. *balāddāsikṛtā ye ca mlecchacāṇḍaladsyobhiś aśubhaṁ kāritaṁ karma gavādiprāṇihiṁsanam. ucchiṣṭamārja.ıaṁ caiva tathā tasyaiva bhojanan kharoṣṭraviḍvarāhāṇāṁ āmiṣasya ca bhakṣaṇam.tatsrīṇām ca tathā saṁgaṁ tābhiś ca saha bhojanam. māsoṣite dvijātau tu prājāpatyaṁ viśodhanam.* Tr. Those who are forcibly kept under captivity by the mlecchas, caṇḍalas and the robbers and are compelled to commit bad deeds, viz. killing of the animals like cows, and are compelled to clean away the left over and to eat the same as well as to eat the meat of the donkey boar and camel, are made to establish union with their women and are made to take food with them; out of them in case of those belonging to 3 classes the prājāpatya vow purifies. (The subsequent verses state the deails for the *āhitāgni*, and *śūdras* under certain conditions)

9. *Mlecchaiḥ sahoṣito yas tu pañcaprabhṛti viṁśatiś.*
varṣāṇi śuddhireṣoktā tasya cāndrāyaṇadvayam.

Tr. Two *cāndrāyaṇas* are prescribed for one who stayed with the mlecchas for five to twenty years.

10. *mātaraṁ ca parityajya pitaraṁ ca tathā sutaḥ*
tataḥ pitāmahaṁ caiva śeṣapiṇḍaṁ tu nirvapet.

Tr. excluding the mother and the father (who have joined the mlecchas) the son should offer a funeral oblations to other forefathers.

11. *anicchantī tu yā bhuktā guptāṁ tāṁ vasayed gṛhe*
malīnāṅgīm adhaś śayyāṁ piṇḍamātropajīvinīm.
kārayen niṣkṛtiṁ kṛcchraṁ parākaṁ vā same gatām.
hīnavarṇopabhuktā yā tyājyā vadhyā ' pi vā bhavet.

Tr. A woman who is enjoyed carnally disregarding her desire should be kept in the house in hide. She should allow to stay in the house with her dirty body to sleep on the ground, to survive with small quantity of rice. When she just goes with (the mleccha), the impurities should be removed by performing parāka if a woman is carnally enjoyed by a person from low caste forcibly, she should be driven away or she deserves death.

12. *brāhmaṇī bhojayen mlecchaṁ abhakṣyaṁ bhaṣayed yadi.*
parākeṇa tataś śuddhir dānena uttaratottarā. 38

Tr. A woman from Brahmin class if gives food to the *mleccha* and if eats the prohibited food then she gets purification by *parāka*. The women from the subsequent ones get purified by giving gifts.

13. *na kṛtaṁ maithunaṁ tābhir abhakṣyaṁ naiva bhakṣitam.*
śuddhis tadā trirātreṇa mlecchannenaiva bhakṣite. 39.
Tr. If she is not enjoyed carnally and if she has not consumed food from the mleccha then she gets purification by *trirātra* vow, provided that the mleccha food is not consumed.

14. *yoṣā garbhaṁ vidhalle yā mlecchāt kāmād akāmataḥ.*
brāhmaṇī kṣatriyā vaiśyā śudrā varṇetarā ca yā.
abhakṣyabhakṣaṇaṁ kuryāt tasyāḥ śuddhiḥ kathaṁ bhavet
kṛcchraṁ sāntapanaṁ śuddhir ghṛtair yoneś ca pācanam. 48-49. Tr. How a purification is possible of a woman may she belongs to Brahmin, kṣatriya, vaiśya or Śūdra or other than this, conceives from a mleccha, out of his lust, even though she doesn't desire? and what purification is possible if she eats a prohibited food? The śuddhi is possible by the kṛcchra sāntapana vow and expiation for the womb is with the ghee.

15. *asavarṇena yo garbhaḥ strīṇāṁ yonau niṣicyate.*
aśuddhā sā bhaven nārī yāvacśalyaṁ na muñcati.
vinihsṛte tataḥ śalye rajaso vāpi darśane.
Tr. That woman is regarded as impure who bears the embryo from the person not belonging to her own class. When that dart comes out or after the menses, that woman becomes as pur as gold.
Here the word used is *'asavarṇa'* and not *mleccha* as it is used distinctly elsewhere. The idea originally is found in the Vasiṣṭha Dharmasūtra 28. 2-3. Which says as follows:-
svayaṁ vipratipannā vā yadi vā vipravāsitā.
baltātkāropabhuktā vā corahastagatāpi vā.
na tyājyā dūṣitā nāri nāsyās tyāgo vidhīyate.
puṣpakālam upāsīta ṛtukālena śudhyati.
Since Devala uses it in the context of the impurities brought out by mleccha we can understand the word *asavarṇa* aiming at mleccha.

16. *sa garbho dīyate, nyasmaeī svayaṁ grāhyo na karhicit.*
svajātau varjayed yasmāt saṁkaraḥ syād ato ' nyathā.
Tr. The child should be given to another women and should never be accepted by the woman herself. It should be kept away from the class of the mother, because in that case it would cause a mixture.

17. *"History of India"* by Mahajan vidyadhara. P. 17.

18. *"Dhāraṇāddharma ity āhur dharmo dhārayatē prajāḥ.*
Tr. They call it *dharma* because it sustains. It is *dharma* that supports the society.

19. Tr. All the sages having gathered together said thus to the great sage Devala who was sitting at ease on the banks of Sindhu.

10

Dharmaśāstra and Inscriptions on *Bhūmidāna*: Its Social Concerns

Manabendu Banerjee

Different kinds of gift and their donors were held in great esteem since the time of the Ṛgveda. The references to *dāna* continued to be included in the later-Vedic literature and elaborate dealings on this topic are seen in the *Anuśāsanaparvan* of the *Mahābhārata* and in the Purāṇas including *Agni* (Chs. 208-215, 217), *Matsya* (Chs. 82-91, 274-289) and the *Varāha-purāṇa* (Chs. 99-111). Hemādri's *Dānakhaṇḍa* of the *Caturvargacintāmaṇi*, Gobindānanda's *Dānakriyā-kaumudī*, Nīlakaṇṭha's *Dānamayūkha*, Vidyāpati's *Dānavākyāvalī*, Ballālasena's *Dānasāgara* and Mitramiśra's *Dānaprakāśa* are prominent digests devoted mainly to the topic of *dāna*.

The *Ṛgveda* contains the *dānastutis* where gifts made by kings as well as the kings themselves have been highly praised by the Brāhmaṇa-donees. The objects that are seen to have been gifted in the *Ṛgveda* are unambiguously some sort of wealth. The prized gifts include cows, chariots, horses, camels, etc. Gifts of young damsels have also been recorded in the *Ṛgveda*[1]. Of these, emphasis has been given on the gifts of cows—their number varying from one hundred to sixty thousand. Gift of land or *bhūmidāna* has not got a noticeable entry in the early Vedic literature where cattle were regarded as synonymous with wealth. It seems that at that time land was not relatively important as an economic unit.

In the Brāhmaṇa literature land along with cows was accommodated in the list of gift-objects, though land-gifting was not acclaimed universally. Thus, when Viśvakarman Bhauvana desired to make a gift of the earth he had conquered through the Aśvamedha to his priest Kaśyapa as a sacrifical fee (*dakṣiṇā*), the earth made herself visible to the king and rebuked him thus:—No human being is authorised to give me away as a gift; so Viśvakarman Bhauvana, as you are willing to give me away, I am going to plunge into the water and for that reason your promise to Kaśyapa will be unprolific[2]. In this portion some has detected the reference to the possibility of 'the clan ownership of land'[3], but this contention cannot perhaps be tenable because of the fact that some portions of the same later Vedic literature show fields and villages being considered to be an object of recognised gift. Thus in the *Chāndogya Upaniṣad* (IV. 2.4-5), Jānaśruti a śūdra by caste is seen to have offering a village along with cows, gold, chariot and a young girl to the Brāhmaṇa Raikva in exchange of the knowledge of 'Brahman' he had received from him. The *Aitarey Brāhmaṇa* (VIII. 20) also mentions land as an appropriate item of *dāna*[4]. However, these references are not very frequent.

Smṛtikāras point out six distinct elements of *dāna*. These are *dātā* (donor), *pratigrahitā* (recipient), *śraddhā* (charitable attitude), *deyaṁ ca dharmayuk* (gift-object that has been procured by the donor in a proper way) and *deśakālau* (a sacred place and an auspicious time)[5]. Among these, a donor may be any one including women and śūdras. As verse has been quoted by Aparārka to substantiate that a rich man not making gifts should be severely punished[6]. The *Bṛhatparāśara-smṛti* (Ch. 10) has signalized a good number of merit achieved by a donor of commendable things. Aparārka, quoting Devala, has remarked that "the donor should be free from incurable or disgusting diseases, be religious, charitably inclined, free from vices, pure and following a blameless profession of livelihood" — *apāparogī dharmātmā ditsur avyasanaḥ śuciḥ/anindyājīvakarmā ca ṣadbhir dātā praśasyeta//*[7]

Iṣṭāpūrta as the subject of *dāna* (and the man who is engaged in this very special kind of *dāna*) own origin in the *Ṛgveda*. In ṚV. X. 14.8 a man who had performed the *iṣṭāpūrta* activities has been praised when he is dead—"May you join the *pitṛs*, may you be united with Yama, and with your *iṣṭāpūrta* in the highest heaven"—*saṁgacchasva pitṛbhiḥ saṁ yamena iṣṭāpūrtena parame vyoman*. The term *iṣṭāpūrta* occurs in the *Atharvaveda* (II. 12.4 and III. 29.1) and in the *Taittirīya Brāhmaṇa* (II. 5.5; III. 9.14). Manu says (IV. 226-227), "one should assiduously offer sacrifices (*iṣṭa*) and perform works of charity (*pūrta*); if these two works are done with *śraddhā* and with lawfully acquired money, they bestow endless rewards." The *Mahābhārata* emphasizes on the distinction between *iṣṭa* and *pūrta*[8].

The *iṣṭa* is that what is offered in the *gṛhya* and *śrauta* ritual fires. *Pūrta* is a larger enterprise and includes dedication of wells, tanks, temples public gardens (*ārāma*) and lands for the welfare of others. "*Pūrta* thus signifies the donation of immovable property and it points to the establishment of an agricultural economy where wells, tanks, gardens and land have a utility which they could not have had in a prominently pastoral economy"[9]. The interesting aspect relating to these two terms is found in the Smṛti literature thus[10]—

> *iṣṭāpūrtau dvijātinām dharmaḥ sāmānya iṣyate /*
> *adhikārī bhavecchūdraḥ pūrte dharme na vaidike / /*

It is specified here that *iṣṭa* and *pūrta* are the *dharma* common to all twice-born classes who ritually pure; but the śūdras who have no authority to perform the *dharma* prescribed by the Vedas can make the *pūrta-dāna* "which in economic terms was more effective". The gift of land can thus be taken as one of the elements of *pūrta-dāna*.

The law-givers have prescribed some specific qualifications for the *pātra* or *pratigrahitā* i.e. the recipients of gifts[11]. A Brāhmaṇa who performs the required ceremonies as indicated in the sacred texts, who is of noble birth and who lives off alms is generally considered to be a deserving recipient of *dāna*. *Manu-saṁhitā* states that a Brāhmaṇa, who is not learned, should not accept as gift, gold, land, horse, cows, food etc.; if he accepts, he is bound to be perished:

> *hiraṇyaṁ bhūmim aśvaṁ gām annaṁ vāsas tilān ghṛtam /*
> *pratigṛhnan avidvāṁstu bhasmībhavati dāruvat / /* (IV. 188).

In return to the gift made to a commendable *pātra*, the donor intends to acquire merit here and hereafter.

Romila Thapar finds in the conception of the acquisition of merit accrued from the *dāna* given to a deserving person "a hint of competition among potential recipients for the acquisition of economic status in a system where, perhaps more attention was being paid to economic status than in earlier times"[12].

Among the *deya* things i.e. which can be the subject of gift, the best, according to *Devala-smṛti* quoted by Aparārka, include food, curds, honey, protection, cows, land, gold, horse and elephants—*a nnaṁ dadhi madhu trāṇaṁ go-bhū-rukmāśvahastinaḥ/ dānāni uttamadānāni uttamadravyadānataḥ/*[13] In the *Smṛti*-texts lands is always hailed as one of the principal objects of gift. Yājñavalkya includes land amongst the objects of gifts which help the donor secure endless happiness (I.210). A verse appearing in the *Vāśiṣṭha-smṛti* (29.16), *Anuśāsanaparvan* (63.19), *Bṛhaspati-smṛti* (verse 7) and *Bhaviṣyapurāṇa* (4. 164. 18) eulogizes the gift of land as the most meritorious:

yat kiñcit kurute pāpaṁ puruṣa vṛttikarṣitaḥ/
api gocarmamātreṇa bhūmidānena śudhyati//

It is suggested here that a man may commit sin under some unavoidable circumstances, but he is purged therefrom by making a gift of land equal to a *gocarma*.[14] The *Anuśāsanaparvan* (59.5) announces that the gifts of land, gold and cows purify even the wicked:

hiraṇyadānaṁ godānaṁ pṛthvīdānam eva ca/
etāni vai pavitrāṇi tārayanty api duṣkṛtam//

The *Vanaparvan* (93.79) has also an almost allied verse. The *Vanaparvan* (186. 15) further says that the gift of a maiden or a land to a brāhmaṇa leads the donor to the blissful world of Indra.

Vaśiṣṭha regards *bhūmidāna* and also the gifts of cows and *vidyā* as *atidāna* i.e. superior to the gift of anything else:

trīṇy āhur atidānāni gāvaḥ pṛthvī sarasvatī/[15]

Manu (IV.233) and Yājñavalkya (I.212) also include land, cows and *vidyā* in the list of the best of *dānas*. The *Anuśāsanaparvan* (62. 2) declares that the gift of land towers over all other gifts—*atidānāni sarvāṇi pṛthidānam ucyate*. It is evidenced from the *Smṛti*-works that land as a *deya*-object has sometimes been praised singularly and sometimes combined with other objects. The *Anuśāsanaparvan* has a whole chapter (Ch.62) on the meritorious benefits achieved from the gift of land. The Puranic literature highly extols the gift of cows, but sometimes *pṛthīvidāna* has also been magnified.

The early Sanskrit literature, while dealing with the subject of gift, has secluded, as we have already noticed, cow and land as the most merited objects of gift. But gradually the gifting of land began to take over other items including cows, as is corroborated by thousands of land-grants issued by kings or royal officers down from the 4th century A.D. The propensity for *bhūmidāna*, showing less concern in cow-gifting, perhaps, indicates that interest was increasing in agriculture and that land had become "more lucrative than herds of cattle". The gift of cows, once regarded as most beneficent, did not become obsolete, but ceased to be a principal items of *dāna*. The gift of land became much attractive to the people because it could stabilize the family of the recipient for several generations and it was considered to be a lasting investment for the posterity. Land-grants issued during the gift or sale of land are in fact records acting as legal claims of the grantees and their families before the future kings or royal administrative officers. The gifts of lands became so prized that the Smṛtis framed rules for their proper execution. Yājñavalkya prescribes that a king, after making a gift of land, should record it in writing for the knowledge of future noble kings on a piece of cloth or on a copper-plate; this would be a permanent edict on the top of which there should be the seal of the donor king; the edict should also contain the names of the king's ancestors and of himself, the measurement and characteristics of the land gifted, verses condemning the confiscation of the gifted property and lastly the signature of the donor and the date on which the gift is being made[16]. Smṛtikāras like Bṛhaspati and Vyāsa are said to have added some other points, such as, a land-grant should contain the identity of the recipient; it should be stated in the record that the possession of the land was to continue till the sun and moon endure, that it was to be free from all future taxes, that it was to continue to the donee's sons and grand-sons, that the edict should be addressed to the Brāhmaṇas, house-holders and other respectable persons of the locality and also to the royal officers; the land-grant should also contain a statement that the gift has been made for accruing merit for the donor's parents as well as for his own self[17].

That the above-mentioned instructions were meticulously followed by thousands of land-grants is evident from the copper-plate inscriptions recording the gifts of land from 5th century A.D. onwards. Even before this time we find evidence of granting villages to Brāhmaṇas along with cows. In the Karle cave inscription (No. 13)[18], and Nasik Cave Inscription (No. 10)[19], Usabhadāta (= Ṛṣabhadatta), who was the son-in-law of the Kṣaharāta king Nahāpana and who belonged probably to the 2nd part of the 2nd century A.D., is said to have given three-hundred-thousand cows and sixteen villages to Brāhmaṇas (*Brāhmaṇebhyaśca ṣoḍaśagrāmadena*) and also given eight ladies as wives to the Brāhmaṇas at Prabhāsatīrtha. The king Ṛṣabhadatta had thus supported the brāhmaṇas by giving valuable gifts including land, assigning proper means of livelihood and arranging their marriage at his own expense.

The Gupta inscriptions are replete with references to grants of lands to learned Brāhmaṇas for sustaining them in their life of learning and religion, and in their regular performance of religious rites, both Vedic and Purāṇic. The land-grants are generally known by the name of *śāsana* or more specifically *dāna-śāsana* meaning 'a royal charter recording gifts' usually engraved on copper-plates. A *śāsana* was indeed a deed generally prepared at the time when a revenue-free land was granted by ancient Indian kings or their officers in favour of persons, deities and religious establishments. The gift of lands and villages to the deserving Brāhmaṇas became so much institutionalised that it was referred to by the special term *agrahāra*. In this sense it occurs in the *Mahābhārata* (*Vanaparvan*, 68. 4) and frequently in the land-grants. In the southern part of our country, the word *agrahāra* was very popular in the context of a rent-free village which was in the possession of a Brāhmaṇa. An *agrahāra* has been explained as a village granted to the *brāhmaṇas* when they returned from the *gurukula* after finishing studies in order to help them in settling themselves as *gṛhasthas*[20]. Such grants were made tax-free to learned Brāhmaṇas in perpetuity in recognition to their proficiency in the sacred texts or religious achievements. That the idea of making such grants as donations to learned Brāhmaṇas is an early feature is corroborated by its references in the *Vanaparva* (68.4) and *Āśramavāsikaparvan* (2.2; 10. 41; 13.11 etc.) of the *Mahābhārata*. Even the inscriptions of the later Gupta period, such as, the grant of the Valabhi king Dhruvasena III, dated 653-654 A.D.[21] and the Madhuvan copper-plate inscription of Harṣa, dated 631 A.D.[22] refer to the brāhmaṇa land-holdings known as *agrahāra*. The donation of *agrahāras* profusely increased in the Gupta period and during this time was created the office of the *agrahārika*, who evidently kept records of such grants[23]. Rent-free holdings under the possession of Brāhmaṇas were also called *brahmadeya*. The expressions-*Brahmadeya-maryādā*[24] and *Brahmadeya-sthiti*[25] bear clear testimony to the custom regarding rent-free property to Brāhmaṇas that was current in the places where the inscriptions were found.

The available land-grants issued from all parts of India contain verses relating to the merit of gifts and sin of resumption of gifted land. Many of these verses are found to be included in the

Smṛti works. The gift of land was regarded so meritorious that the donor of a land is believed to be the receiver of heavenly rewards that cannot be gained by the performance of various sacrifices accompanied by rich wealth as *dakṣiṇā*—

agniṣṭomādibhir yajñair iṣṭvā vipuladakṣiṇaiḥ /
na tat phalam avāpnoti yad dattvā vasudhāṁ nṛpa / /

A very popular imprecatory verse found in the land-grants is—

svadattām paradattāṁ vā yo hareta vasundharām /
svaviṣṭāyāṁ kṛmir bhūtvā pitṛbhiḥ saha majjati / /

This verse gives the warning that the person, who confiscates a land that has been given by himself or by any other, becomes a worm in ordure, and is tormented together with his ancestors[27].

In the earlier records, verses eulogising gifts and deprecating their forceful resumption are few, but gradually they swell in number. In most of the inscriptions these laudatory and imprecatory verses are said to have been quoted from the *Mahābhārata* or Vyāsa or Manu or some other works on the Dharmaśāstra. Successful attempts have been made to trace these inscriptional verses to the *Mahābhārata*, the Purāṇas and the Dharmaśāstra literature[28].

In spite of such warnings we can notice some evidences of confiscation of lands already gifted to Brāhmaṇas. The Rāṣṭrakūṭa king Indra III, in an inscription, dated 915 A.D., is said to have restored four hundred villages that were confiscated by previous kings (*pūrvapṛthvīpāla-viluptāni catvāri grāma-śatāni*)[29]. The Cālukya king Vikramaditya I has been praised in an inscription, dated 660 A.D., as having re-established the property of temples and the grants to Brāhmaṇas that had been lost in three kingdoms (*rājyatraye vinaṣṭāni devasvabrahmadeyāni*)[30].

When a village or villages were granted to Brāhmaṇas, kings excluded portions already donated to gods or Brāhmaṇas. The expressions like—*devabhoga-halavarjam*[31] and *pūrva-pratta-deva-brahma-dāya-rahitaḥ*[32] are pointers to this system. The grant of a village was made by the Candella king Paramardideva for the increase of his religious merit and of his parents (*mātā-pitror ātmanaśca puṇya-yaśovivṛddhaye*) to a number of Brāhmaṇas in about 1178 A.D. It is interesting to note here that in the gift-village, exception was made of the five *halas* (land-measure) of land already gifted to Buddha (*devaśrī-bauddha-saika-pañcahalāni bahiṣkṛtya śeṣabhūmiḥ śāsanīkṛtya pradattā*)[33]. This grant shows that a Buddhist monastery was already in existence in that village. Here we find a reference to a healthy co-existence of different faiths in the same locality.

Many instances of purchasing lands from their owners by the king and bestowing them on learned Brāhmaṇas as gifts are to be found in the land-grants[34]. In this connexion the question of the ownership of land has been discussed by various scholars. The lawgivers (like Jaimini and Śabara) hold the view that the earth is common to the king as well as to those who cultivate or make use of it; the kings are entitled to collect taxes from the land. So when the king makes what is technically called the gift of land, the gift (of soil) is not disturbed there, 'but only provision is made for the maintenance of the donee from the taxes which are alienated by the king'[35]. That the Indian king as theoretically the lord of all lands is evidenced from the Bhitari inscription of Skandagupta,[36] the Khoh copper-plate inscription of Mahārāja Hastin,[37] the Karitalai plates of Jayanātha[38] and many other inscriptions. In case of the donation of a village or a part of it made to a Brāhmaṇa by the king, the villagers were advised to pay revenues payable to the king to the Brāhmaṇa donees. There is also the view that the king was the owner of lands and the privileges of making a gift of land belonged only to the king—*anena bhūpater eva bhūmidāna-nibandhadāne vādhikāraḥ*[39]. The *Mitākṣarā* further maintains that while gift of land was to be made by the king, the consent of the village elders and *sāmantas* (neighbours) is to be sought[40]. But a private person, at the time of donating a land to a Brāhmaṇa, will have to take permission of the king.

Instances of individual right over land can be ascertained from some land-grants. From the Pipardula (Raipur District, M.P.) copper-plate inscription of Narendra[41] we know that Rāhudeva, a subordinate of king Narendra of Śarabhapura, granted a portion of land out of his *jāgir* or a portion purchased from the king; but it is to be noted that the king sanctioned the creation of a rent-free holding (lines-4-7 in page 489). The Paharpur inscription, dated 479 A.D.[42] supplies us with the interesting information that the person who purchased land from the king for its donating to some religious institution (might have) offered to the king some money. The inscription says that the purchaser-donor received 5/6th of the religious merit of the gift, and only 1/6th of the merit and some money went to the king (*parama-bhaṭṭāraka pādānām arthopacayo dharmaṣad-bhāgāpyāyanaṁ ca*). The Khoh copper-plate inscription of Mahārāja Sarvanātha, dated 533 A.D., records the sanction of the Mahārāja to the transfer of two villages for the purpose of constructing a temple of the goddess Piṣṭapurikādevī[43].

Villages gifted to Brāhmaṇas often carried exceptions (*parihāra*) i.e. the donees enjoyed some benefits and immunities, such as, the revenues known as *udraṅga* (of doubtful meaning),[44] *uparikara* (a tax levied on cultivators), *dhānya, hiraṇya* (gold), *adeya* (what is to be surrendered), etc. The Brāhmaṇa donees henceforth could perform their religious activities on the gifted lands and make the lands cultivated without giving taxes. Kauṭilya advises that lands (cultivable or uncultivable) should be given to priests, preceptors and Brāhmaṇas, well-versed in the Vedas; these lands should be exempted from fines or taxes, and inheritence should pass on to corresponding heirs.—

> *ṛtvigācārya-purohita-śrotriyebhyo brahmadeyāny*
> *adaṇḍakarāṇy abhirūpadāyakāni prayacchet*
>
> —*Arthaśāstra*, II. 1

Inscriptions often inform us that lands or villages are granted with eight *bhogas*, i.e., objects to be enjoyed along with the lands by the donees. These *bogas*, according to the Śrīśailam plates of Virūpākṣa, dated 1466 A.D., are *nidhi* (treasure trove), *nikṣepa* (what remains deposited on the land), *vāri* (water), *aśman* (stones and mines), *akṣiṇī* (actual privileges), *āgāmi* (further profits), *siddha* (what is already achieved through cultivation) and *sādhya* (waste land that may be made fit for cultivation)[45]. The donee could also enjoy 'the irrigation channels, gardens and all other sources of income' (*kulyārāmādi-saṁyuktaṁ samastabalisaṁyutam*). The king, however, reserved his rights over the granted land like the right of imposing fines on thieves (*Coradaṇḍa-varjitam*)[46]. Immunity in the gifted villages from entry of royal soldiers, officers and police-personnels (*a-cāṭa-bhaṭa-prāveśya*), as specified in the Vākāṭaka inscriptions[47] and in the Khoh copper-plate inscription of Sarvanātha, dated 512 A.D.[48] helped the villagers settle peacefully with no fear of being tyranized.

The terms occurring in the land-grants in relation to land tenure like *nīvi-dharma, akṣayanīvidharma*, etc., signify that the donees were not empowered to alienate the donated lands by sale or mortgage. These terms have been interpreted as a perpetual endowment which the donee has no right to destroy by sale, mortgage or lease, but he can utilise its income. It was to be treated as trust-property which was to remain intact for all time without any diminution. The land was granted to the donee with the provision that it would be enjoyed uninterruptedly by the donee's sons, grandsons and other descendants (*putra-pautrānvaya-bhogytvena*)[49]. Land that was granted for charity could not be taken by Government "out of the settled holdings of peasant-proprietors". It was to be taken generally out of the fallow and unsettled land in village without disturbing the existing holdings. Such land has been variously termed as *apradā* (unsettled), *aprahata* (untilled), *khila* (fallow), *apratikara* (not yielding any revenue), etc.[50] One of the Faridpur grants refers to a gift of land which was not *aprahata* or *khila*, but *vāpa-kṣetra* i.e., cultivable land; for this land higher price was charged to the purchaser by the Government.

The land-grants in general enlighten us about the position and prestige of the Brāhmaṇas to whom greater number of grants were made. Lands were donated to the Brāhmaṇas by the donors mainly for the increase of religious merits of themselves and of their parents. In this connexion, the very common expression is—*mātāpitror ātmanaśca puṇyābhivṛddhaye*[51]. At the time of granting a village to a Brāhmaṇa, the village-elders headed by Brāhmaṇa-residents were called for standing as witnesses (*brāhmaṇādīn grāmakuṭumbinaḥ*). This system shows the highest rank enjoyed by the Brāhmaṇas in the society. The Brāhmaṇas are often seen to have been donated lands for their convenience of performing religious activities like the *pañcamahāyajña* (which has been defined and classified in *Manusaṁhitā* III. 69).

The Brāhmaṇa donees are almost every time mentioned along with their *gotras, caraṇas* and *śākhās* under which they were grouped and these are indications of social data as well as the importance of the Brāhmaṇa community in respective regions. A land-grant, issued by the Vākāṭaka king Pravarasena II in his 18th regnal year, was the gift of a village to one thousand Brāhmaṇas belonging to different *gotras* and *caraṇas*; the Brāhmaṇas enjoyed it collectively ; forty nine of these Brāhmaṇas, most probably heads of families, are named[52]. Mahārāja Hastin was a donor of land-grants and he is delineated as extremely devoted to gods and Brāhmaṇas (*atyantadeva-brāhmaṇa-bhaktasya*) in the Khoh copper-plate inscription, dated 475-76 A.D.[53]

A land-grant, found at Penukoṇḍa (Anantapur District, Madras) and dated 475 A.D., speaks of a Brāhmaṇa, Kumāraśarman of the Vatsa *gotra* and Taittiriya *caraṇa*, who was "proficient in penance, fasting' mortification, silent prayer, sacrificing, conducting sacrifice, studying and teaching of the sacred texts, cursing and blessing, an acceptor and receiver of gifts"—*Yamaniyama-tapaḥ-svādhyāya-yajana-yājana-adhyayana-adhyāpana-śāpānugraha-ādāna-pratigrahāya*, etc.[54]

These characteristics of a Brāhmaṇa are in conformity with the six duties prescribed by Manu—

> *adhyāpanam adhyayanaṁ yajanam yājanaṁ tathā /*
> *dānaṁ pratigrahañcaiva brāhmaṇānām akalpayat / /* (1. 88).

A Brāhmaṇa versed in all the four Vedas is called a *Caturvedin* and he was deemed to be a very fit person to be granted a land[55].

When Brāhmaṇa donees are thus eulogised and showed honour in hundreds of land-grants it can be assumed that in the regions where those inscriptions were issued, the Brāhmaṇas moulded their life on the ideal laid by Smṛtis and they enjoyed great respect from the kings, royal officers and villagers alike.

Notes

1. *Ṛgveda*, I. 126. 3; VI. 27. 8; VII. 18. 22.
2. *na mā martyaḥ kaścana dātum arhati viśvakarman bhauvana māṁ didasitha/ nirmakṣyehaṁ salilasya madhye moghas te eṣa kaśyapasya saṅgaraḥ/—Aitareya Brāhmaṇa* - 39. 7; also in a slight changed form in the *Śatapatha Brāhmaṇa*, XIII. 7. 1. 15.
3. Romila Thapar, *Ancient Indian Social History: Some Interpretations*, New Delhi, 1990, p. 110.
4. Vide P.V. Kane's *History of Dharmaśāstra*, Vol.II, pt.II, Poona, 1974, pp. 858f.
5. Devala's verse quoted in P.V. Kane's *H.D.S.*, Vol.II, Pt.II, p. 843.
6. *H.D.S.*, II, pt. II, p. 845, fn. 1994.
7. *H.D.S.*, II, pt. II, p. 845, f.n. 1994.
8. *H.D.S.*, II, Pt. II, p. 884.
9. R. Thapar, *Ancient Indian Social History*, p. 115.
10. *Atrisaṁhitā*, Verse 46, *Likhitasmṛti*, Verse 6.
11. *H.D.S.*, Vol. II, pt. I, pp. 110-115.
12. Thapar, *op. cit.*, pp. 115-116.
13. *H.D.S.*, Vol. II, pt. II, p. 847.
14. According to Bṛhaspati *Gocarma* is equal to ten *nivartanas* and "a *nivartana* is defined by him as land that is thirty rods (square) with a rod of ten cubits:

daśahastena daṇḍena triṁśad daṇḍair nivartanam /
daśa tāny eva vistāro gocarmaitan mahāphalam / /
—*Bṛhaspati-saṁhitā*, verse 8.

15. *Vaśiṣṭha-saṁhitā*, 29. 20.
16. Yājñavalkya, I. 318-320:
dadyādbhūmiṁ nibandhaṁ vā kṛtvā lekhyaṁ tu kārayet /
āgāmi-bhadranṛpatiparijñānāya pārthivaḥ / /
paṭe vā tāmrapaṭṭe vā svamudropacihnitam /
abhilekhyātmano vaṁśyam ātmānaṁ ca mahīpatiḥ / /
pratigrahaparimāṇaṁ dānacchedopavarnanam /
svahastakālasampannaṁ śāsanaṁ kārayet sthiram / /
17. *H.D.S.*, II, pt. II, p. 861.
18. *Epigraphia Indica*, Vol. VII, p. 57.
19. *Ep. Ind.*, Vol. VIII, p. 78.
20. D.C. Sircar, *Select Inscriptions*, Vol. I, Calcutta, 1965, p. 108.
21. *Ep. Ind.*, I, p. 88.
22. *Ep. Ind.*, I. p. 73.
23. J.F. Fleet, *Corpus Inscriptionum Indicarum*, Vol. III, Varanasi, 1970, p. 50, 1. 29; ibid., p. 257, 1. 12.
24. Chendalur grant (Nellore Dsit.) of Sarvalokāśraya, dated 673 A.D.; *Ep. Ind.*, VIII, p. 240, 1. 30.
25. Bhamodra-Mohota (Gujarat) Copper-plate Inscription of Droṇasiṁha, dated 502 A.D.; *Ep. Ind.*, XVI, p. 19, 1. 6.
26. *Ep. Ind.*, XXV, p.218, verse 41; this praise of gifting lands has been taken from the *Anuśāsanaparvan* (62. 73) with only some minor changes.
27. Vide, Majhejawam copper-plate inscription of Mahārāja Hstin, *CII*, III, No.23, p.108, 1.16; this verse is the same as the verse 28 of the *Bṛhaspati-saṁhitā*.
28. D.G. Sircar, *Indian Epigraphy*, Delhi, 1965, pp. 174ff.; *HDS*, Vol. II, pt. II, pp. 1271ff.
29. *Ep. Ind.*, IX, p. 33, 1. 56.
30. *Ep. Ind.*, IX, p. 100, 1. 16.
31. *Ep. Ind.*, VII, p. 162, 1. 17.
32. *Ep. Ind.*, X, p. 88, 1. 45.
33. *Ep. Ind.*, XX, p. 130, 1. 14.
34. *Ep. Ind.*, XVII, pp. 345ff.; XXIII, pp 159ff.; VII, pp. 57ff.; VIII, pp. 78ff., etc.
35. *HDS* II, pt. II, p. 866.
36. D.C. Sircar, *Select Inscriptions*, Vol I. pp. 321-324.
37. *CII*, III, No. 21, pp. 93ff.
38. *CII*, III, No. 26, pp. 117ff.
39. Mitākṣrā on *Yājñavalkya*, I. 318.
40. Mitā. on *Yājñ.*, II. 114.
41. *Sel. Ins.*, pp. 488ff.
42. *Ep. Ind.*, XX, pp. 61ff.
43. *CII*, III. No. 31, p. 136.
44. D.C. Sircar takes it as 'a fixed tax or tax on permanent tenants, assessing the total revenue of a village upon the chief proprietor who is entitled to distribute the propertions.' —*Sel. Ins.*, p. 391, f.n. 5.

45. *Ep. Ind.*, XV, p. 22, ll. 60-62.
46. *CII*, III, p. 136, l. 10.
47. *Sel. Ins.*, pp. 135ff.
48. *CII*, III, p. 127, l. 9.
49. *Sel. Ins.*, p. 374, l. 9.
50. R.K Mookerji, *The Gupta Empire*, Delhi, 1973, p. 156.
51. *Sel. Ins.*, p. 374, l. 9.
52. *CII*, III, No. 55, pp. 236ff.
53. *CII*, III, No. 21, pp. 95ff.
54. *Ep. Ind.*, XIV, p. 335, 12-13.
55. *CII*, III, Nos. 16, 39, 55.

11

Marriage Rites and Social Obligations

Radhavallabh Tripathi

Marriage has been viewed as an irrevocable contract in Indian tradition. The Dharmaśāstras establish it as one of the most important sacraments in our society. Marriage in fact, has been a dynamic institution, embodying the kinetic relationships between the individual and the society. It also plays a vital role by helping an individual to realise his aspirations at the physical, the psychological and the spiritual levels and also in fulfilling his duties for the society.

Rituals invest the institution of marriage with sanctity and authenticity. It is here that Dharmaśāstra steps in to provide firm basis for the life-long companionship of the spouses. The ceremony of marriage comprising an intricate set of rituals thus becomes very significant in our tradition. Kālidāsa has treated this ceremony at par with a *yajña*. Addressing the *saptarṣis* as bridegroom, Śiva tells them in Kālidāsa's epic:

विवाहयज्ञे विततेऽत्र यूयमध्वर्यवः पूर्ववृता मयेति ।।

(*Kumārasambhava*, VII. 47)

The philosophy of marriage is inherent in the very concept of evolution which our tradition has maintained. The *Bṛhadāraṇyaka Upanisad* says—The One who was born in the beginning could not enjoy himself, because no one can enjoy oneself alone. Therefore he wanted the second one. He then divided himself into two — a man and a woman. They became the husband and the wife. Dharmaśāstras have accepted this notion, i.e., the husband and the wife both are parts of One and the same Supreme Being. Manu says—

द्विधा कृत्वात्मनो देहमर्धेन पुरुषोऽभवत्।
अर्धेन नारी तस्यां स विराजमसृत् प्रभुः।।

(*Ms*, I. 32)

Kālidāsa has echoed the same idea in his eulogy to Śiva—

स्त्रीपुंसावात्मभागौ ते भिन्न मूर्तेः सिसृक्षया।
प्रसूतिभाजः सर्गस्य तावेव पितारौ स्मृतौ।।

(*Kumārasambhava*, II. 7)

No nation can survive without an organised system of marriage. Marriage not only helps men to subdue their wild instincts, it stops them from becoming animals.

Basically, marriage is a bond between the husband and the wife. They are bound to each other by social obligations, mutual understanding and their inter-dependence. If there is no love between the two, they cannot fulfil their duties for the society properly. At the same time, they must depend on each other. Mārkaṇḍeya lays down the principle of *parasparavaśānugatva* as the core of marriage:

यदा भार्या च भर्ता च परस्परवशानुगौ।
तदा धर्मार्थकामानां त्रयाणामपि सङ्गतम्।
कथं भार्यामृते धर्ममर्थं वा पुरूष प्रभो।
प्राप्नोति काममथवा तस्यां त्रितयमाहितम्।।
तथैव भर्तार मृते वा भार्या धर्मादिसाधने।
न समर्था त्रिवर्गोऽयं दाम्पत्यं समुपाश्रितः।।

(*Mārkaṇḍeya Purāṇa*, XXI. 69-72)

Kālidāsa has also echoed the idea of the wife being regarded as a desideratum for performing all religious duties:

क्रियाणां खलु धर्म्याणां सत्पत्न्यो मूलकारणम्।

(*Kumārasambhava*, VI. 13)

The inter-dependence between the husband and the wife has been sublimated in our tradition as a supreme ideal. They are both commanders to each other, and at the same time they are both subordinates to each other. The wife is called *bhāryā* because the husband is her master. But in fact, a good wife is the supreme commander for a man. She is the only solace in the moments of great distress and crisis. This is the true image of a wife which Nala presents out of his feelings for Damayanti:

भार्या हि परमो नाथः पुरुषस्येह पठ्यते।
असहायस्य लोकेऽस्मिन् लोकयात्रासहायिनी।।
तथा रोगाभिभूतस्य नित्यं कृच्छ्रगतस्य च।
नास्ति भार्यासमं किंचिन्नरस्यार्तस्य भेषजम्।।
नास्ति भार्यासमो बन्धुर्नास्ति भार्यासमा गतिः।
नास्ति भार्यासमो लोके सहायो धर्मसाधनः।।

(Mahābhārata, XII. 142.6-10)

Imbued as he was in this tradition, Kālidāsa makes Mārica utter this blessing for Śakuntalā-*bhartaryapetatamasi prabhutā tavaiva*-now you are the only controller of your lord'. The words 'bhartā' (for the husband) and *prabhutā* (for the wife) have been used here very significantly.

Bhavabhūti has summed up this high ideal of matrimony in the advice of Kāmandakī to the newly wedded couple in his *Mālatīmādhavam*—

प्रेयो मित्रं बन्धुता वा समग्रा
सर्वे कामाः शेवधिर्जीवितं वा।
स्त्रीणां भर्ता धर्मदाराश्च पुंसा-
मित्यन्योन्यं वत्सयोर्ज्ञातमस्तु।।

(Let it be known to you my children that the husband to a wife and the lawful wife to a man are the dearest objects to each other, they are friends, all relations put together, all the things that the heart carves for, a treasure and the life itself.)

Manu says that progeny, religious duties, service to elders, sexual intercourse in the best way and finally entry to heaven (for the husband and his forefathers)-all these depend on a wife (IX. 28).

Ṛgveda not only brings out some of the essential rites that were performed during the course of marriage ceremony it also lays down the aims of marriages as *yajña* and progeny[1]. Kālidāsa also says that the kings of solar dynasty married for progeny[2]. And Bhavabhuti finds the *summum bonum* of all marital relationships in powering one's filial feelings on one's own child[3]. To Manu progeny stands for the continuity of creation[4].

A close scrutiny of the set of marriage rites would reveal that these rites have been evolved in consideration to the basic concepts and philosophy of marriage.

Pāṇigrahaṇa or grabing the hand of the bride by the groom and making a vow (in front of the holy fire) are very essential rites that have been referred as early as Ṛg. X. 85. From the *Gṛhyasūtras* we can understand the process of gradual sublimation and idealisation of the these simple marriage rites and also their development into an integrated complex set of rituals. The essential rites which can be deduced from the detailed descriptions from the *Gṛhyasūtras* are as under:

1. Sending messangers or wooers to the bride's parents by the bridegroom himself, or by his guardians, to be followed by the betrothal (*Vāgdāna*).
2. Auspicious bath by the bride, the bridegroom and the decoration of the bride.
3. *Pāṇigrahaṇa*,
4. *Aśmārohaṇa*
5. Sitting on a platform smeared with *dūrvas*.
6. Glancing each other by the couple being wedded (*parasparasamīkṣaṇa*).
7. *Saptapadī* or taking seven steps together.
8. Bharāmari or circumumbulations around the fire,
9. *Lājāhoma*.
10. *Dhruvadarśana*.
11. Discourse by the elders to the bride.

Norms for finding our a suitable match have been discussed by many *sūtrakāras*. Āśvalāyana regards wisdom as a desideratum for the bridegroom (1.5.2), while Āpastambha (3.20) requisitions good family, noble character, virtues, knowledge and health. For the bride also Āśvalāyana would recommend wisdom, beauty, virtue, health and auspicious characteristics. Kālidāsa summerises all these views by suggesting *tulyaguṇayoga* or equality in qualities as a criteria for a match. He has repeatedly emphasised over the idea of equality between the bride and the bridegroom, viz.:

सङ्कल्पितं प्रथममेव मया तवार्थे भर्तारमात्मसदृशं सकृतैर्गतात्वम् ।

(*Abhijñānaśākuntalam*, IV. 13)

परस्परेण स्पृहणीयशोभं न चेदिदं द्वन्द्वमयोजयिष्यत्।

(*Raghuvaṁśa*, VII. 14, also repeated in *Kumārasambhava*, VII. 66)

गुरोः पुनरनुपवरपदाने सङ्कल्पः।

(*Abhijñānaśākuntala*, Act I)

A young girl is also allowed to search for her own suitable match. Rg. (X. 27. 12) indicates a custom under which she was asked to speel out her choice or to select her companion:

भद्रा वधूर्भवति यत् सुनेशाः स्वयं सा मित्रं वृणुते जनेचित्।

The parents of Sāvitrī had allowed her to wander and select her man.

Normally, bridegroom or his relatives were supposed to take initiative or make a firm proposal for soleminising a marriage. In Ṛg. Aśvinau approach Savitā and ask for his daughter to be married to Soma (X. 85. 9), which is said to be the source of the custom of *varaprekṣaṇa* or *Vāgdāna*. In *Kumārasambhava*, Śiva sends the seven sages to Himalaya and make a firm proposal for his marriage with Pārvatī. This custom has been described at length by the *Gṛhyasūtras*. Śānkhyāyana (1.6. 1-6) prescribed that the persons belonging to the groom's party should approach the bride's father with fruits, flowers, *yava* and a pot of water in their hands.

Naturally, the persons approaching the bride's father for such a proposal were elderly and responsible people, and their role for the solemnisation of the marriage was sonially very important. Kālidāsa hints upon the significancs of sending great sages for a talk with Himalaya in the following way—

विक्रियायै न कल्पन्ते सम्बन्धाः सदनुष्ठिताः।

(*Kumārasaṁbhava*, VI. 29)

The company of a lady with the group going for the *Vāgdana* ceremony was supposed to be advantageous, as Śiva specifically wanted Arundhatī to accompany the sages.

The custom of *varaprekṣaṇa* or *Vāgdāna* is confirmed by later writers also. In the *Ratnāvalī Nāṭikā* of Śrīharṣa Yaugandhārayaṇa sends a minister to the King of Simbala for this purpose. In Bāṇa's *Harṣacarita,* Grahavarman is said to have sent a messanger for begging the hand of Rājyaśri.

Maṅgalasnāna or auspicious bath (termed as *Indrāṇikarma* in *Śānkhāyana Gṛhyasūtra)* is the first essential custom to be performed before the ceremony of marriage. Almost all the *Gṛhyasūtras* which deal with the marriage rites prescribe *maṅgalasnāna* to be performed essentially and the bride be attired with new garments thereafter. The custom finds earliest reference in the *Atharvaveda* (14.1.31). Kālidāsa refers to the *maṅgalasnāna* and the new clothing for the bride Umā—

सा मङ्गलस्नानाविशुद्धगात्री गृहीतप्रत्युद्गमनीयवस्त्रा ।

(*Kumārasaṁbhava* VII. 11)

Pāraskara and Gobhila also prescribe anointation of the bride to be done with the *maṅgalasnāna*. This is called *samanjana*, and is said to have been originated from Rg. X. 85. 47 which is recited during the course of its performance.

A silver cloth was supposed to be essential for the attire of the bride. Kālidāsa indicates its use as veil (*avaguṇṭhana*). Both Mālavikā and Śakuntalā in his plays wear silken garments to form their *avaguṇṭhana*. Queen Dhāriṇi even offers apologies to Parivrājikā for having forgotten to put the *avaguṇṭhana-vasana* on the face of the bride due to her overjoy in the last act of *Mālavrikāgnimitram*. Jivānanda, the commentator interprets this veiling of the bride as a ceremony indicating the cessation of the virginity of the bride- *kaumāryāpanodanasūcaka ācāraviśeṣaḥ*).

In *Śākuntalā*, the *kṣauma* or silken garment being put up on by the bride Śakuntalā is called as *Māṇgalya* or auspicious. Although Śakuntalā has already joined hands with Duṣyanta secretly in *Gandharva vivāha*, she is presented as a bride before him in the V act of the play and her face is veiled, so that Duṣyanta cannot have a full view of her face:

केयमवगुण्ठनवती नातिपरिस्फुटशरीरलावण्या ।

(*Abhijñānaśākuntala* V. 13)

Pārvati also wore a new silken garment called *navakṣauma* or *vadhūdukūla*, on the eve of her marriage in *Kumārasaṁbhava* (VII. 26). In the *Viddhaśālabhañjikā* of Rājaśekhara also, the bride appears with a veil on her face. All these descriptions by the poets are on the lines of the ancient custom called *antaṁpaṭa* or *parasparasamīksaṇa*. Kālidāsa has also describ d the decoration of the bride. Her hair were dressed with the garlands of *madhūka* flowers and *dūrvās* and sprouts of *yava* were tied on her ears. The *Kautukasūtra* or *Kaṅkaṇa* is the most essential ornament connected with the marriage rites. Kālidāsa calls it *'Kautuka hastasūtra'* prepared out of wool[5].

Vallabhadeva translates *hastasūtra* as *kaṅkaṇa*[6]. Bhavabhūti refers to this *Kaṅkana* a number of times in two of his plays in connection with marriage ceremonies[7]. From his descriptions, it is clear that putting a knot in this *hastasūtra* and then opening it formed two customs of marriage rites. These have been refered to in the *Gṛhyasūtras* as '*Pratisaravidhāna*'.

Kālidāsa refers to an arrow placed in the garment of Pārvatī, before her decoration[8]. Baudhayāna Gṛhya Sūtra (5.1.25) prescribes that the bride should hold an arrow in her hand after the auspicious bath.

Garlends of flowers for the bride and the groom as well were very much in vogue. In Bhāsa's *Svapnavāsavadattam*, Vāsavadattā, living in disguise as Avantikā is asked to weave garlends for the marriage of her own husband with princess Padmāvatī; and two herbs called *spatnimardana* (killer of the co-wife) and *avidhvakarana* (bestower of long life for the husband) are also handed over to her for being emblemed therein. Both Kālidāsa and Bhavabhūti refer to the custom of *godāna* (showing of head of the groom)[9]. The *Gṛhyasūtras* do not strictly incorporate this custom in the set of marriage rites. Perhaps in the times these poets were writing, the *keśānta saṁskāra* was mixed with the marriage rituals. Some other rites and customs described by Kālidāsa in his very vivid picture of the marriage of Śiva with Pārvatī, are off course confirmed by the *Gṛhyasūtras*. As soon as the groom (Śiva) entered the house of his father-in-law, he was greeted with *madhuparka* and a pait of garments[10]. Pāṇigrahaṇa has been described by Kālidāsa and Bhavabhūti[11], and Kālidāsa has refered to circumumbulations around fire to be done three times only[12]. *Lājāhoma* and *dhruvadraśana* are also very significant rites described by Kālidāsa and Rajaśekhara[13]. The groom should show dhruva to the bride and ask her whether she has seen it, and the bride after visualising *dhruva*, should reply — yes I have seen.

The last custom at the time of the departure of the bride with the groom consisted of the blessings to be given to her by her elders and the last words of advice to her by some of them. The custom appears to have its origin in the following *mantra* of Rg. (X.85. 33)

सुमङ्गलीरियं वधुरिमां समेत पश्यत ।
सौभाग्यमस्यै दत्वा याथास्तं परंतन ।।

Pāraskara and other *Gṛhyasūtras* confirm the desirability of this custom. Kālidāsa has utilised the occasion on the eve of Śakuntalā's departure for expressing foundations of married life in ancient Indian society in Kaṇva's advice to her. From the woods of Kaṇva which precede this advice-'*Vanaukaso ' pi santo laukikajñā vayam*'-though we live in the forest, but we know the worldly customs it is clear that such an advice was held to be very essential. Gautamī rightly confirms Kaṇva's words-*etāvan vadhūjanas upadeśaḥ*' this much the bride should be advised. In *Kumārasambhava* (VI. 87), the bride Pārvatī is blessed by Brahma himself. In *Bālarāmāyaṇa* of *Rājaśekhara*, both Janaka and Śatānanda speak last words to the bride Sītā in the similar fashion.

The descriptions of the marriage rites by some of the savants of Sanskrit poetry brings out their continuity in Indian tradition from Vedic age. The significance of these marriage rites is evident. They are meant to inculcate the philosophy and values of matrimony in the minds of individuals being married, and also to make them aware of their rights, duties and responsibilities. The santity and the social sanction for the marriage are the marks of these rites.

References

1. See *Ṛgveda* X. 85.36, V.3.2; II. 55.4
2. प्रजायै गृहमेधिनाम्।

   (*Reghuvaṁśa* 1.7)
3. अन्तः करणतत्वस्य दम्पत्योः स्नेहसंश्रयात्।

   आनन्दग्रन्थिरेकोऽयमपत्यमिति पठ्यते।।

   (*Uttararāmacarita* III.17)
4. *Manu* IX.137
5. *Kumārasaṁbhava* VII. 25)
6. Vallabhadeva's Commentary on above, Ed. G. Patel, 1986; Pt. II. P. 10
7. अयमागृहीतकमनीयकङ्कण-

   स्तवम्मिानिवनहोत्सवः करः।। (*Uttararāmacarita*, I. 18)
8. आबद्धकेङ्कणवरप्रणयप्रसादमारीय(*Mālatīmādhava*, VI. 14)

   देव्यः कङ्कणमोचनाभ मिलिता

   राजन् वरेः प्रेष्यताम्। (*Mahāvīracarita* II. 50)

9. *Kumārasaṁbhava* VII. 7
10. *Raghuvaṁśa* III. 33; Sītā's comment *'ete yūyam tatkālakṛta-godānamaṅgalāḥ*—etc. in the I act of *Uttararāmacarita*.
11. *Kumārasaṁbhava* 7.72, 73
12. Ibid, VII. 78, 80
13. Ibid VII. 80
14. Ibid VII. 80, 81; Last acts of Viddhaśālabhañjikā and *Karpūramañjarī*.

12

Four Puruṣārthas and Their Role in Society

A.C. Sarangi

O.Introductory

An individual is a representative of his society and both the society and individual have an equal bearing upon each other. Both of them can coordinate their course of action, once the individuals constituting the society are able to determine their fundamental values of life. The concept of value is significant as it forms the very basis of a social structure. The term *puruṣārtha* literally means what is sought consciously by human beings[1]. Unlike other lower creatures, the human beings rationally think of a set of well-defined goals of life and accordingly they develop stage by stage till they achieve the highest and the most supreme goal i.e., self-realization, though achievable rarely by a few. Still the very endeavour in right direction towards its attainment solves the purpose. It is the uniqueness of the Hindu mind that they have integrated in themselves, the material and mental values along with the spiritual and moral values and precisely for this, the Hindu society has stood the test of time as a formidable force for millennia of years whereas other such great civilizations in the world have been ruined even beyond their recognition.

1. The Puruṣārtha Doctrine

1.0 A sociological analysis of the ancient Indian institutions based on the Dharmaśāstras clearly points out to the fact that the early Indians were very much concerned with their four-fold values of life i.e., *Puruṣārthas* consisting of *Dharma* (an ethical value of life), *Artha* (an economic value of life, *Kāma* (an aesthetic as well as sensuous value of life and lastly the supreme goal, *Mokṣa* (the spiritual value of life). This *Puruṣārtha*-concept is the principal motive of the Hindu-attitude. It is nothing but the four-fold objectives of human existence. Most of the western scholars with a few exceptions like Kant, Plato and Wittgenstein have not gone beyond the intellectual level. Almost all of them have remained either in the physical or psychological level. Initially the first three goals of life (i.e., *Dharma*, *Artha* and Kāma) were given prime significance as they were related with human beings in their mundane and empirical levels. This three-fold nature of man i.e., *sattva, rajas* and *tamas* represent the three levels of human existence i.e., of intellectual, physical and psychical levels. All these three goals are achievable by any ordinary human being and the pursuit of these in their right perspective brings to the society distinction. Although wealth (*Artha*) and pleasure (*Kāma*) are nothing but material goods which are just the means to some end; they become ends in themselves when acquired not in conflict with ethical value (*Dharma*). Thus the instinct is enlightened and then elevated to a value system. The highest and the supreme goal is *Mokṣa* which was set apart as an ab-extra not only in the early Vedic times but also neglected in the present materialistic society, simply because it belongs to the transcendental level. However, there would be discrepancy and disagreement in the societies once this goal is kept apart from the value-system. A human being is not only a social or political being as Plato and Aristotle try to make us believe, but he is a spiritual being too striving for the self-realization. The person thus liberated even in his life-time (*jīvanmukta*) may not be called social as an individual but he is not an anti-social too. He adds to the well being of the society by his spiritual influences.

1.1 C.T. Taylor lists a few values which include pleasure, wealth, fame, power, freedom, love, knowledge, stability, humor and beauty etc., all of which can be covered under our four-fold objectives. As the term *Puruṣārtha* literally signifies, all these four-fold objectives are deliberately sought to be realized in one's life-time[2]. M. Hyriyanna aptly explains, "we may thus define a *Puruṣārtha* as an end which is consciously sought to be accomplished either for its own sake or for the sake of utilizing it as a mean to the accomplishment of a further end"[3].

1.2 The Vedic seers have given as an early glimpse of the Vedic view regarding the *Puruṣārthas*. In the early Vedic age, the people enjoyed a very high degree of material comfort. They prayed for physical health, happiness and a life of hundred years to enjoy their life[4]. Later in the Brāhmaṇa-period, the rituals became be all and end all of life. The rules were laid down elaborately and offerings were made to Gods compelling them to grant the sacrificer what he needed. Accordingly the ultimate goal was to offer sacrifices and only through them, they tried to obtain pleasure and wealth. However, in the Upaniṣadic age the teachings brought a revolution in the thought-process of early Indians. The elaborate rituals were compared with Leaky boats[5]. Thus the values pursued in life took a significant turn in the Vedic society stage by stage from moral, economic and hedonistic good to spiritual good i.e., *Mokṣa* or liberation.

1.2 As a suffering being in the mundane world, it is natural that man must desire to put an end to his suffering and he and other members of his society individually or collectively must strive for putting an end to all their sufferings forever. Thus a concept of heaven (i.e., *svarga*) is discovered which a person endeavoured to achieve in the Brāhmaṇa-age through complex rituals. However, this *svarga*-concept has been treated later as non-permanent and hence in the quest of eternal pleasure man has discovered the *Mokṣa*-doctrine which assures him for relieving the pains permanently.

1.3 In the preface to *Ṛk-prātiśākhya* four-fold *Puruṣārthas* are referred to as stated in the *Ṛg-vidhāna: pavamāna-nābhānediṣṭha-hṛdya-puruṣa-sūktādiṣv* i.e., *Pavamāna*-hymns (*RV* 9.1-67) representatively stand for *Dharma, Nāvānediṣṭha*-hymns (*RV* 10. 61) for *Artha; Hṛdya*-hymns (*RV* 10. 83-84) for *Kāma* and *Puruṣā-sūkta* (*RV* 10.9) for *Mokṣa*. *Puruṣārthas* are also treated as two-fold viz., *śreya* (the good) and *preya* (the pleasant). And the seer in the *Kaṭhopaniṣad* warns a person to properly discriminate between the two and accept the good which will lead to the eternal bliss and to avoid the pleasant which is likely to lead one to bondage[6]. The Vedic concept of *pravṛtti* and *nivṛtti* leading respectively to a pleasurable life and the liberation gets extended in *Dharma Śāstras* including *Manusmṛti* (XII. 88-89) and the *Mahābhārata* (*Anuśāsanaparva*, Ch. 146. 76-80).

1.4 Besides the four-fold division of human-values, one more value is added by a few philosophers viz., Brahman or the self. Self is the end of all activities, the object of all volitions. Self is the dearest and the most valuable object of the world. As *Bṛhadāraṇyaka Upaniṣad* declares, "it is the love of self (*ātmakāma*) that reflects itself in all other forms of desires. Thus, the husband is dear to the wife not because of the wife's love for the husband, but for the love with which she loves her ownself. Gods are dear to us because of self[7].

1.5 The ordering principle in the tetrad of *Puruṣārthas* is based on the significant role of a particular human value played for the society as a whole. Although the concept of *Dharma* has undergone various changes, it is considered as the root of all other values. Both *Dharma* and *Artha* are primarily instrumental for bringing happiness to the individual as well as society. Although ontologically they are considered as means, they are axiologically ends in themselves. However, *Kāma* and *Mokṣa* are proper human goals as the subject of happiness (*viṣayatvena puruṣārthatvam*). In the *Mahābhārata*, *Dharma* is hailed as the most significant *Puruṣārtha*, i.e., the best, *Artha* is the middling and *Kāma* the lowest. Further in case of conflict *Dharma* must supersede both *Artha* and *Kāma*[8]. Unlike in *Mokṣa*, sorrow is mixed up with pleasure with regard to *Kāma*. Hence *Mokṣa* is treated as the supreme goal of life and naturally remains as a final goal. However, in their respective Śāstras, both *Artha* and *Kāma* are treated as essential[9]. *Arthaśāstra* hails *Artha* as the best *Puruṣārtha* since it is the basis of both *Dharma* and *Kāma*. A social organization is successful only if its members are economically conscious and pursue for an independent economic value. Similarly, *Kāma* too is acclaimed as an essential goal in Vātsyāyana's *Kāmasūtra* where the pursuit of love and pleasure is prescribed for the healthy life of a householder.

2. Dharma and its Social Relevance

Although the word *Dharma* has passed through several vicissitudes and thus possesses various meanings like virtue, righteousness, duty, order, justice, morality, religion and the eternal law etc., Manu defines this with its four principal characteristics: The Vedas, the Smṛti, the approved Usage and last but not the least what is agreeable to one's self[10]. *Dharma* as a moral value has been acknowledged as a principle which maintains the stability of the society[11]. Manu has recommended a four-fold division of the span of life (*āśrama*) with *Dharma* as the basis of each stage. Thus *Dharma* regulates the individual life throughout. A man is born as a biological organism but slowly is brought up having been reared by a small social group called family with its own customs and traditions. Then he as a social being gets well acquainted with all the *Dhārmic* regulations of the concerned society. Thus he develops himself into a full citizen, ready for contributing his mite for the sake of his society, although in his student life (*Brahmacaryāśrama*) as well as in the last two stages of life as a hermit (*Vānaprasthin*) and an ascetic (*Sanyāsin*), he is benefited by the society. He as a householder (*gṛhastha*) repays all his three debts (*ṛṇa*): (i) *ṛṣi-ṛṇa* (obligation he owes to the sages) by studying, teaching and advancing the knowledge by research, (ii) *pitṛ-ṛṇa* (obligation he owes to his ancestors) by begetting children and bringing them up as good citizens for the society, (iii) *deva-ṛṇa* (obligation he owes to Divine-powers) by following various religious practices[12]. The earlier concept of *ṛta* 'the cosmic order' was replaced by *satya* and then *Dharma* as a more comprehensive concept was more and more emphasized to keep the individual fully equipped to achieve the highest goal i.e., *Mokṣa*. Once this later developed concept is accepted as the goal of all goals (*Paramapuruṣārtha,Dharma* had a new transformation as an instrumental value although the significance of *Mokṣa* never diminished for the fear of very anihilation of the society[13]. Dharma as moral duty has been highly acclaimed in the *Bhagavad Gītā* which warns the people confused of their own duty to mind their own business to which they are entitled. The four-fold classification of the society (*cāturvarṇam*) based upon *guṇa* and *Karma* (aptitude and action) is regulated through *Dharma* only. *Gītā* teaches *Dharma* as detachment for fruit of any action. Duty for duty sake is the sole motto of the teaching of the *Gītā*. The disinterestedness taught by *Gītā* prepares the people of the society for a gradual training to achieve the highest goal i.e. self-realisation. Gitā brings a synthesis of all the paths towards God-realization, be it the path of knowledge (*jñāna-mārga*), path of action (*karma-mārga*) or the path of devotion (*bhakti-mārga*).

Man is a part and parcel of human society. He should not be treated in isolation. He influences the society through his moral actions and in return the society influences him too. Bradley rightly says, 'the true self is the social self' and it is the social organizm which is higher than the subjective self. The higher self is the man who has identified his will with the moral spirit of the community[14].

3. Artha as a Social-value

Kauṭilya's *Arthaśāstra* is a representative Sanskrit text devoted to *Artha* as a social value. From among four-fold *Puruṣārthas, Artha* has been acclaimed as the principal goal of life[15]. Our *Dharmaśāstras* do not prescribe asceticism for all, rather they have recognized a scale of values. Our famous law-maker Manu recommends that 'one should accumulate wealth for securing only his needs by actions proper to his station (*Varṇāśramadharma*) and without harm to his body. One should not acquire wealth by excessive attachment nor by actions condemned by Śāstra nor when he has enough wealth nor from any kind of person (a sinner or like), even when he is in straightened circumstances[16]. This human goal *Artha* signifies tow aspects: (i) the pursuit of wealth and (ii) the pursuit of power. In the *Ṛgveda* we come across various hymns addressed to Gods for granting wealth. In the *Mahābhārata* there are many stanzas glorifying wealth. In the *Śānti parvan*, the importance of wealth is stressed: "poverty is a state of sinfulness. All kinds of meritorious acts flow from the possession of great wealth, as from wealth spring all religious acts, all pleasures and heaven itself. Wealth brings about accession of wealth, as elephants capture elephants. . ."[17] It is actually wealth as a power which brings stability to the society. Manu has advised people to save for the future. He has referred to a class of people called *Kusūladhānyaka*, those who are desirous of maintaining their livelihood for three years or more from their accumulated food[18]. He has also advised the ladies to avoid spending at their sweet will[19]. All these only go to prove that Manu and others were creating an economic awareness in the society. Hence *Artha* as a value brings moral control in the society and makes the society free from exploitation. Then *Artha* as a political goal of life makes the society politically conscious by referring to the social role played both by the king and his subjects. Through a systematic presentation, Kauṭilya goes on describing about the ideal of power. Plato's ideals in his great work *The Republic*, resemble those of Kauṭilya. Harmony is sought in various functions both of individual capacities as well as classes of society. The success in a social organization depends upon the economic prosperity of the society. *Artha* is at the root for both social good and pleasure. Thus *Artha* as an independent goal of life brigs social harmony, stability and justice. Although *Dharma* is axiologically higher than *Artha*, it is *Artha* which is ontologically superior to *Dharma*. Despite the outcry of Buddhists and Jains against this as a value, from the mundane considerations, it is preferred as the basis for all values belonging to life. Thus, it is intrinsic, absolute and independent in its own right responsible for the well being of the society.

4. Kāma as a Value for the Society

Kāma as a hedonistic value has been appreciated in our ancient Indian tradition. Vātsyāyana's *Kāmasūtra* is a systematic exposition of the hedonistic culture of human beings. *Kāma* as an intrinsic value refers to the pursuit of pleasure, pursuit of sex and pursuit of aesthetic experience. Vātsyāyana warns the people to desist from detestable vices. He, therefore, recommends the people to have a normal healthy sex-life. A society remains healthy when its members have a rightful gratification in their sex-life. Kauṭilya too recommends the life of enjoyment when it is not in conflict with *Dharma*. Even *Āpastamba Dharmasūtra* (II. 8.20; 22-23) declares that man should enjoy all such pleasures as are not against *Dharma*. Similar idea is echoed in other *Dharmaśāstra* works[21]. In the *Bhagavad Gītā* also Kṛṣṇa refers to himself as *Kāma*[22]. Though *Manusmṛti* lays emphasis on abstention, it does not treat the inclination towards eating flesh, drinking wine or indulgence in sex as sin[23]. Vātsyāyana lays proper emphasis on the healthy and rightful satisfaction of one of the primary instincts of man i.e., sex-urge. If this urge is not properly satisfied it is bound to cause perversion. Vātsyāyana condemns those desires which are not sanctified on moral and social grounds. Thus, as an intrinsic and absolute value, *Kāma* too is a social value in its own right and hence is cherished and sought by the men of test and culture.

4. Mokṣa: The Supreme Goal of Life

Mokṣa is regarded as the ultimate aim of life. Unlike other three goals of mundane nature, it belongs to the transcendental order. It is only from the view of trinity of human values (i.e., *Dharma, Artha* and *Kāma*) that one can assert. "The east is east and west is west and the twin can never meet". However, a man becomes universal when as a spiritual being, he strives for the final emancipation. Although it is the highest goal of human life, other goals are stepping stones to achieve it. It is true that each goal from axiological stand-point is independent absolute and underivable and hence autonomous. The monistic approach that *Mokṣa* is the only goal, is in a way anti-thesis of the system of values where pluralism of value is not inconsistent with an integrated approach. In the final analysis all other mundance values are assimilated in *Mokṣa*. It is a state of pure bliss, a value par excellence. Although it presupposes an annihilation of all mundance values, appearing negative in form, it is positive in intention. The social organism as such is inherently weak and for this only it bears a demand for the ultimate value to come to its rescue. However, this is not a path that can be traversed by any human being. As *Kathopaniṣad* remarks, it is a very difficult path like a razor's edge[24] and one can only achieve this goal if he gives up his egoism, selfishness and worldly attachments. The attitude of renunciation is wrongly construed as escapism. Rather the disinterestedness as well as detachment practised even by a few human beings influence the society. It is not a mere co-existence with people, it is rather an inter-existence.

5. Concluding Remarks

Our ancient Indian thinkers have looked upon man as an integrated whole consisting of body, mind, intellect and soul and his personality has thus developed by adopting all the four objectives of life. A man continues to strive for satisfying his desires for pleasure, wealth and power and once he fails to satisfy these he develops tension in himself and causes social tension too. Hence it is his bounden duty to satisfy his desires on ethical means. To maintain stability in the society, *Dharma* plays a significant role. *Artha* and *Kāma*, though themselves are material values, society remains stable and peaceful for these only if these two ends in their right perspectives are adopted by the society. *Manusmṛti* refers to various views about the preference for anyone of these three goods of life (i.e., *Dharma, Artha* and *Kāma*), but finally concludes that all these are important in their own positions[25]. Although *Mokṣa* has been upheld as the final goal of life, Manu warns the people to accept this as the only goal in their stage of householder for fear of the destruction of the very society.

One is only advised to strive for this when he fulfils all his moral obligations in the society. If the final aim of life is to promote harmony between individual and social needs, all these four objectives must be endeavoured to be achieved without sacrificing one for the other.

References

1. Cp. *Pūrvamīmāṁsā-sūtra* 4.1.2: *yasmin prītiḥ puruṣasya tasya lipsā artha-lakṣaṇā avibhaktatvāt*.
2. C.T. Taylor, *The Values*, New York, The Philosophical Library, 1977, PP. 6-7.
3. M. Hyriyanna, *Popular Essays in Indian Philosophy*, Mysore, Karyalaya, 1952, P. 66.
4. Cp. *RV* 1.89.8:
   bhadraṁ karṇebhiḥ śṛṇuyāma devāḥ
   bhadraṁ paśyemākṣabhir yajatrāḥ /
   sthirair aṅgais tuṣṭvāṁsas tanubhir
   vyaśema devahitaṁ yadāyuḥ / /
5. Vide *Muṇḍaka-Upaniṣad* 1.2.7:
   plavā hyete adṛḍhā yajnarūpā aṣṭādaśoktam avaraṁ yeṣu karma /
   etac cheryo ye ' bhinandanti mūdhā jarā-mṛtyuṁ te punar evāpi yanti
6. See *Kaṭhopaniṣad* 11.2:
   sreyaś ca preyaś ca manuṣyam etas
   tau saṁparītya vivinakti dhīraḥ /
   śreyo hi dhīro ' bhipreyaso vṛṇīte
   preyomando yogakṣemād vṛṇīte / /
7. For details see Santi Natha Gupta, *The Indian Concept of Values*, New Delhi, Manohar Book Service, 1978, PP. 127-43.
8. See *Santi parvan* of *Mahābhārata* (12.161.26)
   dharmaṁ samācaret pūrvaṁ tathārthaṁ dharmasaṁyutam /
   tataḥ kāmaṁ caret paścāt siddhārthasya hi tat phalam / /
9. Cp.Kauṭilya's *Arthaśāstra* 1.7.16.17:
   artha eva pradhāna iti kauṭilyaḥ /
   arthamūlau hi dharma-kāmau iti / /
   Cp. also *Kāmasūtra* 1.2.39:
   evam artham ca kāmaṁ ca dharmaṁ copācaran naraḥ /
   ihāmutra ca niḥśalyam atyantaṁ sukham aśnute / /
10. See *Manusmṛti* (11.12):
   vedaḥ smṛtiḥ sadācāraḥ svasya ca priyam ātmanaḥ /
   etac caturvidham prāhuḥ sākṣād dharmasya lakṣaṇam / /
11. See *Uddyoga parvan* of *Mahābhārata* (89.67):
   dhāraṇād dharma ityāhu dharmo dhārayate prajāḥ /
12. Cp. *TS* 6.3.10.15:
   jāyamāno vai brāhmaṇās tribhi ṛṇavā jāyate bramacaryeṇa

ṛṣibhyo yajñena devebhyaḥ prajayā pitṛbhya eṣa vā anṛṇo
yaḥ putraṁ yajvā brahma cārīvāsī

13. See *Manusmṛti*, VIII. 15:
dharma eva hato hanti
dharmo rakṣati rakṣitaḥ/
tasmād dharmo na hantavyo
mā no dharmo hato ' vadhīt//
14. See for details F.H. Bradley, *Ethical Studies*, Oxford, Clarendon Press, 1935.
15. Vide Fn. 8.
16. Cp. *Manusmṛti*, IV. 15:
nehetārthān prasaṅgena na viruddhena karmaṇā/
na vidyamāneṣv artheṣu nārtyām api yatas tataḥ//
17. English translation quoted in B. Kuppuswamy, *Dharma* and *Society*, Madras, The Macmillan Co. of India Limited, 1977, P. 53.
18. See *Manusmṛti* (IV. 7):
kusūladhānyako vā syāt kumbhīdhānyaka eva vā/
tryahaihiko vāpi bhaved asvastanika eva vā//
19. *Ibid.*, (5.150):
sadā prahṛṣṭayā bhāvyaṁ gṛhakāryeṣu dakṣayā/
susaṁskṛtopaskarayā vyaye cāmuktahastayā//
20. Cp. *Arthaśāstra* of Kauṭilya (1.7.12):
dharmārthāvirodhena kāmaṁ seveta
21. For details see *Gautama-Dharmasūtra*, IX. 46-47:
kuryāt yathā-śakti dharmārtha-kāmebhyaḥ
Yājñavalkya-Smṛti, 1.115:
dharmārthakāmān svocitakāle yathā śakti no parityajet
Anuśāsana-parva of Mahābhārata (Ch. III. 18-19):
dharmārthaśca kāmaśca tritayaṁ jīvite phalam/
etat trayam avaptavyam adharmaparivarjitam//
22. *Bhagavad Gītā*, 10.28:
āyudhānām ahaṁ vajraṁ dhenūnām asmi kāmadhuk/
prajanaścāsmi kandarpaḥ sarpāṇām asmi vāsukiḥ//
23. *Manusmṛti* (V. 56):
na māṁsabhakṣaṇe doṣo no madye na ca maithune/
pravṛttir eṣā bhūtānāṃ nivṛttis tu mahāphalā//
24. *Kaṭhopaniṣad* (III. 14):
kṣurasya dhāra niśitā duratyayā durgaṁ pathas tat kavayo vadanti
25. *Manusmṛti* (2.224):
dharmārthāv ucyate śreyaḥ kāmārthau dharma eva ca/
artha evāha vā śreyas trivarga iti to sthitiḥ//

13

Education in Ancient India and Dharmaśāstras

R.N. Aralikatti

Modern thinkers regard *education* "as the dynamic side of *Philosophy* and "*Dharmaśāstra*" as *queen of sciences* in view of the significant role played by both education and Dharmaśāstra. In ancient India, education, culture, science, Philosophy and religion were all interrelated concepts as they fulfilled one or more of the fundamental fourfold objectives of life viz., Dharma, Artha, Kāma and Mokṣa. Religion and philosophy were not divorced from the sciences-like education and *Dharmaśāstra* in particular. The writers on *Dharmaśāstra* were, in a sense more than one, were social scientists and cultural ambassadors. The *Dharmaśāstras* in particular, testify to the fact that people in ancient India were fully aware of the society, its beliefs and its surroundings and their entire life both individual and social was governed by a social cum religious code of conduct[1] to quote Dr. P.V. Kane (*History of Dharmaśāstras* Vol. I Part II, PP.980) "The writers on Dharmaśāstra were actuated by the laudable motives of regulating the Aryan society in all civil, religious and moral life and of securing for the members of society happiness in this world and next.[1a] They laid great emphasis on duties of everyman as a member of society and as a member of particular class (Varṇa). They created great solidarity and cohision among several classes in spite of their conflicting interests and inclinations. By Dharma, they meant religious ordinances or rites, fixed principles and rules of conduct, whole body of religious duties, duties and privileges of a person as a member of Aryan Society and[1b] classified them as *varṇadharma, āśāramadharma, varṇāśrama dharma, naimittika dharma* and *guṇa dharma*. "As rightly pointed by Prof. Keval Motiwan (*Manu-A study in Hindu social theory-Intro.*) `Dharma' is cohesive element and on human plane it is the principle of organisation. From the standpoint of the individual, it is the implementing of the intellectual perceptions of his proper place and duties in the social cosmos. From the standpoint of group, it is the reason or intelligence as the basis of social life. It is developed in juxtraposition with the instinct which forms the basis of animal social life. In these days of conflicting social theories and materialistic interpretation of history the world needs to listen to voice of '*Manu*' which though it belongs to the ancient past embodies the wisdom of the ages".[2]

Dharmaśāstras are primary source for history of education in ancient India which can be broadly divided into four periods According to A.S. Alatekar they are—*Vedic period* upto C. 1000 B.C., the '*Upanishad-Sutra*' period C. 1200 B.C. to 200 B.C., *Dharmaśāstra* period C. 200 B.C. to 500 A.D., '*Pauranic* period' C. 500 A.D. to 1200 A.D. Apart from *Dharmaśāstras* the floating mass of verses of unknown authorship from *Subhāṣita-ratnabhāṇḍāgāra* provides information about aims and objectives, and methods of education and qualities and duties of teacher and taught and other aspects of education in ancient India. Since ideals in life are generally reflected in any system of education, the ideals of education in ancient India were predominantly influenced by the religious and spiritual factors. Purpose of life was to attain salvation or Mukti and education was a means to achieve this end-*sā vidyā yā vimuktaye*. Religion was also a means of attaining the highest ends of life-*puruṣārtha catuṣṭaya*. And hence the intimate relation between Education and Religion in its wider sense is *dharma*. Perpetuation of *dharma*-the cultural citadel and preservation and transmission of our Cultural Heritage was the concern of one and all i.e., all the four classes of the society. Education as the dynamic side of philosophy and Dharmaśāstra as the queen of science played key roles.[3]

Aims of Education

Education was considered essentially a process of illumination. And knowledge is the third eye which gives a man insight into all the affairs and teaches him how to act in life.[4]

A person who does not possess the light of the education is described as blind. It is education which removes all doubts and is a gateway to the world of abstract thoughts.[5] Education nourishes us like a mother, directs us to the proper path like a father and gives us delight and confort like a wife.[6] Education is veritable desire yielding tree. It increases our efficiency and enables us to get fame and wealth by enhancing our reputation.[7] It promotes our material as well as spiritual welfare both in this life as well as in after life.[8] *Budha smṛti* says that it is dharma which is a means to attain material and spiritual welfare.[9]

Contents of Education

The *upanayanam* ritual marked the beginning of the Vedic education. Vedic education was made obligatory. Vedic literature became very extensive in course of time and a student has to study not only four *Vedas*, but also six Vedāṅgas and Purāṇas, Nyāyaśāstra (logic) Mīmāṁsāśāstra.[10] As Vedas were regarded as revealed they had to be preserved with meticulous care both with regard to the accent and intonation of its words. Although the act of writing was well known in India by 800 B.C., its services could not be utilised in the cause of education owing to the absence of paper and printing. Books were written on birch leaves and were very fragile. They were beyond the means of average teacher or student. Students therefore had to learn by heart a number of texts in their subjects from the lips of the teachers and not from pages of a book. Students who studied grammar, sacred law (*dharmaśāstra*), philosophy etc. devoted only 2 or 3 years for the study of vedic hymns, necessary for performing daily duties and spent atleast 8 to 9 years for specialisation in their particular subject. Although memorisation was very important method for Vedic study, critical reflection and development of creative intellect was the hall mark of this period. Metaphysics made remarkable progress as evidenced by the Upanishadic, Bhuddistic and Jain works. The beginning of all later system of philosophy can be traced to this period (*dharmaśāstra* period). Philosophy and grammar were developed, and literary activity in legal literature (*dharmaśāstra*) commenced. Speculations in the realm of political thought were fruitful. Kauṭilya wrote his *Arthaśāstra*. Similarly, Varāhamihira wrote Astronomy and Bhāskāracharya wrote Mathematics and Caraka and Suśruta wrote books on medicine and surgery. Similarly, branches of learning like mining and metellargy were also developed.

Gurukula System

This system where a large number of students had to live together under the direct Superintendence of an inspiring teacher, attached great importance to the code of conduct for students through strict observance of daily routine framed both for the purpose of prohibiting a student from undesirable acts and habits and for forming good and valuable habits leading to the formation of good character. Offering of dairly prayers both morning and evening, showing courtesy to teachers and elders, observing strict celibacy, and diet prohibiting meats, sweet-meats, spicies etc., were a part of their code of conduct and rules of discipline to be observed. "Plain living and high thinking" was the motto that was followed. Students were required to live by begging with a view to inculcating in them the spirit of humility and to make them realise that they owe their achievements and excellence in their learning to the society which has fashioned their careers.

Qualities and duties of a teacher

The teacher was the pivot round which the education system rotated. He was an ideal personality, a person well versed in Vedic and shastric learning. There were three types of teachers termed as Guru, Upādhyāya and Ācārya as per *Dharmaśāstra*. A person who initiates the student into Vedic studies and teaches him Vedāṅgas and Upaniṣads etc., is termed as Ācārya.[11] A person who teaches only a part of Veda or vedāṅga and that to for the sake of livilihood is termed as Upādyāya.[12] A person is termed as *guru* if he maintains himself by officiating as Purohit or priest during the religious ceremonies and rites like nupital night etc..[13] A teacher was held in high esteem., because of his both scholarship and excellence of character. Mostly, Brahmins were teachers and if a Brahmin has not learned Vedas or śāstras, he is a Brahmin only for names sake just as wooden elephant or leather-made deer do not possess the qualities associated with their names.[14] Brahmins were commissioned to perform six functions, viz., teaching and learning, performing sacrifice and officiating over the ritual, accepting and giving the gifts.[15] A brāhmin should know both *śruti* (*vedas*) and *Smṛiti* (*Purāṇas*, *dharmaśāstra* etc.).[16] A teacher was expected not only to teach the subjects but to discipline his students according to the code of conduct prescribed for them.[17] A teacher should select his students and those that are worthy of receiving his learning alone should be taught.[18] Study of *vedas* including Brāhmaṇas, Āraṇyakas, Upaniṣads, Vedāṅgas was a must for a Brahmin and this study was five fold-Recitation of Vedas, contemplating on its meaning, constant repetition, and meditation and then imparting it to the deserving students.[19] A study of *dharmaśāstra* was considered necessary for a Brāhmin for the purpose of knowing his duties and performing according to prescribed procedures.[20] A teacher should impart his learning only to those students who are intellectually well-qualified and morally sound.[21] Such of the students as are grateful free from prejudices, intelligent, averse to fault finding and of high moral characters alone should be accepted for imparting learning.[22]

Scholarship and excellent character were considered the twin requisites for a teacher. Character as crown and glory of life was rated higher than scholarship. A teacher who has control over his sense and has excellent character though with less scholarship with mastery of mere *Gāyatrī mantra* is to be prefered to the teacher who has profound scholarship but no characte.[23] Thus, the qualities of an ideal teacher cited in the Dharmaśāstra text have all time relevance and need to be highlighted in modern context.

Period of the Course

Generally, period of Vedic study was 12 years and for others studies it varied from 9 years to 18 years to 36 years or till a student masters his lore.[24]

Qualities and duties of a Student

As already stated a student had to follow a rigorous code of conduct-'*do's* and *don'ts*. He had to observe a stict decipline and routine and render service to his teacher. Among the '*don'ts*' may be mentioned taboo for use of meats, spices. garlands, contact with ladies etc. Both Manu and Yājñavalkya and other *Dharmaśāstra kāras* lay down the same prohibitory injunctions regarding the code of conduct of the student.[25] A student has to follow his course of study of *Vedas* and *Śāstras* along with the code of conduct which alone would lead to successful completion of his education in Gurukula.[26]

Methods of Study

Memorization, recitation, Recapitulation formed the methods of vedic studies. Chinese traveller (675 A.D.) refers to the wonderful feats of memory of these Vedic scholars since everything had to be at the tip of his tongue. For the study of śāstra and other subjects, exposition was an accepted method for explaining the concepts in subjects, like philosophy, logic, law, grammar. It was accompanied by extensive lectures, discussing exhaustively the opponent's views and establishing one's own stand. Chinese pilgrim again praise Indian teachers for their unsurpassed ability in explaining difficult passages and offering illuminating suggestions on doubtful points.

Dilogues and Parables

They formed the important parts of the method. From upaniṣadic texts and great commentaries on grammer etc., it is evident that the dialogue method was followed. The Mahābhāṣya of Patañjali, for example, uses frequently this method of continuous questions and answers. This method makes the reading of the text very interesting, enlighting and instructive as it is a *two way traffic*. The use of parables was often resorted to in expounding obscure principles especially to juniors. '*Panchatantra* and *Hithopadesa*' are an instance in point. Another feature or the ancient system was use of monitorial system where advanced students were asked to teach the juniors. This system had great educational value in training youngsters to become good teachers. It substituted, in a way, the modern teacher training courses. It also helped the teacher to minimise his expenses on teaching.

Critical Reflection

It was a very important method of learning employed in higher courses. Sanskrit education acquired characteristic thoroughness with the development of the method of critical reflection and specialisation. Inspite of specialisation in one branch, One expected to be fairly conversant with fundamentals of other disciplines and learning.[27]

Thus from a brief presentation, education and some of its aspects as cited in *DharmaŚāstra,* we may conclude that non-vedic disciplines viz., philosophy, law, epic, literature, classical Sanskrit, poetics, astronomy, mathematics were developed and were eagerly studied by one and all irrespective of any caste or class distinction during this period. Women's education received a set back again during this period as their marriageable age was lowered down to 12 years. Secular subjects arts and crafts were studied through hereditory apprentice system. Sculpture, paining, metallurgy were developed as professions along with medicine and engineering. Thus, this was a period of remarkable intellectual activity as attested to by the progress in both religious and secular learning i.e., both humanities, and arts and sciences.

To sum up, we may say that the qualities of an ideal teacher and those of students, plain living and high thinking intellectual freedom, individual attention to the students, residential system of education (i.e., *gurukula* system) monitorial system as a substitute for training course, location of educational institute away from the din and dust of city life and maddening crowds are some of the features which are worthy of emulation even today since they have relevance even in modern times with suitable modifications wherever necessary.

Notes and References

1a. युगे युगे च ये धर्मास्तत्र तत्र च ये द्विजाः ।
तेषां निन्दा न कर्तव्या युगरूपा हि ते द्विजाः ।। (म. स्मृ. I-33)
वेदः स्मृतिः सदाचारः स्वस्य च प्रियमात्मनः ।

1b. एतच्चतुर्विधं प्राहुः साक्षाद्धर्मस्य लक्षणम् । (म. स्मृ. II-12)

2. विद्वद्भिः सेवितः सद्भिनित्यमद्वेषरागभिः ।
हृदयेनाभ्युनुज्ञातो यो धर्मस्तं निबोधत ।।(म. स्मृ. II-i)

3.a. धारणाद्धर्मीमित्याहुयेन धारयते प्रजा ।

b. धर्मार्थावुच्यते क्षेयः कामार्थौ धर्म एव च ।
अर्थ एवेह वा श्रेयस्त्रिवर्ग इति तु स्थितिः ।। (म. स्मृ. II-224)

4. ज्ञानं तृतीयं मनुजस्य नेत्रं समस्ततत्वार्थीविलोकदक्षम् ।
तेजोनपेक्ष विगतान्तरायं प्रवृत्तिमत्सर्वजगत्त्रयेऽपि (सु. र. भा.)

I. Aralikatti, R.N. : Vedānta Education apropos caste system", B.R. Sharma Fellicitation volume, 1989

II. Altekar, A.S.: *Education in Ancient India* Manohar Prakashan, 1975, Varanasi

III. Bhatt Rameswar (Ed.): *Manusmṛti,* Chaukhamba Sanskrit Prakashan, 1990 Delhi.

IV. Pandey, UmeshchandraK Yājñavalkyasmṛti, (Hindi Translation) Chaukhamba Sanskrit Series, 1967, Varanasi.

5. अनेकसंशयोच्छेदी परोक्षार्थस्य दर्शकम्।
सर्वस्य लोचनं शास्त्रं यस्य नास्त्यंध एव सः (सु. र. भा-२)

6. मातेव रक्षति, पितेव हिते नियुक्ते
कान्तेव चापि रमयन्त्यंपनीयस्वेदम् (सु. र. भा)

7. श्रियः प्रदुग्धे, विपदं रुणद्धि यशांसि सूते मलिनप्रमार्ष्टि
संस्कार शौचेन नरं पुनीते शुद्धा हि बुद्धिः किल कामधेनुः (सु.र.भा)

8. विद्यातु वैदुष्यमुपार्जयन्ती जागर्ति लोकद्वयसाधनाय।

9. श्रेयोभ्युदयसाधनोधर्मः (बु. स्मृ. 1)
वेदःस्मृतिसदाचारःस्वस्य च प्रियमात्मनः।
एतच्चतुर्विधिमाहुः साक्षाद्धर्मस्यलक्षणम्।। (म. स्मृ. II-12)

10. पुराणन्यायमीमांसा धर्मशास्त्राङ्गमिश्रिता।
वेदास्थानानि विद्यानां धर्मस्य च चतुर्ददश।। (म. स्मृ. I-3)

11. उपनीय तु यः शिष्ये वेदमध्यापयेद्विजः।
सफल्ये सरहस्ये च तमाचार्यं प्रचक्षते।। (म. स्मृ. II-140)

12 एकदेशं तु वेदस्य वेदाङ्गान्यपि वा पुनः।
योऽध्यापयति वृत्यर्थमुपाध्याय स उच्यते। (म. स्मृ. II-141)

13. निषेकादीनि कर्माणि यः करोति यथाविधि
सम्भावयति चान्नेन स विप्रो गुरुरुच्यते (म. स्मृ. II-142)

14. यथाकाष्ठमयो हस्ती यथा चर्ममयो मृगः।
यश्चविप्रोऽनधीयानः त्रयस्ते नाम बिभ्रति (म. स्मृ. II-157)

15. अध्यायनं चाध्ययनं याजनं यजनं तथा।
दानं प्रतिग्रहश्चेति षट् कर्माणीति चोच्यते। (ल. हा. स्मृ. I-18)

16. श्रुतिस्मृति च विप्राणां चक्षुषी देवनिर्मिति। (म. स्मृ. 10-76)
काणस्मैकयाहीनो द्वाभ्यामन्धः प्रकीर्तितः। (ल. हा. स्मृ. I-24)

श्रुतिस्मृत्युदितं सम्यङ्निबद्धं स्वेषु कर्मसु।
धर्ममूलं निषेवेत सदाचारमतन्द्रितः। (म. स्मृ. IV-155)

17. उपनीय गुरुःशिष्यं महाव्याहृतिपूर्वकम्। (या. स्मृ. I-15)
वेदमध्यापयेदेवं शौचाचारं०चशिक्षयेत्।। (म. स्मृ. II-69)

18. योग्यानध्यापयेच्छिष्यानयोग्यानपि वर्जयेत् (ल. हा. स्मृ. I-21))

19. वेदस्वीकरणं पूर्वं विचारोऽभ्यसनं जपः
ततो दानञ्च शिष्येभ्यो वेदाभ्यासो हि पञ्चधा (द. स्मृ. II-27)
मीमांसते च यो वेदान् षा्डभिरङ्गैसविस्तरैः।
इतिहासपुराणानि सभवेद्वेदपारगः (शेख. स्मृ. IV-45)

20. शौचाचारविचारार्थं धर्मशास्त्रमपि द्विजः।
पठेत् गुरुतः सम्यक् कर्मतद्दिष्टमाचरेत्। (व्या. स्मृ. I-25)

21. धर्माथौ यत्र नस्यातां शुश्रूषा वापि तद्विधा।
तत्र विद्या न वक्तव्या शुभबीजिमिविपरे। (म. स्मृ. II-112)
विघा ब्राम्हणमेत्याह शेवधिष्टेऽस्मि रक्ष माम्।
असूयकाय मां मा दा तथा स्यां वीर्यवत्तमा।। (म. स्मृ. II-114)
तस्मै मां बूहि विप्राय निधिपायाप्रमादिने (म. स्मृ. II-115)

22. कृतज्ञा द्रोहिमेधावि शुचिकल्यानसूयकाः।
अध्याप्याः धर्मतः साधुशक्ताप्तज्ञानवित्तदा। (या. स्मृ. I-28)

23. सावित्रीमात्रसारोऽपि वरं विप्रः सुयन्त्रितः।
नायन्त्रितस्त्रिवेदोऽपि सर्वाशा सर्वविक्रया। (म. स्मृ. II-118)

24. षट्त्रिशाब्दिकं चर्यं गुरो त्रैवोदिकं ब्रतम् (म. स्मृ. III-1)
तदोर्धिकं पादिकं वा ग्रहणान्तिकमेव वा।।
नैष्ठिको ब्रम्हचारी तु वसेदाचार्यसन्निधौ।। (या. स्मृ. I-49)

25. मधुमांसाञ्जनोच्छेष्टशुक्रस्त्रीप्रणिहिंसनम् (या. स्मृ. I-33)
भस्करालोकनाश्लील परिवादादि वर्जयेत् (या. स्मृ. II-177)

26. तस्माद्वेव्रतानीह चरेत् स्वाध्यायसिद्धये।
शौचाचारमशेषे तु शिक्षयेद्गुरुसन्निधौ।। (ल.हा. स्मृ. III-4-10 to 15)

एवमन्वहमभ्यासी ब्रम्हचारी व्रतं चरेत।
हितोपवाद: प्रियवाक् सम्यग्गुर्वर्यसाधके। (व्या. स्मृ. I-35)
अनेन विधिनाधीतो वेदमन्त्रो द्विजं नयेत्।
शास्त्रानुग्रहसामर्थ्यमर्षीणां च सलोकताम्।। (व्या. स्मृ. I-36)
कुर्यादध्ययनं चैव ब्रम्हचारी यथाविधि
विधिं त्यक्त्वा प्रकुर्वाणो न सध्यायफलं लभेत्। (ल. स्मृ. III-2)

27. सम्यक् शास्त्रमधीयानो न विद्याच्छास्त्रनिश्चय:
तस्माद्बहुश्रुत: शास्त्रं विजानीयच्चिकित्सक:।। (कुश्रुते)

14

The Concept of an Ideal Teacher and His Role in the Society

Nirmala Kulkarni

1.0. Any society in the world had reckoned the significance of *Guru* either in the form of a teacher who imparts knowledge or in the form of a priest who possesses mystic powers. Thus, any person who commands considerable knowledge either of the material world or of the spiritual world is acknowledged by the society.

A teacher was paid more attention by Indian culture because of the predominance of the oral transmission of the Vedic texts. It was highly improbable to learn those sacred texts without direct oral instructions. Moreover, it was considered a sin called *Brahmasteya*. The texts were kept intact because of the painstaking efforts of several generations of teachers in the direct oral transmission and in contributing exegetical texts. Therefore, even this initial picture of a teacher had sought the most important position in the society. Later on the spiritual teachers were at the top of the scale. The significance attached to a teacher in general is revealed in the deification of the concept as Bṛhaspati in Vedic lore and as Dattatreya in the later Indian religion.

Keeping in front the social framework of the then society the ancient Indian Dharmaśāstra (DŚ) texts have laid down rules and regulations for a teacher and towards a teacher. The present article tries to focus the image of an ancient Indian teacher painted by these texts. The conclusive part of the article tries to search the impetus behind these. It also tries to highlight how the then society was benefited by these rules. At the same time it also discusses its treatment in ancient mythological descriptions.

1.1. The Teachers

In those days Vedic texual studies formed the syllabus for the formal education. Apart from the formal training moral and spiritual upliftment of a child was desired. One who trains a child to become a responsible member of a society on any plain was treated as a teacher. The *Dś* texts use various technical terms to distinguish these varied role of different types of teachers.

(i) *Guru* was a wider term which included teachers as well as elders. Five persons are said to be *guru*, more respectable.

गुरूणामपि सर्वेषां पूज्याः पञ्च विशेषतः ।
यो भावयति या सूते येन विद्योपदिश्यते ।।
ज्येष्ठो भ्राता च भर्ता च पञ्चैते गुरवस्स्मृताः ।।

Devalasmṛti
quoted in *smṛticandrikā*

Manu defines a *Guru* as

निषेकादीनि कर्माणि यः करोति यथाविधि ।
सम्भावयति चान्नेन स विप्रो गुरुच्यते ।। 2.142

Tr.: One who performs the *saṁskāras* beginning from *garbhādhāna* and one who nurtures a child is called a *guru*.

This verse labels father as *guru* who may or may not be the formal teacher of a child.

Manu further extends the scope of the term to any person who helps in increasing knowledge or information.

अल्पं वा बहु वा यस्थ श्रुतस्योपकरोति यः ।
तमपीह गुरुं विद्यात् श्रुतोपक्रियया तया ।।

Manu 2.124

(ii) The term *ācārya* was specially reserved for the teacher of the Veda. He was supposed to be the most honourable person among teachers. The Upaniṣadic statements आचार्यवान् पुरुषो वेद or आचार्यद्धैव विद्यां साधिष्ठां प्रापत् proclaim his invariable presence in the process of learning. The interpretation of the term given by Yāska as आचारान् आचिनोति अर्थान् वा speaks of his contribution in the scholarly and moral behaviour of a student. A hymn from the *Atharvaveda* (AV) expects complete transformation of a child at his hands and therefore, he is called a spiritual father. As per the definitions of the *Dś* he must have mastered the entire Vedic literature along with the ancillary texts. He must have talent in exploring the secrets of the Veda. Besides, he must formally initiate the child. To quote a representative definition by Manu—

उपनीय तु यः शिष्यं वेदमध्यापयेद्विजः ।
सकल्पं सरहस्यं च तमाचार्यं प्रचक्षते ।। 2.115

(iii) *Upādhyāya* also had a major role in the teaching of the veda. However, he was always supposed to be inferior to *ācārya*, because (a) he was not expert in the entire Vedic lore (b) he used to maintain himself by teaching and thirdly (c) he was not competent enough to elucidate the secrete of the Vedas-Manu defines such a teacher as—

एकदेशं तु वेदस्य वेदाङ्गान्यपि वा पुनः ।
योऽध्यापयति वृत्त्यर्थमुपाध्यायः स उच्यते ।। 2.116

Besides these main technical terms other terms such as *adhyāpaka, śiṣṭādhyāpaka, pravaktā, bhṛtakādhyāpaka* were also in practice but are scarcely defined in the *Dś*.

Thus, excellency in the Vedic studies was the mark of superiority among the professional teachers. But when it comes to moral training parents supersede them. A famous verse from Manu shows the hierarchy among them as—

उपाध्यायान्दशाचार्यः दशाचार्यान्शतं पिता ।
पितुर्दशशतं माता गौरवेणातिरिच्यते ।। 2.145

We also come across exactly opposite of the above statement which keeps a teacher especially an *ācārya* on a higher plain, most probably keeping in view the spiritual training bestowed up on the student. To quote—

गुरुर्गरीयान्पितृतो मातृतश्चेति मे मतिः ।
उभौ हि मातापितरौ जन्मन्येवोपयुज्यतः ।
आचार्यशिष्टा या जातिः सा दिव्या साजरामरा ।

MBh.

This view gives secondary importance to the efforts taken by parents in the development of a child.

1.2 Qualities of a Teacher in General

A teacher next to parents brings up a child and transforms

him into a learned and perfect person. One who introduces others into ethics and etiquettes, himself must possess some basic qualities which would be indirectly transferred to a student. The following are the indispensable qualities expected from a teacher.

(i) Excellency in the subject

A teacher must be proficient in the subject he teaches. Adjectives like *Vedaikaniṣṭhaḥ, abhijanavidyāsamudetaḥ* accompany descriptions of a teacher in the *Dś*. The hierarchy among them also says that one who knows more is respected more. The biographies of renouned teachers in the epics and *purāṇas* read that they were masters of more than one branch of learning. Such interdisciplinary approach i.e. बहुश्रुतत्व kept them update in their own branch. They have tried hard to achieve supremacy in a particular subject. Droṇa, teacher of archery was well versed in the *Veda* and Vedāṅgas and in the *Arthaśāstra*. To quote:

वेदं षडङ्गं वेदाहमर्थविद्यां च मानवीम्।
त्रैयम्बकमथेष्वस्त्रमस्त्राणि विविधानि च।।

(ii) *Knowledge of Ethics and Etequettes*

A teacher, whose instructions were not limited to classroom teachings must know minutely the standard moral behaviour of a society. He must know what is benifical to the society and to an individual as well. Being included in the *śiṣṭas*, he must be competent enough to interpret law. He is generally described as *dharmajña* and *śuciḥ* and therefore was eligible to teach *śaucācāras*.

(iii) Besides these he must be zealous and hard working and must concentrate in further readings of his subject. Manu says:

आ हैव स नरवाग्रेभ्यः परमं तप्यते तपः।
स स्रग्व्यपि द्विजोऽधीते स्वाध्यायः शक्तितोऽन्वहम्।।

Manu- 2.142

(iv) *Simple living devoid of greed*

A teacher is expected to have minimum necessities which are generally met with by royal grants and donations. *'Dama'* restrain is said to be obligatory to a brahmin. Even then if by sheer luck he gets money he may bring up many children, or he must donate it and perform sacrifices and should distribute his money. To quote—

दममेव महाराज धर्ममाहुः पुरातनम्।
स्वाध्यायोऽध्यापनं चैव तत्र कर्म समाप्यते।।
तं चेद्वित्तमुपागच्छेत् वर्तमानं स्वकर्मणि।
अकुर्वाणं विकर्माणि शान्तं प्रज्ञानतर्पितम्।।
कुर्वीतापत्यसन्तानमथो दद्याद्यजेत च।
संविभज्य हि भोक्तव्यं धनं सद्भिरितीष्यते।।

MBh 12.60.9-11

For the same reason *ācārya* who does not expect anything from his student is praised. *Upādhyāya* was placed next to him. *Bhṛtakādhyāpaka* i.e. who teaches on contract basis is condemned. Expiations are enjoined for such students and teachers.

Greed invites all types of calamities. A brahmin who is the sole protector of knowledge if caught in such calamities, knowledge would be at stake. A brahmin well controlled but knowing only the *gāyatrī mantra* is said to be superior to a person who knows all the Vedas having uncontrolled behaviour.

सावित्रीमात्रसारोऽपि वरं विप्रः सुयन्त्रितः।
नायन्त्रितस्त्रिवेदोऽपि सर्वाशी सर्वविक्रयी।।

Manu 2.118

Such restrictions prompted knowledge for knowledge sake, and prevented commercialisation of knowledge. The reverse of it is experienced today especially in the sale of patents.

(v) *A teacher must be a brahmin*

Though all the three classes were entitled to learn Vedas only a brahmin was confered the privilege of teaching. The *Viṣṇusmṛti* prescribes duties of brahmin as द्विजानां यजनाध्ययने। ब्राह्मणस्याध्यापनं धर्मः। Upgradation of a *Kṣatriya* as a brahmin by penance is seen only in the case of Viṣvāmitra. He along with his descendents had acquired the status of a brahmin. However, the *DŚ* does not prescribe any rule for such cases and therefore teaching by a *kṣatriya* or *Vaiśya* appeared as only an *āpaddharma*. To quote *Āpastamba Dharmasūtra*:

आपदि ब्राह्मणेन राजन्ये वैश्ये वाध्ययनम्। 2.2.4.25

The *Gautama Dś* says आपत्कल्पो ब्राह्मणस्य आब्राह्मणात् विद्योपयोग:। समाप्ते ब्राह्मणो गुरु:। Manu retells नाब्राह्मणे गुरौ शिष्यो वासमात्यन्तिकं वसेत्। 2. 242 Very rarely even a *śūdra* is said to be entitled to teach *śubhā vidyā* i.e. a benifical knowledge. श्रद्दधान: शुभां विद्याम् आददीतावरादपि। Manu 2.2.13. However, from the available evidence one can say that a *śūdra* was never appointed as an official teacher.

1.3. Duties of a teacher

(1) Teaching of the Vedas and moral upbringing of a student was the foremost duty of a teacher.

(2) Preservation of the Vedic texts was the core of education. A teacher was expected to transmit it to such a student who would not do any harm to it. Therefore, selection of a student was expected. It is said, नापरीक्षितमध्यापयेत्। नोपनयेत्। नापृष्ट: कस्यचिद्ब्रूयात्।

(3) While selecting a student he must see that he is a hardworking, straighforward and benevolent one. The education must not be inspired by unpious motives. These expectations from a student led the *Dś* to enjoin restrictions on a *brahmacarin* and led teachers to test his tenacity.

(4) A teacher must select a student who is a *dvija*. *Śūdras* were eliminated most probably for the following reasons—

(1) Basically, they were nonaryans and aryanised in course of time. It is said that Indra had converted them into the Aryan clan. The Vedas were assets of the Aryans. The myth of Śaṅkhāsura who had stollen the Vedic texts confirms that there were attempts to take away the Vedic texts. Transmission of the most coveted secret to a defeated foreigner does not fit in any political policy. Because one cannot deny the possibility of misusing it. This political stand continued to centuries and turned into a cruel practice. Several legends are introduced to

justify it and to prompt deprivation of *Śūdra* class from Vedic knowledge. None of these legends puts forth convincing justification. Still there are some scanty references by which one can infer that some Ācārya's desired enlightenment even of a *Śūdra*. To quote these—

(1) The *MBh* says श्रावयेच्चतुरो वर्णान् We do not know whether this rule turned into practice.

(2) Suśruta quotes a view which though denies Vedic instructions to a *Śūdra*, but offers essential education most probably *Śaucācārās*, *Śilpa's* etc. by official initiation ceremony. शूद्रमपि कुलगुणसम्पन्नं मन्त्रवर्ज्यमुपनीतमध्यायपये-दित्येके ।

(3) Thirdly, we do get references of one *Śūdra* class i.e. *sūtas* in learning and preservation of *purāṇas*. However, *sūta* is a *saṅkara* caste born of a brahmin father and a *Śūdra* mother. Thus, they have not confered the responsibility to a pure *Śūdra*.

Thus, one can say that the *Śūdra* were deprived especially of Vedic knowledge. As it is pointed out earlier it might be a political policy turned into practice.

Another reason for eliminating *Śūdra* class from Vedic education was his association with impure deeds. Mental and physical purity was obligatory for any student. It is said—

द्वावेव वर्जयेन्नित्यमनध्यायौ प्रयत्नतः ।
स्वाध्यायभूमिं चाशुद्धामात्मानं चाशुचिं द्विजः ।

Manu 2.127

Physical purity was supposed to be impossible for a *Śūdra* child. Of course, this might be the secondary reason.

1.4. Duties Towards Teachers

Thus, one who keeps aside his personal pleasures and transmits highest knowledge was always respected. Inclusion of teachers in the list of chief guests, touching his feet in a particular mode speak of the respect paid to them. Those who do not respect a teacher were cursed as

अध्यापिता ये गुरुं नाद्रियन्ते।
विप्रा वाचा मनसा कर्मणा वा।
यथैव ते न गुरोर्भोजनीयाः।
तथैव तान्न भुनक्ति श्रुतं तत्।। वासि. धर्म. सू. 2.11

Gurutalpaga, Guruhan and *Gurunindaka* etc. are said to be the most sinful persons and therefore severe punishments are cited for them.

Not only the students but the whole society was obliged to a teacher. Maintenance was from the fees, sacrificial fees or from royal donations. Teachers were not expected to pay taxes. नाभिरूपस्य ब्राह्मणस्य आहरेत्। वासि. धर्म. सू.

Thus, effort of a teacher in developing a child into a responsible member of a society were duly acknowledged and he was placed on a higher level. At the sametime if a teacher does not behave properly the right student had a right to punish him. To quote:

गुरोरप्यवलिप्तस्य कार्याकार्यमजानतः।
उत्पथप्रतिपन्नस्य न्याय्यं भवति शासनम्।।

Nītiśataka

1.5. Conclusion

The following paragraphs aim at evaluating the above description in terms of social awareness i.e. the social requirements of the then society. Social awareness is a relative concept which changes from time to time. We just have to see whether they have legalised the social changes or not. And here I am concerned with the concept of a teacher.

At the very outset let me admit that birth oriented caste system was the background of the *Dś*. Therefore, a brahmin teacher was prefered. The *Dśs* do not project a woman teacher. We have to infer them on the basis of the difference between the pair of words आचार्या and आचार्यानी. With this background let us see how the then society was benifited by the class of teachers projected by the Dś.

If one analyses the general frame work of the society, a fact would be revealed that any individual was treated as a part of the cosmos. Protection of the cosmic order i.e. *ṛta* or *dharma* was the highest goal of the society. In their view unobstructed cosmic order smoothens life of an individual and continuity of it depends up on the perfection of an individual. Any individual is not a born perfect. He needs proper training. The task to train him properly for the sake of the society was shared by teachers and elders. Therefore, a teacher was called ऋतस्य दाता. Complete transformation of a student was expected at his hands. It is symbolically expressed in the त्रिरात्रिव्रत which a *brahmacārin* performs at the time of *upanayana*. By this he gets his second birth.

तं रात्रीस्तिस्रः उदरे बिभर्ति। तं जातं द्रष्टुमभिसंयन्ति देवाः।

Such transformation which cannot be called merely material was the aim of the education. स दाधार पृथिवीं दिवं च or तस्मै देवा संमनसा भवन्ति such sentences speak that high achievement was expected after education.

Such expectancies resulted into restrictions on both the teacher and the taught. Ultimately, it resulted into a class of thinkers who keeping themselves with bare minimum necessities and by overlooking the contempt by others because of their low economic status have developed the masses (of course the *traivarṇikas*) in the responsible and conscious members of the society. This itself was the expectation of the Dś. Needless to say they have also preserved the Vedic tradition intact, till today.

The concept of a formal teacher was not much changed because the core of education i.e. the text oriented Vedic study did not change. In the Vedic times the spiritual teachers were not separated from the formal teachers. However, later on at the advent of different *sampradayas* a spiritual teacher got a separate and higher plain wherein the relation of a *Guru* and *Śiṣya* crossed almost all barriers.

15

Rights and Duties of the Individual in Ancient India

Khagendra Patra

Rights are the sum total of social conditions in the form of essential privileges which help the individual to build up his personality and to lead a cultured life in the society. The enjoyment of rights by an individual implies corresponding duty of others to honour and not to infringe upon such rights. In this way rights and duties of the individual go hand in hand. Both arise out of social awareness of the people. They contribute a healthy social life.

However, rights and duties of the individual are as old as human civilization. It is known from the history of Indian Civilization that in ancient time, specially during the Age of Dharmaśāstra, i.e. the later vedic period, the people of India were quite conscious about their contemporary society and different aspects of life. Depending upon their surroundings, they had been entrusted with various duties violation of which invited punishment and hence certain laws were promulgated. So the people of that Age were more conscious about their duties. Duty was then very important factor for building up the personal as well as the social life. So importance was given on duties and as such the attainment of perfection in duty was the source of rights. In other words performance of duty envisaged the enjoyment of rights of the individual. Accordingly individuals of Dharmaśāstra Age were enjoying rights through the performance of their duties. In this way rights and duties had a co-relation in the practical social life of individuals. All those rights and duties were based upon the prevalent beliefs and traditions which were socially recognized.

Information in this regard is available from Dharmaśāstras of Gautama. Baudhāyana, Āpastamba, Manu, Parāśara and others among which *Manusmṛti* of Manu is considered to be the most outstanding as well as authoritative work on various aspects of social life of ancient India.

During the Age of Dharmaśāstra "Varṇāśramadharma" or the caste system was the base of social organization. At that time rights were existed in duties in term of Dharma. Secondly, the concept of right was something different from that of modern times. Moreover, without duties rights had no separate existence. Yet the-then Indians were enjoying certain limited rights according to their own classes. For example, the Kshatriya was entrusted with the duty to protect the subjects from internal confusion and external disturbances. As regards the right, for maintaining peace and order in the State, the Kshatriya had the right to take part in defence, political and judicial affairs and administration. Such type of Political right stemmed forth from the duty to protect the subjects. In order to enjoy the so-called Political right the individual belonging to Kshatriya class had to perform the duty to take care of the subjects under his control.

In this way, for improving the social conditions of the-then India all the members of the society had taken some responsibilities in different aspects of life as per the instructions mentioned in Dharmaśāstras which supply data regarding the prevalent social system in term of social awareness. So, in this connection it is essential to draw an outline, on the basis of *Manusmṛti*, of rights and duties of the individual during the Age of Dharmaśāstra.

In modern times the rights of the individual are regarded as essential privileges or reasonable claims which are recognized by the society for building up the individual personality and the development of society[1]. And accordingly individuals are enjoying privileges in the form of rights. In this connection if we observe the social condition of Dharmaśāstra Age then it becomes clear that the-then individuals had also certain privileges according to their own classes. Although at that time their privileges were not called as rights or claims yet individuals of that Age were enjoying certain rights through the performance of duty which was considered to be the best means for the refinement of the individual and the society. So with a view to maintaining peace and order in different aspects of life importance was then given to duties. And thus, authors of Dharmaśāstras had focus their attention more on duties than rights.

However, duties of Dharma had been prescribed by the exponents of social norms like Manu and others with a view to building up the individual personality and making the social life happy and prosperous. Dharma, in fact, was meant for the welfare of the society and for the smooth management of every aspect of human life. Accordingly, Dharma was earnestly adhered to without envy, vice, jealosy or hatred towards others in the society[2]. Such type of Dharma was also meant for the development of morality, dutifulness and ability or eligibility on the basis of which rights were then granted to individuals. For example, although the individual belonging to Brahmaṇa class of the society was granted right to vedic education yet it could not be claimed by virtue of one's birth. In order to enjoy such right one had to perform his educational duty like daily practice of vedic study sincerely. Otherwise he was not liked by others. Moreover, the Brahmaṇa without the knowledge of the Vedas was not respected like learned Brahmaṇas in the society. He was regarded as a useless fellow like a baren woman or baren cow[3]. Again, a Brahmaṇa who would not perform his prescribed duty like studying the Vedas was treated as a *śūdra* in the-then Indian Society[4]. On the other hand, those who performed their prescribed duties were praised and liked by all[5]. Thus, the sanction of rights was based on the performance of duty which was considered to be more vital than hypothetical rights in the society.

However, in order to make the human life happy and refined the authors of Dharmaśāstras have dealt with different aspects of social life like education, occupation, marriage and family, political and judicial affairs, administration, religion etc.. All such aspects of life were regulated through certain rights and duties in the form of Dharma which were recognised and sanctioned to individuals of different classes. Moreover, since rights were existed in the form of Dharma or duty it is essential to point out a few rights of the-then individual in relation to the above aspects of social life, such as (1) right to education, (2) right to occupation, (3) right to wages, (4) right to participate in administration (5) right to private property and (6) right to justice etc.

1. Right to Education

According to the-then caste system of India right to education was granted to individuals belonging to the classes of Brāhmaṇa,

Kshatriya and Vaiśya. Brāhmaṇas had the right to study and teach the Vedas[6]. They had the Privilege to perform sacrifices for their personal development and social welfare as well. Kshatriyas like princes had the right to receive education of arts and sciences after their initiation which marked the beginning of their student life[7]. They had been also granted the right to learn the principle of punishment (दण्डनीतिविद्या), the science of reasoning (आन्वीक्षिकी विद्या or तर्कविद्या), the principles of trade, agriculture and animal husbandary (कृषि-वाणिज्यपशुपालनादिविद्या)[8].

Vaiśyas were enjoying the right to commercial education and animal husbandary. So they possessed a sense of qualitative discrimination of material products, of making a distinction between good and evil traits of various countries, of assessing profits or loses incurred in the transaction of finished products, of an expertise in selling and buying articles[9].

However, in connection with their commercial education they had the privilege to learn arithmatic, some languages of the people of different races and practical details of trade. Their right to education had social value since their practical commercial education was contributing to social development. So they were allowed to amass wealth for all others in the society[10].

2. Right to Occupation

According to the Fundamental Rights as mentioned in the Constitution of India, right to work provides that all citizens shall have the right to practise any profession, or to carry on any occupation, trade or business. But such type of freedom was not given to all in ancient India.

Since "caste system" was the dominating factor in the society during the Age of Dharmaśāstra individuals of four castes were not granted equal rights to occupation. Every individual had the right to occupation or to earn livelihood according to his own class. Individuals of each caste had their prescribed rights to work. For example, (a) the Brāhmaṇas had the right to work in the field of academics and religion, (b) the Kshatriyas in political and administrative affairs, (c) the Vaiśyas in trading and (d) the *Śūdras* in serving all other classes of the society through physical labour[11].

In Dharmaśāstras right to occupation has been mentioned in the term of duty or sacred principles of life. According to Manu teaching अध्यापनं, officiating sacrifice as priest याजनं and receipt of gifts प्रतिग्रहः were prescribed means of livelihood for Brāhmaṇas[12].

Kshatriyas or the royal class people had the right to take up arms and to earn their livelihood by participating in defence, political, judicial and administrative affairs of the State. The Vaiśyas or the merchant class people had the right to work in trade, agriculture and animal husbandary[13].

3. Right to Wages

Right to wages was granted to individuals in order to enable them to maintain the standard of living. In this connection the King had to fix up the wages of servants. Normally maid servants were paid one paṇa daily, two sarees for six months and one droṇa of paddy for a month[14].

Right to wages was then enforceable by the law of the State. So this right was included in eighteen types of judicial disputes as mentioned in the 5th verse of Chapter-VIII of *Manusmṛti* (वेतनस्यैव चादानमिति).

4. Right to Participate in Administration

According to the-then caste system of social organization Kshatriyas had been entrusted with the responsibility of protecting all subjects of the State. They were granted the right to take part in defence, political and judicial affairs and administration for the safeguard of the State. So the sacred duty of the King was to take care of the subjects of the Kingdom[15].

However, not only the Kshatriyas but also the Brāhmaṇas had the right to take part in judicial affairs. Generally the learned Brāhmaṇas were then given the privilege to become the adviser of the King in the administrative affairs of the State. So they were associated with the king for the settlement of judicial disputes[16]. The king used to appoint learned Brāhmaṇas for the same in his absence. However, he was deciding judicial disputes with the association of three learned Brāhmaṇas[17].

5. Right to Private Property

Every individual had the right to private property either by purchase or inheritance and partition of paternal property after the death of parents[18]. The right to private property by partition was also granted to some extent to unmarried daughter. There was provision for giving her one fourth of the total property which belong to her brothers[19].

It is very interesting to note that morality or the code of conduct was then strictly followed in granting the right to private property by partition. So the brothers who were given to prohibited activities like gambling, drinking, prostitution etc. were deprived of such rights by the shares accruing from their paternal property[20].

6. Right to Justice

It is a fact of social awareness during the Age of Dharmaśāstra that right to justice was granted to each and every individual in the society. All were equal in the eyes of law. So none was considered to be above punishment for any crime due to deviation from one's Dharma, not even a father, mother, guru, priest, friend, wife and son or any near relation[21]. Even the King was not exempted from being punished. He was rather penalized a hundred times more than an ordinary culprit for his crime[22].

In this way individuals of ancient India were enjoying their limited rights which are the evidence of social awareness of those days.

However, it has been observed that the above-mentioned rights were granted to individuals with certain limitations according to their own classes. Moreover, while enjoying rights individuals of a particular class were also adhering to their duty to honour the same rights of others of their own class. So rights and duties of the-then individuals went hand in hand according to the division of society.

Since the "Varṇāśramadharma" was the dominating factor in the society members of all classes were not granted equal rights. But it is a fact that inspite of all the discriminations pertaining to rights and duties of individuals in ancient India there was unity in diversity in practising common *dharmas* or duties like non-violence, truthfulness, non-stealing, purity in body and mind and controlling the sense organs which according to Manu, were granted to individuals belonging to all classes in the society. Thus the very words of the Master run like this:

अहिंसा सत्यमस्तेयं शौचमिन्द्रियनिग्रहः ।
एतं सामासिकं धर्मं चातुर्वर्ण्येऽब्रवीन्मनुः ।।

—Manu. X/63.

Taking in to consideration the social value of non-violence and truthfulness it can be pointed out that the above dharmas in connection with the duties of individuals are not only the evidence of social awareness of the past but also a guiding principle for all times to come.

Notes

1.(a) According to H.J. Laski "Rights, in fact, are those conditions of social life without which no man can seek, in general, to be at his best".—*Grammar of Politics*, London, Allen and Unwin, 1925, P. 21.

(b) According to Bosanquet "A right is a claim recognized by the society and enforced by the State".—Quoted by A.P. Padhi, J.K. Baral and S.C. Hazary in *Political Theory*, P. 199.

2. विद्वद्भिः सेवितः सद्भिर्नित्यमद्वेषरागिभिः ।
हृदयेनाभ्यनुज्ञातो यो धर्मस्तं निबोधत ।।

—Manu. II/1

3. यथा षण्ढोऽफलः स्त्रीषु यथा गौर्गवि चाफला
यथा चाज्ञेऽफलं दानं तथा विप्रोऽनृचोऽफलः ।।

—Manu.II/158.

4. योऽनधीत्य द्विजो वेदमन्यत्र कुरुते श्रमम् ।
स जीवन्नेव शूद्रत्वमाशु गच्छति सान्वयः ।।

—Manu. II/168.

5. स्वानि कर्माणि कुर्वाणा दूरे सन्तोऽपि मानवाः ।
प्रिया भवन्ति लोकस्य स्वे स्वे कर्मण्यवस्थिताः ।।

—Manu. VIII/42.

6. अध्यापनमध्ययनं यजनं याजनं तथा।
दानं प्रतिग्रहश्चैव षट्कर्माण्यग्रजन्मनः।।

— Manu. X/75.

7. ब्राह्मं प्राप्तेन संस्कारं क्षत्रियेण यथाविधि।
सर्वस्यास्य यथान्यायं कर्त्तव्यं परिरक्षणम्।

— Manu. VII/2.

8. त्रैविद्येभ्यस्त्रयीं विद्यां दण्ड़नीतिं च शाश्वतीम्।
आन्वीक्षिकीं चात्मविद्यां वार्त्तारभ्यांश्च लोकतः।।

— Manu. VII/43.

9. सारासारं च भाण्ड़ानां देशानां च गुणागुणान्।
लाभालाभं च पण्यानां पशूनां परिवर्धनम्।।
भृत्यानां भृतिं विद्यां भाषाश्च विविधा नृणाम्।
द्रव्याणां स्थानयोगांश्च क्रयविक्रयमेव च।।

— Manu. IX/331-332.

10. धर्मेण च द्रव्यवृद्धावातिष्ठेद्यत्नमुत्तमम्।
दद्याच्च सर्वभूतानामन्नमेव प्रयत्नतः।।

— Manu IX/333.

11.(a) (i) अध्यापनमध्ययनं यजनं याजनं तथा।
दानं प्रतिग्रहश्चैव षट्कर्माण्यग्रजन्मनः।।

— Manu. X/75.

(ii) अध्यापनमध्ययनं यजनं याजनं तथा।
दानं प्रतिग्रहं चैव ब्राह्मणानामकल्पयत्।।

—Manu. I/88.

(b) प्रजानं रक्षणं दानमिज्याध्ययनमेव च।
विषयेष्वप्रसक्तिश्च क्षत्रियस्य समासतः।।

(c) पशूनां रक्षणं दानमिज्याध्ययनमेव च।
वणिक्पथं कुसीदं च वैश्चस्य कृषिमेव च।।

(d) एकमेव तु शूद्रस्य प्रभुःकर्म समादिशत्।
एतेषामेव वर्णानां शुश्रूषामनसूयया।।

—Manu I/89-91

12. षणां तु कर्मणामस्य त्रीणि कर्माणि जीविका।
याजनाध्यापने चैव विशुद्धाच्च प्रतिग्रहः।।

— Manu. X/76.

13. शस्त्रास्त्रभृत्त्वं क्षत्रस्य वणिक्पशुकृषिर्विशः।
आजीवनार्थं धर्मस्तु दानमध्ययनं यजिः।।

— Manu. X/79.

14. राजा कर्मसु युक्तानां स्त्रीणां प्रेष्यजनस्य च।
प्रत्यहं कल्पयेद् वृत्तिं स्थानं कर्मानुरुपतः।।
पणो देयोऽवकृष्टस्य षड्डुत्कृष्टस्य वेतनम्।
षाण्मासिकस्तथाच्छादो धान्यद्रोणस्तु मासिकः।।

— Manu. VII/125-126.

15. क्षत्रियस्य परो धर्मः प्रजानामेव पालनम्।
निर्दिष्टफलभोक्ता हि राजा धर्मेण युज्यते।।

— Manu. VII/144.

16. व्यवहारान्दिदृक्षुस्तु ब्राह्मणैः सह पार्थिवः।
मन्त्रज्ञैर्मन्त्रिभिश्चैव विनीतः प्रविशेत्सभाम्।।

— Manu. VII/1.

17. (a) यदा स्वयं न कुर्यात्तु नृपतिः कार्यदर्शनम्।
तदा नियुञ्ज्याद्विद्वांसं ब्राह्मणं कार्यदर्शने।।
(b) सोऽस्य कार्याणि संपश्येत्सभ्यैरेव त्रिभिर्वृतः।
सभामेव प्रविश्यास्यामासीनः स्थित एव वा।।

—Manu. VIII /9-10.

18. उर्ध्वं पितुश्च मातुश्च समेत्य भ्रातरः समम्।
भजेरन्पैतृकं रिक्थमनीशास्ते हि जीवतोः।।

— Manu. IX/104.

19. स्वेभ्योंऽशेभ्यस्तु कन्याभ्यः प्रदद्युर्भातरः पृथक्।
स्वात्स्वादंशाच्चतुर्भागं पतिताः स्युरदित्सवः।।

— Manu. IX/118

20. सर्व एव विकर्मस्था नार्हन्ति भ्रातरो धनम्।
(न चादत्त्वा कनिष्ठेभ्यो ज्येष्ठः कुर्वीत यौतकम्।।)

21. पिताऽऽचार्यः सुहृन्माता भार्या पुत्रः पुरोहितः।
नादण्डयो नाम राज्ञोऽस्ति यः स्वधर्मे न तिष्ठति।।

— Manu. VIII/335

22. कार्षापणं भवेद्दण्डयो यत्रान्यः प्राकृतो जनः।
तत्र राजा भवेद्दण्डयः सहस्रमिति धारणा।।

— Manu. VII/336.

16

Caste System and Division of Labour

C. Panduranga Bhatta

It is difficult to say in what manner and at what time exactly the caste system originated. In the Ṛgvedic Age there were only two classes of people in society, he Aryans and the non-Aryans. In the later Vedic period religion became more ritualistic and provided sufficient work for a class of specialists and this led to the rise of priestly class. The priests devoted their life for mastering the vastly elaborate rule and rituals of sacrificial worship. The extension of their territories and constant wars forced the Aryan rulers to keep a body of trained and skilled soldiers in constant attendance so that their services could be requisitioned at any moment of emergency. This class of fighters in due course formed themselves into a separate independent class called *Kṣatriyas*. The rest of the Aryans, engaged in odd jobs namely trade, crafts, agriculture and industry were called *Vaiśyas* and obtained a lower status than that of the *Kṣatriyas*. The fourth group called *Śūdras* were treated as servants and their main function was to serve the other three main classes. This is the historical origin of the caste system which was in the beginning based on a division of labour. It may be said that the division of the Vedic society into four orders was intended for properly distributing throughout the community the various duties connected with the ritual.

The *puruṣasūkta*[1] found in the *Ṛgveda* refers to the four *'varṇas'* collectively for the first time. The whole social organisation is here conceived symbolically as one human being with its limbs representing the social classes based on the the principle of division of labour.

In order to ensure social harmony, society was divided into number of communities, each community being assigned particular duties (*svadharma*), to be discharged by it for the common welfare of all communities, without-prejudicially infringing the duties and rights of other communities. In short, society was evolved on an economic basis which was well suited to the exigencies of those days.

Manu briefly enumerates the duties of the four castes[2]. According to him teaching and studies, performing sacrifices for himself and for others, bestowing and accepting gifts are the duties of the Brāhmaṇa. Protection of the people, charity, performance of sacrifices, studies are the duties of a Kṣatriya. Rearing of animals, charity, performance of sacrifices, practice of trade and commerce on land and sea and agriculture are the duties of the Vaiśya. The service of the three castes is the only one duty of the *Śūdras*. Similar lists of the duties of various castes are to be found in all the Dharmaśāstra s. In the *Bhagavad Gītā* it is said that the four-fold '*varṇa*' was created by the lord according to '*Guṇa*' (quality) and '*Karma*' (action, more in particular action resulting from past action[3] "and the duties of *Brāhmaṇas, Kṣatriyas, Vaiśyas* and also of *Śūdras* are distributed according to their '*Guṇas*' (qualities) born cf their nature"[4].

ब्राह्मण क्षत्रियविशां शूद्राणां च परंतप।
कर्माणि प्रविभक्तानि स्वभवप्रभवैर्गणैः।।
शमो दमस्तपः शौचं शान्तिरार्जवमेव च।
ज्ञानं विज्ञानमास्तिक्यं ब्रह्मकर्म स्वभावजम्।।
शौचं तेजो धृतिर्दाक्ष्यं युद्धे चाप्यपलायनम्।
दानमीश्वरभावश्च क्षात्रं कर्म स्वभावजम्।
कृषिगोरक्ष्यवाणिज्यं वैश्यकर्म स्वभावजम्।
परिचर्यात्मकं कर्म शूद्रस्यापि स्वभावजम्।।

According to *Gautamadharmasūtra* a Brāhmaṇa would not be a valuable acquisition to the army, as he is unused to the horrors of war[5]. According to Kauṭilya Brāhmaṇas were not considered very good soldiers because an enemy could win them over by prostrating himself before them[6]. Thus Gautama and Kauṭilya justify the fact that the duties of the four castes were in accordance with the nature of the castes concerned.

The word 'dharma' literally means 'what holds together' and signifies that it is the basis of all other, whether social or moral;

'dhāraṇāt dharmam ityāhuḥ, dharmeṇa vidhṛtāḥ prajāḥ[7]'. The term *'varṇadharma'* means the duties of the several classes of society. They form an integral whole of society, and that the co-operation of each is equally necessary for its well being. Social solidarity is their essential aim. Sureśvara, the great Advaita teacher while speaking of the duties of the four classes (*Varṇas*) as conducing to common welfare, compares them to the carrying of a palanquin which requires co-operative effort[8].

The *Bhagavadgītā* also emphasises the principles of ethical interdependence involved in the caste system. Society can progress only if its various units properly perform the functions assigned to them. The consideration whether a function is high or low is not of any real value. The feeling that, you observing 'svadharma' (one's own caste duties) one actively promotes the solidarity and progress of the society is in itself a reward. The idea gained ground that to follow one's own *'dharma'* and to sacrifice one's own life, if need be, in the prosecution of that *'dharma'*, was the highest duty expected of every citizen, to whatever caste he belonged. This is the plain teaching of the *Bhagavadgītā*;

क्षेयान्स्व धर्मो विगुणः परधर्मात्स्वनुष्ठितात् ।
स्वधर्मे निधनं क्षेयः परधर्मो भयावहः ।।

This insistence on *'svadharma'* is a sound economic concept because it makes the individual to realise his responsibility and duty to himself, his family and country[10]. This also made every caste to realise its dependence on the other castes, and this tended to avoid caste wars.

Manu lays down the strictest code of conduct for a Brāhmaṇa. According to him a Brāhmaṇa is a born lover of learning and pursues the study of the sacred texts throughout of his life. Manu declares that the *Brāhmaṇa* who, forsaking the study of the Vedas, exerts in other directions soon sinks with his family, even while living, to the level of the *śūdra*[11];

योऽनधीत्य द्विजो वेदमन्यत्र कुरुते क्षमम् ।
स जीवन्नेव शूद्रत्वमाशु गच्छति सान्वयः ।।

It may be said that 'Varna-dharma' is social planning, in which the spiritual, educational, military, administrative and economic functions are attached permanently to certain hereditary groups ensuring the transmission of professional ideals and standards of efficiency[12].

Thus in the initial stages a man's class or caste was decided by his profession and conduct and not by his birth. It was not at all difficult for man to change from one caste to another. Change of profession could lead to a change of caste. Individuals as well as families could pass from caste to caste. Paraśurāma, a *Brāhmaṇa,* became a *Kṣatriya.* Droṇācārya, the military instructor of the Pāṇḍavas was a *Brāhmaṇa* and Vidura, the guide, philosopher and friend of the king Dhṛtarāṣṭra was a *dāsi-putra.*

By gradually modifying his conduct Viśvāmitra, who was a *Kṣatriya* by birth succeeded in becoming a *brahmarṣi*[13]. Occupation can also exercise an influence on the nature of a person. If a Brāhmaṇa gives up his traditional occupation and takes to that of a Kṣatriya, a fall in his status is postulated. The transformation of the Kadamba dynasty, which started with the Brāhmaṇa, to a Kṣatriya is a classical instance of the operation of the principles in demotion[14].

The caste system took an organic view of society and no tribe or caste was believed to deserve obliteration in the living organism of society. It points out that all work is social useful, and from an economic standpoint equally important.

Tulādhāra, one of the teachers mentioned in the *Mahābhārata* belonged to the third caste. Yet in the epic he figures as an ideal person[15].

It is worth noting that in Vālmiki 's *Rāmāyaṇa* Daśaratha asks Sumantra to invite to his sacrifice the *Śūdras* also, along with the other three `*varṇas'*[16].

The qualifications expected of a commander-in-chief were many-sided. Though *Vaiśyas* and *Śūdras* were debarred, still Śukra would select this officer from any caste, if he happened to be a śūra or a great hero;

सेनापतिश्शूर एव योज्यस्सर्वासु जातिषु ।[17]

The caste system, introduced on the basis of the division of labour in society, promoted economic strength and efficiency in professions and functions. It helped to preserve the skilled labour by transmitting vocational skill from generation to generation. Thus the caste system has made progress possible and maintained the continuity of professions and crafts. The caste system fostered a spirit of brotherhood among the members of the same caste. In time of distress the persons of the same caste used to help each other and thus the system promoted civic virtues of self-sacrifice, love and service. One more advantage of restricting certain work to a particular caste may be pointed out here. The compulsory military service was confined to one particular caste namely Kṣatriyas. This prevented the militant attitude from spreading to other communities.

Kauṭilya[18] recognizes the productive role of the three lowers '*varṇas*' and hence according to him when settling people in virgin territory, preference must be given to the three lower 'varṇas' because of the benefits that farmers, cow-herds and traders brought to the economy.

In the course of its consolidation by accepting heredity as the only criterion which determined one's caste, the caste system completely blocked they way for individual progress. Whatever his ability and attainment, an individual could not even think of being up-graded in the social scale during his life-time. In the *Mahābhārata* itself the propriety of the division of men into rigid castes based on their birth has been questioned. Replying to the questions put by the king Nahuṣa in the form of a snake, Yudhiṣṭhira expresses his doubt in regard to the purity of different castes. In his opinion it is not possible to ascertain the caste of a man because the different castes have got mixed together beyond the possibility of making correct distinctions. According to him 'Truthfulness, generosity, freedom from hatred and wickedness, humility, kindness, and *tapas* make a person *brāhmaṇa*. If these signs are seen in a Śūdra and they do not exist in a brāhmaṇa then the Śūdra would not be a Śūdra and the brāhmaṇa would not be a brāhmaṇa;

सत्यं दानमथाद्रोह आनृशंस्यं त्रपा घृष्णा।
तपश्च दृश्यते यत्र स ब्राह्मण इति स्मृतः।।
शूद्रे चैतद्भवेल्लक्ष्म द्विजे तच्च न विद्यते
न वै शूद्रो भवेच्छूद्रो ब्राह्मणो न च ब्राह्मणः।।[19]

Another verse found in the Vana parva declares that a Śūdra who is always struggling for self-restraint, truthfulness and 'dharma' is a brāhmaṇa, for a brāhmaṇa is so by his character;

यस्तु शूद्रो दमे सत्ये धर्मे च सततोत्थितः।
तं ब्राह्मणमहं मन्ये वृत्ते न हि भवेद् द्विजः।।

It goes to the credit of the Brahmin copyists of the *Mahābhārata* epic who have not removed these verses from the body of that work even though these verses convey revolutionary ideas in respect of caste.

According to a verse quoted by Patañjali in his *Mahābhāṣya* '*tapas*', Vedic study and birth make a person brāhmaṇa, he who is devoid of '*tapas*' and Vedic study is a brāhmaṇa only by birth (and not a real brāhmaṇa);

तपः श्रुतं च योनिश्च एतत् ब्राह्मणकारकम् ।
तपश्रुताभ्यां यो हीनो जातिब्राह्मण एव सः ।।

Bhavabhūti in his *Uttararāmacarita* has represented that when a Śūdra began to practise austerities in the dominion of Rāma, that impious act resulted in the premature death of a Brāhmaṇa boy in Āyodhyā. When Rāma noticed that Śūdra ascetic in the Daṇḍakāraṇya he put him to death and the Brāhmaṇa boy was brought back to life. Bhavabhūti who was very proud of his own Vedic learning must have felt the injustice of Rāma's action. So he has given the stage direction '*Kathañcit prahṛtya*' (having somehow dealt a blow) and made Rāma exclaim sadly, '*kṛtam Rāmasadṛaśṁ karma*' (I have done a deed worthy only of Rāma)[22]. Thus here and there we come across statements made by Sanskrit writers which indicate their unhappiness over the caste system based on birth alone.

Originally the caste system was introduced to meet the needs of the time when different races had to live together in amity and peace. This system minimised the evils of competition in trade and industry and helped to maintain the professional discipline and honour.

In later times it became a check on the economic progress because it kept economic and intellectual opportunities confined to a certain section of the population only and denied them to others. The caste system did not make proper provision for low-born talents or high-born incompetents and therefore it failed to become a successful institution.

References

1. *Ṛgveda*, X. 90.12.
2. *Manusmṛti*, I. 89-91.

3. *Bhagavadgītā*, IV. 13; चातुर्वर्ण्यं मया सृष्टं गुणकर्मविभागशः ।
4. Ibid, XVIII, 41-44.
5. V.R. Ramachandra Dikshitar, *War in Ancient Inaia*, P. 197
6. *Arthaśāstra* IX. 2.23.
7. *Mahābhārata*, XII. 109.14.
8. *Bṛhadāraṇyaka Vārttika*, I.`iv. 1600
9. *Bhagavadgītā*, II. 35; स्वधर्मे निधनं श्रेयः परधर्मो भयावहः ।
10. See Dikshitar, *Hindu Administrative Institutions*, pp. 40-41.
11. *Manusmṛti*, II. 168.
12. K.V.R. Aiyangar : *Some aspects of the Hindu view of life*, pp. 105.
13. *Rāmāyaṇa*, I. 51.61.
14. K.R. Basavaraja, *History and Culture of Karnataka*, p. 34.
15. *Mahābhārata*, Śānti, 262, 264.
16. *Rāmāyaṇa*, I. 9.77.
17. *Śukranīti*, II. 434.
18. *Arthaśāstra*, VII. 11.21.
19. *Mahābhārata*, Śānti, 189.4.
20. Ibid. 8
21. *Mahābhāṣya* on Pāṇini, II. 2.6.
22. *Uttararāmacarita*, II Act after verse no. 10.

17

Kauṭilya's Views on Punishment

Shailaja Bapat

Hindu Dharmaśāstra illumines the *dharma* (code of conducts) of four *Varṇas* viz. *Brāhmaṇa, Kṣatrīya, Vaiśya* and *Śūdra* and *dharma* of four *Āśramas* viz. *Brahmacharya, gārhasthya, vānaprastha* and *sannyāsa*. *Varṇa* and *Āśrama dharmas* characterise the Hindu Society. Besides, Hindu Dharmaśāstra considers *adharma* or prohibited actions (*akartavya*) which lead to undesirable results. The man who wants himself to be cultivated, he should know *dharma* and *adharma*. Manu has proclaimed-"*Na Māṅsabhakṣaṇe doṣo na madye na ca maithune / pravṛttireṣā bhūtānāṁ nivṛttistu mahaphalā*". To live according to nature is a living like animal-life while to live according to rules and regulation is a cultured life of human being. If man wants himself to live distinct from animal life, he should live according to the duties and should avoid the anti-duties. Dharmaśāstra informs the man the results of prohibited actions. The man is called '*patita*'[1] who does not follow the way of duties, and fulfills his desires by following prohibited path of actions. He looses his rights and status in the society, and they are restored to only by performing rites etc. which are called punishments.

Present paper tries to elaborate the nature of punishment in view of Kauṭilya's Arthaśāstra. Arthaśāstra is recognised as a branch of Dharmaśāstra, since it deals with *Rājadharma* which is one of the *varṇadharmas* in the Hindu Dharmaśāstra[2]. Yet, Kauṭilya in his Arthaśāstra deals with punishment as one of the aspect of *Rājadharma* in a distinct manner. Kauṭilya guides the king regarding the difficult task of analysis and use of punishment for some person's sinful action.

It is true that punishment is employed for sinful action, but, what is the nature of that action which is valued as a sin? Let us see the nature of human action. Kauṭilya takes the cognision of the importance of man and his action in the achievements of social needs such as stability and peace and welfare. Kauṭilya says—'पुरुषवद्धिराज्यम्'. (K.A. P. 420) Rājya is of पुरुष or मनुष्य ('मनुष्यवती पृथिवी.' K.A. P. 616) *puruṣa* or man is not without action and capacities. Man's action has two aspects. One of that aspect of human-action is desirable by which there can be achievement of social needs. Such types of action is virtuous and is favoured in the social life, while human-action that causes unstability and disorder or chaous, is not desirable. Dharmaśāstrakāras and Kauṭilya who are social thinkers, try to get over the social problems raised by human actions, and make a way to restore the order and peace in social life. These thinkers try to determine virtuous actions and harmful actions by the parameters of social needs. Virtuous actions are duties and non virtuous actions are anti-duties. Man is social being as well as animal also. Manu has rightly said that दुर्लभो हि शुचिर्नरः । That is due to his selfish nature and lack of social awareness, he tries to fulfill his desire by that way of life which is against social life. These anti-social actions are of various types such as theft, *atichāra, pāruṣya* and actions, which are against one's own duties, and some of them are illegal contracts. Social thinkers, have seriously thought of various types of remedies for serious anti-social actions of persons who are the members of society. The cream of their thinking is the preventive motif, which is called 'दण्ड'-the king's power that protects virtuous actions of man and prevents anti-social action. Lord Śrikrisṇa also says- 'दण्डो दमयितामस्मि' । Gautama in his Dharmasūtras (G.D.S.) describes the duties of the concecreted king[2], Gautama says that king should withdraw those people who deviate from the right path of *dharma*,-'*chalatas-chaitānsvadharma sthāpayet*', (2.2.10). He protects the duties of varṇāśramas in proper way and controls the illegal actions of sinners, by his supra power called punishment. (दण्ड).[3] Manu also has described the *daṇḍa* that controls human conducts. Due to forceful *daṇḍa*, there is order in social life[4]. Kauṭilya also has said that the discriminate use of *daṇḍa* protects common people in the society[5]. On the contrary, if the king fails in his duty of protecting the common people, and punishing the sinners, G.D.S. says that, then the king deserves to have the प्रायाश्चित्त.[6] While Kauṭilya says, that as the king fails in giving justice to the person he should offer *daṇḍa* (30 paṇas) to God *Varuṇa* who is the Sovereign Ruler of the kings who are sinful[7].

Manu explains the notion of the king and his supra power of controlling. He says that the God has created the king and his *daṇḍa*, in extra-ordinary way[8]. Kauṭilya , however, holds different view from that of Manu. Kauṭilya says that, the man becomes king who has *vinaya*[9]. *Vinaya* means study of Śāstras, self-control, and consultation with the learned. *Vinaya*, in addition to that depends on the assistance of *Purohita*, Ministers and Heads[10]. The king's spies and officers create the impression that king is *sarvajña* and he possesses the power of suppressing the offenders[11]. Thus, king is *Iśvara* of all subjects because of his assistants.

The *daṇḍa* whether it is a power created by God, by which king can do his duty, or as Kauṭilya says it, as a result of *Vinaya* of king, is used as an instrument to obtain social needs. Therefore, it should be used discriminately. Kauṭilya has mentioned consequences of the misuse of the power. Severe use of *daṇḍa* excites the people, while extremely polite use of *daṇḍa* is not honoured by the people. Hence, proper use of *daṇḍa* is honoured by all. It helps subjects to obtain their desirable goals[12]. That is why, Kauṭilya , guides the king to use *daṇḍa* discriminately, and by which king can control human actions and would establish stability and peace in country and in state.

Kauṭilya describes the pre-requisites of the employment of दण्ड. That is, the knowledge of man (पुरुष) with his distinct characteristics and the knowledge of the distinct offences of sinner. Kauṭilya says, 'पुरुषापराधविशेषेण दण्डविशेषः कार्यः ।' (Kangle's Artha Shastram (K.A., p. 285)[13]

Let us try to know in what manner Kauṭilya helps the king by illustrating distinct characteristics and types of sinners, and their offences.

Kauṭilya has basically considered the different categories of sinners as follows. (1) Sinners among the government officers and servants [14], (2) Criminals who contract illegally[15]. (3) The sinners, the thorns of city and country, are thieves in disguise[16]. (4) Enemies of king in disguise, viz. *Rajavallabhas* and who are in league with king's enemy[17].

Government Servants and their Offences

Treasury is one of the important *prakriti* of state. Yet the government servants who are *'arthachara'* cause the deplation of treasury-such as hindrance, lending, treading, concealment, causing loss, use, interchange and embezzlement[18]. Kauṭilya mentions about forty ways of embezzlement[19], for example, what is to be carried out is not carried out, and what is not to be carried out is carried. — etc. Kauṭilya has pointed out that government servants commit the crimes due to following reasons[20]-the person (viz. the officer) if not conversant with the activity, customs and fixed rules, causes loss of revenue through ignorance, if unable to endure the trouble of (energetic) activity, through laziness, if addicted to the pleasures of the senses, sound and others, through remissness if afraid of an uproar (among subjects) or of an unrighteous or harmful act through fear, if inclined to show favour to those who have work with him, through love, if inclined to do them harm, through anger, because of reliance on learning or wealth, or the support of a (royal) favourite, through ignorance and because of (deceit in) introducing a difference in weight, measure, assessment or counting he causes loss through greed. Kauṭilya has classified the servants as patrimony-squanderer, the immediate spender and the niggardly[21].

Criminals-Thorns in City and Country

Kauṭilya also has considered criminals in the city and country. Thieves who are not known as thieves such as traders, artisans, actors, medicants, jugglers are harmful to the country[22]. These person have secret ways of income. They are, for example, extortioner, false witness, user of accult means for winning love, practisers of black magic and sorcery, an utterer of false coins, dealer in artificial gold, remover of colour from precious metals[23].

Besides the *arthacharas* and *guḍhajīvins*, Kauṭilya also pays special attention to the criminal thorns of kingdom and the king. He describes them as *rājānamavagrhyopajīvin* and *śatrusādhāraṇāḥ duṣyāḥ* and are united to *rajyopaghātin*, rājavallab has are principal officers. These thorns are such, which are not possible to be weeded out openly[24].

Crimes Due to Illegal Contracts and Misconduct

Kauṭilya has made other significant category of criminal *puruṣas* among the citizens. This category is different from the criminal government servants, and thieves in disguise. Government servants are representative of the king's power, and are related to king's administration. While citizens have no political authority. From the political point of view, government servants are mainly characterised by king's political powers. Their duties have been ordered by the king. On the contrary, in view of Kauṭilya , citizens are mainly characterised by their duties of *varṇa* and *aśramas*, while Kauṭilya does not take into consideration these social structural characteristics of king's officers and servants as he considers their offences.

Furthermore, regarding the criminal citizens, Kauṭilya also has given stress on the gender, age, physical in capability etc. Citizens being characterised with social duties, gender, age, physical incapabilities etc., may commit the crimes regarding the illegal contracts with other person. Regarding the contracts there arise more than one parties. The party or parties become criminal if they settle the illegal contracts. These contracts are mainly based on human capacities, actions and inter-relationships with each other. They are determined by the individual's duties and common duties also. If the persons interact and develop the relationships against these duties or determiners of duties, and if the other party suffers or complaints, the accused one becomes criminal. For example, illegal marriage between man and woman, illegal sexual relationship between man and woman, and theft, blaming, killing etc. are offences of citizens because of which they deserve the punishment[25].

From the above discussion it becomes clear that Kauṭilya considers the sinful actions (*aparādha*) of the sinners as government servants and citizens and also persons who are sinners in disguise in the country and in the city and in the rulership. To prevent their misbehaviour against king and his rulership and sinful actions of one person to other, it is necessary to confess the sinner and their harmful conducts.

The confession of an offences is possible in the following manner—

(1) Individual's confession of his sin.
(2) King's assertainment of particular crime of particular person.G.D.S. refers to first type of individual's confession—'स्तेन: प्रकीर्णकेशो मुसली राजानामियात्वुर्माऽऽचक्षाण: ।' 2.3.40, 'तस्याजिनमूर्ध्वबालपरिधाय लोहितपात्र: सप्तगृहान्भैक्षं चरेत् कर्माऽऽचक्षाण: ।' 3.5.18.

Here, the pharase, 'कर्माऽऽचक्षाण:' is significant which indicates that sinner himself approaches the king to confess his sinful act. It throws light on particular human nature. Man is selfish as well as he is social in nature. He has conscience but due to uncontrolled passions he does injury to other person. But he also fears of deprival of social rights and ashamed of his misconduct with other. Therefore, he wants himself to be pure of sin and wants his previous status as, a man free from sin. King and the committee of Vedavids, purify the sinner by employing the punishment for his sin[26]. King makes him pure of sin by killing him or also by making him free from sin[27].

While Kauṭilya holds objective view regarding the confession of the sin. Kauṭilya emphasises, that aspect of, human nature which is cultivated in the social circumstances. Man has particular prestigious status in the society. Man likes praise, honour. He wants that others should understand him as ideal righteous man in the society. Because of this pride and prejudices of himself, he tries to conceal his crime instead of it's open confession. He fears of infamy in the society. Therefore, in view of Kauṭilya , man himself does not confess his sin. The sinner is passive. Hence, according to Kauṭilya, it is the responsibility of the king to determine the sin of sinful person. The king has the authority to confess the particular man as a criminal. Kauṭilya gives stress on that confession which is the result of king's powerful administration. Kauṭilya in this respect gives valuable suggestions about the factual confession of sin. How will the king be in a position to confess the sin of a sinner in scienfic manner? and how will the king make an impartial justice to the other party (plaintiff) in particular offence?

Kauṭilya has suggested different factual ways of finding out the sins so that king would logically confess sinner's sin.

In regards with the search of sins of government officers, heads and servants, the king appoints the various spies. These spies keep watch on the doubtful behaviour of government people[28].

Besides king should appoint *Samāhartā* (Administrator), and *Pradeṣṭā* (Magistrate)[29]. *Samāhartā* should station his spies. They would find out whether officers and servants and also citizens are honest to their work or not. Administrator has also right to punish the heads and officers such as Magistrate, Judge and village Chief if they would make harm to others. Magistrate along with the village and Divisional officers should make search of thieves outside and the city-superintendent should do it inside the fort[30].

In this manner king with his power, through his officers, spies should investigate the *'arthacharas'* and then they viz. Judge and others should search the sinners among the citizens[31]. Investigation of the sinners and their sins begins under certain conditions. If there is doubt of crime, due to finding of stolen things, then there is scope for investigation of sin[32]. Kauṭilya in the *Adhikaraṇa* called *Kaṇṭakaśodhanam* has demonstrated the methods of investigation of the sinners in the city and country.

Thus, Kauṭilya gives much importance to the king's confession of sinner's sin on the basis of factual investigation. The reason can be possible as follows—Kauṭilya does not believe in confession of sin by the sinner himself. Since, the man may confess himself as sinner even though he had not committed the crime due to fear. Kauṭilya for example, points out that due to the fear of query *Aṇimāṇḍavya* had confessed himself as a sinner[33]. Therefore, Kauṭilya advises that without determination of sin, person will not be punished.

Further more, the scientific investigation of sin, makes possible the king to punish to the sinner only and not to sinless person. The subjects and righteous servants would believe king's power of preventing from injustice. Besides, the entire method of investigation into sin may influence on subjects that the king gives the impartial justice.

Investigation into sinful act and query of injustice becomes necessary if there would not be complaint. Therefore, Kauṭilya suggests that Judge, should ask about injustice to learneds, orphans, and olds, who are not inclined to complaint against the injustice upon them, or sin due to which they suffer[34].

The investigation is required to determine the sin of a sinner. It is determined by the plaintiff's complaint of sin against him. Judge, on the basis of witness's information and written papers of contracts, or indications of harmful injuries, determine the sinful act of sinner. After, complete scientific search of sin and dermination of the offence, the king can employ the punishment for sin of sinful person.

Types of Daṇḍas (Punishment)

Now it would be proper to take into consideration the Kauṭilya's information about the distinct types of punishment, regarding distinct types of sinful actions and according to severe consequence of sins.

Daṇḍa is the last type of punishment. Kauṭilya has stated various aspects of *daṇḍa* as follows—

(1) *Dravya* (*paṇa*)[35]: It is of three grades (a) *Prathama sāhasa daṇḍa*. (b) *Madhyama sāhasa daṇḍa* (c) *Uttama sāhasa daṇḍa*. These forms of daṇḍas are employed according to the severity of offences. This aspect of daṇḍa is also a substitute to corporal punishment and *nirviṣaya* punishment.

(2) *Vadha daṇḍa*: (Corporal punishment). It is of two fold—
(a) *Chitraghāta* (causing death in injurious way)
(b) *Śuddha vadha*-Injury to the limb by which the sinner commits a crime. Kauṭilya mentions many types of corporal punishments as mentioned by *smṛtikāras*. Yet, Kauṭilya does not agree the cruel punishments mentioned by smṛti Śāstrakāras. He accepts only *śuddhavadha* for simple offences[36]. Kauṭilya mentions other type of corporal type of *daṇḍa*. It is significantly called *upānśu daṇḍa* or *tūṣṇī daṇḍa*[37]. It is like a चित्रघात yet, it is different from it, because it is used secretly.
(c) Kauṭilya also mentions other type of corporal punishment as *śiphāprahāra* by not iron stick instead of fine[38].
(d) Kauṭilya describes uninjurious corporal punishments. These are also effective, yet are not injurious. This type of uninjurious corporal *daṇḍa* is characterised as the making of the indicatory marks (*chinha*) on the sinner's body, particularly on his forehead[39]. In some cases these types of daṇḍa are substituted by *dravya daṇḍa*[40].

(3) *Social types of punishments*: Kauṭilya also refers to another significant type of punishment called *'pravrājanam'*[41]. He mentions it by the other expressions *'pravāsayet'*, *'nirviṣaya'* and *sthānādvyavaropaṇa*. It means driving the sinner away from the society, i.e. deprival of membership of the society.

(4) *Religious type of punishment*: Kauṭilya describes the deprival of death-rituals to man or woman for committing suucide[42]. Kauṭilya also refers to *vrata, abhiṣeka, agnikārya, upavāsa mahākaccha* etc.[43]. According to Kauṭilya , these types of punishment are not intended for the purity of sins while Gautama Dharmasūtrakāra meant them for the purity of sins[44]. Dharmasūtras refer to प्रायाश्चीत,[45] तप,[46] उपवास,[47] होम,[48] दानऽ[59] and दिव्यऽ[50]. These punishment are aimed at the purity of sins[51]. Some of these punishments are mainly capital and cause the purity of sin only after death even in case of *Brāhmaṇa* who commits adultery to his guru's wife[52].

Kauṭilya, however, does not mention these ritualistic punishments in general with the exception of vānaprastha. Yet, according to Kauṭilya vānaprastha, and pāṣaṇḍa who are sinners should not observe the ritualistic punishment for the sake of own's purity of sins, on other hand, they should enjoy such punishments for the sake of king's welfare and prosperity[53]. Kauṭilya , however does not mention प्रायाश्चित, दान and दिव्य, types of punishment[54].

Why does Kauṭilya not mention प्रायश्चित, दिव्य etc., as Gautama mentions? The reasons can be said as follows—(1) These types of punishments are peculiar in nature. These punishments are enjoyed by the sinner himself. Sinner is active in a sense that he desires to enjoy the punishment[55]. Besides, these punishments are enjoyed for the sake of purity. The purpose of such punishment is the purity of sin according the Dharmaśāstra[56]. In addition to that these punishments are private in nature. Such types of punishments are their purpose of purity are abstract in nature. There is no way except sinner who alone could know the enjoyment of punishment and the purity of sin. It is well-known that Seetā, Śriāma's wife enjoys अग्निदिव्य to assertain her purity and loyality to her husband. Yet, the citizens of Ayodhyā raise the doubt about her purity of sin. Similarly, drinking the poison is a *divya* type of punishment[57], but in case of a person who can digest the poison it would not be the determiner of his purity of sin.

Furthermore, after enjoying the punishments such as fast, vrata etc., sinner is also free to do wrong behaviour. Besides, such type of punishments are spiritual and abstract in nature therefore, they would not be effective regarding the person who is habitual in bed conduct and the one who is heterodox will not be ready to enjoy such punishments. Kauṭilya, therefore does not describe such punishments, which may not prevent anti-duties of the any human being as such. In view of Kauṭilya , sinner is passive, who does not want to enjoy the punishment. He, therefore, does not describe the punishments which are purifier. On the other hand, Kauṭilya has described these punishment which prevent the sinner from the sinful acts for ever, and at the same time the sinner's enjoyment of punishment prohibits the sinless person from doing sinful act, since these punishments are mainly corporal in nature, and therefore are known by others also. We have seen above the various types punishments which are different in nature from those mentioned in G.D.S. These punishments are forceful, therefore, before the employment of daṇḍa[58], the king who wants to protect his subjects and his servants like a father, he should use other means which are different from दण्ड and are also useful in the primary stage. They are for examples as follows:

1. King should endure the small offence of government servants and honour them who are honest and righteous servants[59]. This behaviour of king may inspire others to be honest to the king and may prevent them from being disloyal to the king.
2. King should stop the sinner from his negligible offence of him, who has credited income[60], while he should properly punish the severe offence of a servant.
3. King should not punish who is ignorantly associated with the crime. Instead, king should give only warning to such a person[61].
4. King also should use the devices such as *sāma, dāna, bheda* etc. to check the embezzlement of the government servants[62].
5. King should appoint more than one officers in one department and transfer them from department to department so that they will get little chance to make a fraud[63].
6. King should appoint the different spies to keep watch on the doubtful activities of servants, since as it is difficult to know the fishes as drinking the water in ocean, so also the

act of stealing etc. of government servants could not be pointed out easily[64].

Furthermore, king should use his spy-organization to prevent the misconduct of the subjects. For example, the spies should organise the assembly near crowdy place such as chowk bazars etc. They will present the psecudo dramatic dialogues and preach the subjects to pay the tax to king and should prevent them from the hatred to king[65].

The spy-organization should also try to check the mis-conduct of common people. The spies should organize the dramatic events which may create an impression that the king is capable to search the criminal and he has also acquired the art of finding out the thieves[66].

These pre-punishments devices have been mainly used to prevent the anti-duties of subjects in general and of government servants in particular. Even then, if they do not stop their anti-duties then they are to be punished. In that case Kauṭilya gives distinct valuable information to the king for the employment of various types of punishments. It would be relevant to turn to this point in the following manner:

1. Kauṭilya has described the manner by which punishment will be used. In this regard, Kauṭilya takes into consideration the knowledge of human nature. Man as a social being, likes, prestigious status in the society. He wants renown, and he wants the honour as he is rich, generous in the society. Therefore, he tries to conceal his animal nature, which requires high efforts to control. He may fail there, and commits the crimes secretly[67], yet, sins never keep mum, and come to the foreground. Such sinful person who is recognised as righteous, wealthy man, should be punished in such a manner, that he will be ashamed of his misconduct. Kauṭilya, therefore emphasises that, king should use punishment for the sinful person by public declaration of his sin i.e. *avaghoṣaṇa* or *'udghuṣya'* of sins[68]. Besides, if we look the features of the punishments, it would become clear that the sinner's enjoyment of punishment could be easily known by the others, who will also know him as a sinner. Further more, people will also come to know the nature of enjoyments of punishment of

sins, and would not incline to commit the sin. Man enjoys the results of his social activities in the society only. Thus, king should declare the punishment, and employ them discriminately. Kauṭilya says— 'पुरुष' चापराधं च कारणं गुरुलाधवम्। अनुबन्धं तदात्वं च देशकालौ समीक्ष्य च। ऽत्तमावरमध्यत्वं प्रदेष्टा दण्डकर्मणि। राज्ञश्च प्रकृतीनां च कल्पदन्तरास्थितः (K.A. p. 322)

King should employ the punishment for sin with the discrimination of sin, and sinner's social status, age, gender, cause of the sin, object of the sin, severity of sin's results etc. In this regard, due to vastness of the subject, it would be better to deal with such illustrations which will illuminate Kauṭilya 's views in this respect.

King, in general, punishes in the form of *paṇa* (*dravya daṇḍa*) to the criminal government officers and servants yet, in case, the servant who commits a crime of stealing of precious stones from king's treasury, is punished by *chitraghāta*[69]. Similarly, sinner is killed for his sexual relationship with king's wife[70].

2. Regarding, the punishment to government servants, Kauṭilya does not take into consideration the caste, age gender of a criminal. Yet, he considers the caste, gender of the other party. For example, prison-officer is killed as he commits a crime of adultery regarding the Ārya lady prisoner[71].

King should use *upāṅṣu daṇḍa* for the principal government officers who are treasons and have league with king's enemy, since it is not possible to punish them in public[72].

Regarding the punishment for offences due to illegal contracts between or among the persons, Kauṭilya emphasises the sinner's social characteristics as caste, *āśrama*, gender, intention and nature of sin.

G.D.S. Manusmṛti say partial use of punishment. G.D.S. says, 'न शारीरो ब्राह्मणदण्डः ।' (2.3.43) Kauṭilya follows Dharmaśāstra by saying—सर्वापराधेष्वपीडनीयो ब्राह्मणः । (K.A; P. 314) Yet, he adds that king should declare the enjoyment of punishment as making the indicatory mark (चिन्ह) of his sin on Brāhmaṇa's forehead[73].

Kauṭilya describes the corporal punishment of *Brāhmaṇa* for his crime against king, or for having the desire of kingdom[74]. Thus, regarding sin against the king, Kauṭilya describes severe punishment to the sinner irrespect of his being a Brāhmaṇa or śūdra.

According to Kauṭilya, king should not severely punish the sinner who admits his sin due to his ignorance, hate, anger or because of having taken a drink[75].

Kauṭilya says also to consider gender of sinner before the employment of punishment[76]. Regarding the offences such as illegal sexual relationship between man and woman, Kauṭilya describes different punishments to man and woman. Woman is punished half of the fine of that fine to the man, for the same crime[77].

Kauṭilya considers woman offender simphathetically. If she is pregnant or who has given birth to infant, should not be cross-examined. In her case verbal examination only is prefered[78]. Yet, the woman looses her right of स्त्रीधन and शुल्क if she hates the king[79].

According to Kauṭilya, suicide is severe crime, the person whether man or woman would be punished by the punishment of deprival of rites after death[80].

Kauṭilya says that the judge should employ the punishment sympathetically, regarding virtueous people, asetics, diseased one, hungry, thirsty, tired, foreigner and the poor one[81].

Kauṭilya also describes different types of punishment only to वानप्रस्थ and पाषण्ड sinners[82]. It is the punishment of fast, and oblation for the sake of king's welfare.

Kauṭilya describes distinct punishment to the king who gives injustice, and does not punish to the sinner. Kauṭilya describes the punishment as fine to the king for his sin. King should offer that fine to the Lord *Varuṇa* who is the sovereign ruler of all kings[83]. While, G.D.S. describes प्रायश्चित्त as punishment to the king for the same sin.

Conclusion

Thus we have seen Kauṭilya's treatment to the notion of punishment. To put in brief, punishment is the king's power who has *vinaya*. King should employ the distinct punishments for sin with the knowledge of particularity of sinner and particularity of his sin. With this view Kauṭilya has given distinct categories of the sinners and distincts types and kinds of their offences.

Kauṭilya holds a view which is distinct from Gautama regarding the punishment. Gautama describes the purpose of purity of sin by the enjoyment of punishment. He gives much emphasis on expiatory punishments, and *prayaschittas, dānas, homas* rituals etc. Besides, Gautama emphasises sinner's self-confession of his sin in presence of king. While, Kauṭilya interprets the notion of punishment with the emphasis on the exhibition of king's political power through his employment of punishment. He does not however, emphasise the purity of sin. Further, Kauṭilya does not give stress on the sinner's self-confession of his sin, but on the king's scientific investigation into sin of a sinner. In addition to that, Kauṭilya differs from Gautama in employment of different types of punishment to the same person for the same offence, as it is said above. It explicitly shows the purpose of punishment according to Kauṭilya . He thinks of the economic growth of the state. Therefore, he has interest in finding out the sources of acquiring the money such as different taxes. With this view also he describes the punishment in the form of money (पण). All other types of punishment are substitutable with some special exceptions by the punishment of fine (द्रव्यदण्ड). He describes injurious punishment (*vadha* or *chitraghāta*) for sin against king or government servant's crimes against Ārya lady (prisoner). Kauṭilya holds also a distinct view from Manu. Manu thinks of welfare of particular class of the society. He interprets social welfare in terms of particular class of society, while welfare of other than that class and of its members is subordinate to it. On the contrary, Kauṭilya thinks, that society which does not emphasise the welfare of particular class of society as such, yet according to him entire society is to be uplifted. Further, Kauṭilya mentions severe punishments even to Brāhmaṇa for his sin like that of śūdra against the king and has successfully tried to soften the awareness of social differences among the members of the society. He considers the society from economic point of view. Economic growth of the state is achieved only when there is equity among the members. Kauṭilya tries to establish equity among members through political power. He considers the human beings as a unit of state who help to achieve the stability of king's power and social welfare.

In this regard, the person whether *Brāhmaṇa* or *Śūdra,* man or woman, have their valuable contribution to the State. Therefore, Kauṭilya gives stress on chanellising the human action so that it would lead to welfare and stability of state, with this view, punishment is one of the means to the fulfillment of the social needs. Kauṭilya's perspective of human knowledge and his cognisance of man's importance, should be a guide-line to the modern social thinkers also who want to get the solutions to the social problems and find ways to social progress through human capacities and human relationships.

Notes

1. 'ब्रह्महसुरापगुरुतल्पगमातृपितृयोनिसंबन्धगास्तेन नास्तिकनिन्दित-कर्माभ्यासिपतितान्याग्यपतितत्यागीनः पतिताः ।', 'पातकसंयोजकाश्च', तैश्चाब्दं समाचरन् । G.D.S. 3.3., 2,3. Patita is the one who is deviated from his own's duties. G.D.S. describes deviation i.e. पतन saying द्विजातिकर्मभ्यो हानिः पतनम्, तथा परत्र चासिद्धिः । 3.3.4-5.
2. पञ्चविधो धर्मः वर्णधर्म, आश्रमधर्म उभयधर्मो गुणधर्मो नौमित्तिक (धर्म) श्चेति ।– अभिषेकगुणयुक्तस्य प्रजापालनादि गुणधर्मः । मिताक्षरा, G.D.S., 3.1.1.
3. वर्णधर्मांश्च हि न्यायतो अभिरक्षेत् । दमनादित्याहुस्तेनादान्तान् दमयेत् ।, G.D.S., 2.2.9, 28
4. दण्डस्य हि भयात् सर्व जगद्भोगाय कल्पते ।, म. स्मृ., 7.22.
5. सुविज्ञातप्रणीतो हि दण्डः प्रजा धर्मार्थकामैर्योजयति ।, K.A., p.12.
6. अप्रवृत्तौ प्रायश्चित्ती सः ।, G.D.S., 2.3.45. see- प्राप्तानिमित्तदण्डाकर्मणि राजानमेनः स्पृशति ।, Ā.D.S., 2.11.28.
7. अदण्डयदण्डने राज्ञो दण्डस्त्रिंशद्गुणोऽम्भसि ।
   वरुणाय प्रदातव्यो ब्राह्मणेभ्यस्ततः परम् ।
   शास्ता हि वरुणो राज्ञां मिथ्या व्याचरतां नृषु ।।
   (K.A. p. 334)
8. रक्षार्थमस्य सर्वस्य राजानमसृजत्प्रभुः ।,
   इन्द्रानिलयमाकणिामग्नेश्च वरुणस्य च ।
   चन्द्रवित्तेशयोश्चैव मात्रा निर्हृत्य शाश्वती । ।, M. 7.3,4

यस्मादेषां सुरेन्द्राणां मात्राभ्यो निर्मितो नृपः ।
तस्मादभिभवत्येष सर्वभूतानि तेजसा ।। M.S. 7.5

तस्यार्थे सर्वभूतानां गोप्तारं धर्ममात्मजम् ।
ब्रह्मतेजोमयं दण्डमसृजत्पूर्वमीश्वरः ।। M.S. 7.14

9. विद्याविनीतो राजा हि प्रजानां विनये रतः ।
अनन्यां पृथिवीं भुङ्क्ते सर्वभूत हिते रतः ।।, K.A., p. 14

10. महायसाध्यं राजन्वं चमुमेक न वर्तते ।, K.A. p. 17

11. चोरग्रहणी विद्यामधीते राजा, तस्योपदेशादिमे चोरा गृहीताः, भूयश्च ग्रहीष्यामि---एष राज्ञः प्रभावः ।, K.A. p. 302-303.

12. तीक्ष्णदण्डा हि भूतानामुद्वेजनीयो भवति । मृदुदण्डः परिभूयते । यथार्हदण्डः पूज्यते । सुविज्ञानप्रणीतो हि दण्डः प्रजा धमर्थिकामैर्योजयति । स तेन गुप्तः प्रभवतीति ।, K.A.., p. 12.

13. Compare
पुरुषशक्त्यपराधानुबन्धविज्ञानाद्दण्डानियोगः ।,
G.D.S., 2.3.48.

14. K.A. Adhyakṣapracāra, (Adhikaraṇa, 2) Kaṇṭaka śadhanam (Adhikaraṇa, 4)

15. K.A. Dharmasthiyam, K.A. (Adhikaraṇa 3)

16. K.A., Kaṅṭakaśodhanam (Adhikaraṇa 4)

17. K.A. Daṇḍakarmika m (Adhikaraṇa. 5)

18. प्रतिबन्धः प्रयोगो व्यवहारोऽवस्तारः परिहापणमुपभोगः परिवर्तनमपहारश्चेति कोशक्षयः ।, K.A., p. 92

19. तेषां हरणोपायाश्च त्वारिंशत् ।, K.A., p. 94.

20. प्रचारचरित्रसंस्थानान्यनुपलभमानो हि प्रकृतः समुदय मज्ञानेन परिहापयति, उत्थान क्लेशासहत्वादात्वस्थेन शब्दादिष्वन्द्रियार्थेषु प्रसक्तः प्रमादेन, संक्रोशाधर्मानर्थभीरुभयेन, कार्यार्थिष्वनुग्रहबुद्धिः कामेन, हिंसाबुद्धिः कोपेन, विद्याद्रव्यवल्लभापश्रयाद् दर्पेण, तुलामान तर्कगणितान्तरोपाधानास्त्लोभेन ।,
K.A., p., 9.

21. मूलहरतादावित्वकदर्याश्च प्रतिषेधयेत् ।, K.A. p., 98

22. एवं चोरानचोराख्यान् वणिक्काकुशीलवान् ।
भिक्षुकान् कुहकांश्चान्यान् वारयेद्देशपीडनात् ।।,

K.A.. p. 291.

23. आरब्धारस्तु हिंसायां गूढाजीवस्त्रयोदश ।, K.A., p. 301

24. राजानमवगृह्योपजीविनः शत्रुसाधारणा वा ये मुख्याः राज्योपघातिनस्तु वल्लभाः संहता वा ये मुख्याः ।, K.A., p. 335.

See, त्यजेत्---राजधातकं---, G.D.S., 3.2.1.

25. K.A. Dharmasṭhiyam (Adhikaraṇa 3)

26. अनुज्ञानं वा वेदवित्समावायवचनाद्वेदवित्समवाय वचनात् ।, G.D.S. 2.3.49

27. पूतो वधमोक्षाभ्याम् ।, G.D.S., 2.3.48.

28. शौचाशौचममात्यानां राजा मार्गेत सत्त्रिभिः ।, K.A., p. 25., अपसर्पेणैवोपलभ्येतेति कौटिल्यः ।, K.A., p. 97.

29. प्रदेष्टारस्त्रयोऽमात्याः कण्टकशोधनं कुर्युः । K.A., p. 286

30. सगोपस्थानिको बाह्यं प्रदेष्टा चोरमार्गणम् ।
कुर्यान्नागारिकश्चान्तदुर्गे निर्दिष्टहेतुभिः ।। K.A., p. 308.

31. एवमर्थचरान् पूर्वं राजा दण्डेन शोधयेत् ।

K.A. p., 319.

32. See topics – गूदजीविनां रक्षा
सिद्धव्यंजनैर्माणवप्रकाशनम् ।
शंकारूपकर्माभिग्रहः आशुमृत परीक्षा
वाक्कर्मानुयोगः । K.A. Chapter – Kanṭakaśodhanaṁ

33. दृश्यते ह्यचोरोऽपि चोरमार्गे यद्दच्छया संनिपाते चोरवेषभाण्डसामान्येन गृह्यमाणश्चोरस्योपवासेन वा यथाऽणिमाण्डव्यः कर्मक्लेशभयादचोरः 'चोरोऽस्मि' इति ब्रुवाणः । K.A., p., 312-313.

34. देवब्राह्मणतपस्विबालवृद्धव्याधितानामभिसरतां धर्मस्थां कार्याणि कुर्युः, न च देशकालभोगच्छलेनातिहरेयुः । K.A., p. 285.

35. Kauṭilya considers daṇḍa as one of the sources of income. He says 'शुल्कं दण्डः....आदेयं च दुर्गम् ।' K.A., p. 83. Therefore, He gives much more importance to this type of daṇḍa.

36. एते शास्त्रेष्वनुगताः क्लेशदण्डाः महात्मनाम् ।
अक्लिष्टानां तु पापानां धर्म्यः शुद्धवधः स्मृतः ।। K.A., p. 325.

37. .....प्रकाशमशक्याः प्रतिषेद्धुं दूष्याः तेषु धर्मरुचिरुपांशुदण्डं प्रयुञ्जीत ।, K.A., p. 335.
38. तेषामयः शुलेन यावतः पणानभिवदेयुस्तावन्तः शिफापप्रहाराः दण्डः ।, K.A., p. 291.
39. K.A. p. 314, 316.
40. आद्विपादमूल्यादिति षट्पणः गोमयभस्मना वा प्रलिप्यावघोषणम् ।, K.A. p. 316.
41. K.A. p. 316
42. -----न स्मशानविधिस्तेषां न संबन्धिक्रियास्तथा । K.A., p. 311
43. -----यावन्तः पणा दण्डास्तावती रात्रीः क्षपणाभिषेकाग्निकार्यमहाकच्छवर्धनानि राज्ञश्चरेयुः । – – – –
ते यथास्वमुपवासव्रतैराराधयेयुः.... ।, K.A., p. 274.
44. तस्य निष्क्रियणानि जपस्तपो होम उपवासो दानम् ।, G.D.S., 3.1.11.
45. निश्चित्य तपसोऽनुष्ठानं प्रायश्चित्तम् । तथा चाङ्गिराः प्रायो नाम तपः प्रोक्तं चित्तं निश्चय उच्यते । तपो निश्चयसंयोगात्प्रायश्चित्तमिति स्मृतम् । Mitākṣarā on G.D.S., 3.4.1.
46. आक्रोशानृतहिंसासु त्रिरात्रं परमं तपः ।, G.D.S., 3.4.1.
47. अभोज्यभोजनेऽमेध्यप्राशने वा निष्पुरीषीभावः ।, G.D.S. 3.5.23.
48. असत्यवाक्ये वारुणीमानवीभिर्होमः ।, G.S.S., 3.5.28.
49. हिरण्यं गौर्वासौऽश्वो भूमिस्तिला घृतमन्नमिति देयानीति ।, G.D.S., 3.1.16.
50. अग्नौ सक्ति ब्रह्मघ्नास्त्रिरवच्छातस्य ।, G.D.S., 3.4.2.
51. सुरापस्य ब्राह्मणस्योष्णामासिञ्चेयुः सुरामास्ये मृतः शुद्ध्येत् ।, G.D.S., 3.5.1.
52. लिङ्गं वा सवृषणमुत्कृत्याञ्जलावाधाय दक्षिणाप्रतीचीं व्रजेदजिह्ममाशरीरनिपातात् ।, मृतः शुध्येत् । G.D.S 3.5.10-11.
53. अभिषेकाग्निकार्यमहाकच्छवर्धनानि राज्ञश्चरेयुः ।
– – – – ते यथा स्वमुपवासव्रतैराराधयेयुः । ....K.A., p. 274.
54. Hivargaon kar, B.R., Kauṭiliya Arthaśāstra, Introduction, (J.S. Karandikar) p. 35.
55. See, above page 9.
56. Footnote No. 51.
57. Kaṇe, P.V.
58. पितेव अनुगृह्णीयात् ।, K.A. p. 67

59. अपराधं सहेताल्पं तुष्येदस्पेऽपि चोदये।
महोपकारं चाध्यक्षं प्रग्रहेणाभिपूजयेत्।, K.A.; p. 95.
यश्चैषां यथादिष्टमर्थं सविशेषं वा करोति स्थानमानौ लभते। p. 97.

60. सचेद्राजार्थमुपनयत्यल्पापराधे वारयितव्यः महति यथापराधं दण्डयितव्यः।, K.A.., p. 97.

61. अज्ञाते परिभाषणम्।; K.A. p. 82.

62. अतुष्टान् सामदानभेददण्डैः साधयेत्। K.A., p. 34.

63. बहुमुख्यमनित्यं चाधिकरणं स्थापयेत्। K.A., p. 99.

64. अर्थस्तथा ह्यर्थचरेण राज्ञः स्वल्पोऽप्यनाचरन्तो ज्ञातुं न शक्याः सालिलं पिबन्तः। युक्तास्तथा कार्यविधौ नियुक्ता ज्ञातुं न शक्या धनमाददानाः।, K.A., p. 99

65. K.A., p. 32-33.

66. See footnote 11.

67. Compare the phrase 'कर्माऽऽचक्षाणः' occurred in G.D.S. which emphasises sinner's confession of his sin.

68. K.A., p. 316.

69. चोराणामभिप्रघर्षणे चित्रो घातः।, K.A., p. 83.

70. सर्वत्र राजभार्यागमने कुम्भीपाकः।, K.A., p. 333

71. K.A; p. 319

72. K.A. p. 34, 335, 341.

73. तस्याभिशस्ताङ्को ललाटे स्याद् व्यवहारपातनाय, स्तेयेश्वा, मनुष्यवधे कबन्धः, गुरुतल्पे भगम्, सुरापाने मद्यध्वजः (G.D.S. declaires death punishment to Brāhmaṇa by pouring hot wine in his mouth.). ब्राह्मणं पापकर्माण मुद्घुष्याङ्कृतव्रणम्। K.A., p., 314-315.

74. राज्यकामुकमन्तःपुरप्रघर्षकमटव्यमित्रोत्साहकं दुर्गराष्ट्रकोपकं...ब्राह्मणं तमः प्रवेशयेत्। K.A., p. 324.

75. सचेत्कोपं मदं मोहं वाऽपदिशेद् यथोक्तवधदण्डमेनं कुर्यादिति कौटिल्यः।, K.A; p. 276.

76. पुरुषं चापराधं च कारणं गुरुलाघवम्।
अनुबन्धं तदात्वं च देशकालौ समीक्ष्य च।।

अुत्तमावरमध्यत्वं प्रदेष्टा दण्डकर्मणि ।

राज्ञश्च प्रकृतीनां च कल्पयेदन्तरास्थितः । K.A., p. 322

77. सकामायां चतुष्पञ्चाशत्पणो दण्डः स्त्रियास्त्वर्धदण्डः ।, K.A. p. 326

78. विषदायकं पुरुषं स्त्रियं च पुरुषघ्नीमपः प्रवेशयेदगर्भिणीम्, गर्भिणीं मासावरप्रजाताम् ।, ...K.A; p. 325.

आप्तदोषं कर्म न कारयेत्, न त्वेव स्त्रियं गर्भिणीं सूतिकां वा मासावरप्रजाताम्, स्त्रियास्त्वर्धकर्म, वाक्यानुयोगो वा । p. 313.

79. राजाद्विष्य.....स्त्रीधनानीतशुल्कानामस्वाम्यं जायते स्त्रियाः ।, K.A., p.224

80. K.A., p. 311

81. तीर्थकरतपस्वी व्याधितः क्षुत्पिपासाध्वक्लान्तस्तिरोजनपदो दण्डखेदी निष्किंचनश्चानुग्राह्याः ।, K.A., p. 285.

82. See footnote 43.

83. See footnote 7.

References

1. Bhat, Yashvant A., (Tr.): (1970), Kane P.V., History of Dharma Śastra (Marathi), Maharashtra rajya sahitya sanskriti Manal, Bombay
2. Belvalkar S.K. (Edr): Śantiparva (Mahabharat), BORI, Pune.
3. Bühler, G. (Edr.): (1932): Āpastambadharmasūtram. (Ā.D.S.)
4. Das, Motilal B. (Pubr): (1964), Shrimad Bhagavadgītā, Śrī Śankarācārya granthāvali, 2nd volume Delhi
5. Hivargaonkar, V.B. (Tr.) (New Ed. 1988) Kauṭilīyam Arthaśāstram.
6. Kangle R.P. (Tr.), : (1982): Kautiliyom Arthaśāstram. (K.A.) (Marathi), Maharashtrarajya sahitya sanskriti Mandal Bombay.
7. Pandey, Umeshchandra, (Tr.): (1966) Gautama dharmasūtra mitāksarāvrttisahitā, (G.D.S.) Kashi Sanskrit book series, No. 172, Varansi.
8. Panshikar, V.L. (Edr.): (1920) Shri Manusmṛti (M.S.), Nirnay Sagar Press, Bombay.

18

Priests and their Role in the Society

Ganesh Prasad Panda

Priesthood is found in almost all civilizations in the world. Even among the uncivilized, as 'Encyclopaedia of Religion and Ethics' observes-"Priesthood among uncivilized includes not only the priests proper, who conduct the religious rites and the communication with gods, but also magicians, sorceresrs, etc., who practice magic i.e. utilize impersonal forces acting in accordance with certain fixed rules"[1]. It is a very common tendency existing among people that they expect some kind of superhuman assistance for the better results in their life. But, in many cases they themselves think unable to communicate directly with the gods or supernatural beings. Acknowledging their inability in this respect they regard certain higher personalities trained in such deeds, as their only medicators. This is the psychology behind the origination of priesthood in different civilizations of the world. Therefore, the origin of priesthood certainly goes back to Pre-historic age.

Thus in a way Priests are the protectors of common man. They protect ordinary persons from misfortunes arising out of the anger of the god or witchcraft. So, the principal duty of the priests is to administer, or give advice as to, worship of gods. As all gods do not stand in the same relation to men, the assistance of the priests must often be called into point out the special deities to whom people shall offer their sacrifices[2].

In Hinduism, the Sanskrit term *'purohita'* for priest and the concept of priesthood *'purohiti'* or *'purohitya'*[3] are certainly pre-vedic. The first *mantra* of Ṛgveda begins as: ॐ अग्निमीळे पुरोहितं यज्ञस्य देवमृत्विजम्। होतारं रत्नधातमम् (Ṛv. 1.1.1). The etymologies of the two terms *'Purohita'*[4] and *'purodhas'*[5] as found in the ancient *Kośas* and their commentaries for priest reveal the importance of him. The *Sāyaṇabhāṣya* on Ṛv. I 55.3 explains the term *purohita* as

पुरोहितः पुरस्थादवस्थापितः 'he who is placed in front'. Sāyaṇa explains all the grammatical peculiarities of the term[6] under *Ṛv* I.44.10. The etymology and definition of the term *'purohita'* found collected in various classical lexicographical works[7] almost repeat similar qualities of a *purohita*.

The present paper is a retrospective study of the position of priest and priesthood in Hinduism with relation to society starting from early Vedic times. The paper aims at studying the relevant points of such references available through textual sources. Each significant point here is supported with textual evidences. For the sake a systematic representation, the paper has been divided into three parts: I, II, and III. The first part discusses the role of priests as found in Vedic literature. The second part deals with the position in Post-Vedic works and the third one deals with the Priests and priesthood in recent times..

Section I

(i) *The ability and importance of priests as found in Vedic literature*

Priests were playing predominant role in Vedic Society. So, certainly their qualifications, ability and morale were high. *Ṛgveda* IV, 50.8 declares that people themselves pay respect to the king, of whom the Brahmin goes before[8]. Priests were always shown side by side with the kings. As kings were having authority over political matters so the priests over all spiritual or sacred matters. The relation between kings and *purohitas* is so much close as their relation has been described as between husband and wife[9]. The *Aitareya Brāhmaṇa* 7.26.[10] speaks of *purohitas* as half of the king. This shows their association. A *purohita* in the *Śukla-Yajurveda* 11.81 speaks of his ability and importance as under:

संशितं मे ब्रह्म संशितं वीर्यं बलम् ।
संशितं क्षत्रं जिष्णुः यस्याहमस्मि पुरोहितः ।।

Again, the *Śukla-Yajurveda* 9.23 declares the self-reliance and awareness of *purohitas* as: 'वयं राष्ट्रे जागृयामः पुरोहिताः ।।' There are numerous stories telling about the kings saved by their *purohitas* while the former were in distress. For instance, Divodāsa, the king was saved by his *purohita* Bhāradwaja, while he was in trouble[11].

The office of Priests was so much dignified that the sacrifices like *Vājapeya* and *Bṛhaspatisava* were prescribed for one who desired for this office[12]. It shows the importance of that office. But, we do not have sufficient evidence to say that the persons other than a Brāhmin (by cast) were ever empowered to have controlled this office. Moreover, we also cannot say that among the Brāhmins all were able to carry on this dignified profession of priesthood. So, only a few Brāhmin students were initiated into this profession only after an approved term of appenticeship with a master[13]. The scanning was again in two levels, i.e. during the training in *gurukula* and during the selection of priests by *Yajamāna* before any ritual begins[14]. This reminds us the kinds of priests appointed for ritualistic matter.

Kinds of Priests

Among the priests, some were accepted as regular priests called domestic priests or *Kula-purohitas* and other kinds of priests were irregular or occasional; called for rituals if they are qualified for it. The term *'Purohita'* mainly refers to the first kind of priests whereas the terms like *Ṛtvij* or *Yājaka* are found for this officiating priests[15]. Each family or dynasty had a family priest[16].

Priest and Priesthood or Prominent Duties of Priests

Some of the prominent duties of a priest can be listed as followed: (i) Officiating at sacrifices (ii) to accompany kings to battle-field or prayers for the king (iii) to act as Ratnin at the caronations of the king (iv) Receiving of gifts etc.

(1) During the sacrifices, the *Purohita* of that particular king or *jajamāna* was engaging other officiating priests[15A] and he himself was acting as a superintendent. It is known from the literary sources that in the early vedic times, when the function of *hotā* was very important one, the *purohita* himself was retaining that in his hand[16], but later when on account of the complications in the sacrifices the office of the Brahman became more important, he himself took the charge of that office leaving the earlier office[17]. Accordingly, other officiating Priests were chosen.

Normally, it is observed that Sacrifices were performed on

behalf of *kṣtriyas*, particularly kings or by Brāhmins[18]. It was the principal duty of the king's chaplian (another word for priest) to look after the sacrifices on behalf of the kings for the sake of welfare and prosperity of both cattle and agriculture of the king himself and the people[19]. Many such vedic passages speak about the effect of sacrifice and sacrificial prayers. Through the sacrifices, the priest has made kings worthy of heaven and full of life[20]. The vedic prayers of priest has eradicated epidemics from the society[21]. There are also a number of Ṛgvedic references which speak of gods being pleased by his prayers showered rain for the crops[22] and drought was averted through the magical *mantras*. These are also corroborated with Atharvavedic hymns[23].

(2) Apart from taking part in Sacrifices, *purohita* was accompanying king to battle-field[24]. *Purohita* was needed to decide the right hour and right direction etc. for war. In *Aitareya Brāhmaṇa*[25], the *purohita* is also called as *rāṣṭragopā* (Protector of the realm), the protector of king's power over his subjects and his safty and victory in the battles. It has already been stated[26] that there are examples in the Vedas which speak of kings saved their *purohitas*. There are references of *purohitas* taking part in actual war along with their kings. For instance, Viswamitra joined Sudās enemies and took part in the attack of ten kings against him, while Vaśiṣṭa assisted him[27]. But, leaving apart a few instances like this, priests were praying god for the victory of the kings so that the spiritual power can help kings in winning the war.

(3) Another importance of king's chaplain (*purohita*) was that he was a dynamic and leading member of *ratnahabiṁsi*[28] (a rite at the time of consecreation ceremony). Ṛgveda X. 173. 4-6 mentions that a priest was supposed to consecrate the king at the coronation ceremony[29]. The important thing there is along with the consecration of the new king, the descent (*ārṣeva*) of his *purohita* is also declared[30].

(4) A *Purohita* is also famous as an *ādāyī* 'receiver of gifts'[31]. *Aitareya Brāhmaṇa* 6.45 describes the necessity of *dakṣiṇā* (gift) in following words: Just as cart does not move without a bull, similarly a sacrifice does not move without *dakṣiṇā* (gift). Emphasising the importance of offering gifts to Brahmins the *Śat. Brāhmaṇa* II. 2.2.6 (also IV. 3.4.4.) says—"the sacrificial gifts are for gods and gifts are for human gods. . . these two gods, if satisfied, can transfer them into heaven".

Apart from these above duties, a *purohita* is also famous as a well-wisher of kings[32] and common people. He is an advisor to king[33]. He always keeps vigilant watch over the polity so that no *adharma* can creep in.

Section II: Priests in Post Vedic Literature

As we shift to Post vedic literature, we find the same as due importance was given to *purohitas*. But, as the nature of propitiating god was changing into more and more in the form of idol worships, the *purohitas* were appointed for such activities apart from fire worship. Priests in Post-vedic literature are found with more defined character and qualities. Over and above the rituals related to more spiritualistic results, a *purohita* was related to king as a practical guide. A *purohita* was a real friend, philosopher and guide to the king. Kauṭilya has defined the nature and qualities of a *purohita* in following words— "Him whose family and character are regulated by the rules as laid down in the Śāstras, who is fully trained in the Vedas and the *aṅgas*, in the reading of portents providential and accidential; in the prevention of calamities providential and human, in performing such expiatory rites as one prescribed in the *Atharvaveda*, the king shall employ as a high priest[34]".

Kings were advised to obey their *purohita* as a student his teacher, a son his father or a servant to his master[35].

As it has been already stated that a *purohita* was related to king with various capacities, so naturally he was discharging his duties from various levels. In addition to his regular priesthood, he was also an ideal teacher for the prince. It is said that a prince can be prevented from wrong or evil deeds only by ministers or *purohita*[36]. Purohita was guiding prince in *Śāstra* and in conducting necessary rites upto *cūḍākaraṇa*[37].

Again as he was discharging the multi-farious duties, due to his knowledge in Astrology, he was also expected to guide kings the proper timings of starting auspicious works[38].

Further, the art of battle was, in part, based on magical practices originating from *Atharvaveda*, so naturally the *purohita* had to be proficient in this art also[39]. Thus, *purohita* was a great guide to king in preparation of war.

In addition to these above duties, a *purohita* was also a guide to king while latter was falling sick. A Vaidya was approaching king through *purohita*. Purohita was there called a *mantraviśārada*[40] as the *vaidya* is called a *rasaviśārada*[41].

Section III: The Priests and Priesthood in our Recent Times

Those were the days of kings and whatever has been said so far in two sections is a part of history. Coming to our recent times, we generally find two types of priests i.e.

(1) Priests in temples (also in other charitable organizations)
(2) and Priests working in rural and urban life of people.

The first kinds of priests are seen working in Hindu temples and in other such pilgrimages. Their rights and duties are guided by the instructions of the concerned administrations or by the tradition existing therein. The other types of priests work for people in general. They are invited for ceremonial rites and for different Hindu rituals performed time to time by the people.

The designations of priests in general are named differently as: *paṇḍā* (not to be confused with surname), *baḍapaṇḍā, purohita, nanā, paṇḍit, bhatji, brāhmaṇa, pūjārī, gurava* etc. Every term has significance in its circumstances. But, they all mean the mediatorship between human beings and supernatural world. Generally, these priests are brahmins except a few worshipping Śiva and different forms of *śakti* in some places.

In changing era of science and Technology, the Hindu rituals are slowly loosing their significance; so also the importance of priests is decaying day by day. Priests hold priesthood just because it is one of the ways of earning livelihood. The understanding of *mantras* is almost absent. *Mantras* are uttered almost in a parrot-like way, so also their follow ups are carried out in a mechanical way. But in spite of all, a longer part of Hindus believe in the traditions of this land. So, in this critical juncture of time, priests have a greater role to play. They must try to understand the significance of sacrificial and ceremonial rites to uphold the faith of people. The proper utterances of *mantras* with their applications must be kept intact with the tradition. This way they can revive the faith of people again. So far the priesthood in temples is concerned, it is one of the foremost duties of the concerned temple authorities (Endowments etc.) to look after the upliftment of the moral and spiritual standard of the priests working there in the temple. The exploitations of the priests in some of the Hindu temples in India today are well-known. The bad treatments of the priests or priestly class towards the devotees may create a stigma in the temple history of future India. Such bad treatments must be stopped with immediate effect. Thus, an atmosphere will be created in temple premises to have a free and fair thinking of God.

A kind of encouragement shown by the Central Government by instituting Priests (designated as Paṇḍits) and priesthood at Regimental temples is praiseworthy. Such Priests, apart from their regular worship at temples, attend soldiers under sentence, give special instructions to children and enlisted boys, minister to the sick in hospitals etc. and work for the welfare of the defence personals in general. However, the question again remains about their honesty and dedication. But it is certainly an evenue of a new opportunity which is to be explored by the priests.

Concluding Observations

From first two sections, we definitely can conclude that the role of *purohita* was very important one through the ages. He has served this land in various capacities as *ṛtvik*, jurist*, advisor, well-wisher, teacher, astrologer, technician and also as doctor (*mantraviśārada*). So far the third section is concerned, what more can be expected is—the betterment of present situation.

The main purpose behind instituting a spiritual authority even over the kings** was making a kingdom sound-functioning. It is because, all the political systems those directly contravene the law of the nature and liberties of spiritual power, are certainly short-lived. So, the great minds prepared a system where temporal power which a king symbolizes and the spiritual authority to which *Purohita* represents can work together for the betterment of society. Further, it can be noted that neither the kings, nor the *purohitas* were over and above the law, but, under certain conditions they had some privileges of enjoying more power and freedom than a common man. Moreover, the grivious mistake even in the part of a *purohita* was also noted down in the system of law and

* *Gau. Dh.* Su. 13.36

** Rolland, "A Few Vedico-Cettic Concordances", *VIJ*, XII, 1974: "The most striking feature is that the royal class and the sacredotal class in India go together as in celtic countries... But, the priests are given more dignity and importance than the kings. In numerous vedic passages mention is made of the superiority of the priest in relation to the king".

punishments were prescribed. It shows that Indian culture is basically democratic and never a plutocratic.

Of course, there are cases of exploitations, ill-treatments, etc. between kings and *purohitas*, *purohitas* and common man, but all such cases in turn were hazardous to the development of society. Kauṭilya in later times calls it an internal problem of a kingdom. The exploitations of Brāhmaṇas, particularly of *purohitas* as recorded in Buddhist *Jātakas* in a certain point of history, if any happened, due to the ill-practices of what has been prescribed in Hindu law.

Thus, *purohitas* have brought invisible result (*adṛṣṭa-phala*) i.e. through invoking mercy of God, and also created visible results (*dṛṣṭaphala*) in guiding the kings and kingdom at various capacities. What pitiable is the role and personality of *purohitas* today. His role in the society in our hoary past never meant what it generally means to a common man belonging to atler part of 20th century, but Indian heritage had a privilege of seeing him with dignity and never with mockery. Therefore, the personality and role of priests in recent times must be upgraded to the extent of reviving same faith (free from superstitions) and wisdom set by the Seers in this land of great culture. In this regard, it is not only *Purohitas* who are responsible for such degradation but also many other factors, i.e. time, lack of patronage etc.

Remarks

By the by, the study has given rise to five problems in my mind which I want to pose before the scholars:

(1) If it is a fact that Mahāmahopādhyaya P.V. Kane has exhausted all the materials and hardly anything remains to be said now, then the problem is whether all that we do are to be considered as futile exercises?

(2) Whether the धर्मशास्त्रिन्ऽ of present day who are लोके स्थित्वाऽपि न लौकिकाः as against वनौकसोऽपि लौकिकज्ञाः:can meet the challenges of the present day need. The question is also related to the compartmentalization of studies in educational pattern.

(3) Whether Dharmaśāstra here should essentially mean classical Hindu laws propounded in श्रुति and स्मृति literature or other *āgamic* and non-aryan sources can be sanctioned?

(4) Whether only on the basis of literature that are of Prescriptory in nature, can we decide a thing that was prevalent there or not?

(5) In what way this sort of seminars, discussions etc. which are confined to four walls can become effective in bringing about the real awareness among people in practical life?

Notes

1. *"Encyclopaedia of Religion and Ethics"*. Vol. X, P. 278.
2. *Ibid.*
3. *'Patyanta-purohitādibhyo yak'* (P.V. 1.128
4. Vide *Vyākhyāsudhā* (*Ramāśramī*) Commentary on *Amarakośa* 2.8.5: *puro dhīyate sma / ktaḥ* (P. 3.2.102)
5. Loc. cit.: *Puro ' gre dhīyate / `purasi ca* (U. 4.2.31) *iti dhāño ' siḥ*
6. *"Purohitaḥ / 'purvādharāvarāṇāmasi puradhavaścaiṣām* (P. 5.3.39) *iti asi pratyayāntaḥ puras Śabdaḥ / 'taddhitaścāsarvavibhaktiḥ* (P. 1.1.38) *iti avyayatvāt 'puro ' vyayam'* (P. 1.4.67) *iti gati samjñāyāṁ satyām Samāse 'gatiramantaraḥ' iti purvapadaprakṛtisvaratvam*.
7. Vide *Śabdacintāmaṇi* under the term *purohita*: *purodṛṣṭādṛṣṭaphaleṣu karmasu dhiyate āropyate yaḥ* (*ḍudhāñ/ktaḥ/dadhāter hiḥ*; also vide the definition under the same: *vedavedāṇgatattvajño japahoma-parāyaṇaḥ/āśirvādavacoyukto eṣa rājapurohitaḥ / / trayyāñ ca daṇḍanityāñ ca kuśalaḥ syāt purohitaḥ / atharvuvihitaṁ kuryānnityaṁ-śāntikapauṣṭikam / /*; The *Śabdakalpadruma* (3rd Part) notes the etymology of the term *prohita* as: *pura adav eva hitaṁ maṅgalam yasmāt /* The characteristic of a *purohita*, it points out as: *kāṇaṁ vyaṅgamaputraṁ vā ' nabhijñamajitendriyam / na hrasvaṁ vyādhitaṁ vā ' pi nṛpaḥ kuryāt purohitam / / purohito hito vedasmṛtijñaḥ satyavāk śuciḥ / brahmaṇyo vimalācāraḥ pratikarttā ' padāmṛjuḥ / /*
8. Vide Ṛv. 4.50.8: *"tasmai viśaḥ svayamevā namante yasmin brahmā rājani pūrva eti"*
9. Coomarswamy, A.K., *Spiritual Authority and Temporal power in the Indian Theory of Government*: "It may be said that the role of Indian theory implied and subsumed in the words of the marriage formula "I am that, than art This, I am sky, thow art Earth", etc. addressed by the Brāhman priest, the *purohita*, to the king in *AB*. VIII, 27", P.1.
10. *AB*. 7.26: *ardhāmo ha eṣa kṣatriyasya yat purohitaḥ*
11. *Pañcaviṁśa Brāhmaṇa* XV. 3.7; In *Jaiminīya Brāhmaṇa* III. 244-47 there is also another story narrating how king Kṣatra (son of Pratardana) was saved by Bhāradwaja (Indra came at Bharadwaja's request and saved Kṣatra).
12. *Sat*. V. 1.11.11; also *Tai. Br*. II. 7.1.2; *Pañ Br*. XVII. 11.4.
13. *Kauṣitaki Sūtra* 55; also vide *Āpastamba Dh. Sū*.(S.B.E.) P. 3.
14. (i) The *Āśvalāyana Gṛhyasūtra* 1.23, 1-2 emphasises on the physical fitness of the persons who are to act as priests and mentions that a sacrificer should select only those possesses neither loss or superfluous limbs,

taking into account the physique of the priest's mother and father. They should be young and strong.

(ii) Similarly, *Sāṅkhāyana* 5.1. 1-2 laid emphasis on the physical fitness of priests. Moreover, it also emphasises on intellectual requisite of the priests stating that a *yajamāna* should choose both young and learned as his priests.

15. *Manusaṁhitā* 7.78 refers to domestic and officiating priests as *purohita* and *Ṛtvij* respectively.

15A. Sharma, Rajendra Nath, *Brahmins Through the Ages* (P. 31) records the names of 17 vedic officiating priests as follows: *hotā, maitrāvaruṇa, acchāvaka, grabhāstubha, udgātṛ, prastotṛ pratihartṛ, Subrahmaṇya, adhvaryu, pratiṣṭhātṛ, neṣṭṛ, unnetṛ brahman, brahmanācchanŝin, agnidh, potṛ and Sadasya.*

16. Vide Macdonell and Keith, *Vedic Index*, Vol. II, 7.8.78.

17. *Ṛv.* II. 24.9, X. 143.3; *Ait. Br* 7.26; Tait. Saṁ III. 5.2.1.

18. P.II. 2.9: *'Yājakādibhiŝca'* implies that *'yājaka'* is compounded with the words Brāhmaṇa or kṣatriya (as *Brāhmaṇa-yājaka* or *kṣtriya-yājaka*)

19. *Vāj. Saṁ* XXIII. 2; *Tait. Saṁ* VII. 5.18; *Mait. Saṁ* III. 12.6; *Kāthaka Saṁ*, V. 5.14.

20. *Ait. Br.* VIII. 24

21 *Rv.* X. 98.

22. Ibid.

23. Vide Bloomfield: *Hymns of the Atharvaveda*, Introduction, 1XVII-1XVIII.

24. *Ṛgveda* VII. 18; *Āŝvalāyana Gr.* 3.12.

25. *AB* VIII. 18.24.25.

26. Vide *fn.* 11.

27. *Ṛgveda* VIII. 18.

28. *Tait. Saṁ* 1.8.9.1 and *Tait Br.* 17.3.1 mention the 9 *ratnins* as follows: *Brāhmaṇa (purohita, rājanya, senānī, suta, grāmaṇī kṣattr, Saṁgrāhitṛ, bhāgadugha* and *akṣavāka.*

29. also vide *Ŝat Br.* V. 3.1. 1-2 and *Ait. Br.* VIII. 21-23.

30. *Ait. Br.* VII. 25.

31. *Op. cit* 7.29.2.

32. *Ibid.* on 10.122.4: *Purohitaṁ purato hitakāriṇam.*

33. Vide *Sāyaṇabhāṣya* on 8.102.12: *kiṁ ca tvam devānāṁ purohitaḥ hitopadeṣṭāsi.*

34. *Arthaŝāstra* (*AŜ*) 1.9.5.

35. *Ibid* 1.9.10; but this also restricts monopoly in the part of a *purohita*

36. *AŜ.* 8.4.26.

37. *Manusaṁhitā* 2.140; *Yājñavalkyasmṛti* 1.34.

38. *AŜ.* 5.3.

39. *AŜ.* 10.3; 12.5; 14.3.15.

40. *Suŝrutasaṁhitā* (*sūtrasthāna*) ch. 34.
doṣāgantujamṛtyubhyo rasamantravŝāradau /
rakṣetāṁ nṛpatiṁ nityaṁ yatnād vaodyapurohitau / /
brahmāvedaṅgamaṣṭāṅgamāyurvedamabhāṣata / /
purohitamate tasmād varteta bhiṣagātmavān / /

41. *Ibid.*

19

Construction of the Court-Building Nyāyaśālā

Mrs. Rajani Patki

Natural instincts like hunger, thirst, sex etc.; are common to both: human beings and other animated world. Human beings are successful in subjugating these instincts. They formed a society and made the rules and regulations for their own behaviour, i.e. the code of conduct. Separate science is developed for formation of this code which is called Dharmaśāstra. With reference to Sanskrit literature, the Dharmasūtras discuss the rules of behaviour for the betterment of the humanity. The discussion contains various factors of the behaviour, such as day to day living, rules of Government, rules of social conduct and criminal laws. This discussion also occurs in the eighth chapter of Manusmṛti. There is a separate judicial branch of the Government which controls the behaviour of members of the social community. There is a separate forum for the convenience of the authorities who work in this judicial branch. That forum is called court, i.e. Nāyaśālā. The Nyāyaśālā is constructed according to the needs of operational working. Different types of constructions are cited in different Sanskrit books pertaining to that science, namely Viśvakarmā Vāstuśātra, Samarāṅgaṇa Śilpa, Mayamata etc. A brief introduction to the arrangement of Nyāyaśālā detailed out in Viśvakarmā Vāstuśātra is attempted in this paper.

The sixteenth and seventeenth chapter of the book 'Viśvakarmā Vāstuśātra', a book ascribed to Viśvakarmā, deals with the details of the construction of Nyāyaśālā. The author defines the Nyāyaśālā as:—

(i) It is a place, honoured by the kings, for the welfare of the world.
(ii) It is a sacred place, worthy for performance of religious vows

rather it is constructed at such a location, therefore, it is a 'Vratasthala' in its ethical sense.

(iii) It is accepted that there is presence of Gods at this place and it is endowed with all might, created for the protection of all beings.

The Nyāyaśālā has the following tasks to perform:—

1.—To ascertain/establish Dharma. 2.—To frame rules and administer them. 3.—To code ethics and enforce it. 4.—To protect the interest of the people. 5.—To preserve the character and integrity of the country.

To achieve these objectives of Nyāyaśālā, some proper authority is needed. The book describes the qualities of such an authorised person as follow—

He should be born in Kṣatriya race; he should possess the virtues like compassion, forbearance etc. He must be cool and calm by temperament; he should have the knowledge of laws and regulations. He must be aware of different branches of knowledge; he must have with him different kinds of eligible persons like Āmātya, Purohita i.e. minister and priests who know the procedures of law.

The different authorities appropriate for administration of justice: Nyāyaśālā are enumerated below—

1. Cakravarti-The sovereign emperor with unaccountable wealth.
2. Sārvabhaum a Universal monarch whose income is above hundred crores (of gold coins)
3. Mahārāja-A sovereign king whose income is upto hundred crores.
4. Bhūpāla-A king whose income is upto ten crores.
5. Sāmanta-A feudatory, tributory king or prince whose income is below one crore.
6. Pattadhara Yuvarāja-Heir apparent of the king.
7. Narendra-A petty king.

The different personalities who can associate with the presiding judge during the Nyāya session are enlisted as—

Sāmanta, Bhūpāla, Parivrājaka (a recluse or wandering sanyāsi), Naiṣṭhika Yogi, Taṭastha (impartial), Āmātya (minister), Senādhipati, Saciva (secretory), Kulaguru (master of the race), scholars in the different fields of knowledge, the heroes of the wars (occasional presence), apparent heir of the king.

The judging authorities are prescribed as per the status of the jurisdiction of the Nyāyaśālā. Cakravarti and Sārvabhauma king presides over in appex court (Pradhāna Nyāyaśālā). Other lower grade kings or head of the states chair in the Nyāyaśālā of their respective jurisdiction i.e. district level courts (Mukhya Nyāyaśālā). The other dignitories who are not kings preside over in Sādhāraṇa Nyāyaśālā, but in this case, they actually do not sit on the throne but discharge judicial duties in front of the empty throne kept on elevated platform (i.e. they act on behalf of the authority of the throne in representative capacity).

In every Nyāyaśālā throne is said to be compulsory, whether it is being actually occupied during the session or not. The thrones have specific designs and characteristic to indicate the status of the judiciary. The different designs prescribed for different levels of judges, also different designs of chairs (Āsana) are prescribed for particular kind of dignitories. Some of them are as—

Bhadrāsana for Sāmanta and Bhūpala; Kurmāsana for Yogi, Parivrājaka and Niyamavān; Vīrāsana for Senāpati; separate types of chairs for saciva, Kulagurun and scholars; Vijayāsana for heir apparent; benches for observers and witnesses. This is a standard pattern of seats in each type of Nyāyaśālā.

The Nyāyaśālā exists in palace as well as it is built in capital, city, town and villages etc.

1. Nyāyaśālā in the Palace

1. *Deśyā*—This is also called Sādhāraṇasabhā / Mānuṣi Sabhā / Grāmasabhā. It is held in the main building of the residence of the head of the village.
2. *Paurā*—It is also called Mukhyasabhā / Rājñi Sabhā / Paura Sabhā. It is held in the residence of the head of the city / town.
3. *Court in the Palace of the King*—It is also called Pradhānasabhā / Daivi Sabhā / Mahāśabhā.

2. Nyāyaśālā Outside the Palace

1. *Sādhāraṇasabhā*—It is held in the public place in village.
2. *Mukhyasabhā*—It is held in the public place in the city or town.
3. *Pradhānaśabhā*—It is held in the public place in the capital city.

Each of the six classes of Nyāyaśālā mentioned in the above paragraph are detailed out as below:—

1. Nyāyaśālā in the Palace

1 *Deśyā*

The platform of the Simhāsana is designed in different artistic forms, namely, Jagatipaṭṭa, Padmadala, Kampavājana etc. It is a raised platform called Vedikā. The main Simhāsana formed in the name of Sarvabhauma is thirty steps high, inspite of the presence of a sovereign ruler, this Simhāsana must be situated. The chair for chair person is fifteen or more steps high. The four doors of the main building are located at four directions. The construction of Nyāya centre and indoor arrangements should be useful for the working needs. The building should be constructed as per the instructions of the Bhūpāla, considering the standard rules. Upaśālā, Kośāgāra-treasury are the sub-parts of the main building. The architectural design can be circular, quandrangular or as the Bhūpāla prefers.

2. *Paurā* .

The construction of this Nyāyaśālā is respective to the person's designation and the work load. The specific design is prescribed for each one: Cakravarti, Sārvabhauma, Paṭṭadhara Yuvarāja, Narendra, Mahārāja, Māṇḍalika, Sāmanta and Bhūpāla. A particular design is identified with a particular chair person. The seats are also peculiar for each one. The seats are to be decorated with providing the design on the top called Śikhara, Vimāna; the artistic sculpture i.e. design of couples, peacock, swan, a creeper plant with flowers etc. The seat of Paṭṭadhara Yuvarāja and Bhūpāla do not have this artistic features.

Upaśālā, Bhadraśālā, Pūrvaśālā are constructed according to work load. Pūrvaśālā is designed half with the measurement of Madhyaśālā. It is located at the front of Madhyaśālā which is measured twelve daṇḍas. Upaśālā is designed with the half measurement of Pūrvaśālā.

The seat of Sāmanta and Bhūpāla is ten steps high, it has three tier structure. It has a pole for flag. The Vedikā where the chair person sits is called Devāsana. The seats for other important persons are arranged along all the sides. The design of the Vedikā is named as Āvartā, Padmadala, Kampavājana. Interior decoration shows the difference between them.

3. Court in the Palace of the King

This court is constructed in the inner part of the palace or in front of the temple of Kuldevatā. Or it should be a place where religious acts can be performed. This is a place where the Vedic scholars can have free access. The author recommends 'Vrata-Ratnākara' for further details.

These three types pertain to the inside parts of the residential building of the head of the village or town or capital. Therefore, no special architectural features are specified for the building of those structures. However, in case of the Nyāyaśālā in the public places, which will be discussed here-after, exaustive details of architectural arrangements of the building are specified.

2. Nyāyaśālā Outside the Palace

1. *Sādhāraṇa Sabhā*

It is also called Mānuṣi Sabhā / Grāma Sabhā. The idol of deity is placed in this court. The court exercises on tax collection, acceptance of taxes, enquiries of crimes etc. The judge belongs to that particular village, he must be a scholar in ethics; should not be lazy and he should possess qualities like compassion, forbearance etc.

The building of the court is built on the frame of twenty columns. Four columns are built at the four directions i.e. on East, West etc. Four columns should be placed in the centre of the building. Upaśālā and Kośāgāra should be posited as per directions. Arrangement of Āsanas is standard.

2. *Mukhya Sabhā*

It is called Rājñi-Sabhā / Paurā Sabhā. The idol of Bhūmipāla should be kept in that court. The throne of Sārvabhauma is placed here. This court works for the affairs, transactions, tax collections of hundred and eight towns. The judge is Bhūpāla or a Jurist or Mahipāla or educated and intelligent person.

The building of the court is constructed on twentyfour columns. Eight columns are located at the front portion, eight on back side, eight columns are build in circular arrangement. In that circle the Vedikā and throne above it should be built. The building must contain Kośāgāra, Upaśālā and Bhadraśālā. The arrangement of other seats is standard.

3. *Pradhāna Śālā*

It is also called Daivi Sabhā/Mahāśālā. The throne of Sārvabhauma is placed in this court. This court has to work for the affairs of many towns and villages situated nearby and far away. This court also enquires the matters concerned with Deśyā and Paurā court, as well as those connected with the Māḍalika court.

The judge is Cakravarti or Mahārāja, the main or supreme king. If the chair of a judge remains empty and no eligible king is available, then the judge should be elected according to the instructions given by Manusmṛti.

There are other persons who take part in actual working with the judge. Those are: the clerks who take notes etc.; saciva, impartial persons, Government officers; the representatives of Paurā and Deśyā Sabhas; Māṇḍalikas and other revered juries.

The building of the court is constructed on forty columns. This is a large building. The sixteen columns are placed in two rows at left side and two rows at right side. Eight columns are placed where the Simhāsana is recommended. These eight columns are covered with a roof. Four columns are located near the front main door of east, which is an entrance of the court. The building requires two floors or five or more, as per requirement of the working capabilities.

The Vedikā is forty steps high. The design of Kalaśa is decorated on the top of the Vedikā. The design of Simhāsana is made with Pāncāla style or with blending of many other styles of construction. The entrance of Vedi is decorated with Śikhara, Vimāna etc. The building has two and more main and sub entrances. The vast place is recommended for the arrangement of many seats, benches along with mats. Each seat is decorated with carving the designs of faces of lion, elephant, horse etc.; along with other beautiful art. The Vedikā is also fully decorated with sculpture, carvings etc.

The author details out the specifications of the throne: Simhāsana of Supreme court in a separate section. The description follows:

Simhāsana

A Simhāsana or the judicial throne has the shape of a lion, its hight is prescribed to be one, two or three hand meters or suitable for the size of the hall. There should be pieces of wood fixed as hand rests. There should be border planks called 'Catuṣkūta'. It is four pinnacles. Jewels should be inled in the frontal of the hand rest called 'Caturnetra'. The hight of the back rest should be more than half, that is three hand meters if the seat is two hand meters above the surface or else the hight should be proportionate to five meters. There should be a top for resting the head and around that there should be varied pictures of the Sun, the Moon or circular halow, and the top should have a crowning. Below the plank of the seat there should be series of Bambara (dwarfs?), motifs holding supporting planks on all the four sides. There should be two or three planks with pictures. On the faceds of the supporting planks on the four legs there should be fixtures of golden and silver jingling bells. On the throne, having prepared a silken cushion cover, nine gems should be woven on four sides in the order : on the left five Rubies, one Gomeda one cat's eye gem (Vaiḍurya), one diamond and one Padmarāga (Topaz). In the middle plank, their should be a chain woven with various gems and golden bells in the shape of an arch. On the rear plank there should be one white staff meant to support a canopy. On that canopy there should be a decorative pattern of Aṅga, Vaṅga, Kaliṅga, Kosala, Pāñcāla, Magadha, Śūrasena, Kuru, Kekaya and other styles.

The pedastle of the throne-It should have generally one meter measurement on all four sides or it should have six golden steps on front side and two bands on back side, or it may have three golden bands on all the four sides and nine jewels studded silver or gold plates on four corners. There may be a pictursque motif named 'Catuṣkarṇa'. There should be the motifs of Indrs, his son Jayanta, Vaiśravaṇa or Kuber, serpent or cobra faces and deities in pairs. On the pedastle, there should be a small platform on the left side for placing the sword. It should be constructed with conventional characteristics.

20

Worship of Deities and its Social Relevance

P.K. Acharya

Man's development depends upon worship, because man is not satisfied with *Karma* which results into both pain and pleasure. If matter is developed into consciousness due to the motion of matter-as a materialist propounds, then the consciousness further opens its unlimited realm of bliss by its own expansion called 'worship' or "*upāsanā*". "*Samāna-cittavṛtti-santānakaraṇam*,-as writes Acharya Sankar in his introduction to the *Chāndogya upanisadbhāsya*[1].

Three things are exposed in the Vedas: *Karma, Upāsanā* and *Jñāna*. In a *Karma,* the performance is predominantly physical. When the physical ingredients are ommited and the act is purely mental, it is called *upāsanā*. Further, when the existing fact is spontaneously revealed by the fulfillment of the conditions for its rise, it is called *jñāna*[2].

Leaving aside the measurement of the cultural, political, economical or social purposes of deity worship, such as the great Balagangadhara Tilak started the worship of Gaṇeśa in Maharastra, if we limit the scope of this topic to the philosophical aspects of social relevance of deity worship, and if at east two or three schools of thought on each of these three important words (*worship, deity and society*) are taken into consideration, then the topic will cover at least (2 x 2 x 2) eight or (3 x 3 x 3) twenty seven schools of thought. For, each of these three concepts is as much complex as these three words owe to their different schools of thought. For example, the concept 'society' in a Community Society differs from that of a Humanistic Society. Therefore, the topic will be limited to the worship as it is prevalent amongst the present Hindu societies with special reference to the Advaita Vedānta and Kashmir Śaiva scriptures.

There are various types of worship like determinate (*saguṇa*) or inderterminate (*nirguṇa*); *bheda* or *abheda*; in difference (*aparā*) or *parā* (absolute); vide, *prathamā pratimā pūjā,japastotraṇi madhyamā, uttamā mānasipūjā, sohampūjottamottamā.*

Whatever may be the mode of worship, just as raising one's hand or led is though an action, yet it turns to be a step of Yoga when that action, say raising leg (*Śirśāsana*), is performed with the awareness of it. Otherwise, a monkey's *Śirśāsana* could also be called yoga. Similarly, all modes of worship must be oriented towards the transformation of the worshipper's consciousness. Otherwise, an elephant's garlanding the statue of Gaṇeśa in circus, could also be called worship.

History

The present procedure for worshipping the deities, mainly the five viz, Śiva, Śakti, Viṣṇu, Gaṇeśa and Sūrya, the deities of the five Hindu Tantras, follows a common system. Whether its origin is whether Vedic or non-Vedic is a matter of dispute. Worship was a common practice in the Vedas for which the *Nighanṭu* enumerates forty four verbs that have the sense of 'worship'. Among these, *Yajāmahe* (Ṛg. 7.59.12), *dhīmahi* (Rg. 3.62.10), ile (1.1.1) *arādhi, pūjayati* etc. are included. The common words for worship are *āradhanā, arcanā, ūpāsanā, paricaryā, varivasyā and samāsrayaṇa* etc. The *Nirukta* explains *supāṇi* and says people worship gods by joining their hands together. "Long before Panini there had arisen professional men who made their livelihood by attending on images and that temples of deities must have existed even in the fourth-fifth century B.C.[3]. About idols, Pāṇini's *sūtra* (*jīvikārthe cāpanye*, 5.3.99) speaks about those images which are to be sold. Patañjali explains that the images of the deities of the Maurya are not for selling. The word "*devapūjā*" occurs in the Vārtika on Pāṇini (1.3.25). The digest try to show that *pūjā* is one type of *yāga*. Śabara distinguishes *yāga, homa and dāna on jaimini's sūtra : Yajati codanādravyadevatākriyāṁ samudāye kṛtārthatvāt* (IV 2.27-28). In another place Śabara refers to (on *Jaimini* IX. 1.6) the argument that *yāga* is nothing but the worship of deity (*Api ca yāgo nāma devatāpūjā*) (Śabara on Jaimini IV. 2.28). *Viṣṇudharmottara* observes that those who perform upavāsavrata, should inaudibly mutter the *mantras* of that deity; should mediatate on that deity and worship the image of that deity etc. In the *Mahābhārata* Bhiṣma says images tremble, shed tears etc. Manu and Yājñavalkya (1.100) speak of the worship of gods to be followed immediately after *tarpaṇa* and include *homa* among the five *yajñas*. In the latter *Smṛtis* a distinction is made between homa (*devayajña*) and *deva-pūjā*. Medieval writers on *dharmaśāstras* came to look upon vaiśvānara as *devayajña* while others made that *homa* to god is different from *vaiśvānara*. (*Vide Marīci* and *Hārita* : *Atha devapūjanam. Tacca prātarhomānantaram iti kecit. Vidheyā devatāpūjā prātar homādanantaram-iti marīci smaraṇāt*, as quoted in *Smṛtimuktāphala* (P. 383).

Smṛtimuktāphala, Smṛticandrikā, the *Pūjāprakāśa* etc. devote considerable space to the subject of *devapūjā* in its various aspects. Elaborate discussions on the construction of the images, consecretion and principal deities etc. are dealt in *Bṛhatsaṁhitā, Matsyapurāṇa, Agnipurāṇa, Mānasāra* etc.

What It Is

The nature of worship could better be studied from its constituents and procedures rather than from literature. Many a book is published on how to perform a worship, say of Visṇu or Śakti. These are supported by all the *Purāṇas* and other treatise. They prescribe that a *pūjā* must follow the steps like *bhūta śuddhi, prāṇāyāma, nyāsa and meditations* etc.

Upāsanā is Not a Karma

1. It is not a *Karma* as *karma and upāsti* are counted as two separate methods (*karmopāsti vicāryete*)[5]
2. Worship is considered to be a higher means than Karma : (*pāmarāṇām vyavahṛteḥ varaṁ karmādyanuṣṭhitiḥ tatopi saguṇopāsti nirguṇopāsanā tataḥ* (pan IX. 121).
3. Whether *saguna* or *nirgunopāsana*, meditation is the sole means of all worships.
4. *Upāsanā* is a common word in the Vedānta and everywhere it denotes *dhyāna* or *Vidyā*[6]. "*Vidyupāstyośca Vedānteṣvavyatirekeṇa prayogaḥ dṛśyate*".
5. The English translation of *upāsanā* has ever been made as meditation by all translators.

6. "As there is no other means except digging to get a gem buried in the ground, so also meditation, or upāsanā is the sole means of getting the gem like 'self'. (Pan. IX. 153)
7. The definition of upāsanā differs from that of *Karma* : "continuation of thought is worship." (*pratyayavṛtti rupāsanā*-speaks Vidyaranya IX. 55; so also Acharya Śaṅkara in Ch. up. and Br.S.Bh. 4.1.1).
8. Swāmi Swāhānanda in his translation and notes toe *Pañcadasi* defines; "*Upāsanā*, meditation or worship is the process of keeping the mind in the thought of the object worshipped. As a result the mind takes the form of the objective".
9. The differences between worship and *karma* should be remembered. Perfection is not possible through *karma*, since action is dual and the ever existing self can't be produced from anything. Therefore the self is revealed either by worship or by knowledge. *Upāsanā* is thus called a yoga:

   Upāsakānāmapyevaṁ vicāratyāgato yadi.
   Bāḍham tasmād vicārasyāsambhava yoga iritah. (IX. 131)
10. Then what is the difference between worship and knowledge?

   Vidyopāstyorviśsaḥ ka iti ceducyate śṛṇu
   Vastutantro bhavedbodhaḥ kartutantramupāsanam.

Worship depends on the worshipper, whereas knowledge depends upon the object of knowledge. In a beautiful way the kingly sage illustrates that a lady attached to a paramour can't fully satisfy her husband and household activities, as does a chaste lady attached to her domestic duties. Similarly a man of meditation indifferently performs his worldly affairs; whereas a man who has realized, fulfills his duty well, as they don't come in conflict.

Gṛhakṛtyavyasaninī yathā samyakkaroti tat
Paravysaninī tadvanna karotyeva sarvathā (IX. 86-87)

Philosophy of Worship

The Supreme self becoming the world entered into it as the *jiva*:

"Svechhayā Svavittau viśvamunmilayati"

All the scriptures declare one thing : The transitories or transiences in the world are pervaded by the Lord. Object has no meaning without the subject and vice versa. Beyond the subject and object is the third, from which the two flow. Thus the object is covered by the subject. From that subject whatever comes forth, enjoy that. Don't search the object any where else (i.e. except the subject). You can't get anything from anybody. Implore Him. If pleased, He will grant you all (*tena tyaktena*).

> Worship is the realization of one's own divinity:
> Upāsakastu satataṁ dhyāyannaiva vasedyataḥ
> *dhyānenaiva kṛtaṁ tasya brahmatvam Viṣṇutādivat*[6].

In Tantra, worship is said "*Svasvarūpaparāmaśraḥ*"-as says Abhinavagupta. Worship in *Upanisads* is *Vidyā*or *Vedana*, knowledge. *Vidi* and *Upāsti* are same in the Vedas.[8] Aṣṭāvakra assures:

> Yadi deham pṛthakkṛtya citi visrāmya tiṣṭhasi
> Adhunaiva sukhī śānto bandhamukto bhaviṣyasi:
> Dehābhimānaṁ vidhvasya dhyānādātmānamadvayam
> Paśyan mṛtyo amṛto bhutvāhyatra brahmasamaśnute.
>
> Pan. IX-157.

"God is knowable; you can know him just now through meditation", says Paramahansa Yogānandaji. Worship or meditation unifies the missing link between individual soul and cosmos. Mind can be transcended. Mind is an energy, not merely a psychological stuff. The uninterrupted practice of the awareness of the man is the means of dispersion of *avidyā* (Y.s. II. 26)

Methodology of Worship

The indeterminate grasp of all determinate ideas such as the awareness of different parts of body is one of the simple methods accepted in the *aṅganyāsa* of worship[9]. The worshipper realizes that the entire objectivity rests on the *Cit (MM 193,112,113)*. Abhinavagupta in *Tantrāloka* (111.119) points out the mystic method of worship: *Samvidekātmanā avasthānaṁ Pūjā*. Jayaratha explains: *Pūjā nāma na pusādyai* —[10]

Maheswarananda points out that worship consists not in offering flowers etc. to any images but in the grasp of the true nature of the self : "*tasmāt svarūpa parāmarśa eva paramāpūjā*". Otherwise an elephant garlanding Ganeśa in a circus would also be a worship.

The performance of worship is in successive stage from obscurity to perfect clarity (TA 3,4,5) as is done in *Bhūta śuddhi*. The worldly multiplicity represented by sensuous objects such as touch, smell, sound etc. ordinarily supposed to be binding, turns out to be unfailing means of self realization[11].

"A man with the axe like intellect, should remove the stones like body consciousness, dig the field like mind and then he can get the gem like `Me' the self[12]:

> "*Dehopalamapākṛtya buddhikuddālakātpunaḥ*
> *Khātvā manobhūvaṁ bhuyo gṛhniyān mām nidhiṁ pumān*"
>
> (Pan. IX. 154)

Pūjā and Spanda

Material images call up the mental idea and vice versa, since there is no thought without mental image or language.

It is the free will that makes one appear limited[12]. When the individual soul, out of his own free will, identifies himself with Universal consciousness, all his chains drop down[13].

The realisation of that power of the free will of the consciousness is within an easy reach of him who watches and observes clearly his own free conscious nature.

The subject becoming the object is the theory of *spanda*. Observance of this *spanda* is *Bhairava*, the power of consciousness, which infuses life into the physical senses, otherwise apparantly insentient. The realisation of that *Bhairava* state places above fears of creative and destructive forces. When complete cessation of mental activity is achieved, the associationless entity *(ātmā) remains: "nirodha-lābhe puṁso ntarasangaṁvastu śiśyate*" (Pan. IX-127).

The whole theory, methodology and ritual of worship is seconded by the latest Scientists who find nothing objective. Scientists like T. Kuhns, Talbet, Davices, Hoyle, whitehead and others felft the reality being created in every moment. As matter is dissolved in *bhūtaśuddhi*, the photens with a velocity more than light are discovered, bombarding in Quark to confirm the science or worship that 'idea is the source of power house of creation'.

Worship for a Society of Materiality, Humanity and Divinity

Worship is a transformer of object into subject; a synthesiser of *Karma* and *Kaula*; action and knowledge; a *yoga* of *Tantra* and *Vedanta*; *Āṇava* and *Śākta Upāyas*. *Śāmbhava* is the Pratyabhijñā, the *Viveka* of Vedānta.

Material production is the basement of society. Production is ineffective unless the humanity is developed. The humanity is a limited one: *Janmanā jāyate śūdraḥ*. Man seeks for infinity and eternity. Humanity of an individual becomes a nucleus of that potentially universal divinity. A society with a mere material production shatters and breaks down as the world has witnessed in a dehumanised and ueurotic personalities resorting to a culture of gun, sex and drug. It is not due to political or economical imbalances. But due to the disfunct of discriminating power of the neurons. Therefore, a society for mere material productivity must have to be reconciled for a higher human consciousness. Progress is not stopped with Human Resource Development (HRD). This has been foretold in *Pañcadasi*, where the word *pāmara* is ascribed to a society aspiring for more material growth and HRD to "live in a lawful activity". Morethan these two is divinity:

> *Pāmarāṇām vyavahrteḥ varaṁ karmādyanuṣṭhitiḥ;*
> *tatopi saguṇopāsti nirguṇopāsanā tataḥ.*
>
> (Pan. IX. 121)

The way to divinity is the same what paved the way from materiality like the Marxism in China to the Humanity in Japan. That in India is called a Yoga, a worshipping society, transforming the object into the subject or vice versa.

HRD Movement

Human Resources Development is the key philosophy of Industrial Management in Japan. It is being followed by all countries. Material production does not depend upon the scientific theory and discovery alone; but it also depends on managerial efficiency and work culture. "It is not the profit nor production which should be the main target of any organisation". Capital money or advanced machines can come over night. All these are useless if the workers are not developed. Gold or bread alone is not the criterion of human satisfaction. Selfishness, frustration, passion, individualism, petty motives, ego, unrest etc. shoot out in the form of demanding higher pay revision or service security". Man has higher expectations. He is aware of his freedom and rights, and is far more capable and determined to protect these where he sees them threated". (*Vide, Not Bread Alone,* Baldev Sharma). "Better people, not better technology, is the surest way to a better society" (TV Rao andD.F. Percire, *Recent Experience in HRD*). If development of the man is not aimed at, no one can associate himself with any organisation. Feeling of normlessness is one of the dimentions of alienation. "It is not the knowledge, skill or capabilities, but the humanity which is to be counted". It is who you know rather than what you know that counts for a society. In an HRD system there is no class between the afluent and the have-nots.

In this way the exponents go on accounting for the HRD system. They conclude: "Discharge of social responsibility by business and industry too is not merely a means to some end but and end in itself". Most of the problems of the present society, such as, student unrest, employees agitation, family disturbances, provincialism, social injustice and inharmony etc. are nothing but the eruption of stress and strain evolved due to some hormonal, electrical or chemical imbalances in the brain chambers linked with discriminating centres of the brain which can never be toned by theoritical or explanatory studies. Soundness in the discriminating centres may be called humanity which is the 'life' of all success. Humanity is the pillar upon which all the plans and projects, their execution and implementation of a nation are depended and the whole "roof" of the nation rests on it. If this humanity pillar is collapsed, the whole construction and *production-force* is ruined. The development of humanity is nothing except the expansion, or clearing of the awareness of an individual soul. Throwing of poison by a man into the fiscery ponds, the incidents happening in our societies, are the instances of lack of awareness or humanity. In the terms of HRD, when an electrician or a technician is allowed to make himself an engineer in Japan, we in India call it in a Vedantic or SW. Vivekananda's words: *"Each soul is potentially DIVINE"*.

This is what HRD is. And in Vedantic term it is called worship of deities in the human soul or expansion of awareness to the higher levels.

Conclusion

The source of milk is not limited to the swellen udder of a cow-as a materialistic society would think of; nor is the source of milk confined to the cow only-as the HRD system would present it. A materialist would kill the 'hen' to obtain all her golden eggs at a time. The source of milk lies in many: the food, the air, the season, the environment, the emotion, the age, the gene, and so on. The society of materiality have to ascend to the absolute through humanity: *Yoga or worship*. Pure materiality, pure humanity or pure divinity may not be the essence of a society; but the three combined "Divine Life Society" may be a best possible one. That's why the *Gītā*, the appex of wisdom, arrived at its climax in the "Universal citizenship" proclaiming:

> *"Yasmāt Kṣara matitohamakṣarādapi cottamḥ*
> *atosmi loke veda ca prathitaḥ puruṣottamah".*

The trinity, Balabhadra, Subhadra and Jagannatha-Puruṣottama is the highest stage-as says the *Puruṣasūkta or Īśā*:*"Yosā Vasau puruṣaḥ sohamasami"*.

To a Sanskritist, worship is not a question of enquiry, *"Naciketo maranaṃ mānuprākṣi"*, rather he should say *"Tavaiva vāhāstava nṛtyagīte"*. Then sing the 18 cities, a slogan of the Divine Life Society of Rishikesh.

The worshipping dictum is: *Upāsanā* serves as a science of perfection, an applied science of the Technology of *Tantra* and *Vedanta*. The transcendence is in immanence and immanence in transcendence : In whom everything is, from who, everything comes, who is everything and everywhere, who is immanent in all things eternal, Him the self of all, do I adore:

> Yasmin sarvaṃ yataḥ sarvaṃ sarvaṃ sarvataśca yaḥ
> *Yaśca sarvamayo nityaṃ tasmai sarvātmane namaḥ.*

References

1. Chāndogyopaniṣad with Śaṅkara bhāṣya, Gitapress, Gorakhpur.
2. Vidyāraṇya, Pāñcedaśi; Eng. tr. by Sw. Swahananda, Ramkrishna Mission.

3. Kane, P.V. History of Dharmaśāstra, BORI, Vol. V.
4. Ivid.
5. Pan. IX. 26.
6. Brahamasūtra Śāṅkara-Bhāsyaṃ 4.1.1.
7. Pan.
8. Br. S. 4.1.1.
9. Mahārtha-mañjari, *Sivasūtra*. 1.1.1.
10. Jayaratha's Com. *Tantrāloka*, 2.1.1.
11. Rastogi, N.J. *Karma Tantrism of Kashmir*.
12. Pan. XI. III, 113.
13. *Spandakārikā*, Kashmir Text Series, P.8

21

Anadhyāya and its Social Relevance

Subas Chandra Dash*

Introduction

In ancient India, the pupil used to go to the house of his preceptor and was initiated to the Vedic Study. He was staying with the teacher in his house. To serve the preceptor was considered as the sacred duty along with the study. The student was considered as a *brahmacārī* and had to obey what the teacher says. A *brahmacārī* was expected to avoid large gatherings, all sorts of pleasures and luxuries and association of woman. These were some cardinal principles of self-discipline. So the student had to undergo a rigorous training in the preceptor's house and the duties were prescribed accordingly as mentioned above. Along with such prescribed duties there are some occasions on which cessation of study was prescribed. This suspension or cessation of vedic study was considered as *anadhyāya* and for that various rules have been prescribed about the days and times which were treated *anadhyāya* days. Let us go into detail to see what *anadhyāya* is, when it is observed and for what purpose?

Anadhyāya plays an important role since ancient period. It means not to study *Veda* at certain times or on certain days. During this time the vedic study is completely suspended. It is regarded as holiday for both the student and the teacher as well. There are various factors responsible to decide the *anadhyāya* days like impurity, natural phenomena and various *tithis* etc. Let us look into those one by one:

---

* I am indebted to Prof. Sadashiba Praharaj, G.M. College, Sambalpur, Orissa for his constructive suggestions regarding this topic.

Impurity

Vedic Study is suspended when the person is impure either by the impurity caused by the birth and death of any family member or relatives or the place of study is impure. To this, the *Taittirīya Āraṇyaka* gives a description in the *yajña* i.e. *brahmayajña*, there are two occasions when the Vedic study is suspended namely, when the man is impure or when the place of study is impure[1].

The *Dharmasūtras* also describe in the same manner. The *Gautama Dharmasūtra* mentions—one should not study in a burial ground, or at the end of a village or on a high road or during impurity or when a foul smell is coming from a nearby place or there is a dead body nearby or near a *sūdra*[2]. In another *sūtra*[3] it is stated that, when the student is impure, he should not even recite the *Veda* mentally. *Āpastamba Dharma sūtra* also says this when there is impurity in a place, from which foul smell comes, one should not study Vedas[4]. In the later period, Manu and Yājñavalkya also have taken those points and described carefully. Manu[5] says: a brahmin should stop vedic study when the place of recital is impure and he himself is defiled.

According to *Baudhāyana Dha sū*. also, when there is impurity nearby or a rotting smell in the wind, study should be discontinued[6]. At birth and death, one should not do even the mental study[7]. The *Ābastamba Dha. Sū*. provides 3 days *anadhyāya* at the death of near relatives, 12 days if parents and teachers have died[8]. He records that according to some, upon the death of the teacher-*anadhyāya* of 3 days and 3 nights are prescribed.

Manu[9] holds that-when there is foul smell coming, or in a village through which corpse has passed and in the presence of वृषाल (शूद्र) there is no study. He further states that one must not study *Veda* in water, at midnight, when one attends to the call of nature and takes food in the mouth etc.[10].

Natural Phenomena

Gautama Dha. sūtra[11] narrates the student shall not recite the *Vedas* if wind whirls up the dust in day-time, when there is noise of musical instruments, noise of chariot or if the barking of many dogs and jackels or the braying of many donkeys is heard, or if the sky appears red, a rainbow is seen or if unseasoned cloud arise. Again he mentions one should not study *Veda* when he feels the necessity to attend the calls of nature (urine and excrements), or at midnight, in the twilight while rain falls, when the planets Jupiter and Venus are surrounded by a halo and even to Sun and Moon. In the above cases the Vedic study is suspended as long as the disturbance remains. Again it gives various natural phenomena like lighting, earthquake, an eclipse and the fall of meteors are reasons for discontinuing the Vedic study until the same time next day[12]. If rains and lightening are in a rainy season, it should be stopped for a day or a night. If lightening is observed in the night, study shall be stopped until the third watch[13]. If it appears in the third part of the day or night, the *Veda* should not be studied during the entire following night. If thunder is heard before midnight the study is interrupted during the night. If it is heard during the early part of the day the interruption must continue as long as the sun shines[14].

Vaśiṣṭha Dha. Sūtra also records in the similar way. Study should be suspended when there is thunder, earthquake, solar or lunar eclipse, when there is rumbling inthe quarters or in the mountains or shaking of mountains till the same time next day[15]. When meteors and lightning appear together, study is suspended for three days[16].

Baudhāyana Dha. Sūtra[17] states that-one should not study for three days, when there are thunder, rain and lightening, except during the rainy season.

Āpastamba Dha. Sūtra gives the *anadhyāya* days as follows: The text records when rain, thunder and lightening occur together out of season, the study is suspended for three days[18]. It continues this description and gives that—in case of an eclipse of the sun or the moon, or of an earthquake or of a whirl-wind, of the fall of a meteor, or of a fire in the village at whatever time these natural events happen, the study of all sciences must be interrupted from that period until the same time of the next day. If a cloud appears out of season, if the sun or the moon is surrounded by the halo, if a rainbow or a comet appears, if a high wind blows, or hoar frost lies on the ground, at all these cases the study is entirely stopped[19].

Let us come to Manu. He has dealt with this *anadhyāya* and also describes that Vedic study is stopped to the same time next day when there is lightening, thunder, rains and the fall of great meteors[20]. He also records in the same way as we have seen earlier that study is suspended when there is storm, an earth quake, or an eclipse of the stars[21].

Tithis

Among *tithis* mostly—अष्टमी, अमावास्या, चतुर्दशी and पूर्णिमा are considered as *anadhyāya* days. Manu states:-

नीहरे वाणशब्देन संध्ययोरेव चोभयोः।
अमावास्याचतुर्दश्योः पौर्णमास्यष्टकासु च।। 4.113

one should not study the *Veda* when there is fog, or sound of arrows, or at the morning and evening twilights, or at the conjunction of sun and moon or on the fourteenth (lunar) day, or on the day of the full moon or on the eight (lunar) day. In the next verse he states that if one studies, the following will happen.

अमावास्या गुरुं हन्ति शिष्यं हन्ति चतुर्दशी।
ब्रह्माष्टकापौर्णमास्यो तस्मात्ताः परिवर्जयेत्।। 4.114

The day of conjunction destroys the Guru, the fourteenth day destroys the pupil, the eighth and full moon day destroy the *Veda*. Therefore, one should avoid these days and hence considered as the days of *anadhyāya*.

The similar type of description also we get in *Baudhāyana Dha. sū*. 1.11: 43.

हन्यष्टमी ह्युपाध्यायं हन्ति शिष्यं चतुर्दशी।
हन्ति पञ्चदशी विद्यां तस्मात्पर्वाणि वर्जयेत्।।

In the *Vasiṣṭha Dha. Sū*. in these days vedic studies were suspended. (when somebodies hands are wet, while the flute is being played etc.) on the fourteenth day on the moonless day, on the *aṣṭaka* days these are considered as *anadhyāya* days[22].

Yājñavalkya also prescribed *anadhyāya* in the days of पञ्चदशी (i.e.-अमावास्या or पूर्णिमा चतुर्दशी) or in the solar and lunar eclipses or ऋतुसंधिऽ or when a person partakes of *śrāddha* food or accepts a gift on *śrāddha*. Mitākṣarā here points out that—

ऋतुसंधिगतासु च प्रतिपत्सु श्राद्धिकभोजने तत्प्रतिग्रहे च ह्युशमन-ध्यायः।

In the earlier cases, nowhere प्रतिपद् is mentioned. But it is also accepted that प्रतिपद् पाठनाशिनी, it destroys the *vidyā* i.e. *Vedas*. In the *Rāmāyaṇa*[23], also we get a reference where प्रतिपद् is considered as *anadhyāya* day, because on these days, *Vidyā* is destroyed. These *tithis* as we have mentioned are regarded as the regular holidays i.e. नित्य अनध्याय days, on which complete study of all sciences were suspended. Even now we find that in the traditional *pāṭhaśālās*, they observe these days as holidays for them. These rules are also observed now that Vaidik pandits don't study the *śāstras* in these days.

It is also recorded in the texts that-if a person studies *Veda* in *anadhyāya* days, then it destroys one's life, cattle, intelligence and merit accumulated by him.

छिद्राण्याहु द्विजातीनामनध्यायात्मनीषिणः ।
छिद्रेभ्यः स्रवति ब्रह्म ब्राह्मणेन यदर्जितम् ।।
आयुः प्रजां पशुन्मेघां कृन्तामि सुकृतं च यत् ।
अनध्यायेष्वभ्यसतः ब्रह्मण्याहरतस्तथा ।।

अपराकौंत्तिं याज्ञव. 1.142-151

स्मृतिचद्रिका- I. p. 61

Outside factors which cause-*anadhyāya*: Less Light caused-non study

Āpastamba Dha. Sū. records that at night one shall not study in a forest, where there is no fire nor gold[24]. Because light is required for study. In the above case, there may be less of light, for which study is suspended.

Manu[25] and Yājñavalkya[26] say that when there is dust shower or redness of the quarters (horizon), when a jackel houls, or dogs, asses and camel bray and in a gathering, one must not study. These are the instances which either is not conducive or suitable for concentrating our mind on vedic study. According to *Āp. Dh. sū*, 1.3.11.33. if there is howl of a wolf or of a jackel is heard, one shall stop study until he has slept[27]. Gautama 16.45 states that the *Veda* cannot be studied in a city. Manu also equally refers to such description. He says—Vedic study should not be done as long as there is an assembly of people[28]. Manu (4.126) and Yājñavalkya[29] refer to such *anadhyāya* days (one day and night) when a beast, frog, mongoose, dog, snake, cat or mouse passes between the teacher and pupil.

Yājñavalkya[30] and Manu[31] also prescribe 3 days *anadhyāya* on the death of a pupil or *Ṛtvig* or a fellow pupil or a teacher or at the time of *upākarma* and *utsarga* ceremonies or a *śrotriya* of one's own branch of *Veda*. However, *Āp. Dh. Sū* (1.3.10.4) prescribes 12 days *anadhyāya* on the death of one's parents and *ācārya*. Baudhāyaya (1.11. 3-2) prescribes 3 days *anadhyāya* on the death of one's father. These are called as the *naimittika anadhyāya* days.

In these days, one is certainly impure but at the same time the mind is not in a position to grasp properly. Hence these days were considered as the days of *anadhyāya*. It may be the psychological reason for which such a long duration is prescribed.

The Relevance of Anadhyāya in Different Tithis from Scientific Point of View

We also get support in favour of *Anadhyāya* form scientific investigations. The relation between man and moon which is described in *Veda* and *Purāṇas* is proved by the medical science. Dr. Candeśvara Prasad Thakur, who was a medicine Professor in Patna Medical College and studied much regarding this topic. In his thesis—*Full moon and Poisoning,* he pointed out that the poisoning accidents are more in comparison to other *tithis*. Patients or their relatives seek medical advice usually on the same day that the poison has been taken and the time of poisoning can be established easily. The relative position of the sun and moon on the *Puraṇimā* day are such that their gravitational forces on the earth act almost in a straight line, causing higher tides. The effect of the moon and the sun creates tides in the sea including the watermass of the earth. Human blood is a fluid. The moon's longitude has direct effect on human blood causing tides and regulating hormone secretion[32].

Water contains 50-60 per cent of the body weight of the human beings. Possibly, as with the sea water, body water might also generate some sort of tidal wave that increases on *purṇimā* days. These human tidal waves might cause physical, Psychological or bio-chemical changes in the body. The brain is also affected by the process. As well as other factors that influence an individual to take poison, this phenomenon might affect the incidence of poisoning on *pūrṇimā* days[33].

Dr. C.P. Thakur with the help of one of his students analysed all the case of acute poisoning admitted to the medical ward of Patana Medical College Hospital from January 1976 to December 1979. It is observed that 49 *pūrṇimā* days occurred during the study period and 45 cases of poisoning were admitted on those days. The total number of non-*pūrṇimā* days were 1412 and the number of cases admitted on these days are 796. It is found that in 16 *pūrṇimā* cases, no case; in 23 *pūrṇimās*, 1 case; in 8 *pūrṇimās*, 2 cases and in 2 *pūrṇimās*, 3 cases were admitted to the hospital.

So from this investigation it is observed that the poisoning accidents are more in *pūrṇimā* days in comparison to non-*pūrṇimā* days. The impulse to take or to give poison may be increased on *pūrṇimā* days owing to increased human tidal waves[34].

Full Moon and Crime

Dr. C.P. Thakur also proved that not only the impulse to take or to give poison is increased but also the ill-intention for theft and murder etc. are also increased in this day. The incidents of crimes reported to three police stations in different towns (one rural, one urban, one industrial) was studied to see if it varied with the day of lunar cycle. The period of study covered 1968-1982. It found that the incidence of crime committed on full moon days was much higher on all other days. The increased incidents of crimes on full moon days may be due to humna tidal waves caused by the gravitational pull of the moon.

Analysis

Many modern scientists have found a significant co-relation between phases of moon and aggressive behaviour,injury, accidents, mental imbalance and sucides. As the human body contains 60 per cent water and when moon creates tidal waves in sea water it must have some impact on human beings too. It creates also human tidal waves which causes physical. psychological and bio-chemical reactions or changes in the body resulting in behaving different ways. That is why the ancient Indian scientists knew this psychological states of human beings on those days and considering those points which generates imbalance in the mind, they thought of not encouraging vedic study during such periods. Hence the different days of *anadhyāya* were prescribed.

It is also necessary to study the happenings and mental status in other days which are prescribed as the days of *anadhyāya* from scientific and astrological stand point.

Conclusion

As per our above discussion the following observations are made:

1. The *anadhyāya* days are regarded as holiday both for the pupil and teacher since ancient period.
2. The factors which cause disturbance in the mind are the occasions regarded as the days or times of *anadhyāya*. The sounds of thunder, rains and other natural phenomena and also of various animals create disturbance in mind. So these times are not good for study. It is very practical even now.
3. Impurities plays a great role in this regard. When the place of study or the person is impure, it is not proper to study. It is true that purity not only is an outside phenomena, but internal too. When the surrounding or atmosphere where one sits for study is clean, automatically liking (श्रद्धा) becomes more and one indulges himself fully for study. Hence our *Dharmaśāstra* Texts have taken care of those facts.
4. If somebody studies *Veda* in the *anadhyāya* days, it is mentioned that Gods would become angry if the sanctity of *Vedas* was defiled by being studied. The result thereby is—one incurres loss as to life, cattle, intelligence and merit accumulated by him. If we look seriously to this, it has a strong point behind this. It points out to pay respect to the scriptures and abide the rules prescribed in it. It serves the purpose both ways. But there are some points which are not relevant today, which we can drop from today's standpoint like seeing a *sūdra* or some animal when passes in your front.
5. The *tithis* which are mentioned earlier, are regarded as the regular holidays (नित्य अनध्याय days) on which Vedic study is suspended. On the otherhand, in other days which are *anadhyāya* days either due to impurity or natural disorders

or disturbances are regarded as occasional holidays, (नैमित्तिक अनध्याय days).

6. Vedic study requires attention and concentration for memorising. When the body and mind both are stable then only study is possible. So the *tithis* play a vital role. It has a strong impact on human system as per the movements of stars. We are part and parcel of the whole universe, hence we are also disturbed when the positions of the stars change or when there is earth quake, eclipse which are considered as natural phenomena. Since these periods cause some adjustments in the whole Eco system, we are not an exception to it. Hence, the impact is on our organism. It is a kind of rest to our body and mind and both when we take rest during the holidays. We are refreshed during that time and work better in the next day. So the *anadhyāya* days are not only meant stop the study but as a result, we rest completely.
7. As the scientific study of *tithis* are concerned the full moon day is considered as the day when much crime, mental imbalance, accidents occur. It is true that moon creates tidal waves on human body and hence the imbalance in mind. The ancient thinkers noted and examined this and came to a conclusion that such time is not good for memorising or grasping Vedic knowledge. So it was treated as the day of non-study.
8. It is true that our mind requires some rest for sometime and the holidays are given. This is quite logical. And hence they have prescribed different days of *anadhyāya*. Even today, there are different types of holidays given to teachers and students for non-study. But so far as the believes are concerned which have no present concern should be avoided even if it is mentioned in the *Dharmaśāstras*. If something is directly related to the upliftment of an individual and society at large, let us accept that and that which is not related or has no social concern, let us not accept that.

Notes and References

1. तस्य वा एतस्य यज्ञस्य द्वावनध्यायौ यदात्माशुचिर्यदिशः ।

Tai Āra., II. 15

2. श्मशान ग्रामान्त महापथाशौचेषु। 16-18
पूतिगन्धान्तश्शवदिवाकीर्त्य शूद्रसंनिधाने।। 16-19
3. मानसम्प्यशुचिः। Ibid 16-47
4. पूतीगन्धः। 1.3.10:24
5. द्वावेव वर्जयेन्नित्यमनध्यायौ प्रयत्नतः।
स्वाध्यायभूमिं चाशुद्धामात्मानं चाशुचिं द्विजः।। 4.127
6. वातेपूतिगन्धे.....1.11.24
7. मानसेऽपि जननमरणयोरनध्यायः। Ibid. 1.11:41
8. तथ सम्वन्धेषु ज्ञातिषु। Āp. Dha. Sū, 1.3.10:3
मातरि पितर्याचार्यइति द्वादशाहाः। 1.3.10 : 4
9. 4.107. 108
10. 4.109.
11. नाधीयीत वायौ दिवा पांसुहरे। 16.5-16
12. आकालिका निर्घात भूमिकम्प राहुदर्शनोल्काः। Gau. Ibid. 16.22
13. विद्युति नक्तं चापररात्रात्।
त्रिभागादि प्रवृतौ सर्वम्। 16.25-26
14. 16-30.
15. *Vas. Dha.Sū.* 13-8.
16. उल्का विद्यत् समासे त्रिरात्रम्। 13.9
17. *Bau. Dha. Sū,* 1.11.25.
18. वायुर्घोषवान् भूमौ वा तृणसंवाहो
वर्षीति वा यत्र धाराः प्रवहेत्। *Āp Dha. Sū,* 1.3.11:8
19. सूर्याचन्द्रमसोर्ग्रहणे भूमि च लेपखान उल्कायामग्न्युत्पाते च। *Āp. Dha. Sū,* 1.3.11-30
सर्वासां विद्यानां सार्वकालिकमाकालम्।
अभ्रं चापती सूर्याचन्द्रमसोः परिवेष इन्द्रघनुः प्रतिसूर्यमत्स्यश्च वाते पूतिगन्धे नीहारे च सर्वेष्वेतेषु तावन्तं कालम्। Ibid, 1.3.11-31
20. 4.103
21. 4.105
22. चतुर्दश्याममावास्यामषृभ्यामषृकासु प्रसारितपदोपस्थकृतस्थोपाश्रित्य। 13:8

23. सा प्रकृत्यैव तन्वङ्गी तद्वियोगाच्च कार्शिता।
प्रतिपत्पाठशीलस्य विद्येव तनुतां गता।।

सुन्दरकाण्ड, 59:32

24. नक्तं चारण्येनग्नावहिरण्ये वा। 1.3.11:34

25. पांसुवर्षे दिशां दाहे गोमायुविरुते तथा।
श्वखरोष्ट्रे च रुवति पङ्क्तौ च न पठेद्विजः।। 4.115

26. 1.150

27. सलावृक्यामेकसृक इति स्वप्नपर्यन्तम्।

28. अनध्यायो रुद्यमाने समवाये जनस्य च।। 1.8

29. पशुमण्डूकनकुलश्वाहिमार्जारमूषिकैः।
कृतेऽन्तरे त्वहोरात्रं शक्रपाते तथोच्छ्रये।। 1.147.

30. 1.144

3.1 4.119

32. *Planets and Forecast*, Ed. by Nimai Banergee, March 1983. P. 138, Pithapur, Cuttack.

33. *British Medical Journal*—20-27, Dec. 1980, Great Britain.

34. Ibid.

22

Dharmaśāstra and the Study of Logic

Mrinal Kanti Gangopadhyay

I shall begin with a story. It occurs in the *Mahābhārata*, Śāntiparvan, Chapter one hundred eighty. While awaiting death, lying on his bed of arrows, Bhiṣma delivered long sermons to Yudhiṣṭhira on a variety of topics ranging from *rājadharma* to *mokṣadharma*. In the course of such a sermon, he narrates one parable, which is known as Indra-Kaśyapa-saṃvāda.

Once upon a time, a merchant (*vaiśya*), arrogant because of his immense wealth, runs his chariot over a Brahmin of the Kaśyapa clan. Deeply mortified and finding no way to redress the injustice, he resolves to put an end to the wretched life. But, as he is about to do so, Indra, the lord of the gods, takes pity upon him and appears there in the guise of a jackal. He advises him not to take such a drastic step. Human life is too precious to be wilfully destroyed. He is moreover a Brahmin, who is accorded the highest place of honour in the society. At great length, Indra described, on the one hand, the excellences of being born as a human being and on the other, the intolerable miseries of being born as a low animal.

If the story would have ended here, it would have been a simple story, denouncing suicide or extolling the virtues of human life over animal life. But the fact is that the story does not end here. Indra, the jackal, continues. He informs further that in the previous birth he had not been such a wretched jackal; he had been a human being. But, what, indeed, has led him to this pitiable condition? Is it the result of some grave sin committed in the past life?

Let us hear the answer in his own words. He says: "Previously, I had been a pseudo-intellectual (*paṇḍitaka*), always proceeding on the basis of reasoning (*haituka*), a vilifier of the Vedas, deeply attached to logic (*ānvīkṣikī*) which embodies only the techniques of fruitless argumentation. I was in the habit of starting logical debates (*hetuvāda*) and, in the assemblies, I used to emphasise what was strictly based on reasoning (*hetumat*). I shouted at the Brahmins hostilely and controverted their statements. I was a disbeliever (*nāstika*) and raised doubts about everything. Though really a fool, I looked upon myself as a man of learning. O Brahmin ! this life of the jackal that I am suffering now is the result of all that "(*Mahābhārata*, Śāntiparvan, Chapter 180, Verses 47-49, *aham āsaṃ paṇḍitako* etc.).

So, finally, the implication is that it is not safe of indulge in the study of practice of logic; an attachment to logic is a dangerous thing and some great misfortune is sure to befall a man attached to logic.

Almost the same attitude is to be found in the other epic, the *Rāmāyaṇa*, also. When Bharata goes to meet Rāma in the forest, he advises Bharata on how to rule the kingdom. He warns him particularly against the Laukāyatika Brahmins. Why? Because they ignore the Dharmaśāstra, they are guided by logic and lead people to fruitless exercises (*śāstreṣu mukhyeṣu vidyamāneṣu durvadhāḥ/ buddhim ānvīkṣikīṃ prāpya pravadanti nirarthakam// Rāmāyaṇa, Ayodhyākāṇḍa*, Chapter 100, Verse 99).

This is also more or less representative of the attitude of the authors of Dharmaśāstra or law-givers to involvement with logic. One should not put too much reliance on reason and logic. However, one point should be clearly noted here. The law-givers do not reject the relevance of logic outright. They are ready to show tolerance for logic, but only in so far as it may be an aid to the understanding of the scriptural doctrines. The only legitimate function of logic, according to them, is to defend the supreme wisdom contained in the Veda. Thus, for example, in an oft-quoted verse, Manu says (iv. 30): One should not even speak with the heretics, the transgressors of the caste discipline, the hypocrites, the logicians and the double dealers' (*pāṣaṇḍino vikarmasthān baiḍālavratikān śaṭhān/ haitukān bakavṛttiṃśca vāṅmātreṇāpi nārcayet//*).

We have taken the word *haituka* in the above verse in the sense of a logician. But it has been pointed out by scholars that at least in the context of the law-givers the word should rather be taken in a restricted sense. It should not be taken in its ordinary sense to mean logicians in general. It should be taken to mean specifically sophists or logicians who indulge in all kinds of free discussions and controvert the Vedic doctrines (cf. Surendranath Dasgupta, *A History of Indian Philosophy*, volume three, P. 518).

Thus, it has been urged that *haituka* means a free thinker, who instead of making logic scrupulously subservient to the scriptures, insists on allowing it an independent efficacy of its own. But the law-givers can hardly look favourably upon such a tendency, for they cannot allow the right to question the authority of the scriptures. In fact, it is clear from many other statements of Manu that he has nothing against those who agree to allow logic the restricted function of following a course determined and sanctioned by the scriptures.

Naturally, the commentators cannot but endorse the view of the original. Commenting on the verse of Manu just quoted, Medhātithi says that the *haitukas* are none but the disbelievers; these people have the firm conviction that there is no after-life, no merit in practising charity, and no efficacy of the sacrificial oblations (*haitukā nāstikāḥ, nāsti paralokah, nāsti dattam, nāsti hutam ityevaṃ sthitaprajñn$ḥ*). According to Kullūkabhaṭṭa, the *haitukas* are those who are in the habit of advancing arguments opposing the doctrines of the Vedas (*veda-virodhi-tarka-vyavahārin*). Of course, the difference between the two interpretations does not amount to much. Acceptance of afterlife, performance of sacrifices, practising charity etc. are all enjoined by the Vedas. Questioning the belief in all these is as good as questioning the authority or the validity of the Vedas themselves.

Again, in the twelvth and last chapter of his work Manu (xvii. 111) speaks of constituting a council (*pariṣat*), having at least ten members, which would advise the king on the true course of *dharma* in case of doubt. There, among the members Manu includes a *haituka* and a *tarkin*. Both the words may mean logicians in general. But, as Kullūkabhaṭṭa points out, that is not the intention of Manu. There the two words mean respectively a Naiyāyika who does not controvert *śruti* and *smṛti*, and a Mīmāṃsaka (*śruti-smṛti-aviruddha-nyāyaśāstrajña* and *mīmāṃsātmaka-tarkavit*).

At least on one occasion Manu also refers to *ānvīkṣikī* as a branch of study. In a quite well known verse, enumerating the subjects to be studied by the king, he says (vii. 43):

traividyebhyas trayīṃ vidyād daṇḍanītiṃ ca śāśvatīm /
ānvīkṣikīṃ cātmavidyāṃ vārtārambhāṃśca lokataḥ //

It is true that there is a difference of opinion regarding the interpretation of the expression *ānvīkṣikiṃ cātmavidyām*. Some commentators take it to mean two separate branches of study, the science of dialectics and the doctrine of the supreme self, while others take it to represent a single branch of study, namely, logic as conducive to the study of the true nature of the soul, considering *ātmavidyām* an adjective to *ānvīkṣikīm*. However, Medhātithi is categorical in adhering to the second interpretation. He says that the word for logic (*ānvikṣikī = tarkavidyā*), as occurring in the verse, is to be understood strictly as related to *adhyātmavidyā* or *ātmavidyā*, the doctrine of the soul and its salvation, and it should not be taken in the sense of free thinking, the sense in which the heretics and materialists may like to take it.

That this may be the real intention of Manu is corroborated by many of his other statements. It is not difficult to prove that he attaches supreme importance to the study of the Vedas, performance of the Vedic rites and vindication of the Vedic tenets. Thus, for example, the means for realising the true nature of *dharma* is said to be reasoning not in conflict with the Vedas (*veda-śāstrāvirodhinā tarkeṇa*: *Manu* xii. 106). Explaining the norm of right conduct, Manu says (iv. 163), one should avoid disbelief, *cavilling at the Veda*, contempt for gods, malice, conceit, anger and cruelty. Further, he declares (xii. 109), those Brahmins are to be considered ideals who, in accordance with the sacred law, have studied the Veda along with its appendages, and who live such a model life as to adduce by it perceptual proof, as it were, for the true character of the revealed scriptures (*śruti-pratyakṣa-hetu*). In fact, Manu is never tried of eulogising the Veda; for him Veda is Brahman, the only ultimate means for all ends, for the ignorant and the learned alike, for one desiring heaven and for one desiring liberation (*Manu* vi. 83-84).

In this connection, it would perhaps be interesting to refer to a remark of Kauṭilya . Almost at the begining of the *Arthaśāstra*, (1.2.1f) he has given a classification of the different branches of learning. Before recording his own opinion that they are definitely four in number, namely, *ānvīkṣikī*, *trayī*, *vārtā* and *daṇḍanīti*, he notes the views of others who do not agree with him. Thus, he notes that, according to the Mānavas, the branches of learning are only three, the reason being that logic is really included in the Vedic lore (*trayīviśeṣa hyānvīkṣikī*). If it can be established that the Mānavas here are the followers of Manusmṛti, it can be taken as corroborating the view that, according to Manu, logic should not be independent of the Veda.

Manu's veneration for the Vedas and his bias against independent logic, it has been argued, had a far-reaching effect upon the development of the philosophical tradition. An easy, palpable instance of how the Indian philosophers fall under the spell of Manu is the most widely accepted classification of the systems of Indian Philosophy, namely, the Āstika-Nāstika classification. It is invariably given a prominent status and all the text books on Indian philosophy generally start, even today, with it.

Popularly, the *āstika* and *nāstika* mean respectively the theist and the atheist. The former carries with it a sense of honour and respect, and the latter a stigma. But, as we all know, these meanings have not been taken into consideration, perhaps because in that case the two well known Brahmanical systems, the Sāṃkhya and Mīmāṃsā, would go into the Nāstika group along with the Cārvāka, the Bauddha and the Jaina. In fact, it may rather become difficult to find at least one system genuinely and indisputably Āstika.

Pāṇini, the grammaraian, says (4.4.60) that the words *āstika* and *nāstika* may be formed by the addition of the suffix *ṭhak* to the words *asti* and *nāsti*, meaning respectively, one who believes that 'it' exists and one who believes that 'it' does not exist. Commentators more or less agree that 'it' here means *paraloka*. Thus, etymologically, an *āstika* is one who accepts *paraloka*, rebirth, transmigration of the soul, and a *nāstika* would be the opposite. However, just like the major Brahmanical systems, the Bauddha and the Jaina also accept the immortality of the soul and its journey through births and therefore, these two also would become *āstika*, making, in fact, the Cārvāka the lone representative of the Nāstika group. Perhaps that is why these meanings also have not been taken into consideration.

Thus, while classifying the systems of philosophy into *astika* and *nāstika* special meanings have been attached to the terms. *Āstika* means one who has faith in the Veda, one who believes in the absolute authority and infallibility of the scriptures. *Nāstika* means the opposite, one who has no faith in the Veda and is rather a vilifier of the scriptures. But who is responsible for such a shift of meaning, such a specialisation? Few scholars seem to have concerned themselves with the question. S. Kuppuswami Sastri (*A Primer of*

Indian Logic, introduction, P. vii), after noting the various meanings, remarks non-commitally that "a post-Buddhistic but pre-Christian tradition" fixed those special meanings for the terms. The only scholar to make a categorical statement is Surendranath Dasgupta, who writes (*A History of Indian Philosophy*, volume three, P. 518): "But we have the definition of *nāstika* in Manu's own words as one who controverts the Vedic doctrines (*vedanindaka*)".

Obviously, Dasgupta's reference is to the following verses of Manu (ii. 10-11):

> *śrutis tu veda vijñeyo dharmaśātraṃ tu vai smṛtiḥ /*
> *te sarvārtheṣvamimāṃsye tābhyāṃ dharmo hi nirbabhau / /*
> *yo ' vamanyeta te mūle hetuśāstrāśrayād dvijaḥ /*
> *sa sādhubhir bahiṣkāryo nāstiko vedanindakaḥ / /*

By *śruti* is to be understood the Veda and *smṛti* is nothing but the legal code. In no way are these two to be judged by adverse arguments, for *dharma* in its entirety is revealed through them. if a person having greater confidence in logic shows contempt for these two basic sources, he is to be considered a disbeliever, a vilifier of the Veda; he is to be thrown out of society by the righteous even though he is a Brahmin. In other words, preoccupation with logic is almost a crime. Manu would not ordinarily talk of punishing a Brahmin. But if a Brahmin is imprudent enough to challenge the authority of *śruti* and *smṛti*, what can he do? He has to provide for an exemplary punishment, excommunication.

By way of illustrating how this spell of absolute Vedic authority held away over the classical Indian Philosophers we may refer to the remarks of two of them, one early and the other late. Praśastapāda (c. 5th cent. A.D.) classifies false knowledge or *avidyā* into four forms, one of which is *viparyaya*, the contradictory, false knowledge totally opposed to right knowledge. One of his illustrations for it is *trayī-darśana-viparīteṣu śākyādi-darśaneṣv idaṃ śreya iti mithyā-pratyayaḥ*, the notion that even the doctrines of the Śākyas and others which are opposed to the teachings of *trayī* may be beneficial. In his *Prasthānabheda*, Madhusūdana Sarasvatī (1540 A.D.) again rejects outright the possibility that the Buddhist or the Cārvāka or the Jaina doctrines may be conducive to human welfare even in the least degree, even in an indirect way, simply because they do not conform to Vedic orthodoxy (*veda-bāhyatvāt teṣāṃ mlecchādi-prasthānavat paramparayāpi puruṣārthānupayogitvād upekṣaṇīyatvam eva*).

Manu's mandate on logicians for not violating the Vedas and the acceptance of the classification of philosophies based upon it have been assailed with a number of objections.

An obvious objection against the special interpretation of the words *āstika*and *nāstika* would be that it goes against etymology. At least in the case of Sanskrit words, etymology is often regarded as the standard means for determining the meaning of words. But so far as grammatical derivation is concerned there is nothing about pledging or not pledging loyalty to the scriptures. It is true that words do not always retain their etymological significance. Meanings of words may change and etymology may be forgotten. But instances are perhaps rare where the meaning of a word is fixed just on the whim of on individual.

Secondly, the classification originates from a non-philosopher, a law-maker, whose own interest in philosophy may be extra-philosophical. Unlike the philosopher, the law-maker may not be concerned with an essentially rational approach to reality. Rather he may be interested in the security of a social structure he considers to be the most desirable and ideal.

Thirdly, the Vedas are the scriptures of a particular religion and philosophers are asked to have absolute allegiance to them. What would be the situation if a similar stand is taken by others owing loyalty to other religions and their sacred texts? If the Cārvākas urge that the only criterion for being *āstika* is faith in the *Bṛhaspatisūtra*, what would be the fate of the other systems? Similarly, if the Buddhists or the Jainas decide to consider as *āstika* only one who devoutly follows the precepts as laid down by he Buddha or Mahāvira, we shall we different sets of *āstika* and *nāstika*.

Finally, what is the situation among the Āstikas themselves? Let us take a concrete illustration. Śaṅkara, the great advaita Vedāntin, is full of admiration and reverence for Manu. He sincerely believes that *yad vai kiñca manur avadat tad bheṣajam*. (on *Brahmasūtra* 2.1.2). So what does he do? He quotes the authority of the law-giver as decisive proof, in refuting or in substantiating philosophical positions. Thus, as against the doctrine of the Sāṃkhya, his supreme adversary (*pradhānamalla*), he time and again declares that it cannot be accepted, because it is in contradiction with not only the Veda, but also the assertions of Manu. The relevance of the Yoga system also is rejected on the same ground (on *Brahmasūtra* 2.1.3) and the Vaiśeṣika theory of atomism becomes unacceptable, finally because it is not in the least approved of by the noble people having reverence for the Veda, such as Manu and others (*śruti-pravaṇaiśca śiṣṭair manvādibhir aparigṛhītatvāt* etc., on *Brahmasūtra* 2.2.17).

In short, the mandate of the law-givers would stifle the spirit of free thinking and prevent as essentially rational approach to reality. It would bring about a climate of intellectual sectarianism, which would thwart attempts to understand and assess properly the interactions of the various systems and the growth and development of the Indian Philosophical tradition. It may also compel us to ignore even what is valuable in our tradition.

Others however argue that all this criticism is unnecessarily adverse and seem to miss the real point. As the guardians of the society, the law-givers cannot remain totally indifferent to the impact that may be made on the people in generally by a certain view advocated by philosopher or a logician. Their involvement with philosopher may not be direct, but indirect, for they cannot absolve themselves from the obligation of guiding the people to the right way of life. It is not so much a question of curbing free thinking or making logic totally subservient to the scripture; the question rather is to what extent liberty is to be accorded to logic. The point is whether logic should be allowed to play havoc even with the accepted norms of the society and create chaos. For example, for the good of the society the law-giver may prohibit drinking. But the logician may challenge it by arguing that liquor also may be drunk, since it is a kind of drink, like water, milk, fruit-justice etc. In other words some sort of limit or curb against excessive attachment to logic, so that it may not degenerate into mere perverse argumentation, has to be admitted and this limit, according to the law-givers, is provided by the dictates of the scripture. Logic is necessary, but it should play a positive, constructive role, and one must be cautious about its destructive role.

It appears that the fact is recognised by the logicians themselves in their own way. They deny validity to inferences contradicted by the scripture or do not at all permit the formulation of such an inference, Thus, while explaining the nature of logic and giving the etymological meaning of the term *ānīkṣikī* (logic), Vātsyāyana, the author of the *Nyāyabhāṣya* remarks (on *Nyāyasūtra* 1.1.1): "An inference (*anumāna*) which proceeds on the basis of (i.e. is not contradicted by) perception (*pratyakṣa*) and the scripture (*āgama*) is called *anvīkṣā*, that is, knowing over again that which is already known through perception and the scripture... An inference which is contradicted by (*viruddha*) either perception, or the scripture is a pseudo-*nyāya* (*nyāyābhāsa*)".

It is absurd, for example, to advance an inference in the form that fire is cold, because it is a substance (*dravya*), like water etc. for it is contradicted by perception. Perception, through the cutaneous sense, gives us the knowledge that fire is hot and there is no ground to doubt the validity of this perception. Similarly, it would be unjustified to put forward an inference which may go against the scriptural injunction. As an example, Uddyotakara (*Nyāyavārtika* on *Nyāyasūtra* 1.1.1) mentions an inference advanced by the sect known as the Kāpālika: "The human skull is sacred, because it is the part of an animal body, like the conch-shell (*śaṅkha*)". Just as the conch-shell is considered to be sacred, by the followers of the Veda, in spite of its forming a part of a dead animal, so also, let the human skull be considered sacred on the same ground, inferentially. But this inference is to be rejected as invalid, because the Dharmaśāstras based on the Veda declare the skull to be profane and the touching of a corpse in prohibited (cf. *Manu*v. 7).

Again, the very first step in the formulation of an inference is to make a statement of the thesis, technically called *pratijñā*. Praśsatapāda says that as a rule it must be free from contradiction with the scripture (*āgama*). Thus there is no possibility of formulating an inference with the thesis *brāhmaṇena surā peyā*, because drinking of liquor by an Brahmin is prohibited. Similar examples are available in Buddhist and Jaina works on logic also. (See, for example *Nyāyapraveśa* of Diṅnāga and *Prameyakamalamārtaṇḍa* of Prabhācandra Suri).

Moreover, there is the perennial question of the supremacy of reason or faith. If reason alone capable of solving the riddles and answering the queries concerning human existence, or of delivering the final verdict in matters Philosophical? Does faith also have a role to play in this regard? The Indian tradition does not seem to discard faith altogether. We may take the case of the idea of God. Undeniably, the overwhelming majority of the Indian Philosophers are atheists. Atheism may be said to represent one of the rare fields of close agreement among the representatives of traditional Indian wisdom. But had it been possible to do away with the notion of God? As a modern scholar of Indian Philosophy notes: "Our

Philosophers do their best to argue that logically speaking the idea of God is only an illusion, an empty assumption entrenched only in certain recognised forms of fallacious thinking. Yet they reach nowhere near their desires objective, which is nothing but the full eradication of the idea of God from the Indian mind. In the Indian mind the idea of God survives-and survives in a big way-notwithstanding all the philosophical considerations urging for its rejection. This is a situation which it is impossible for our philosophers to understand. How is it that in spite of being illusory God can have such a living grip on human consciousness?"

Thus, if faith is not totally irrelevant, what, then, would be its foundation, the ultimate basis? The authors of Dharmaśāstra believe that it is nothing other than the scriptures. There are truths that are *tarkagamya*, and there are also truths that are *āgamagamya*. The domain of *āgama* should not be invaded by the expedient of *śuṣkatarka* (cf. Śaṅkara on *Brahmasūtra* 2.1.11).

23

Revenue and Maintenance of State

V.B. Inamdar

The general subject of the Seminar is of a vital interest as it shows an awareness on the part of its organisers to have a second look at the time-honoured systems of the part from a modern social point of view. The purpose of the symposium is to see whether and to what extent the social awareness is reflected in the works on the Dharmaśāstra; in other words to see whether the framer of this Śāstra have paid equal and adequate attention to the life, customs, traditions and interests of all the sections of the society. The subject certainly is important as there is often a talk, rather a loose talk, on the meaning and contents of this branch of Sanskrit literature.

Dharmaśāstra is the science of Dharma. The word Dharma has several meanings-a religion, a religious rite, a religious ordinance, law, duties enjoined or prescribed by customs and traditions, rules of conduct, moral law etc. etc. The word is in the masculine as well as neuter genders (Tāni Dharmāṇi etc. R.V.). It is derived from Dhṛ to sustain or uphold, hence that which sustains or upholds the society if Dharma. Today, however, Dharma is used, rather misused, in the social and political contexts as it is identified with the Karma-kāṇḍa and the attendant evils of exploitation by the priesty class. It is, therefore, to be seen whether this is a correct understanding of our Dharmaśāstra or whether it had a brighter side also in the form of a constructive outlook on the society of those times.

The ancient thinkers prescribed for all, the fourfold aim of life viz. Dharma, Artha, kāma and if possible Mokṣa, at least the first trivarga. There too Dharma is the basis for all the actions and *artha* and *kāma* opposed to Dharma are not commended. From this it is clear that by Dharma was and is meant moral or ethical code of behaviour. The definitions given by the Sūtrakāras and Smṛtikāras are—

गौतमधर्मसूत्र–वेदो धर्ममूलम्। तद्विदां च स्मृतिशीले। I-i-2

आपस्तम्ब–धर्मज्ञसमयः प्रमाणं वेदाश्च। I-1-i, 2

मनुस्मृति–वेदोऽखिलो धर्ममूलं स्मृतिशीले च तद्विदाम्।
आचारश्चैव साधूनामात्मनस्तुष्टिरेव च।। II-6

याज्ञवल्क्यस्मृति–श्रुतिः स्मृतिः सदाचारः स्वस्य च प्रियमात्मनः।
सम्यक् संकल्पजः कामो धर्ममूलमिदं स्मृतम्।। I-7

All these definitions are very comprehensive and broad-based. In the scriptural works, there are directions and instructions regarding the duties of men and women in the various stages of life. These are collected and codified by several Dharmasūtrakāras and Smṛtikāras. The sūtras and rules laid down in these works form the Dharmaśāstra. Most prominent of these works are following:-

(1) Portions of Ṛgveda and Atharvaveda forming the basis of Dharma.

(2) गौतमधर्मसूत्र of Sāmaveda-28 chapters in prose-700 B.C.

(3) बौधायनधर्मसूत्र of कृष्णयजुर्वेद. Mixed with other Sūtra-works 500 B.C.

(4) आपस्तम्बधर्मसूत्र of कृष्णयजुर्वेद. Mixed with other Sūtra-works 600 B.C.

(5) हिरण्यकेशिधर्मसूत्र of कृष्णयजुर्वेद continuation of आपस्तम्ब ध र्मसूत्र

(6) वसिष्ठधर्मसूत्र of ऋग्वेद —300 B.C. Many topics.

(7) विष्णुधर्मसूत्र of ऋग्वेद —300 B.C.

(8) हारीतधर्मसूत्र later than मनुस्मृति

(9) शंखलिखितधर्मसूत्र of शुक्लयजुर्वेद –300 B.C.

(10) मानवधर्मसूत्र of कृष्णयजुर्वेद

(11) वैखानसधर्मसूत्र of कृष्णयजुर्वेद

(12) अर्थशास्त्र of कौटिल्य 300 B.C.

(13) मनुस्मृति of कौटिल्य 200 B.C.

(14) याज्ञवल्क्य-स्मृति with मिताक्षरा 200 B.C.

(15) पराशरस्मृति, नारदस्मृति and many other स्मृतिs
(16) Rāmāyaṇa and Mahābhārata and Purāṇas
(17) The works of अत्रि, उशनस्, देवल, बृहस्पति, भरद्वाज, कात्यायन and others.

A host of commentators and Nibandhakāras also have written voluminous treatises. Bh. Rtn. Mr. Dr. P.V. Kane has listed as many as 4614 works on the subject of Dharmaśāstra written during the last 2600 years and more. Some of these are small tracts while others are books dealing with a number of topics coming under Dharma. These lay down the rules of conduct, religious observances and duties of persons belonging to each of the four Varṇas in every stage of their life. Thus, these are the rules for the whole of the society framed with a view to ensure a smooth well-regulated social life-as per ideas existing then.

The duties are classified into Varṇa-Dharmas, Āśrama-Dharmas, Varṇāśrama-Dharmas, Naimittika-Dharmas and Guṇa-Dharmas (e.g.the duty of a crowned king-to protect). The king was elected and appointed by the Sabhā (also called नरिष्टा) and the Samiti of representatives (vide The Atharva Veda VII-12-1). Without their sanction we could not spend money from the state treasury. They are said to be his daughters who protect him and the subject i.e. they ensure peace and amity. The A. Veda lays down the qualifications and duties of the members of these two bodies. The king cannot rule during their displeasure. Though periodically a theory about the divine origin of the king is put forward, the king is never seen as an absolute owner of the people. He and his government with various departments were responsible to the people. This cannot happen without a social awareness.

The writers of these Dharmaśāstṛa works were mostly from the priestly class-the Brahmins. They provided in the rules certain privileges for their community e.g. The गौतमधर्मसूत्र says— राजा वै सर्वस्येष्टे ब्राह्मणवर्जम्। I-ii. 'न वै अपुरोहितस्य देवा बलिमश्नुवन्ति। ऐतरेय ब्राह्मण VII-5-24 or नृपः यन्नमो ब्रह्मणे-इति त्रिष्कृत्वो ब्रह्मणे नमस्करोति, ब्रह्मणः एव तत् क्षत्रं वशमेति, तद्राष्ट्रं समृद्धं तद्वीरवदाह।' ऐतरेय ब्राह्मणे-VI-II-i. These statements clearly show that the—priestly class was trying to establish its superiority and domination of the ruling क्षत्रिय

Class. "Wherever क्षत्रिय is under the thumb of the Brahmin-that nation becomes prosperous"-so on and so forth. They claimed special privileges such as exemption from tax-payment and from capital punishment etc. The Viśvāmitra-Vasiṣṭha feud in the Vedas is indicative of the same situation. It, however, appears that in actual practice, considering the human nature, all this could not and did not happen. There are instances where the priests were punished and removed by the क्षत्रिय kings. Their cows were taken back (vide Aitareya Br. VII-29) Even the Taittirīya Br. says- 'यदा वै राजा कामयते, अथ ब्राह्मणं जिनाति।'– III-9-14 'Whenever the king desires, he can remove a Brahmin from his office'. The बृहदारण्यकोपनिषत् says—'तस्मात् क्षत्रात् परं नास्ति, तस्मात् ब्राह्मणः क्षत्रियमधस्तादुपास्ते।' 1-4-10. The ancient literature contains several stories of the rivalry between the two varṇas and the ultimate decisions in favour of the क्षत्रिय. It is true that learned Brahmins were exempted from tax-payment. But those who were not learned and not observing the prescribed holy code of conduct were regarded as Śūdras and had no exemption from tax-payment and had no privileges. Vide Mb. 'एतेभ्यो बलिमादद्याद्धीनकोशो महीपतिः।' XII-76-21- 'एते शूद्रसमा राजन् ब्राह्मणानां भवन्त्युत।' XII-76-7 एते ब्राह्मणचाण्डाला महापथिकपांचालाः।' Ibid-9. This means that exemption was only an encouragement to learning, pursuit of knowledge and practice of austerities. Therefore, it would not be quite correct to assume the existence of a theocratic state in our country at any time. The priestly class was always in high esteem for its learning, knowledge and austerities. Their advice was always sought. A Purohita had the status of a minister in the royal court e.g. (अथ सर्वाणि कुर्वीथाः कार्याणि सपुरोहितः। Mbh. XII-71-47)but he never supplanted the king. There might have been some struggle for supremacy between the brain and the brawn. But if the Indian society was always torn by the war of ideas and had only a theocratic leadership, there would not have flourished on this soil, great empires like those of Maurya, Gupta, Vākāṭaka, Shilāhāras, Harṣa Vijay-nagar and others. The Brahmin priest was a preceptor (e.g. Kauṭilya), a teacher (e.g. Yajñavalkya) and a guide (e.g.

Vidyāraṇya, Mādhava) but not a ruler, with a few negligible exceptions. Therefore the Church did not rule.

In the beginning there were large clans formed by large families of agnates and cognates. The peter families was the head. Then there were Viśas, then Janas, then Gaṇas, then Republics and ultimately state with the king as the head. Various experiments were made., new forms of government were evolved, but ultimately monarch was found to be the best by the ancient people. If we minutely observe the office and the position of the king, it will be clear that it was not a bed of roses. He had to keep a constant vigil to see that all his people got their due. This he secured by means of दण्ड which was symbolic. He had to see that there was no difficulty for any one in achieving the पुरुषार्थ–त्रिवर्ग. Vide. नात्मप्रियंहितं राज्ञः प्रजानां तु प्रियं हितम्। को. I-20. कार्यार्थिनामद्वारासङ्ग कारयेत्। दुर्दर्शो हि राजा कार्याकार्यविपर्यासमासन्नैः कार्यति। कौ. I-19. or vide मनुस्मृति VII-123-

राज्ञो हि रक्षाधिकृताः परस्वादायिनः शठाः।
भृत्या भवन्ति प्रायेण तेभ्यो रक्षेदिमाः प्रजाः।।

He had to be watchful about corruption among his officers (eternal-truth !)

The fourfold Varṇa system was there. The ancient thinkers felt that by such a division, they could regulate the society and thus ensure an ideal social order. Nothing, however, has any finality as time has proved. The duties of each one were fixed. It was an experiment. In such a rigid para-military social order the type of social awareness we have in our mind was there and also was not there. The equality (समता) which is the modern concept and is a finding of the democratic thinking and experiment and is more or less a graft from the west, could not exist, in the form in which we cherish it, in that rigid and regulated society in which the status and standard of each one were fixed by Dharmaśāstra. One however, wonders whether it existed at any moment of time or, like philosophers searching a black cat in a dark room where it is not, it is only a futile exercise on our part.

Let us now turn to the particular topic assigned viz.-'Revenue and Maintenance of State'. We can get information about this important subject from many sources. The chief sources allied to the Dharmaśāstra are the following:—The AtharvavedaKāṇḍ III-

4,29 and Kāṇḍa IV-22, the Mahābhārata-Śāntiparvan chapters 62,71,76,87,88,119,120,130 and 131 (Bhiṣma explaining Rājadharma to Yudhiṣṭhira.), the Arthaśāstra of Kauṭilya (the whole of Adhikaraṇa II and parts of V and VI where Kośa and Janapada are described in great detail), Gautama Dharmaśāstra II and X Āpastamba (sporadic references to king's role), Manusmṛti Adhyāya VII verses 80,106,121,127,129,130,131,132,133,134,137,139 Adhyāya VIII-31,33,35,36,37,38,39,40 and verses 140 to 188, Śukraniti I 316,317, IV-3, 22,23,116 (revenue reserves), Yājñavalkya Smṛti with Mitākaṣarā. The institution of kingship was in existence since Vedic times and the idea of State went on slowly evolving.

The main source of revenue was Bali or 'Kara' or Udraṅga (Tax or cess) i.e. land-tax. It was not rent but tax because individual ownership of land was there and the king was not the owner of all lands, though he was called भूमिपति. The waste-land and unoccupied land, however belonged to him. People had to pay tax in return for the protection (of rights, interests, life etc.) All the Śāstrakāras have categorically emphasised that the royal Kośa must always be full. It is said to be the Mūla i.e. the basis of the stability of the state. Kauṭilya says—कोशपूर्णाः सर्वारम्भाः तस्मात् पूर्वं कोशमवेक्षेत। II-8-2

In the Mbh. Bhiṣma says-XII-130

राज्ञः कोशक्षयादेव जायते बलसंक्षयः।
कोशं संजनयेद्राजा नित्यमेभ्यो यथाबलम्।। १३।।
कोशश्च सततं रक्ष्यो यत्नमास्थाय राजभिः।
कोशमूला हि राजानः कोशवृद्धिकरो भवेत्।। १६।।
राज्ञः कोशबलं मूलं कोशमूलं पुनर्बलम्।
तन्मूलं सर्वधर्माणां धर्ममूलाः पुनः प्रजाः। ३६।।

अध्याय १३१-हीनकोशं हि राजानमवजानन्ति मानवाः। ४
श्रियो हि कारणाद्राजा सक्रियां लभते पराम्। ७

The rate at which the part of the produce was to be paid to the king varies 1/16 part acc. to the Atharvaveda vide—

यद्राजानो विभजन्त इष्टापूर्तस्य षोडशं यमस्यामी सभासदः। III-29

1. This was later on increased. Manu says—

पञ्चाशद्भाग आदेयो राज्ञा पशुहिरण्ययोः।

धान्यानामष्टमोगः षष्ठो द्वादश एव वा।। VII-130

1/16, 1/8 or 1/12 part should go to the royal granary. The maximum rate suggested is 33 per cent. This divergence must be due to quality of the land. Śukraniti has a realistic approach vide—

राजभागादिव्ययतो द्विगुणं लभ्यते यतः।
कृषिकृत्यं तु तच्छ्रेष्ठं यन्न्यूनं दुःखदं नृणाम्।। IV - 2-115

After paying the state-tax and the cost of production, the cultivator must be left with some gain at least. Tax was paid in king also and there were huge granaries in the Capital and other big towns. From the cattle-yield and the gold (and perhaps other precious metals) 50 per cent had to go the state Treasury. Present (Nazarāṇās) also were given to the king vide Atharva V. III-4-3, बहुं बलिं प्रतिं पश्यासा उग्रः। On the whole from the annual income one-sixth used to go to the king vide also Kālidāsa's Abh. Śākuntala—

तपःषड्भागमक्षय्यं ददत्यारण्यका हि नः। II-13

The Śāstrakāras have laid down the tax-policy. Though the king is always eager to replenish the Kośa, rate-reduction and exemption must be made acc. to circumstances. In case of drought or very heavy rains or famine or locusts and other the king has to be liberal and considerate. Exemption was also granted to dumb. dealf and disabled persons and widows and helpless people. Bhiṣma says to Yuddhiṣṭhira—

बलिषष्ठेन शुल्केन दण्डेनाथापराधिनाम्।
शास्त्रानीतेन लिप्सेथा वेतनेन धनानेमम्।। XII - 71-10

Restraint is advised while collecting revenue. It is further advised that money should be extracted from people with utmost skill and without creating a feeling of extraction. vide

मधुदोहं दुहेद्राष्ट्रं भ्रमरान्न प्रपातयेत्।
वत्सापेक्षी दुहेच्चैव स्तनांश्च न विकुट्टयेत्।। XII - 88-4

The honey should be taken without raising the bees; the cow should be milked in such a way that some milk will remain for the calf and the udders also will not be pressed too much. At another place (88-7) it is said that slowly and silently the taxes should be increased so that people will not feel the burden. Also an article should be taxed only once. Vide—

वस्तुजातस्यैकवारं शुल्कं ग्राह्यं प्रयत्नतः । शुक्रनीति IV-2-III

A very healthy principle of taxing the merchants is suggested—

प्रचारं भृत्यभरणं व्ययं संग्रामतो भयम् ।
योगक्षेमं च संप्रेक्ष्य गोमिनः (वैश्यान्) कारयेत करम् ।

—Mbh. XII-87-35

Before levying the tax the reasonable expenditure on the items listed in the verse should be taken into consideration एवं राष्ट्रमयोगेन पीडितं न विवर्धति । Thus suppressed by heavy taxes the nation will never prosper (17-16).

There are other sources for the king's revenue. The officer भयधुक् collected taxes in cash and समाहर्ता collected taxes in kind-cows bulls, horses, goats, food-grains etc. Traders used to bring several articles from various lands (upātta) and at the entry point they had to pay the octroi. This was a big source of income for the state. Road-tax was another source. vide— मार्गसंस्काररक्षार्थं मार्गिभ्यः फलं हरेत् । Śukraniti IV-2-25. The customs duty on gold, silver and jewels was very heavy. It was also charged on various articles vide मनु. VII-131, 132.

आददीताथ षड्भागं द्रुमांसमधुसर्पिषाम् ।
गन्धौषधिरसानां च पुष्पमूलफलस्य च ।।
पयशाकतृणानां च चर्मणां वैदलस्य च ।
मृन्मयाजां च भाण्डानां सर्वस्याश्ममयस्य च ।।

6 per cent of the profit was to go to the royal treasury. Fuel, meat, wine, ghee, scents, medicines, juices, flowers, roots, fruits, leaves, vegetables, grass, leather, articles of cane (baskets etc.) earthen vessels, stone articles cotton and silkcloth, in short all articles of daily or occasional use were taxed-cases of exemptions also are given. Public vehicles on road and water had to pay annual

tax-shops and business centres were taxed. Artists and artisans had to pay tax in the form of one day's free labour in a month to the state (vide Gautama Dharma S-II-1-31) Smiths, carpenters, barbers, and all such workers had to pay small taxes. Kauṭilya has given a very very long list of fines and penalties for small and big offences. All this amount went to the state exchequer.

The mines were a source of revenue. They were owned by the state. In case they were leased out, excise duty was imposed and the rates proposed by Śukra were 50 per cent of the value in the case of gold and diamonds, 33 per cent in the case of silver and copper and 25 per cent in the case of other metals. Forest-wealth was a rich source of income कुप्यवन (Vide कौटिल्य II-17-duties of a कुप्याध्यक्ष). Sections of the forests were reserved for the breeding of cattle, elephants and other useful animals that would again yield rich revenue to the state. Expenses of the inspection tours of the state officers were to be borne by the respective towns and villages. Sometimes special taxes for developmental schemes or for meeting emergency situations were also levied. Kauṭilya has written a whole chapter (II-90) on how to enrich the depleted royal treasury.

As the king was the 'Bhoomi-Pati', the unclaimed buried wealth, lands and all else which was not owned by anybody went to the state-treasury (vide-Śākuntala Act VI-the account of the sea-faring merchant-Dhanamitra who died without a child.) Lincence-fee was charged for giving permission to start and carry on various businesses, small and big. These are some of the notable sources of revenue for the state. Income, however, was trickling from several other sources to the royal treasury. All this of course—आदानं हि विसर्गाय।

Maintenance of State

So far as the maintenance of the state is concerned, it is only the Arthaśāstra of Kauṭilya and the Śukraniti that give us some information. Only broad outlines of the State-departments, their infrastructures, the distribution of state revenue. The pay-scales etc. are given. In the भृत्यभरणीयम् (Prakaraṇa 91 of Adhikaraṇa V) salaries of several officers are given. On military (Balam), half the state-income was spent. Constant warfare and constant plans to conquer new countries seem to be the reasons for this. The very name-vijigiṣu for every king suggests this. For encouragement to learning and pursuit of knowledge and for charity (Dana-dharma) 1/12th part, kings privy purse 1/12th part, Administrative machinery 1/12th part, for public utility works and amenities 1/12th part (such as hospitals, rest-houses, public wells, parks, roads etc.) The remaining part as Reserve Fund. This was a broad division which may be taken only as a guideline. The detailed infra-structure must have been thee since large, long-lived and neatly administered empires are known to history.

Kauṭilya gives the salaries (annual) of some top and middle-rank officers of the state. They are (i) 48000 paṇas per annum for the royal priest, the royal preceptor, ministers, Purohita, army-general, prince in office, king's mother and the chief queen. (ii) 24000 paṇas per annum for the chief Dwārapāla, the chief of the palace-guards, Organiser of the army camps, Samāhartā and Sannidhātā. (iii) 12000 paṇas per annum for the king's sons, other queens, leader of the army, arbiter for the complaints of city folk, factory-manager, members of the minister's council and the state-boundary guards (iv) 8000 paṇas per annum for heads of army battalions, commandants of elephant corps, cavalry and chariot-section (v) 4000 paṇas for infantry leaders, cavalry leaders, chariot section officers, elephant-soldiers chiefs, guards of the elephant forests and wealth-producing forests, (vi) 2000 paṇas for chariot warriors, elephant-tramers, physicians, horse-tamers, building-workers, cattle breaders and managers of harlot-homes etc. The list is very long. The provisions made here appear to be of a doubtful nature. An astute statesman and an experienced politician like Kauṭilya can hardly make such absurd provisions. Such dubious provisions have made scholars entertain doubts about the genuineness of many of the statements found in this work. The information available about the various heads of state-expenditure is very scrappy and we have to admit this fact. This, however does not mean that the ancient people had no idea about scientific budgets, account, relative importance of various departments and other aspects of state-maintenance. There were rich and prosperous kingdoms, brave and enlightened rulers cherishing the ideal of Rāmarājya where every member of the state was happy, brilliant cities with stately buildings and a life that could be happily lived. This could not be done without financial insight. Rāmarājya was their dream. In fact, that was the aim of Dharma and the endeavour of Dharmaśāstra.

Bibliography

1. Atharva Veda
2. Mahābhārata
3. Rāmāyaṇa
4. Gautama-Dharasūtra
5. Arthaśāstra or Kauṭilya
6. Manusmṛti
7. याज्ञवल्क्य-स्मृति
8. History of Dharmaśāstra-Vol.I by Bh. Rtn. Mm. Dr. P.V. Kane
9. State and Government in Ancient India-Dr. A.S. Altekar.
10. धर्मशास्त्र-मंथन-पं.महादेवशास्त्री दिवेकर
11. प्राचीन भारतीय राजनीती-डा.रा.शा.मोरखंडीकर
12. प्राचीन भारतीय शासन-व्यवस्था-लालचंद्र राय
13. प्राचीन भारत में राज्य और न्यायपालिका —हरिहरनाथ त्रिपाठी

24

Legal Aspects of Dharmaśāstra as Viewed by European Jurist/ Orientalists Contributing to Comparative Jurisprudence

Prabhakar Apte

Alexander's temptation to invade India is said to be the result of the reports about India's glory presented by bilateral ambassadors to his father's court. The antiquity of the Europeans being attracted by the cultural advancement of the Hindu civilisation seems to date back at least upto that period. However we do not get any written evidence about the interpretation of the aspects of Hindu life in that age, except whatever information we get through the books like 'Milinda-Pañho'. During last three centuries, however European adventurists seem to have set forth for search, contact or invasion in respect of India. The Dutch, the French, the Portugese and the British succeeded in acquring the land of Hindus to some extent or more. Consequently after subjugation they had to rule over sizable Hindu population and they had to study the Hindu jurisprudence, i.e. the Dharmaśāstra for better administration of justice. Naturally, with preconceived notions of their respective sets jurisprudence, they were confronted with the task of interpretation followed by implementation. Besides, much depended on the political background of the ruler: democratic, autocratic or theocratic etc. It is said that Colebrooke was assisted by several Pandits when he got numerous Dharmaśāstra texts translated into English for the sake of the guidance to be provided to the judges. The cultural gap often created embarrassing situations for the interpreters, as eminent as Sir Henry Maine. He is cited to have wondered why an ascetic like Yājñavalkya laid down a stipulated fine for a courtesan refusing to serve the customer after accepting the fee in advance. The verse runs as: *Necchantī dviguṇam dāpyā*. The cultural answer for this doubt is that cases presented before the royal courts were referred to the ascetics when those were found to be complicated. Because they resorted to meditation and penance, hence they could pass impartial judgment. Duncan J. Derrett has called the Hind law as evolved during British rule, as Anglo-Hindu law. It is said about the Portugese that they practically overpowered Dharmaśāstra and scarcely bothered for its interpretation. About the Dutch not much information is available, since their conquest of Hindus is a matter of remote past. About the French however we get documented recorded of century old reports of consultative committees, working since 1828. The voluminous bulk is a precious store for research, in what may be termed as Franco-Hindu jurisprudence. The French jurists appear to have introduced some principles like legitim in interpretation of Dharmaśāstra. Whereas the British introduced some alien concepts like restitution of conjugal rights and judicial separation in Hindus law, the French refrained from imposing French law even on Hindus converted to Christainity. In Indian context, it may be roughly said that the Portugese were oppressive, the British pursuasive and French appreciative.

In the Fag end of eighteenth century, when a very small part of Indian continent, was under the British rule, Sir William Jones was sent to Calcutta High Court as a presiding judge, sometime in 1783. Soon, he became aware of the need to get acquainted with local customs, for smooth administration of justice among the Hindus. For that sake, he started learning sanskrit and Dharmaśāstra. Soon, he published his edition of Manusmriti, and in the preface to that edition, he observed, "the legislature of Britain, having shown an intention to leave the natives of Indian provinces in possession of their own laws at least on the titles of contracts and inheritance, we may humbly presume that all future provisions for the administration of justice will be confirmable, as far as the natives are affected by them, to the manners and opinions of the natives themselves". It was colebrooke who made a compendium of Dharmaśāstra text as a manual for ready reference for the British jurists. Their outlook towards the intermingling of two streams of jurisprudences, namely British and Hindu developed a sort of Anglo-Indian jurisprudence during the long lenure of British rule in India. Sir William Jones was aware that the areas of personal laws only would be left to the natives for self administration. Recently, an eminent British jurist Prof. J. Duncan M. Derrett succeeded in diving deep into the ocean of Anglo-Hindu law and Dharmaśāstra. Actually even though some provisions inserted by the British jurist in personal law areas of the Hindus like `Restitution of conjugal rights' and `judicial separations were alien to Dharmaśāstra the appreciative jurist in Derrett was shocked and shaken to the core of his heart when the Hindu legislators of free Indian voluntarily embraced a totally alien provision of Divorce by mutual concent in 1976. That amendment cut at the very roots of the milleannice old article of faith and fact that Hindu marriage is a `*sanskāra*' and not a `contract'. It is note worthy that the Hindu jurists of Hindu blood did not react as sharply as Derrett did to that epoch making change.

There were other European countries who had also ruled some territory for sometime in History. They had also to do the job of administration of justice over the Hindus. They were Portugese, French and Dutch. It is said that the Portugese simply extended their law over all areas including personal laws of Hindus. About the Dutch outlook not much information available but, the French have contributed a lot to the area of what may be called Franco-Hindu 'Jurisprudence', which is a close Chapter, now open for researchers of comparative jurisprudence. The French rulers of some parts of Indian territory were aware of the problems of administration of justice over the Hindu population of French India. In the preface to the valuable document 'Avis du Comite Consultatif the Jurisprudence Indienne' by Leen Sorg, it is observed that the French did not have the competence to interpret the Hindu Law, nor the English translations of Dharmaśāstra texts were much helpful. Consequently, as Sorg has observed, the Ignorance of the underlying principles of Hindu jurisprudence have caused major errors in the judicial decisions. To overcome these hardless, the French rulers thought it expedient to appoint a consultative committee to decide the case pertaining to the area of personal laws of the Hindus. They laid down the composition of the committee comprising nine members: two Brahmins, two villagers, one soldier, one chief of lower caste, one shepherd, one komti or labourer, and one chetti or merchant. The remarkable feature of this composition was that it was regardless of the religions conversion of these representatives. In the long course of French rule in South India, Many commoners and dignitories had embraced Christianity. However, as far as the personal law was concerned they were regarded by the rulers as governed by their traditional branch of personal law. As a result, a Chetti, or a Brahmin or a Desai, whether, a Hindu, or a converted Christian was governed by his original traditional Dharmaśāstra. The first reported case law is the case of Kanakarāya Mudaliyar the interpreter of the French governor Dupleix, decided by Dupleix himself. In deciding that case two elements of comparative jurisprudence have emerged. They were, firstly that the succession of a Hindu converted to Christianity was decided according to Dharmaśāstra principles of Mitākśarā joint Hindu family and secondly the priciple of 'legitim' in French jurisprudence. According to the first principle, Tanappā, the brother of Kanakarāya also a convert Christian was given the status of co-parcener of the joint Hindu family and given the right of inheriting the entire property of Kanakarāya. Kanakarāya had left to widows behind him belonging to two generations: his own widow and a widow of his pre-deceased son. The main living house in addition to sizable movable property was granted to her by Dupleix, and the widowed daughter-in-law was given comparatively smaller house and some movable property for her subsistence. In this, regard, Dupleix affected some modification to strict Hindu law and invoked the principle of legitim of French jurisprudence meant for balancing the relative inconvenience.

It is learnt that the French rulers were following Hindu jurisprudence in deciding even criminal cases of the Hindus. But that practice had stopped by the turn of seventeenth century. The practice of invoking Dharmaśāstra provisions for deciding the cases of succession etc. of the Hindu converts to Christianity in Pondicherry, not only until the codification of Hindu Law, or its extension to Pondicherry. But up to A.D. Nineteen eightytwo, when the government of India extended, Indian Succession Act to Pondicherry Christians. Thus during Nineteen Fifty-five to Nineteen Eightytwo, Śāstrie Hindu law happened to be the customary law of the Pondicherry Christians. As eminent Retd. chief-justice of Pondicherry, when specifically asked as to the expediency of extension of Indian succession Act, to Pondicherry........

Christians, apparently found no justification for it and exclaimed, "Ask this question to the President of India". Justice David Annousamy has written a research article entitled, `Common

Civil Code a Pondicherry Experiment'. According to him, Pondicherry treatment of personal laws of heterogeneous groups would be a torch-bearer for common civil code, the desideratum of Indian people and Indian government.

The administration of justice, for the Hindus by the French rulers assisted by the consultative committees constituted from time to time and available in the form of printed book of Leon Sorg in 1896, is now a close chapter, open for researchers. This document would not only help the scholars interested in Franco-Hindu jurisprudence as well as the comparative jurisprudence especially of those foreigners who happended to have ruled Indian over some territory and some period of history. To be specific if the interpretation of various Dharmaśāstra texts by the British interpreters and French interpreters are kept side by side for a comparative study, the outcome would go a long way to assess the meaning of Dharmaśāstra text in the proper perspective. It is hoped that some young scholars undertake this forfile field of research for advanced study.

25

कियदेककुटुम्बत्वं विभागश्च कदा भवेत्
एकत्वे वा विभागे वा किं प्रयोजनमिष्यते

चि. श्रीरामशर्मा

विदितचरमेवैतत् भारते देशे भरतीयसंस्कृतौ च चतुषु, आश्रमेर्षु, गार्हस्थ्यं प्रधान आश्रमः। यतो हि तदन्ये यतिब्रह्मचारिणौ कदाचित् वानप्रस्थोपि एतामुपजीवकाः सन्तः स्वे स्वे धर्मेप्रभवन्ति। तदुक्तम "ग्रामादाहृित्य वाग्रासानष्टौ भुञ्जीत वाग्यतः" (इति याज्ञ. प्राय. ५५) वानप्रस्थधर्मप्रकरणे। एवं "भिक्षार्थी ग्राममाश्रयेत्" (५८) इति यतिधर्मप्रकरणे च। सत्येवं गृहस्थो ग्रामे-नगरे वा वसन् सकलं स्वीयं धर्म मनुतिष्ठन् वर्तते इति।

तर्हि धर्मानुष्ठानाय धनं कम्मात्-संपद्यते इति चेत् तदुक्तं स्मृतिषु।

"गुरुषु त्वभ्यतीतेषु-विना वा तैः, गृहे वसन्
आत्मनो वृत्तिमन्विच्छन् गृह्णीयात् साधुतः सदा"

मनु ४-२५२

इत्यादिभिर्वचनैः पित्रोः मरणान्तरं-अथवा तेषु सजीवेस्वपि तैः विना वा-गृहे वसन् वृत्तिनिर्वाहाय सम्पादनं कार्यम्। अपिच एवं सम्पाद्य ये पोष्याः तान् सम्यक् पालयेत् इत्यपि चोद्यते। तत्र पोष्याणां परिगणनापि कृता। तथाहि-

वृद्धौ च मातापितरौ साध्वी भार्या शिशुः सुतः।
अयाज्यथाजनशूद्रप्रतिग्रहादिनापि पोषणीयाः" इति

धर्मसिन्धौ प्रतिपादितः- ५७९. पृ

पिता माता गुरुर्भार्या प्रजा दीनाः समाश्रिताः।
ज्ञातिः बन्धुजनः क्षीणः तथाऽनाथः समाश्रितः।
अन्येप्यधनयुक्ताश्च पोष्य वर्ग उदाहृतः। इति
तत्रैव टिप्पण्यां दर्शितश्चायंश्लीकः स्मृत्यन्तरात्।

अस्तु अत्र संशयः। पिता माता च यदि वृद्धौ तर्हि पोष्यत्वं नाम तयोः उपचारादिः कर्तव्यः इत्यर्थः युक्तो भवति- यदि न वृद्धौ तर्हि किं नाम तयोः पोषणम् तौ पृथक्कुटुम्बत्वेन वर्तेते एव किल। इति चेत् सत्यम्। परन्तु किं नाम पृथक्कुटुत्बत्वं भिन्नपाकाशित्वं वा-पृथग्गृहनिवासित्वं वा ग्रामान्तनिवासत्वं वा-एवं किं नाम कुटुम्बस्य एकत्वं? इत्यत्र निश्चयः कर्तव्यः। प्रकृते तु यदि तौ निर्धनौ तर्हि यथा पत्नीपुत्राः च तथैव तौ दोष्याविति पोष्यवर्गे प्रत्येकतः कथनम्। पृथक्कुटुम्बत्वं-नाम, यदा परम्परागतं अथवा स्वार्जितं वा पुत्रेभ्यो विभज्य पिता, अथवा ज्येष्ठः कनिष्ठेभ्यः तान् पृथग्भाण्डाशिनः करोति तदा पृथक्कुटुम्बत्वं परिगणनीयमापतति। अन्यथा एककुटुम्बत्वमेव। अयं दायविभागप्रकरणे सूच्यते। तथाहि-

विभागकालः- कः इति प्रश्ने-यजमानः स्वीयं ऋणत्रयं देवर्षिपितॄणां अपाकृत्य तदनन्तरं पुत्रे सर्वं भारं दत्वा उदासीनो वसेत्-इति

"महर्षिपितृदेवानां गत्वानृण्यं यथाविधि।
पुत्रे सर्वं समासज्य वसेन्माध्यस्थ्यमाश्रितः" इति।
मनु.४-२५७.

तस्मिन्नेव समये यदि पिता इच्छेत् तर्हि ऐश्वर्यमपि विभजेत्। तदुक्तम्-

विभागं चेत् पिता कुर्यात् इच्छया विभजेत्सुतान् (इति-याज्ञ-व्यव-११४) इति। यदि पिता नेच्छेत् तर्हि पुत्राणां इच्छया विभागो नैव कार्यः असति निमित्ते तेषां पितुरनन्तरमेव विभागकरणे स्वातन्त्र्यम्। तदुक्तं "अत ऊर्ध्वं पितुः पुत्राः विभजेयुः धनं समम्" इति नारदस्मृतौः १३-३.

ऊर्ध्वं पितश्य मातुश्च समेत्य भ्रातरः समम्।
भजेरन्पैतृकं रिक्थमनीशास्ते हि जीवतोः इति
(मनु. ९-१०४) इति मनुरप्यवोचत्।

परन्तु मातरिजीवन्त्यां पितरि मृते तु कदाचित् विभागस्य अवकाशो दृश्यते- तदुक्तम्

"पितुरुर्ध्वं विभजतां माताप्यंशं समं हरेत्"

(याज्ञ-व्यव-१२३) इति।

परन्तु-असति निमित्ते एव-एवमुक्तरीत्या। यदि
निमित्तं स्यात्-तर्हि अकामेपि पितरि पुत्राः
बलात् विभागे समर्थाः। तदुक्तम्।
मातुर्निवृत्ते रर्जास-प्रत्तासु भगिनीषु य।
निवृत्ते चापि रमणे-पितर्युपरतस्पृहे।

इति-नारदस्मृति-१३-३

एवं-"अकामे पितरि रिक्थविभागः-वृद्धे विपरीतचेतसि-रोगिणि च-" इति शङ्खस्मृतौ।

एवं गौतमोपि "ऊर्ध्वं पितुः पुत्राः रिक्थं विभजेरन् २८-१, निवृत्ते चापि रजसि जीवति चेच्छति २८-२," इति।

एवं सर्वेषु भ्रातॄणां पितरि मृते एव स्वकर्तृको विभागः निर्दिष्टः। स च विभागः सम एव। अतएव "ज्येष्ठं वा श्रेष्ठभागेन सर्वे वास्युः समांशिनः"

(याज्ञ.व्यव.११४)

इत्यत्र-"विषमविभागः स्वार्जितविषयः" इति मिताक्षरा।
अपिचात्र विशेषः-वार्धकावस्थायां एव पिता
स्वेच्छयापि विभजेत् इति नियमोस्ति। यतः
"ऊर्ध्वं विभागाज्जातस्तु पित्र्यमेवहरेद्धनम्"
"संसृष्टास्तेन वा ये स्युः विभजेत स तैः सह" इति

(मनु-९-२१६-) इति विभगोत्तरं जातस्य विषये उक्तत्वात्। एष यो विभागः सः पुनरसंसृष्टः चेत् तद्विषये पृथक्कुटुम्बप्रयोजक इत्यवगन्तव्यम्। अथ को नामायं संसृष्ट इति चेत् प्रथमं विभक्तः पुनः त्वयैव सह वत्स्यामि इति पित्रा सोदरेण अग्रजेन वा सह मिलती स संसृष्ट इति। एवं पृथक्कुटुम्बत्वं एककुटुम्बत्वं वा इति निर्णयः।

एवं सह निवसतां एककुटुम्बिनां विभक्तानां च विप्ये
"एकपाकेन वसतां पितृदेवद्विजार्यनम्।
एकं भवेत्-विभक्तानां तदेव स्यात् गृहे गृहे"
(इति बृहस्पतिस्मृतौ।) इति विभागः।

तत्र पक्षद्वये को वा पक्षः श्रेष्ठ इति चेत्। तदाह मनुः-"एवं सह वसेयुर्वा पृथग्वा धर्मकाम्यया।

पृथग्विवर्धते धर्मः तस्माद्धर्म्या पृथक्क्रिया" इति-९-१११.

तत्र सह वसतां एकपाकत्वात् "पाकमेते वैश्वदेवभेदः" इति धर्मसिन्धु वचनात् (८४६ पृ.) वैश्वदेवादिपृथक्करणे अनवकाश इति तद्दृष्ट्या-यथा धर्मवृद्धिः तथा पृथग्वसेयुः धर्मकाम्यया नत्वन्यकाम्या। इति पित्रोः मरणानन्तरं पृथग्वास एव श्रेष्ठः इति धर्मनिर्णयः। तदेव विभक्ताविभक्तभेदेन कर्मभेदः कीदृशः इति धर्मसिन्धौ वणितः। अविभक्तानान्तु- धननिरपेक्षाणि स्नानसन्ध्या-बध्मयज्ञमन्त्रजपोपवासपारयणादीनि नित्यनैमित्तिक-काम्यानि पृथगेव। अग्निसाध्यं श्रौतस्मार्तनित्यकर्मादि पृथगेव। पञ्चमहायज्ञमध्ये देवभूतपितृयज्ञमनुष्य यज्ञाः ज्येष्ठस्यैव" इत्यादिना। ८४६ पृ.

परन्त्वत्रेदमवधेयम् विमागाविभाग भेदः कुटुम्बभार निर्वहणाधीनः यतोहि न स्त्री स्वातन्त्र्यमर्हतीति यद्यपि मनुना प्रोक्तम्ःतथापि-

"असंस्कृतास्तु संस्कार्या भ्रातृभिः पूर्वसंस्कृतैः।
भगिन्यश्च निजादंशात् दत्वांशन्तु तुरीयकम्"

(याज्ञ-व्यव १२४) इति याज्ञवल्येन

अनुद्वाहिता याः भगिन्यः तासां विवाहः स्वभागे चतुर्थांशं दत्वा कार्य इति प्रतिपादितम् मनुना विभागे यः भिन्नपक्षः प्रतिपादितः-

"ज्येष्ठ एव तु गृहणीयात् पित्र्यं धनमशेषतः
शेषास्तमुपजीवेयुः यथैव पितरं तथा"

९-१०५. इत्यत्र

तत्र-अन्येषां विभागाभावेपि तेषां पोषणं ज्येष्ठेनैव कर्तव्यमिति विहितमेव।

"भक्तच्छादनाद्यर्थं पितरमिवोपजीवेयुः" इति तत्र व्याख्य च। अतएव असंस्कृता इत्यत्र असंस्कृताः पुरुषाः असंस्कृताः स्त्रियः च इति एकशेषेण उभयोः अपि संस्कारः कर्तव्यः विहितः परन्तु तत्र विवाहादौ धनव्ययः केन वोढव्यः इति शंकायाः समाधानमेव तुरीयकममंशं दत्वा भगिन्यः संस्कार्या इति। अपिच कात्यायनस्मृतौ "पत्नी भर्तुः धनहरी-या स्यादव्यभिचारिणी। तदभावे तु दुहिता यद्यनूढा भवेत्तदा" इति एवं "भर्तुर्धनहरी पत्नी-तां विना दुहिता स्मृता"

इति बृहस्पतिरपि (२५.५५) इति प्रावोचत्। गौतमस्तु अत्र विशेषमाह "स्त्रीधनं दुहितृणां अप्रत्तानां-अप्रतिष्ठितानाञ्च" 29-6 इति। अत्र अप्रतिष्ठितानां च इति वचनं श्रद्धेयम्। एवं परिशीलनेन ज्ञायते-यत्-धनस्थितिरेव विभागहेतुः। धनाभावे विभागशब्दः प्रायः न प्रयोजकः। अपिच यावच्छक्यम् तावत् एककुटुम्बता पित्रोः मरणानन्तर-मपि धर्मकाम्ययैव पृथक्कुटुम्बत्वम्। धन-विभगोपि यदा यजमानस्य पुत्रीविवाहादिककर्तव्यसंपूर्तिः तदैव यजमानस्य इच्छावशैनैव सम्पूर्तेः प्राक् चेत् विभागपर्यन्तं तस्यैव स्वामिता। अन्यथा जातपुत्रस्य आधानादौ पित्रार्जितधनविनियोगे अर्नाधिकारप्रसक्तेः।इत्यादि व्याख्यातं व्याख्यानेषु।

अत्रैकोविशेषः।

सपिण्डीकरणान्तानि यानि श्राद्धानि षोडश।
पृथङ्नैव सुताः कुर्युः पृथग्द्रव्या अपिक्वचित्-
इति लघुहारीतः।

अर्वाक् संवत्सरात् ज्येष्ठः श्राद्धं कुर्यात् सयेत्यतु-
ऊर्ध्वं सपिण्डीकरणात् सर्वे कुर्युः पृथक् पृथक्-
इति व्यासः-

नवश्राद्धं सपिण्डत्वं श्राद्धान्यपि च षोडश
एकेनैव तु कार्याणि संविभक्तधनेष्वपि इन्युशनाः-

(एतानि त्रीणि वचनानि धर्मसिन्धौ उाहृतानि-८४६ पृ.) इत्यादिवचनेषु विचारितेषु एवं ज्ञायते विभागः केवलं धर्माचरणायैवेति। तथाहि-संविभक्तानामपि पित्रोः प्रथयवत्सरकृत्यं सोदरैः मिलित्वैव कार्यम्। अनन्तरं पृथक् इति वदता तदनन्तरकालभावि महालयादिव्दादशदैवन्येषु देवतानां भिन्नत्वात् तदा विभागो अवश्यंभावीति। अपिच एावंविधवाक्यपर्यालोचनया प्राचीनौरार्जितं द्रव्यं प्रथमतः कुटुम्बभारनिर्वाहाय उपयुज्य शेषं विभज्य स्वीकर्तव्यमिति च। अत्र एकः प्रश्न उदेति। यत्र धनं वर्तते तत्रेव विभागः प्रायः इत्युक्तम्। यदि धनाभावः तर्हि विभागो नास्तीत्येववा इति-उच्यते। यत्र धनाद्यभावः तत्र एकग्रामे नगरे वा स्वस्वद्रव्योपभोगपूर्वकपृथगभाण्डाशित्वमेव विभागः इत्यपि तत्र तत्र धर्म- शास्त्रेषु निरुपितं वर्तते। तदनुसारेण धर्मानुष्ठानम्। अन्यथा कार्यलोप-प्रसङ्गस्स्यात् इति। अस्तु।

एवञ्च धर्मशास्त्रग्रन्थेषु यद्यपि एककुटुम्बलाभाः साक्षात् न निर्दिष्टाः तथापि तत्तत्प्रसङ्गदर्शनेन कुटुम्बभारपूर्तये एककुटुम्बः लाभदायक इति यदा कुटुम्बभारपूर्तिः तदा पृथक्कुटुम्बः धर्मवृद्धये भविष्यतीति च लौकिकप्रयोजनं मनसि कृत्वैव निर्दिष्ट इति ज्ञायते इदं च प्रयोजनं लौकिकं स्वीकृत्य इदानीन्तनेपि काले व्यवहारः कर्तुं शक्यत एव। परन्तु स्वार्थः किंचित् परित्यक्तव्यो भवति। यदीदं मौलिकं प्रयोजनं दृष्टौ प्रधानया स्वीक्रियेत तर्हि सोदराणां आर्थिकव्यवस्थायां यावच्छक्यं तरतमभेदः परिहर्तुं शक्यत इति शम्–

26

संस्कारास्तेषां सामाजिकी भूमिका च

किशोर चन्द्र महापात्र

समुपसर्गात् कृ-धातोर्घञि प्रत्यये भूषणार्थे सुडागमे च कृते संस्कारशब्दो निष्पद्यते। स च संस्कारशब्दो विभिन्नेषु भारतीयशास्त्रेषु विभिन्नार्थको दृश्यते यथा-[1]यज्ञांगपुरोडाशेषु प्रोक्षणादिजन्यद्रव्यधर्मत्वेन मीमांसकाः स्नानाचमनादिजन्य-जीवधर्मत्वेन वेदान्तिनः, शिक्षा प्रशिक्षण- संस्कृति- संस्करण- परिष्करण-भूषण-स्मरण-शक्ति-शुद्धिक्रियादिरूपत्वेन च साहित्यिकाः संस्कारशब्दं व्यवहरन्तो दृश्यन्ते। आंग्लभाषायामयं संस्कारशब्दः
इत्यादिशब्दैः व्यवह्रियते। वस्तुतो धर्मशास्त्रानुसारेण मानवस्य कायिक-मानसिकवाचिकपरिशुदध्यर्थे धार्मिकक्रियानुष्ठानेनात्मनि जायमानो धर्मविशेषः संस्कार इति संस्कारशब्दार्थः। उक्तं [2]मित्रमिश्रेण-आत्मशरीरान्यतरनिष्ठो विहिताक्रियाजन्योऽतिशयविशेषः संस्कार इति। स च द्विविधः। उपनयनादिजन्यो वेदाध्ययनाधिकारापादकः एकः उत्पन्नदुरितमात्रनाशको जातकर्मादिजन्योऽपरः।

[3]हारीतेन द्विविध एव संस्कारः प्रतिपादितः। ब्राह्मो दैवश्चेति। गर्भाधानादिः स्मार्त्तो ब्राह्मः। पाकयज्ञा हविर्यज्ञाः सौम्याश्चेति दैवः। ब्राह्क्रमेण संस्कारेण संस्कृतो मानवः ऋषीणां सलोकतां गच्छति दैवेन च संस्कृतः देवानां सलोकताम्। [4]मनुमतानुसारेण गर्भाधानादारभ्यान्त्येष्टिं यावत् त्रयोदशसंस्काराः यथा-गर्भाधानं, पुंसवनं, सीमन्तोन्नयनं, जातकर्म, नामकरणं, बहिः निष्क्रमणं, अन्नप्राशनं, चूडाकर्म उपनयनं, केशान्तः, समावर्त्तनं, विवाहः, अन्त्येष्टिश्चेति। [5]याज्ञवल्क्येन केशान्त-संस्कारं विहायान्ये सर्वे मनूक्ताः संस्काराः स्वीकृताः। तेन प्रायशः केशान्तस्य समावर्त्तनेऽन्तर्भावः कृतः। एते सर्वेऽपि संस्कारा ब्राह्मण-क्षत्रिय-वैश्यानां द्विजातीनां समन्त्रका एवानुष्ठीयन्ते। शूद्रस्य

तूपनयनसंस्काराभावात् एकजातित्वात् तदतिरिक्ता अन्यं सर्वे संस्कारा यथाकालममन्त्रका एवोपदिष्टाः। यथोक्तं याज्ञवल्क्येन[६]

ब्रहमक्षत्रियविट्शूद्रा वर्णास्त्वाद्यास्त्रयो द्विजाः।
निषेकाद्याः श्मशानान्तास्तेषां वै मन्त्रतः क्रियाः।।

यमेनापि[७] – शूद्रोप्येवंविधः कार्यो विना मन्त्रेण संस्कृतः।। इति हातुकर्ण्यस्तु[८] – "विवाहमात्रसंस्कारं शूद्रोऽपि लभतां सदेति।।" ब्रह्मपुराणवचनमुदाहृत्य एकस्मिन्नेव विवाहसंस्कारे शूद्रस्याधिकारं प्रतिपादयन् तस्येतरसंस्कारव्यावर्त्तनं विदधाति। वैजवापगृह्यसूत्रे शूद्रस्य निषेकः पुंसवन सीमन्तोन्नयन – जातकर्म – नामकरणान्नप्राशनचौलानीति अमन्त्रकाणि यथाकालमुपदिष्टानीति प्रतिपादितम्।

[१०]व्यासमतानुसारेण षोडशैव संस्काराः। गर्भाधानादारभ्योपनयनान्ताः दशसंस्कारा वेदारभ्यः, केशान्तः, स्नानमुद्वाहः विवाहाग्निपरिग्रहः त्रेताग्निसंग्रहश्चेति षडिति मिलित्वा षोडश। अंगिरास्तु[११] पञ्चविंशतिसंस्कारान् प्रतिपादति । यथा –

गर्भाधानं पुंसवनं सीमन्तो बलिरेव च।
जातकृत्यं नामकर्म निष्क्रमोऽन्नाशनं परम्।।
चौलकर्मोपनयनं तद्व्रतानां चतुष्टयम्।
स्नानोद्वाहौ चाग्रयणमष्टकाश्च यथायथम्।
श्रावण्यामाश्वयुज्याञ्च मार्गशीर्ष्याञ्च पार्वणम्।
उत्सर्गश्चाप्युपाकर्म महायज्ञाश्च नित्यशः।
संस्कारा नियता ह्येते ब्राह्मणस्य विशेषतः।।
पञ्चविंशतिसंसरैः संस्कृतास्ते द्विजातयः।।
त पवित्राश्च योग्याश्च श्राद्धादिषु सुयन्त्रिताः।।

एतेषु पञ्चविंशतिसंस्कारेषु गर्भाधानाद्युद्वाहान्ताः षोडशसंस्कारा नैमित्तिकाः, आग्रयणाद्युपाकर्मान्ता सप्तसंस्कारा वार्षिकाः, पार्वणः मासिकः महायज्ञाश्च नित्या इति संज्ञाभेदेनापि व्यवह्रियन्ते।

[१२]गौतमेन सर्वाधिका अष्टचत्वारिंशत् संस्काराः प्रतिपादिताः तन्मते गर्भाधानं, पुंसवनं, सीमन्तोन्नयनं, जातकर्म, नामकरणमन्नप्राशनं चौलकर्मोपनयनाद्यष्टौ चत्वारि वेदव्रतानि, स्नानं, सहधर्मचारिणीसंयोगः

(विवाह):, पञ्च महायज्ञाः (ब्रह्म, दैव, पितृ, मनुष्य, भूत) सप्त पाकयज्ञाः (अष्टकाः, पार्वणः, श्राद्धं, श्रावणी, अग्रहायणी, चैत्री, आश्वयुजी), सप्त हविर्यज्ञाः। (अग्निहोत्रं, दर्शपूर्णमासौ, चातुर्मास्येष्टिः, आग्रयणेष्टिः, निरूढपशुबन्धः सौत्रामणिः) सप्त सोमसंस्थाः (अग्निष्टोमः, उक्थ्यः, षोडशी, अतिरात्रः, वाजपेयः, आप्तोर्यामश्चेति) इति मिलित्वा चत्वारिंशत् संस्कारास्तैश्च सहाष्टौ आत्मगुणाः (दया, क्षमा, अनसूया, शौचं, शमः, अनायासः मंगलम्) मिलित्वा अष्टचत्वारिंशत् संस्कारा भवन्ति।

एतैः संस्कारैर्नकेवलं मानवस्य नैतिकाध्यात्मिकभौतिक- सांस्कृतिकादिविकासा भवन्ति अपि तु सामाजिकविकाशेन सह व्यक्तित्वस्यापि अभिवृद्धिर्भवति। गर्भाधानादिसंस्काद्वारा मानवः कायिकशुद्धिं प्राप्य समाजे विकसितवैदिकमानवरूपेण परिगण्यते। उक्तं मनुना[13]

गार्भहोम-जातकर्मचौडमौजीनिबन्धनैः।
वैजिकं गार्भिकं चैना द्विजानामपमृज्यते।।

एतेषु संस्कारेषु ये लोकप्रियाः त्रयोदशसंस्कारास्तेषां संक्षेपेण कालविध्यादिनिर्देशपुरःसरं सामाजिकी भूमिका प्रतिपाद्यते।

-गर्भाधानम्

[14]"निषेकादिश्मशानान्ता" [15]"निषेकाद्याः श्मशानान्ताः" इत्यादिमनुयाज्ञवल्क्यादिवचनानुसारेण गर्भाधानस्य संस्कारेषु प्राथम्यं बोध्यते। गर्भ आधीयते येन कर्मणाधा तत् गर्भाधानम् इति। तच्च ऋतावेव भवति "गर्भाधानमृतौ" इति [16]याज्ञवल्क्यवचनात्। इयर्त्ति गर्भधारणं गच्छति इति ऋतुः। तस्य कालः षोडशरात्रयः उक्तं याज्ञवाल्क्येन[17] - षोडशर्त्तुः निशाः स्त्रीणां तस्मिन् युग्मासु संविशेत्। ब्रह्मचार्येव पर्वाण्याद्याश्चतस्रस्तु वर्जयेत्।।

अत्र निशाशब्दप्रयोगात् गर्भाधानाय दिवसे स्त्रीगमनं न केवलं निषिद्ध्यते अपि तु प्रत्यवायोऽपि श्रूयते। यथोक्तं [18]प्रश्नोपनिषदि -"प्राणा वा एते स्कन्दन्ति ये दिवा रत्या संयुजन्ते" इति। तास्वपि निशासु पुत्रार्थीयुग्मासु-कन्यार्थीचायुग्मासु संविशोदिति व्यवस्था विद्यते। एवं यो यथा कामयते स तथा प्रजाः प्राप्नुयात्। तत्र ऋतुकालगमनं नियमेन विधीयतेऽगमनेन प्रत्यवायश्रवणात्। उक्तं वीरमित्रोदये[19]

ऋतुस्नातां तु यो भायं सन्निधौ नोपगज्छति।
घोरायां भ्रूणहत्यायां युज्यते नात्र संशयः।। इति

एवमृतुकाले यथाविधि स्त्रियं गत्वा गर्भ आहिते सति ततः प्रभृति आप्रसवात् रजोदर्शनाभावात् अनृतौ स्त्रीगमनस्य निषेधे प्राप्तेऽपि

यथाकामी भवेद् वापि स्त्रीणां वरमनुस्मरन्।
स्वदारनिरतश्चैव स्त्रियो रक्षा यतः स्मृता।। इति

[२०]याज्ञवल्क्यवचनात् तत् प्रतिप्रसवो दृश्यते। यतो हि स्त्रीणां कृते इन्द्रेण वरो दत्तः यथा भवन्तीनां कामविहन्ता पातकी स्यात्। अतोऽनृतावपि भार्य्याया इच्छायां सत्यां गमनं कार्यमेव। अन्यथा पातकित्वश्रवणात्। अपि च स्वदारनिरतश्चैवेति वचनात् परदारगमनं सर्वथा निषिध्यते। अत एतेषां नियमानां पालनेन स्त्रियो न व्यभिचारं कुर्वन्ति न वा पुरुषाः। तेन समाजः संस्खलितो भवति जारजसन्तानोत्पत्तेः सम्भावनापि न भवति।

पुंसवनम्

पुमान् सूयतेऽनेनेति पुंसवनम्। येन संस्कारेण पुत्रोत्पत्तिः अवश्यमेव भवति स पुंसवनमित्युच्यते। प्राक् काले समाजे पुत्राकांक्षा कन्यापेक्षया अधिकाऽऽसीत्। 'पुत्रेण[२१] लोकान् जयति' 'पौत्रेणानन्त्यमश्नुते' इत्यादि मनुवचनात् पुत्रस्य प्रसंसाऽपि शास्त्रे श्रूयते। अतो गर्भचलनात् प्राक्पुंसवनसंस्कारः क्रियते।

[२२]"गर्भाधानमृतौ पुंसः सवनं स्पन्दनात् पुरा।"

इति योगीश्वरवचनात्। [२३]पुंस्त्वलक्षणानामाविर्भावात् प्रागगर्भस्थशिशोः लिंगपरिवर्त्तनं कर्तुं शक्यत इति स्पष्टमुक्तमायुर्वेदे। अतः तस्मिन्नवसरे गर्भरक्षणार्थं पुत्रोत्पत्तये चायुर्वेदोक्तौषधीनामपि प्रयोगः क्रियते। संस्कारोऽयं गर्भचलनात् प्राक् तृतीये चतुर्थे मासि वानुष्ठीयते। केषांचित् मतानुसारेणायं संस्कारः एकवारं कर्त्तव्यः न प्रति गर्भम्। [२४]आश्वलायनगृह्यसूत्रे पुंसवनविधिरित्थं दृश्यते यत् गर्भाधानात् तृतीये मासि कस्मिंश्चित् पुनर्वसुनक्षत्रे पत्नी उपोष्य स्वकरतले गण्डूषमात्रं दधि संस्थाप्य तन्मध्ये शिम्बिकावीजद्वयं तदन्तरा चैकं यवं संस्थाप्य पिबेत्। यथा तदा पतिः पृच्छति किं पिबति इति पत्नी च पुंसवनमिति उत्तरं दद्यात्। एवं त्रिवारं दधि पिबेत्। अस्य संस्कारस्य कर्त्ता स्वयं पितैव।

सीमन्तोन्नयनम्

अयं संस्कारः गर्भाधानात् षष्ठेऽष्टमे वा मासि क्रियते "षष्ठेऽष्टमे वा सीमन्त" इति [२५]याज्ञवल्क्यवचनरात्। अस्मिन् संस्कारे पतिः गर्भिण्याः पत्न्याः सीमन्तस्य अर्थात् केशपाशस्य उन्नयनं करोति अर्थात् केशपाशमलंकुर्वन् तस्मिन् सीमन्तं रचयति। यतो हि गर्भस्तेन सुस्थितो भवति। [२६]उक्तमाश्वलायनाचार्येण – गर्भिण्या गर्भमत्तुं काश्चित् राक्षस्यः रूधिराशनाः समायान्ति। तासां निरसनाय गर्भिणीपतिः सीमन्तकरगीं श्रियमावाहयेत्। सीमन्तोन्नयनेन सीमन्तश्रितायाः श्रिया आविर्भावेन अलक्ष्म्यः क्रूरा राक्षस्यः पीडिताः पलायन्ते येन गर्भः सुस्थितो भवति। संस्कारस्य अस्यापरमपि प्रयोजनं यत् गर्भिण्याः केशप्रसाधनेन गर्भभरक्लान्ता पत्नी प्रमोदिता भवति तेन गर्भस्थस्य शिशोर्विकासः पुष्टिश्च सुतरां जायते। पुनश्च यदा पतिः सीमन्तं रचयति तदा [२७]अयमूर्जस्वितां वृक्षः ऊर्जेव फलिनी भवेति मन्त्रेण एकामुदुम्वरीशाखां तेन केशपाशेन सह वध्नीयात्! कृत्यमिदं पत्न्याः फलवत्तायाः प्रतीकमिव प्रविभाति। वैदिकयुगे सीमन्तोन्नयनावसरे वीणागाथिनो वीणावाद्यपूर्वकं सोमरागस्य स्तुतिमकुर्वन्तीति [२८]भारतीयसांस्कृतिनिधौ रामजीउपाध्यायेन लिखितम्।

जातकर्म

गर्भकोशात् शिशौ जाते जातकर्म विधीयते। पुत्रमुखदर्शनेन पिता तस्य नाभिवर्द्धनात् प्राक् हिरण्येन चमसेन मधुसर्पिषां प्राशनं मन्त्रवत् पिता कुर्यात्। उक्तं मनुना[२९] – प्राङ्नाभिवर्द्धनात् पुंसो जातकर्म विधीयते।

मन्त्रवत् प्राशनं चास्य हिरण्यमधुसर्पिषाम्।।

यद्यपि वैश्वानरं द्वादशकपालं निर्वपेत् पुत्रजाते इति वेदोक्तो नियमो विद्यते, तथापि जातप्राणवियोगभयात् अशौचान्त तत् कर्म कर्त्तव्यम्। जातंपुत्रं दृष्ट्वा पितर आनन्दी भवन्ति इति हेतोः जातकर्मणि पितृनुद्दिश्य [३०]नान्दीमुखी श्राद्धादिकमपि क्रियते। एतत् सर्व अच्छिन्ननाले कर्त्तव्यम्। यतो हि नाभिच्छेदनसमनंतरमेवाशौचं भवति न ततः पूर्वम्। एवं कुमारे जाते महोत्सवं कुर्वन्ति जनाः यतो हि पुत्रोत्सवतुल्य उत्सवः नान्यो विद्यते। पुत्र एव पितुः नरकनिवर्त्तकः, पिण्डोदकदाता रिक्थग्राही चेति सामाजिकी धारणा।

नामकरणम्

नामकरणसंस्कारस्यातीवमहत्त्वं विद्यते। यथा व्यवहारार्थं कस्यचिद् वस्तुनो नामापेक्षते तथैव मनुष्यस्य नामकरणस्यावश्यकतास्ति। उक्तं बृहदारण्यकोपनिषदि बृहस्पतिवचनत्वेन

नामाखिलस्य व्यवहारहेतुः शुभावहं कर्मसु भाग्यहेतुः।
नाम्नैव कीर्त्तिं लभते मनुष्यस्ततः प्रशस्तं खलु नाम कर्म।।

एवञ्च जन्मतो दशमे द्वादशे वादिनेऽशौचापगते कर्त्तव्यम्। उत्कले एकविंशतिदिवसे नामकरणं सम्प्रति क्रियते। एकं नाम गुह्यं क्रियते अपरं सर्वजनप्रकाशनीयं भवति। चतुरक्षरं द्व्यक्षरं वा घोषवदाद्यन्तस्थं पुंसाम्, ईकारान्तामयुजाक्षरं च स्त्रीणां नाम कर्त्तव्यम्। उक्तं मनुना[३२]

स्त्रीणां सुखोद्यमक्रूरं विस्पष्टार्थं मनोहरम्।
मंगल्यं दीर्घवर्णान्तमाशीर्वादाभिधानवत्।। इति

वर्णभेदेनापि नामकरणे भेदो दृश्यते यथा ब्राह्मणस्य मंगलसूचकं क्षत्रियस्य वलान्वितं वैश्यस्य धनसंयुक्तं शूद्रस्य च जुगुप्सितं स्यात्। पुनश्च ब्राह्मणस्य नाम्नोन्ते शर्मा क्षत्रियस्य वर्मा, वैश्यस्य गुप्ता शूद्रस्य च दास इति उपनामसंयुज्येते। उक्तं [३३]व्यासेन

शर्मेति ब्राह्मणस्योक्तं वर्मेति क्षत्रियस्य तु।
गुप्तदासात्मकं नाम प्रशस्तं वैश्यशूद्रयोः।।

एतच्च नाम देवानां महापुरुषाणां वा यथा स्यात् तथा देयमिति केचित् यतन्ते। तेन न केवलं तन्नामोच्चारणेन पुण्योदयो भवति, अपि तु तेषामादर्शेनाभ्युत्थानेनाय प्रेरणाऽपि भवति। नाम्नः प्राक् श्रीशब्दयोजनस्य परम्परापि वर्त्तते। देशविशेषे स्वनाम्ना सह वंशनाम, ग्रामनाम, पितृनामसंबोजनस्यापि परम्परा विद्यते।

निष्क्रमणम्

[३४]जन्मतश्चतुर्थे मासि शिशुः सूतिकागृहात् बहिरानीयते। प्रथमं मातुर्गर्भान्निष्क्रम्य प्रसूतिगृहं ततश्च निष्क्रम्य बहिरागत्य विश्वात्मकं व्यक्तित्वं संवर्द्धयितुं समाजे तत् तत् नाम्ना परिचीयते। निष्क्रमदिवसे सूर्यस्य दर्शनं रात्रौ च चन्द्रस्य दर्शनं शिशोः कार्यते। सूर्यस्तु सकलशक्तेराधारभूतः। अतस्तस्य दर्शनं कारयन् पिता गायति

[३५]तच्चक्षुदेवहितं पुरस्तात् शुक्रमुच्चरत्।
पश्येम शरदः शतं जीवेम शरदः शतम्।।
शृणुयामः शरदः शतं प्रववाम शरदः शतम् इत्यादि।।

अन्नप्राशनम्

जन्मतः षष्ठे मासेऽन्नप्राशनं क्रियते। षष्ठेऽन्नप्राशनं मासीति मनुवचनात[३६]। सामान्यतः दधिमधुघृतमिश्रमन्नं शिशवेऽन्नप्राशनाय दीयते। तद् भोजनग्राासं पिता भूर्भुवः स्वरिति व्याहृत्युच्चारणं कुर्वन्नेव दद्यात्। अन्नस्य भोजनं न केवलं जीवनधारणाय अपि तु व्यक्तित्वस्य विकाशनाय कल्प्यते। तद्दिनादारभ्य शिशुः बहिष्ठं खाद्यं गृह्णन् मातृस्तन्यपानात् निवृत्तो भवति। एवञ्च कर्म शुभे लग्ने शुभे योगे नक्षत्रे च शुभे चन्द्रे च कार्यम्।

चूडाकर्म

संस्कारोऽयं जन्मतः तृतीये पञ्चमे वाब्दे क्रियते् मनुना प्रथमेऽब्देऽपि चूडाकर्म विहितम्। उक्तं यथा

[३७]चुडाकर्म द्विजातीनां सर्वेषामेव धर्मतः।
प्रथमेब्दे तृतीये वा कर्त्तव्यं श्रुतिचोदनात्।।

चूडाकरणे शिखाव्यवस्थातीव महत्त्वपूर्णा। शिरसः शिखरे शिरासन्धीनां सम्मिलनं भवति। अस्य स्थानस्याधिपतिः रोमावर्त्तः। तच मर्मस्थानं भवति। तत्र केनापि प्रहारेण शीघ्रमेव मृत्युर्भवति। अतः तत्स्थाने शिखां धृत्वा तस्य रक्षा क्रियते। प्रवरसंख्यानुसारे चूडासंख्या कल्प्यते। शिरसो मध्ये वसिष्ठगोत्रीयाः एकां शिखां धाश्यन्ति। अत्रिकाश्यपा उभयतः एकैकां, भृगवो मुण्डाः, अंगिरसगोत्रजाः पञ्चशिखाश्च धारयन्ति। यथाकुलधर्म केशावेशान् कारयेदिति [३८]आश्वलायनवचनाच्च वंशपरम्परया शिखाधारणव्यवथासीत्। अनयैव व्यवस्थया शिखिनं दृष्ट्वा हिन्दूरयं ब्रह्मणश्चायं वेति ज्ञानं समाजिकानां भवति।

उपनयनम्

वेदाध्ययनार्थ शिष्यस्य गुरोराचार्यस्य वा समीपे गमनमुपनयनमुच्यते।

अत्र पितैव मुख्यः संस्कर्त्ता। स यदि वेदमध्यापयितुमसमर्थो भवति तर्हि स्वयं स्वपुत्रमाचार्यस्य समीपं नीत्वा तस्योपनयनाय प्रार्थयेत्। आचार्यस्तमुपनीय शिष्यत्वेन गृहीत्वा तमध्यापयति। [३९]अष्टवर्ष ब्राहमणमुपनयीत तमध्या पयीतेति वचनादुपनयनाध्यापनयोरेककर्त्तृकत्वं बोध्यते।

उपनयनसंस्कारेण द्विजत्वप्राप्तिर्भवति। जन्मना जायते शूद्रः संस्काराद् द्विजः उच्यते इति वचनात्। शूद्रस्य तदभावात् स एकजातिरित्युच्यते। ब्राह्मण-क्षत्रियानामुपनयनाख्ये कर्मणि आचार्यस्य पितृत्वेन सावित्र्याश्च मातृत्वेन कल्पितत्वात् तद् द्वितीयं जन्म तेषाम्। अनेन संस्कारेण संस्कृतस्य मानवस्य सामाजिकं जीवनमारभ्यते। वसन्ते ब्राह्मणं ग्रीष्मे राजन्यं शरदि वैश्यं, गर्भाष्टे ब्राह्मणं गर्भकादशे क्षत्रियं गर्भेद्वादशे च विशमुपनयेदित्यादिना द्विजातीपामुपनयनस्य विभिन्नकाला उक्ताः। विभिन्नायां कामनायां सत्यां विभिन्नवर्षेष्वपि संस्कारोऽयमुपदिष्टः। यथोक्तं [४०]मनुना

ब्रह्मवर्चसकामस्य कार्या विप्रस्य पञ्चमे।
राज्ञो बालार्थिनः षष्ठे वैश्यस्येहार्थिनोऽष्टमे।। इति

उपनयनसंस्कारकालस्य परमावधिरपि शास्त्रकारैर्निर्द्धारितः। तद्यथा - [४१]"आषोडशाद् ब्राह्मणस्य आद्वाविंशत् क्षत्रियस्य आचतुविंशाच्च वैश्यस्योपनयनं कर्त्तुं शक्यते। यथोक्तकालानन्तरं ब्राह्मणक्षत्रिवैश्या अनुपनीताः व्रात्या इत्युच्यन्ते। ये समाजे सर्वस्यात् द्विजकर्मणः। ब्रहिष्कार्या भवन्ति। तदर्थं व्रात्यस्तोमनाम यज्ञानुष्ठानं विहितं येन ते प्रायश्चित्तं कृत्वा पुनः सामाजिका भवितुमर्हन्ति। प्राचीने काले [४२]नारीणामपि उपनयनं भवति स्म। लोपामुद्रा, गार्गी मैत्रेयीप्रभृतीनामुपनयनसंस्कारोऽनुष्ठितः इति ऐतिहासिका वदन्ति। एतेन कृतापनयनो ब्रह्मचारी विद्यालाभेन सह सहनशीतां संयमभावं शैचाचारज्ञानं सामाजिकताञ्चाहरेत। गुरूर्यथावर्णं ब्राह्मणादिशिष्यान् क्रमेणाध्यात्मविद्यां, युद्धविद्यांवार्त्ताञ्च (कृषिवाणिज्यादिविद्यां) शिक्षयेत्। तेऽपि वर्णाश्रमधर्मपालयन्तः विभिन्नान् दण्डाजिनमेखलोपवीतप्रभृतीन् धारयन्तोऽदृश्यन्त। प्राक्काले जडमूकान्धबधिराणामुपनयनं नासीत्। यथोक्तं शंखलिख्तिाभ्यां - [४३]"नोन्मत्तमूकान् संस्कुर्यादिति। परन्तु कालान्तरे यदा ब्राह्मणानामुपनयनमनिर्वार्य्यमभूत्तदा तेषामप्युपनयनं जातम्। यथोक्तं ब्रह्मपुराणे

तस्माच्च षण्ढबधिरकुब्जवामनपंगुषु।
जडगद्दरोगार्त्त शुष्कांगविकलेषु च।।
मत्तोन्मत्तेषु मूकेषु शयनस्थे निरिन्द्रिये।
ध्वंस्तपुंस्त्वेषु चैतेषु संस्कारा: स्युर्यथोदितम्।।

एवं गुरुसमीपे स्थित्वा वेदं वेदौ वेदान् वा यथाशक्ति समधीत्य गुरवेऽभिलषितं वस्तु दक्षिणारूपेण दत्वाऽदत्वा वा तदनुमत्या स्नायात्। तेन स स्नातको भूत्वा गुरुकुलात् स्वगृहं प्रत्यागत्य ब्रह्मचर्यावस्थायां वर्जितानां गन्धालंकारप्रभृतीनामुपयोगं कुर्यात्। स्नातकस्य स्थानं समाजे सर्वोच्चं भवति। राजा तस्य योग्यतानुसारेण वृत्तिं विदध्यात् येन स्नातक: कदाचिदपि क्षुधापीडितो न भवेत्। स राज्ञोऽपि सम्मानं प्राप्नोति। उक्तं [४४]मनुना – राजास्नातकयोश्चैव स्यातको नृपमानमाक् इति।

एवं प्रकारेणोपनयनसंस्कारेण मानव: समाजे प्रवेशार्हतां प्राप्य स्नातकरूपेण सम्पूर्णसमाजिको भवति। तस्य जीवनविन्यास: समाजस्यादर्श इति प्रमाणितम्। ततश्च स गृहस्थाश्रमपरिपालनाय गृहिणीमपेक्षते।

विवाह

सहधर्मचारिणीसंयोगो विवाह:। स्नातक: अविप्लुतब्रह्मचर्य: असगोभाम् असपिण्डाम् अनन्यपूर्विकां कान्तां यवीयसीमुत्तमलक्षणयुक्तां स्त्रियमुद्वहेदिति [४५]याज्ञवल्क्यमतानुसारेण कन्याया या योग्यता प्रदर्शिता तादृर्शी कन्यां गृहीत्वा गृहस्थो भवेत्। वरस्यापि कुलशीलाभिजात्यादिकं दृष्ट्वाकन्यादानं क्रियते। न गृहं गृहमियाहुर्गृहिणी गृहमुच्यते इति भारतीयानां धारणा। तेन गृहिणीसनाथ एव गृहस्थ इत्युच्यते।

विवाहस्य प्रयोजनत्रयं दृश्यते। धर्मार्थ पुत्रार्थ इत्यर्थञ्च भार्या गृह्यते। यागाद्यनुष्ठानार्थ पत्न्या आवश्यकता पुत्रार्थे जायाया: (पुंनामनरक-व्यवर्त्तनाय) सत्यामपि पत्न्यां सत्सु च पुत्रेषु कामतोऽधिकस्त्रीलाभार्थमपि विवाह: क्रियते। अष्टवर्षे भवेद् गौरी, नववर्षे तु रोहिणी दशवर्षे भवेत् कन्या अत ऊर्ध्व रजस्वला इत्यादिवचनात् कन्यावस्थायामेव स्त्रियं गृह्णीयादित्युक्तं भवति। अत: [४६]त्र्यष्टवर्षोष्टवाषाञ्वेत्यादि शास्त्रेषु प्रतिपादितम्। अथवा [४७]"त्रिंशद्वर्षोद्वहेत् कन्यां हृद्यां द्वादशवार्षिकीम्। नाग्निकां तु वहेत् कन्यां

यावन्नर्तुमती भवेत्" इत्यादि वचोभ्यो ज्ञायते यत् प्राचीनकाले बाल्यविवाह-प्रथाऽऽसीत्। [४८]कन्या ऋतुमती सती गृहे त्रीणि वर्षाणि अपेक्षेत। तत्कालाभ्यन्तरे यदि पिता उपयुक्ताय वराय न ददाति तर्हि सा स्व - सदृशं पतिं वरयेत्। प्राचीनसमाजे स्वयंवरस्य प्रचलमासीत्। रामायणकाले सीतायाः महाभारतकाले च द्रौपद्याः स्वयंवरमुल्लेखनीयम्। भारतीया नारी एकवारमेकवराय प्रदीयते विवाहानन्तरं परपुरुषचिन्तनमपि तस्याः पापाय कल्प्यते। संकल्पादारभ्य सप्तपदीकमन्तिं विवाहक्रियाप्रचलति। तेनैव नियमेन सप्तपदीकर्मान्ते वरकन्ये सामाजिकबन्धनेन बद्धे भवतः। ततः प्रभृति उभयोरेकशरीरत्वम् एकधर्मत्वम् एकप्राणत्वञ्च कल्प्यते। अपत्नीको मानवः समाजे कस्मिन्नपि श्रौतस्मार्त्तकर्मणि योग्यो न भवति। अतः सर्वेषां वर्णानां कृते विवाहसंस्कारोऽनिर्वार्य्य एव। विवाहः एकः व्यक्तिगतसंस्कारो न भवति। अयं पारिवारिकः सामाजिको वा संस्कार इत्युच्यते। हिन्दुसमाजे पुरुषः सर्वावस्थायां नार्याः रक्षणं करोति। यथा कौमार्ये पितृरूपेण यौवने भर्त्तृरूपेण वार्द्धक्ये च पुत्ररूपेण रक्षति। उक्तं मनुना[४९]

पिता रक्षति कौमारे भर्त्ता रक्षति यौवने।
रक्षन्ति स्थविरे पुत्रा न स्त्री स्वातन्त्र्यमर्हति।।

अयमेव विवाहः ब्राह्मदैवार्षप्राजापत्यगान्धर्वासुरराक्षसपैशाचनेदेनाष्टविधः। एतेषु प्रथमे चत्वारो धर्म्याः अपरे चत्वारश्चाधर्मा इति। गान्धर्वस्यापि प्रशंसा बहुभिः क्रियते वस्तुतः क्षत्रियाणां कृते स प्रशस्तः। ब्राह्मणश्चतुषु वर्णेषु क्षत्रियः त्रिषु वैश्यः द्वयोः शूद्रश्च शूद्रामेव कन्यां गृह्णाति स्म। सवर्णाभार्या मुख्या। कामतः प्रवृत्तानामानुलोम्येन कन्याग्रहणं कर्त्तु शक्यंते। परन्तु तेन वर्णसंकराः जायन्ते येन कुलधर्मस्य लोपो भवति। अतः समाजे तदर्थ प्रोत्साहनं नासीत्। प्रतिलोमविवाहस्य च सर्वथा निषेधः [५०]शास्त्रेषु दृश्यते तेन कुलान्यकुलता यातीतिहेतोः। एवं विवाहसंस्कारेण स्त्रीपुरुषयोर्मिलनेन यौनसुखलाभेन सह परस्परसौहार्द्येन विभ्निनव्रतोत्सवादीनामनुष्ठानेन विधिवच्च पुत्रोत्पादनेन च न केवलं परिवारस्य वंशस्य वाऽपि-तु देशस्य समाजस्य च कल्याणं साध्यते।

विवाहे यौतकप्रथाऽपि प्राक्कालात् समाजे प्रचलति। कन्यादानाकाले पिता यथाशक्ति कन्यामलंकृत्य ददाति। तदानीं तत् सम्बनिधनोऽप्यनेन कन्यामुद्दिश्य वराय यद्ददति तद् [५१]यौतकमित्युच्यते। 'यु' मिश्रणेमिश्रणे इत्यस्माद्धातोः 'क'

प्रत्ययेन युतमिति पदं तस्य भावः यौतम् स्वार्थे 'क' प्रत्ययेन यौतकं यौतकं यौतुकमिति निघण्टुकाराः। तेन विवाहकाले लब्धं धनं यौतुकमिति कथ्यते। साम्प्रतिकयौतकप्रथा ततो भिन्ना दृश्यते यतो हि वरपिता कन्यापितरं धनं यौतकरूपं याचते। प्राचीनकाले क्वचित् कन्या विक्रयो भवति स्म परन्तु सम्प्रति वरविक्रयो दृश्यते इति महतः रोखेदस्य विषयः। यद् भवतु विवाहसंस्कारेण बहुविधसामाजिक समाजिकसमस्यानां समाधानेन सह यौनसमस्याया अपि नियन्त्रणं क्रियते इत्यत्र नास्ति संशयः अनेन प्रकारेण संस्काराः मानवजीवनस्य विकाशार्थ समाजस्य कल्याणाय परिकल्प्यते।

अन्त्येष्टिः

मनुयाज्ञवल्क्यादिभिरन्त्येष्ट्या अपि मरणोत्तरसंस्कारत्वेन स्वीकारः कृतः। मृतं दाहादिना संस्कृत्य तदुदेश्येन तिलोदकपिण्डदानानि क्रियन्ते, अन्यथा तस्य प्रेतत्वं न गच्छेत्। बालानां सिद्धपुरूषाणां महात्मनाञ्च भूमौ निखननं क्रियते। परन्तु सामान्यतः शवस्य दाहसंस्कारः सर्वमान्यो भवति। ततश्च सपिण्डादयः आशौचं यथाविधि पालयन्तः प्रेतोददेशेन श्राद्धादिकं कुर्वन्ति। सपिण्डीकरणेन प्रेतत्वविनाशेन सह पितृत्वप्राप्तिर्भवतीति शास्त्रेषूक्तम्। पतिमरणे पत्नी विधवा जायते। सा च मृतपत्युः चितामारूह्य दग्धीभूता सती सतीपदवाच्या भवति। सम्प्रति सा प्रथा लुप्ता। परन्तु विधवा यतिधर्मेण स्थित्वा शुक्लवस्त्रं परिधाय गन्धालंकारादिरहिता भर्तृकुलं तदभावे च पितृकुलं समाश्रयेत् अन्यथा समाजे सा निन्दिता भवेत्।

साग्निकनिरग्निकभेदेन ब्राह्मणादिवर्णभेदेन बालवृद्धाद्यवस्थाभेदेन देशकालादिभेदेन चान्त्येष्टिसंस्कारो बहुधा दृश्यते। परन्तु सर्वत्र मृतस्य शुद्धिहेतुत्वेन क्रियमाणत्वात् तस्य संस्कारत्वमेव।

एवं समाजस्य सुरक्षार्थ संस्कार एव मुख्यं साधनं येन संस्कृतो मानवः समाजं सेवितुं शक्नुयात्। अतो यावत्पर्यन्तं सामाजिकानां मनः संस्कृतं न भवेत्, तावत् पर्यन्तं समाजे शृंखला, अनुशासनं च सम्यक् न प्रचलेत्। अस्मात् संस्काराः सामाजिकताया प्रतीकभूताः साधनरूपाश्च भवन्ति। एतावता संस्काराणां सामाजिकी भूमिका कीदृशी कियती चेति तत् सम्यगवगम्यते।

१. वाचस्पत्यम् पृ. ५१८८
२. वी.मि.सं.प्र. पृ. १३२
३. धर्म.इ. प्रथमभाग पृ. १७७
४. मनुस्मृतिः २/२७-२८
५. याज्ञ.स्मृति. आचार ११/१४
६. या.स्मृ. आचा. १०
७. वी.मि. सं.प्र. पृ. १३४
८. वी.मि. सं.प्र. पृ. १३४
९. वी.मि. संप्र. पृ. १३३
१०. हिन्दुसंस्कारः पृ. २४
११. सं.मयूखः पृ. ११
१२. गौ. ध.सू. १/८/१४-२४
१३. म.स्मृ. २/२७
१४. म.स्मृ. २/१६
१५. या.स्मृ. आ.१०
१६. या.स्मृ. आ.११
१७ या.स्मृ. आ.७९
१८. प्रश्नोप. १/१३
१९. वी.मि. सं.प्र. पृ. १५३
२०. या.स्मृ. आ. ८१
२१. मनु. ९/१३७
२२. याज्ञ. आ. ११
२३. चरके शारीरस्थानप्रकरणे ८/३/२५
२४. आ.गृ.सू. १/१३/२/७
२५. या.स्मृ. आ.११
२६. आश्वलायनः – वी.मि. सं.प्र. पृ. १७२
२७. पा.गृ.सू. १/१५/६
२८. भा.सांनि. पृ. १७
२९. म.स्मृ. २/२९
३०. अच्छिन्ननाले कर्त्तव्यं श्राद्धं वै पुत्रजन्मनि (जावालिः) – वी.मि.सं.प्र. पृ. १९२
३१. बृ. उ. ३/२/१२
३२. मनु. २/३३
३३. वी.मि. सं.प्र. पृ. २४३

३४. चतुर्थे मासि कर्त्तव्यं शिशोर्निष्क्रमणं गृहात्। मनु. २०/३४
३५. भा. सां.नि पृ. २०
३६. मनु. २/३४
३७. मनु. २/३५
३८. वी.मि.सं.प्र. पृ.३१५
३९. सं.म. पृ.३२
४०. मनु. २/३७
४१. मनु. २/३८
४२. पुराकल्पे कुमारीणां मौञ्जीबन्धनामिष्यते – धर्मशास्त्र का इतिहास, प्रथमभाग पृ.२१९ पा.गृ.सू. २/२
४३. वी.मि. सं.प्र. पृ.४००
४४. मनु. २/१३९
४५. य.स्मृ. आ.५२
४६. मनु. ९/९४
४७. धर्म.शा.अतिहास पृ.२७४
४८. त्रीणि वर्षाणि ऋतुमती कांक्षेत पितृशासनम् इति पराशरमाधवीये बौधायनोक्तेश्च। – नि.सि. पृ.२२०
४९. मनु. ९/३
५०. मनु. ३/६३
५१. वी.मि. व्यप्र. पृ.५४८

धर्मशास्त्रानुसारं स्त्रीपुरुषाणां कर्तव्याणि

के.नलचक्रवर्ती

धर्मशास्त्रानुगुणं मानवस्यायुः शतवत्सरात्मकम्। शतवत्सरात्मकः काल। चतुर्धाविभक्तः एषः कालः प्रत्येकाश्रमत्वेन व्यवहियते। प्रथम पञ्चविंशति वर्षात्मकः कालः ब्रह्मचर्याश्रम इति, द्वितीय पञ्चविंशति वर्षात्मकः कालः गृहस्थाश्रम इति, अन्तिम पञ्चविंशति वर्षात्मकः कालः सन्यासाश्रम इति व्यवह्रियते। एवंमानव जीवनंम् आश्रमचतुष्टतया विभक्तम्[१]।

एवमेव गुणकर्मानुगुणं ब्रह्मक्षत्रिय वैश्यशूद्राश्चेति मानवाः चतुर्धा विभक्ताः गुणकर्म विभागानुसारं यत् विभाजनं कृतं तदेव विभाजनं वर्णरूपेण व्यवह्रियते। "लोकानां विवृदध्यर्थं मुखबाहरूपादतः ब्राह्मणाः क्षत्रियाः वैश्याः शूद्राश्च ब्रह्मणा सृष्टाः[२]। वर्णश्चत्वारः पञ्चमः वर्णः कोऽपिनास्ति" इति मनुना स्पष्टीकृतम्[३]। पुनः शीरकावयवानां आधारेण वर्णेषुविद्यमानाः स्त्रीपुरुषाश्चेति द्विधाविभक्ताः।

आश्रमानुगुणं वर्णानुगुणं स्त्रीपुरुघाणां कर्तव्यानि धर्मशास्त्रदिशा कानीति लघुप्रबन्धेऽस्मिन् विविच्यन्ते प्रधानतया। प्रायः मानवानां कर्तव्यानि प्रायः चतुर्धा विभक्तुं शक्यन्ते।

I पुरुषाणां कर्तव्यानि। (वर्णानुगुणम्)

१. ब्राह्मणानां कर्तव्यानि। (सामान्यानि, विशवरानि)

२. क्षत्रियाणां कर्तव्यानि। (सामान्यानि, विशवरानि)

३. वैश्यानां कर्तव्यानि।

४. शूद्राणां कर्तव्यानि।

II पुरुषार्ा कर्तव्यानि। (आश्रमदशासु)

१. ब्रह्मचर्याश्रमे कर्तव्यानि।

२. गृहस्थाश्रमे कर्तव्यानि।

३. वानप्रस्थाश्रमे कर्तव्यानि।

४. सन्यासाश्रमे कर्तव्यानि।

III स्त्रीणां कर्तव्यानि।

१. ब्रह्मचर्यदशायाम्।

२. गृहस्थाश्रमे।

IV आनुलोम्य प्रातिलोम्य स्त्री पुरुषाणां सम्बद्धानि कर्तव्यानि।

तत्तत् वर्णाश्रिमेषु विद्यमानानां स्त्रीपुरुघाणां एते गुणाः परिपालनीया आसन्। ते गुणाः यथा–अहिंसा, सत्यं, भूतदया, अनुग्रहबुद्धिः, तीर्थयात्राकरणम्, ब्रह्मचर्यपालनम्, मात्सर्यराहित्यम्, देव ब्राह्मणपूजनम्, गुरुशुश्रूषा, सर्व धर्म श्रवणम्, पितृपूजनम्, राजभक्तिः सर्वदा उत्तमशास्त्राणां साहाय्येन विषयावगाहनम्, क्रोध राहित्यं, सहनम्, अस्तिक्यबुद्धिः इत्यादयः।

चतुर्षु आश्रमेषु वर्णेषुच द्विजानांकृते अधिकानि कर्तव्यानि निर्दिष्टानि। यानि कर्तव्यानि धर्मशास्त्रकारैः निर्दिष्टानि तानि केवलं द्विजानां कृते परिमितान्यासन्। अतः आदौ तेषां कर्तव्यान्युद्दिश्य ईषत् जानीमः।

I.1. ब्राह्मणानां कर्तव्यानि

चतुर्षु वर्णेषु ब्राह्मणवर्णः श्रेष्ठतम आसीत्। समाजे अस्यवर्णस्य उत्कृष्टं स्थानमासीत्। न केवलं प्राचीनकाले अद्यापि उत्तमं स्थानमस्ति ग्रामीण प्रान्तेष्वपि। किमुत पत्तनेषु।

मनोरभिप्रायानुसारं ब्राह्मणानां कर्तव्यानि अध्यायपनम्, अध्ययनम्, यजनम्, दानम्, प्रतिग्रह एतानि षड् कर्माणि ब्राह्मणस्य विहितान्यासन्[१]। अत्रिसंहिताया अनुसारं बाह्मणस्य यजनम्, दानम्, अध्ययनं तप इति चत्वारि कर्तव्यानीति ज्ञायन्ते। प्रतिग्रह, अध्यापनम् याजनम् एतानि त्रीणि आजीविका साधनानि इति ज्ञायन्ते[२]।

ब्राह्मणैः स्वेन कर्मणा स्वजीवनं यापनीयम्। एवं जीवितुमसमर्थाः ब्राह्मणाः क्षत्रियवैश्यशूद्रधर्मान् पालयितुं प्रभवन्ति। आपत्काले ब्राह्मणेन कृषिः, वाणिज्यं गोरक्षणं, वृद्धिव्यापारमपि कर्तुं शक्यते। किन्तु तेनगोक्षीरं, गुडं, लवणम्, क्षारः, मांसम् इत्यादीनां वाणिज्यानि न करणीयानि। ब्राह्मणेभ्यः ऋतम्, मृतम् प्रमृतम्

इति चतुर्विधरीत्या जीवनं यापयितुम् अवकाशः प्रकल्पितः। सेवा वृत्तिः कदापि न आश्रयणीया। अत्रिसंहिता नुसारम् ब्राह्मणेन मांसम्, लाक्षा, लवणम् इत्येतानि त्रीणिन विक्रेतव्यान्यासन्। क्षीरविक्रयणमपि ब्राह्मणस्यनिषिद्धम्[१]। यदि तेन क्षीरविक्रयणं क्रियते तर्हिदिनत्रये शूद्रः भविष्यतीति च स्पष्टीकृतम्। अत्रिमहर्षिणा स्पष्टीकृतं यत् भिक्षाया जीवनं न यापनीयं ब्राह्मणेन। एवं ये जीवेयुः तेदण्डया आसन्[१]।

सन्ध्यास्नानं, जपः, होमः, देवतानां पूजनं, वैश्वदेवयज्ञः अतिथिसत्कार एतानि षट्र कर्माणि दिने दिने ब्राह्मणैर्निर्वर्तनीयान्यासन्।

ब्राह्मणानां सामान्यकर्तव्यानि विवेचितानि। इतःपरं विशिष्टानि कर्तव्यानि विविच्यमानानि भवन्ति। एातनि गुरुणां कर्तव्यानि इति व्यवह्रियन्ते। ब्राह्मणानां गुरु स्थानं प्रदत्तम्। ब्राह्मणा एव ब्राह्मणानां क्षत्रियाणां वैश्यानां गुरव आसन्। स्मृतिकाले त्रिप्रकारकाः गुरव आसन्। ते यथाः- गुरु उपाध्याय आचार्यश्चेति।

यो ब्राह्मणः गर्भादानाद्या उपनयनान्ताः क्रियाः कृत्वा वेदमध्यापयति सः गुरुरिति कीर्त्यतिस्म[२]।

यः वेदे कञ्चन भागं वा वेदाङ्गानि वा आजीवनार्थम् अध्यापयति स उपाध्याय इति परिकीर्त्यतिस्म[३]।

यः शिष्यस्योपनयनं कृत्वा वेदान् कल्चसूत्रै उपनिषद्भिः बोधयति स आचार्य इत्युच्यतेस्म[४]।

य अल्पं वा बहु वा यस्य वेदशास्त्रोपनिमित्तं उपकरोति सोऽपि गुरुरिव भावितो भवतिस्म। एातेषु त्रिषु अध्यापकेषु आचार्य उत्तमोत्तम आसीत्।

शिष्यस्योपनयनं कृत्वा आदौ शौचम् आचारम् प्रातस्सायं सम्बद्धम् अग्निकार्यं सन्ध्योपासनच अध्यापनीयम्। एतत् अध्यापकस्य प्रथमं कर्तव्यम्[१]। महयमिदं वदतु इति केनापि पृष्टं चेत् बोधनीयम्। नपृष्टं चेत् न बोधनीयम्। भक्तिश्रद्धादीन् विना केनापि किमपि पृष्टञ्चेत् न बोधनीयम्। धर्मार्थयोः रहितस्य शुश्रुषा रहितस्य शिक्षा न बोधनीया। योग्य शिष्यः न लव्धश्चेत् शिक्षया सह मर्तव्यम् इति कर्तव्यं निर्दिष्टम् घोरापदि अपात्रस्य शिक्षा नैवाध्यापनीया इतिनियम आसीत्। ये गुरव आसन् तेस्सरहस्यास्सर्वा मन्त्रा बोधनीया आसन्। कश्चन महापण्डित अधीतान् सर्वान् अंशान् नाबोधयत्। फलतस्सः चूतवृक्षस्समभवत् अन्यस्मिन् जन्मनि।

उक्तञ्च:- सचूतवृक्षोऽभवत् विद्वान् वै वेदपारगः।
विद्यान दत्ता विप्रेश्यो तेनैव तरुतांगतः।।

एवमेव शिष्यानुद्दिश्य अद्यआगच्छतु, प्रातरागच्छतु, सायमागच्छतु शिक्षामध्येतुम् इति न वक्तव्यमासीत्। एवं येन केनापि व्याजेन ये शिक्षां नाध्यापितवन्त ते आचार्या अनाचार्या इति परिकीर्तिताः[२]। अतः ये अध्यापका आसन् तैः नियतंत् शिक्षाअध्यापनीया आसीत्।

ये ब्रह्मचारिणः शिक्षाध्ययनाय आगच्छन्तिस्म ते शिक्षाध्ययनाय योग्या उत अयोग्या इति गुरुणा परीक्ष्यमाणा आसन्ः। एकसंवत्सरं यावत् अध्यापकैः परीक्ष्यमाणा आसन् ब्रह्मचारिणः। अध्यापकानां कर्तव्यम् इदमप्यासीद्यत् संवत्सरानन्तरं अवश्यं तेषां कृते शिक्षा बोधनीया[१] इति।

I. २. क्षत्रियाणां कर्तव्यानि

क्षतात् त्रायत इति क्षत्रियः। क्षत्रियाः स्वभुजबलेन सर्ववर्णस्थान् पौरान् रक्षितवन्त आसन्। ब्राह्मणवर्णस्यानन्तरं क्षत्रिय वर्णस्यैव समाजे प्रामुख्यं गौरवञ्चासीत्। क्षत्रियाणां सामान्यानि कर्तव्यानि एवम् आसन्। यथाः- यथाविधि अध्ययनम्, दानम्, यजनम् इति[२]। अत्रिसंहितानुगुणं तप इति कर्तव्यम् अधिकतया अस्ति। शस्त्रोपजीवनं भूतरक्षणञ्चेति द्वे वृत्ती निर्दिष्टे। सामान्य क्षत्रियाणां कर्तव्यानि एवं रीत्या आसन्[३]।

ये राजान आसन् तेषां कर्तव्यानि एवमासन्। राज्ञां सामान्यकर्तव्यैस्साकं प्रजानां रक्षणं, विषयेष्वप्रसक्तिश्च स्याताम्[४]। धर्मार्थिनः राज्ञः आचारः पवित्र आसीत्। तेजः, सत्त्वं, धैर्य, दक्षता, संग्रामेष्वनिवर्तिता, ईश्वर भावः एते सुक्षत्रिय धर्मा आसन्। प्रजापालनं राज्ञां परमं कर्तव्यमासीत् पृयग्विधैः यज्ञैः व्रतैः उपवासैश्च राजानः स्वर्ग नैव प्राप्नुयुः इति, उत्तमप्रजापालनादेव राजानः स्वर्ग प्राप्नुयुः इति शंखस्मृतिः निवेदयति[५]। योगानुसरणम् विप्रजन सन्तृप्त्यै अपेक्षिताचरणम् क्षत्रियाणाम् आवश्यके स्तः। यदि विप्राः सन्तुष्टाः भवन्तिस्म तर्हिराज्ञः राज्यं, कोशागारश्च संवर्धितौ अभवताम्। एवमेव वाणिज्यं, कृषिः, गवाञ्च परिपालनं संवर्धितं भवतिस्म। अर्थात् एातैः क्षत्रियोचितैः कर्तव्यैः देशः सुभिक्षः भवतिस्म।

राजा वयवहारान् द्रष्टुं मन्त्रज्ञैः ब्राह्मणैस्सह विनीतस्सन् सभायां प्रविशतिस्म। सभायाम् अधिकानि कार्याणि भवन्ति चेत् उपविश्य अल्पानि कार्याणि भवन्तिचेत् उत्थायैव विनीतवेषाभरणेन राज्ञा दक्षिणपाणिमुद्यम्य राजव्यवहारा निर्वर्तनीया आसन्। तानि च कार्याणि अष्टादशसु विषयेषु पठितानि देशजातिकुल व्यवहारावगतैः साक्षावगतैः साक्षिद्रव्यादि हेतुभिः पृथक् पृथक् प्रत्यहं विचारणीयान्यासन्। प्रधानतया ऋणविषयेषु शाश्वतं धर्ममाश्रित्य कालनिर्णयः करणीय आसीत्। राजा यदा इतर कार्यैनिमग्नो भवतिस्म रोगपीडितः भवतिस्म तदा एतादृशान् व्यवहारान् द्रष्टुं कश्चन विद्वान् बाह्मणः नियोजनीय आसीत्। यस्यां सभायां निन्दार्हाः दण्डिताः भवन्ति तत्र विद्यमानस्य राज्ञः पापः न लिप्यते इति धर्मशास्त्रकाराणाम् अभिप्राय आसीत्। अनाथबालानां वन्ध्यनिष्कुलपतिव्रतविधवारोगिणां सम्पत्तयः संरक्षणीयाः राज्ञा। जीवन्तीनाम् एतासां धनं ये हरेयुः ते चोराश्च राज्ञा दण्डनीया आसन्। अनाथसम्पत्तीनां विषये। तासां सम्पत्तीनाम् औरसाः सन्ति वा? इति नगरे घोषणां कारयित्वा प्रकटनाफलकेषु वर्षत्रयं यावत् प्रकटीकृत्य औरसा आगमिष्यन्तिचेत् तेभ्यः ताः सम्पत्तीः समर्पणीयाः। नोचेदनन्तरं कोशागारेमेलयितुं निर्णयः स्वीकरणीय आसीत्। पौराणां धनंचोरैरपहृतं चेत् तद्रक्षक भटानामुपलव्धव्न्वेत् तत् कोशाधिपतितः संरक्षणीयम्। धनापहर्तारः चोराः निगृहीताश्चत् ते मत्तगजैः घातनीया आसन्। राज्ञा धनलोभेन व्यवहारविषये उपनेक्षाभावः न प्रदर्शनीयः ग्रामवासिनः देशवासिनः वा संधीभूय अस्माभिः एतत्कार्य करणीयम् इति निश्चित्च अनन्तरं कोऽपि लोभेन कार्यपूरणे असमर्थः भवति चेत् राज्ञा सः देशात् बहिष्करणीय आसीत्। ग्रामद्वयस्य सीमानिर्धारणं ज्येष्ठमासे करणीयमासीत्। सीमानिर्धारणे साक्षिभिः अलीकानि उक्तानिचेत् ते दण्डनीया आसन्। केशललाट नासिकापर्यन्त परिमाणक्रमेण ब्राह्मणानां दण्डाः देयाः। ते दण्डा अव्रणा, अक्षताः शोभनदर्शनाः, सवल्कला अग्निदाहरहिताः भवेयुः। कोऽपि शूद्रःजपहोमतत्परः भवतिचेत् सः राज्ञा घातनीयः। ई दृश कर्तव्यानि राज्ञांकृते निर्दिष्टानि धर्मशास्त्रकारैः।

इतः परं वैश्यानां कर्तव्यानि निर्दिश्यन्ते।

I. ३. वैश्यानां कर्तव्यानि

वैश्याः तृतीयवर्णान्तर्गताः। एतेऽपि द्विजाः। क्षत्रियवैश्ययोः यथाविधि दानम्

अध्ययनम्, यजयचेति समानानि कर्तव्यानि निर्दिष्टान्यासन्[१]। पशूनां रक्षणम्, कृषिः, वणिज्यं, वृद्धिव्यापारः,विशिष्टानि कर्तव्यान्यासन्[२]। एतानि कर्माणि यथाविधि करणीयान्यासन्। दम्भमोहौ त्यक्तवा वचसिनियन्त्रणं करणीयमासीत्। ईर्ष्याभावः न प्रकटनीय आसीत्। ब्राह्मणाः यथा प्रसन्नाः भवन्ति तथा तैः प्रयत्नाः करणीया आसन्। यज्ञसमये ऋत्विजानां प्रीतिपूर्वकं भोजनं देयमासीत्। एवं मरण पर्यन्तं धर्मकार्यरताः भवन्तिस्म। प्रतिदिनमालस्यं त्यक्त्वा यज्ञम्, अध्ययनं, दानञ्च करणीयमासीत्। पितृणां श्राद्धादि कर्माणि निर्वर्त्य नरसिंहर्चनपराः भवन्तिस्म[१]। विष्णुस्मृत्यनुसांर एतैः क्षत्रिय ब्राह्मणयोस्सेवा करणीया आसीत्[२]। शिक्षायाम् अधिकार आसीत्। किन्तु अध्यापनाय अवकाशः न प्रकल्पितः।

एतावत्पर्यन्तं क्षत्रियाणां सामान्यकर्तव्यानि विशिष्टकर्तव्यानि निरूपितानि। इतः पर चतुर्थ वर्णसम्बद्धानां शुद्राणां कर्तव्यानि उद्दिश्य ईषत् जानीमः।

I. ४. शूद्राणां कर्तव्यानि

शूद्रवर्णश्चतुर्थः। शिक्षाध्ययनाधिकारः नास्ति एतेषाम्। अतस्संस्कार अनावश्यक आसीत्। शूद्रे पातकं किचिन्न भवतीति अतस्सः संस्कारानर्ह इति मनुः निवेदितवान्[३]। स्मृतिकारेण विष्णुना उक्तं यत् द्विजानाम् आत्मनिवेदनमेव शूद्राणां विहितः संस्कार इति[४]। एवं शूद्राणाम् आत्मनिवेदनम् (शुश्रूषाकरणम्) कारु कर्मच प्रधाने कर्तव्ये इति अत्रिमहर्षेरभिप्रायः[५]। स्मृतिकारस्य शंखस्याभिप्रायानुसारं सर्वशिल्पकार्याणि शूद्रैः करणीयानीति ज्ञायते[६]। हारीतस्यानुसारं वर्णत्रयस्य कृते सेवा करणीया विशेषतया ब्राह्मणानाम् करणीया इति ज्ञायते। शूद्रस्य प्राणः धनम् स्त्रियश्च ब्राह्मण सेवायै नियोजनीया आसन्। मनोरनुसारं शूद्रस्य सेवा एवमासीत्। अन्तर्बहिरच संशुद्धाःमृदुवचः अहङ्काररहिताः शूद्रा आजीवनं ब्राह्मणस्य सेवां कृतवन्तः।

विष्णुस्मृत्यनुसारं द्विप्रकारकाः शूद्रा आसन्। श्राद्धकर्माधिकारिणः अनधिकरिणश्चेति। श्राद्धकर्माधिकरिणः। शूद्राः ये आसन् तेषां पञ्च यज्ञविधानं निर्दिष्टमासीत्[१]। हरीतस्यानुसारं विनाभ्यर्थनं दानं शूद्रेण देयमिति ज्ञायते। जीविकानिर्वहणार्थ कष्टसहनं करणीयमासीत् शूद्रेण। पाकयज्ञेन देवतानां पूजनं कृत्वा न्यायतत्परो भूत्वा देवतार्चनं करणीयमिति कर्तव्यमपि

विहितं शूद्राणाम्। जीर्णवस्त्रधारणं ब्राह्मणस्योच्छिष्ट भोजनम् शूद्राणां नियमौ आस्ताम्।

वर्णानुगुणं ब्रह्मक्षात्रियविट्शूद्राणां कर्तव्यानि (सामान्यानि विशिष्टानि च) निरुपितानि। इतः परं आश्रमानुगुणं पुरुषाणां कर्तव्यानि कानीति निरूप्यन्ते।

II. १. ब्रह्मचर्याश्रमे कर्तव्यानि

ब्रह्मचर्याश्रमः द्विजानां कृते परिमित आसीत्। शूद्राणां कृते जन्मत आरभ्य सेवाकरणमेव। अतः शूद्राणाम् एष आश्रमः न निर्दिष्टः। स्त्रीणां कृते प्राक्तनस्मृतिकाले एष आश्रमः नासीत्। अर्वाचीनस्मृतिकाले एष आश्रमः प्रकल्पितः स्त्रीणाम्। उपनयनानन्तरं ब्रह्मक्षत्रियविशां पुत्राः द्विजा इति परिगणिता आसन्। उपनयनानन्तरं द्विज बालकाः ब्रह्मचारिण इति व्यवह्रियन्तेस्म। ब्रह्मचारिभिः गुरुकुले ४८ वत्सरपर्यन्तं निवासः करणीय आसीत्। ये नैष्ठिक ब्रह्मचारिण आसन् तेषां कृते एतावान् कालः। ये गृहस्थाश्रमे प्रवेष्टुमिच्छन्तिस्म तेषां द्वादश वत्सरः कालः वा २४ वत्सर कालः वा आसीत्। वेदत्रयं, वेदौ, वेदं वा यथाक्रमं ब्रह्मचर्येण अध्येतव्यमासीत् ब्रह्मचारिभिः[१]। ब्राह्मण ब्रह्मचारिणः कृष्णाजिनम्, क्षत्रिय ब्रह्मचारिणः रुरु चर्म, वैश्यब्रह्मचारिणः बास्तञ्च उत्तरीयानां रूपेण धृतवन्त आसन्। एवमेव ब्राह्मणाः शाणवस्त्रम्, क्षत्रियस्य क्षौमवस्त्रं, वैश्यस्य ऊर्णवस्त्रञ्च अधोवस्त्राणां रूपेण निर्दिष्टान्यासन्। एवंयज्ञोपवीत दण्डधारणेऽपि प्रत्येक वर्णस्य भेद आसीत्। कृतोपनयनानां द्विजानां कृते आसमावर्तनं यावत् गुरुकुले इन्धनानयनम्, अहरहः भैक्षाचरणं, सत्यवाक्पालनम्, अधश्शयनम्, उदकुम्भानयनम्, गोग्रासानयनम्, गवांचारणम्, कर्मणामनसागिरा गुरोः हितचिन्तनम्, न गुरुवचनावधिक्करणम्, सन्ध्याद्वयोपासनम्, पूर्वां सन्ध याम् उत्थायकरणम्, आसीनो पश्चिमसन्ध्याकरणं, अप्सुदण्डवन्मज्जनम्, गुरोः प्रियहिताचरणम्, मेखलदण्डाजिनोपवीत धारणम्, गुरुकुलवर्जं गुणवत्सु भैक्षाचरणम्, गुर्वनुज्ञातो भैक्षाभ्यवहरणम्, श्राद्धकृतलवणशुक्तपर्युषित नृत्यगीत स्त्रीमधु मांसाञ्ज नो च्छिष्ट प्राणिहिंसाशीलपरिवर्जनम्, गुरोः पूर्वोत्थानम्, चरम संवेशनम्, कृतसन्ध्याद्वयोपासानन्तरं गुरोरभिवादनम्, व्यत्यस्तकरेण गुरोः पादोपस्पर्शनम्, अभिवादने नाम्नोऽन्ते भोश्शव्दनिवेशनम्, इत्यादीनि कर्तव्यानि

ब्रह्मचारिणां विहितान्यसन्। गन्धमाल्यदिवास्वप्न यानोपानत्र? कामक्रोध लोभमोहवाद्यवादन हर्षगीतस्त्रीप्रेक्षालापनानि वर्जनीयान्यासन्। एवमेव गुरोरासीनेसति उपतिष्ठन् तिष्ठत अभिगमनं, गच्छतः प्रत्युद्गमनं, धावतः पश्चाद्धावनं, गतिचेष्टा भाषिताधिकम् इत्यादीनि वर्जनीयान्यासन्। एकासने गुरुणासह नैवोपविशन्त आसन् ब्रह्मचारिणः ऋते शिलाफलकयानेभ्यः। गुरो-र्गुरुः सन्निहितेसति गुरुवत् माननीय आसीत्। बालौ समानवयसि वा ऽध्यापके गुरुपुत्रे गुरुवद्वर्तेत। तस्य पदौ न प्रक्षालनीयौ आस्ताम्। तस्योच्छिष्टं न भोक्तव्यमासीत्। गुरोः पुरतः जृम्भनं, हसनं, क्षपणं, प्रावरणं, नरवविस्फोटनम् इत्यदीनि नैव करणीयानीति स्मृतिकारणामाशयः। एतानि कर्तव्यानि परिपालयन्तः वेदं, वेदौ, वेदान्, वेदाङ्गानि वा अधीतवन्त आसन्ब्रह्मचारिणः।

ब्रह्मचर्यदशायां ब्राह्मणस्य सकाशेऽध्येतव्यमिति आपस्तम्बः। बोधायनेन स्पष्टीकृतं यत् अब्राह्मण सकाशे ऽप्यध्येतुं शक्यते इति। मनुरापस्तम्बौ च आपत्काले अब्राह्मणस्य सकाशेप्यध्येतुं शक्यते इति स्पष्टीकृतवन्तौ। श्रद्धासहिताः द्विजाः स्वस्मादवरवर्णात् मनुजात् उत्तमशिक्षाऽध्येतव्या इति आपत्काले अब्राह्मणादपि वेद अध्येतव्य इति तस्याब्राह्मणस्य अध्ययनं यावत् अनुसरणं शुश्रूषा च करणीया इति मनोरभिप्राय[१]: किन्तु पादप्रक्षालनम् उच्छिष्टभोजनम् इत्यादयः न स्वीकरणीया इति

आश्रमदशासु ब्रह्मचर्यदशायां विद्यमानानि कर्तव्यानि विदितानि। गृहस्थाश्रमे पुरुषाणां कर्तव्यानि कानि इति इदानीं निवेद्यन्ते

II. २. गृहस्थाश्रमे कर्तव्याणि (पुरुषाणाम्)

गृहस्थाश्रमः श्रेष्ठोधर्मः। गृहस्थाश्रमधर्मात् परो धर्मः नास्तीति स्मृतिकारस्य व्यासस्याभिप्रायः। त्रिषु आश्रमेषु विद्यमानाः गृहस्थस्य आश्रयेण जीवन्ति। "सर्वोपकारक्षममाश्रमस्ते" इति कालिदासः रघुना वाचितम्। गृहस्थाश्रमे गृहस्थानां प्राथमिकानि कर्तव्यानि यजनम्, तपः करणम्, दानम् इति कर्तव्यानि निर्दिष्टानि। आदौ यथाविधि सायं प्रात औपासनादि क्रियाः वैवाहिकाग्नौ करणीयाः। वैश्वदेवादि क्रियाः पाकक्रियाश्च निर्वर्तनीयाश्च आसन्,। गृहस्थाः दैनन्दिनजीवने चुल्ली, पेषणी, अमस्करः खण्डनी, उदककुम्भ एतान्

उपयुञ्जन्तेस्म। एतेषामुपयोगकरणेन पञ्चहत्यापापानि भवन्तिस्म। एतानि पापानि एव पञ्चसूनदोषा इति व्यवह्रियन्तेस्म। एतेषां दोषाणां निवारणाय गृहस्थैः ब्रह्मयज्ञः, पितृयज्ञः, दैवयज्ञः भूतयज्ञः, नृयज्ञश्च करणीया आसन्। अतिथिसत्कारः गृहस्थस्य प्रथमं कर्तव्यम् आसीत्। स्वाध्यायस्सर्वेषां द्विजानां मुख्यं कर्तव्यमिति निर्दिष्टम्। दारिद्यकारणेन नित्यमतिथिपूजाकरणे योऽसमर्थः भवति तेन स्वाध्यायः करणीय आसीत्।

ऋषयः, पितरः, देवाः, भूतानि, अतिथय एते गृहस्थेभ्यः यानि वस्तूनि वाञ्छन्तिस्म तानि ज्ञात्वा देयान्यासन्। वेदाध्ययनेन ऋष्यः, होमेन देवाः, श्राद्धेनपितरः, अन्नेन अतिथयः, बालिना जन्तवश्च प्रीणनीया आसन्। प्रतिदिनं वैश्वदेवनिमित्तं यत् सिद्धान्नंकृतं तत् गृह्याग्नौ होमः करणीय आसीत्।

एवं गृहस्थेन बलिकर्म कृत्वा गृहमागताय अतिथये भोजनं देयम् आसीत्। तदनन्तरं चतुर्थाश्रमे विद्यमानस्य सन्यासिनः प्रथमाश्रमेविद्यमानस्य ब्रह्मचारिणश्च भिक्षा देया।

अतिथिसत्कारविषये आगतस्यातिथये आसनं देयम्। पादप्रक्षालनायोदकं दत्वा यथाविधि समर्च्य व्यञ्जनसहितान्नं देयमासीत्। यदि भोजनदानासमर्थे मार्गायासापनयाय स्थलं, शयनायतृणनि, हस्त पादौ प्रक्षालनाय पिपासानिवारणाय जलं, सूनृत वचसाच आतिश्यं प्रदेयम् आसीत्। एवं क्रियतेचेत् तस्य समृद्धिः भवेत् इति आश्वासनं प्रदत्तं धर्मशास्त्रकारैः।

वैश्वदेवानन्तरम् अतिथेः भोजनानन्तरं अन्यः कोऽपि अतिथिस्समागतश्चेत् तस्मैबल्यन्नं नैवदेयमासीत्। यथाशक्ति तस्मै अन्नं प्रदेयमासीत्। सुवासिनीः नवोढाः रोगिणः, गर्भिण्य एतासां कृते अतिथेः परिवेषणात् पूर्व भोजनं देयमासीत्। विप्राणाम् अतिथीनां भृत्यानां भोजनान्तरं जायापतीभ्यां भोजनं स्वीकरणीयमासीत्। देवान् ऋषीन्, मनुष्यान्, पितृन्, गृहस्थान्, सर्वान् अन्नेन पूजयित्वा तदनन्तरम् अवशिष्टान्नं भोक्तव्यमासीत्।

II. ३. वानप्रस्थाश्रमे कर्तव्यानि

आयुषः तृतीयभागे एकाकी अथवा भार्यया वा जितेन्द्रियो भूत्वा वानप्रस्थाश्रमे प्रविशन्नासीत्। भार्यया सह गन्तुं नेच्छा अस्तिचेत्, भार्यानैवागच्छति

चेत् भार्यां पुत्राधीनां कृत्वा वानप्रस्थाश्रमे प्रविशातिस्म गृहस्थाश्रमी। यदा शरीरं वलीभिः आक्रान्तं भवतिस्म फलित केशः भवतिस्म पौत्रोत्पत्तिः भवतिस्म तदा गृहस्थाश्रमं त्यक्त्वा गृहयाग्निं स्वीकृत्य वनाश्रमे प्रविशतिस्म नखकेशसित-गात्रत्वग्युतेन तेन वने स्थित्वा शास्त्रोक्तविधिना अग्निहोत्र-पञ्चयज्ञाश्च करणीया आसन्। तस्मिन् वने यत्नपूर्वकं अनिन्दित नीवाराद्यन्न शाकफल मूलानि स्वीकुर्वन् वानप्रस्थधर्मं निर्वहन् होमं कुर्यात्। स्वयं यत् भुज्यते तेन बलिं वैश्वदेवविधिं आचरणीयौ आस्ताम्। आश्रमे समागतानां जलं मूलानि फलानि च भिक्षारूपेण देयान्यासन्।

स्वाध्यायेतरस्सन् शीतवर्षातपसहितः भवतिस्म। नक्षत्रेष्टि आग्रहायणेष्टिश्च करणीयौ आस्ताम्। चातुर्मास्ये उत्तरायणदक्षिणायणयोश्च क्रियमाणे श्रौतकर्माणि करणीयान्यासन् वान प्रस्थेन। वसन्तऋतुगतेभ्यः शरदृतुगतेभ्यः परिशुद्धेभ्यः स्वत आनीतेभ्यः नीवारधान्येभ्यः पुरोडाशा चरवश्च पृथक् पृथक् यथाविधि करणीया आसन्। वनोपलब्धैः नीवारधान्यैः कृतानि पुरोडाशचरुहवींषि देवतानां कृते दत्वा हविश्शेषं स्वीकरणीयम् आसीत्। स्वतः कृतं लवणञ्चोपयोक्तव्यमासीत्। मधुं, मांसं, भौमानि कवनानि, भूस्तृणं, शिग्रुकं श्लेष्मातक फलानि त्यक्तव्यान्यासन्। अटव्यामपि हलकर्षित प्रदेशे समुद्भूतं यजमानेनोपेक्षितं धान्यं नैव स्वीकरणीयमासीत्। हलेनानकर्षितानि ग्रामे समुद्भूतानि मूलफलानि रुजग्रस्तेनापि नैवस्वीकरणीयान्यासन्

सुखविषयेष्वनासक्तः स्त्रीसम्पर्करहितः धराशायी ऊर्णकृमिनिर्मितवस्त्रेषु ममकार सहितः वृक्षमूलनिवासी च स्यात् वानप्रस्थ इति नियम आसीत्। वानप्रस्थनियमपालने उपनिषत्सूक्तानि ब्रह्मप्रतिपादकानि वाक्यानि सर्वाणि परब्रह्मप्राप्त्यै वारं वारम् आवर्तनं कुर्वन् तेषाम् अर्थान् जानीयात्। वानप्रस्थः त्रिषुकालेषु स्नानं कुर्वन् तीव्रतपस्सम्पन्नः स्यादिति स्मृतिकारस्य शंखस्याभिप्रायः। पक्षान्ते अथवा मासान्ते स्वयं भोजनं कृत्वा भोक्तव्यमासीत्। चतुर्थकाले अथवा अष्टमे काले भोजनं स्वीकरणीयमासीत्। नोचेत् उपवासयुतः स्यात्।

ग्रीष्मकाले पञ्चाग्निमध्ये वर्षाकाले निराश्रयभूमौ, शीतकाले जलमध्ये स्थित्वा तपः करणीयमासीत्। अर्थात् त्रिषुऋतुषु ऋतुधर्मानुकूलं उग्र तपश्चर्यानुकूलं कालः यापनीय आसीत्। एवं तपः कुर्वन् शनैश्शनै अधिकाधिकं तपः कुर्वन् स्वीय बुद्धिः यथा स्थिरा भवेत् तथा करणीया। अग्निपक्वं वन्यमन्नं कालपक्वानि फलानि उलूखलमुसलाभ्याम् अचूर्णितं पाषाणैः चूर्णीकृतं

अपक्वमन्नं वानप्रस्थेन भोक्तव्यमासीत्। एवमेतादृशानि कर्तव्यानि स्मृतिकारैः वानप्रस्थानां कृते विहितानि।

इत ऊर्ध्वं सन्यासाश्रमे पुरुषाणां कर्तव्यानि निरुप्यन्ते।

II. ४. सन्यासाश्रमेपुरुषाणां कर्तव्यानि

चतुर्षु आश्रमेषु उत्तमोऽस्ति संन्यासाश्रमः। श्रद्धापूर्वकतया आश्रमेऽस्मिन् स्थित्वा धर्मानुष्ठानं करणीयमासीत्। परम् एष आश्रमः केवलं ब्राह्मणानां कृते निर्दिष्ट इति विष्णोरभिप्रायः। अस्याभिप्रायानुसारं क्षत्रिय वैश्ययोः ब्रह्मचर्यगृहस्थ वानप्रस्थाश्रमाः निर्दिष्टा इति ज्ञायते। आश्रमेऽस्मिन् द्विधा प्रवेष्टुमवकाश आसीत्। धीर यस्मिन् समये वैराग्ययुक्तः भवतिस्म तस्माद्दिनादारभ्य आश्रमेऽस्मिन् प्रविशतिस्मः एषः प्रथमः प्रकारः। एतादृशाः विरला आसन्। वनाश्रमे स्थित्वा समस्तप्रकारपापेभ्यः विमुक्तो भूत्वा आयुर्दायस्य चतुर्थभागे आश्रमेऽस्मिन् प्रवेष्टव्यं ब्राह्मणैः[1]। एषः द्वितीयः प्रकारः। प्रायः बहव एवमेव आश्रमेऽस्मिन् प्रविशन्तिस्म। ईदृशे समये सर्ववितस दक्षिणम् इति प्राजापत्येष्टिं निर्वर्त्य अग्नीन् आत्मन्याशेप्य ब्राह्मणाः स्वगृहात् निष्क्रमेयुः इति नियम आसीत्।

आश्रमेऽस्मिन् पितृभ्यः देवेभ्यः मानवेभ्यः निमित्तं आदानं देयमासीत्। यत्नपूर्वकं पितृभ्यः मानवेभ्य एवमात्मने च श्रांद्धकरणीयमासीत्। पूर्वं अथवा उत्तरदिशाभिमुखो भूत्वा वैश्वानरयज्ञः करणीयः तदनन्तरं स्वयमग्निरिति मत्वा मन्त्रवित्पुरुषः सन्यासाश्रमे प्रविशतिस्म। सन्यासाश्रमे प्रविश्य पुत्रादिषु स्नेहः प्रदर्शनीय आसीत्। पालन पोषणाद्याः याः वृत्तय आसन् ताः त्यक्तव्याः। बन्धूनां तथा समस्तप्राणिनां अभयं देयम् आसीत्। शौचसमये आसनपरिग्रह समये मुनिभिरावेदितं कौपीनं शीतनिवारणार्थं कन्थाच स्वीकरणीये आस्ताम्। अन्यानि वस्तूनि विहाय पादुके धारणीये इति नियमः प्रकल्पितः। एतानि संन्यासाश्रमे विद्यमानानां सन्यासिनां कृते प्रधानानि चिह्नानि। एवंविधः संन्यासी दृष्टिपूतं पादं त्यजेत्, वस्त्रपूतं जलं पिबेत्, सत्यपूतां वाचं वदेत्, मनःपूतं समाचरेत्[2] इति नियमः प्रकल्पितः। मन्त्रोच्चारणसहितं देवतानां तर्पणं कृत्वा सूर्यस्य नमस्कारो विधेय आसीत्। पूर्वदिशाभिमुखोभूत्वा मौनतया त्रिवारं प्राणायामः करणीयः। लौकिकग्निरहित : गृहं विना व्याधिग्रस्तोऽपि व्याधिमनालक्ष्य

स्थिरचित्तो मौनी भूत्वा ब्रह्मध्यायन् अहोरात्रं वने उषित्वा एकाकी चरेदिति कर्तव्यं विहितम्। शिरोजनखश्मश्रवश्चास्थापयित्वा भिक्षापात्रं कमण्डलुञ्च स्वीकृत्य सर्वान् प्राणीन् अबाध्य एकत्रैवास्थित्वा सदानियमैः सञ्चारः करणीय इति निर्दिष्टं धर्मशास्त्रकारैः। अलाबूपात्रं, दारुपात्रं, मृत्पात्रं, वंशीपात्रं एतेषु यत्किमपि पात्रमुपयोक्तव्यमासीत्। प्रायः हस्तौ पात्रतुल्यौ। पुर्वोक्तेषु पात्रेषु सत्स्वपि तेभ्यः हस्तपात्रे एव आहारमुपस्थाप्य भोक्तव्यमासीत्।

हस्तेकपालः, वृक्षमूलनिवासः, मलिनवस्त्रधारणम्, सर्वसमदृष्टि आश्रमेऽस्मिन् विद्यमानानि लक्षणानि। ग्रामगृहेषु धूमोपशान्त्यनन्तरं, मुखलरावस्य स्थगनानन्तरं, अङ्गारकणिकानां निर्वापनानन्तरं, सर्वेषां पौराणां भोजनपरिसमाप्त्यनन्तरं, पात्रपरिमार्जनानन्तरं सन्यासी भिक्षायै ग्रामे प्रविशेत् इति कर्तव्यं विहितम्। मधूकर, संक्लृप्त प्राक्प्रणीत अयाचित तात्कालिकोपपन्नाः पञ्चविधभिक्षाः स्वीकरणीया आसन्। दिने एकबारमेव भोजनं स्वीकरणीयम् इति नियमः प्रकल्पितः। तत्रापि देहरक्षणाय अनेक्षित आहारः स्वीकरणीयः आषाढस्य पौर्णमास्यां चातुर्मास्यव्रतारम्भः करणीय आसीत्। कार्त्तिकशुक्लनवमीतः सञ्चारः करणीय इति कर्तव्यमपि विहितम्।

एतावत्पर्यन्तं वर्णगतानाम् आश्रमगतानां पुरुषाणां कर्तव्यानि धर्मशास्त्रानुगुणं निरूपितानि। इतः परं ब्रह्मचर्य गृहस्थाश्रमदशयोः स्त्रीणां कर्तव्यानि कानि इति विशदीक्रियन्ते।

III. स्त्रीणां कर्तव्यानि

१. ब्रह्मचर्यदशायाम्

"न गृहिणी गृहमुच्यते" "पत्नीमूलं गृहं पुंसाम्," "पत्नीमूलं गृहेसुखम्" इत्यादि भिर्वाक्यैः स्त्रीणां महत्वं स्पष्टतया ज्ञायते। "विनाश्रयो न शोभन्ते कविता वनिता लता" इति नीतिवाक्यमनुसृत्य स्त्रीणां क्वचन आश्श्रय आवश्यकः। स्त्रीणां कृते विद्यमानासु तिसृषु दशासु त्रयः पुरुषाः आश्रयभूताः भवन्ति[१]। एनं निमित्तीकृत्य "न स्त्री स्वातन्त्र्यमर्हति" इतिस्मृतिवाक्यमुदाहरन्ति। स्त्रीणां स्वातन्त्र्यं नास्तीति वक्तुंन शक्यते। स्त्रियः कुसुमकोमलाः अबलाः भीरवश्च। अतएव तासां पुरुषैः रक्षणम् आवश्यकम् इत्येतावन्मात्रमेव वक्तुं शक्यते। किन्तु

तासां स्वातन्त्र्यं नास्ति इति यो अनुवाद अस्ति स असदनुवादः। स्त्रीणां महत्वमुद्दिश्य मनुमहर्षिणा एवमुक्तम्ः-

"यत्र नार्यस्तु पूज्यन्ते रमन्ते तत्रदेवताः।
यत्रैतास्तु न पूज्यन्ते सर्वासस्तत्राफलाः क्रियाः।।

एवमेतादृशं महत्वं स्त्रीणाम् अस्तीति निवेद्य पुनस्तासां स्वातन्त्र्यं नास्तीति कथनं मनोरभिप्रायः नास्ति।

वैदिककाले स्त्रीणां कृते शिक्षायामधिकार आसीदिति वेदोपनिषन्मन्त्रैः ज्ञायते। परन्तु श्रुतीननुसृत्य विरचिताः स्मृतिग्रन्थाः स्त्रीशिक्षाविषये अनादरमेव प्रदर्शितवन्तः। विवाहविधिरेव स्त्रीणां वैदिकसंस्कारो उपनयनाख्य इति मन्वादिभिः स्मृतः। पतिसेवैव गुरुकुल वासः वेदाध्ययनरूपः गृहकृत्यमेव सायं प्रातसमिद्धोमरूपोऽग्निपरिचर्या। अर्वाचीनः स्मृतिकारःयमः ब्रह्मचर्यदशायां मौञ्जी बन्धनमासीत्। वेदाध्ययनं वेदाध्यापनं सावित्रीवचनञ्चासीत्। तासाम् आध्यापनाय पिता पितृव्यो भ्राता वा अध्यापकानां रूपेण आसन्। स्वगृहे भैक्षचर्याच विहिता आसीदिति[1]।

III. २. गृहस्थाश्रमेस्त्रीणांकर्तव्यानि

स्त्रीणां कृते पतिः देववत् आराधनीय इति कर्तव्यं विहितम्। पतिर्विना तासां पृथक् यज्ञः व्रतम् उपोषणञ्च नासन्। पतिशुश्रूषा तासांपरमः धर्मः। पतिशुश्रूषया ते स्वर्गलोकं प्राप्तुमर्हाः आसन्।

स्त्रीणां दैनान्दिनकर्तव्यानि स्मृतिकारैरेवं निर्दिष्टानि। पत्युःपूर्वं शय्यातः समुत्थाय देहशुद्धिं विधाय गृहस्य मार्जनं करणीयम्। यज्ञशालायां मार्जनं लेपनं यज्ञकर्माणि अपेक्षितानांपात्राणां मन्त्रपूर्वकम् उष्णोदकेन शुभ्रं कृत्वा स्थाने स्थापनीयानि। भर्त्रापित्रा भ्रातृमातुलबन्धवैर्यानि वस्त्रालङ्काराणि दत्तानि तानि धारणीयानि मनोवाक्कायकर्मभिः शुद्धा भूत्वा पत्यादेशानुवर्तिनी छायेवानुगता सती हितकर्मसु सखीव नपयादिष्ट कर्मसु दासीव स्यात्। समनन्तरं भोजनं संपच्य भर्त्रे समर्प्य वैश्वदेवयज्ञं कृत्वा अवशिष्टान्नं भृत्यानां प्रदेयम्। तदनन्तरं भर्तुः परिवेषणं करणीयम्। भर्त्रोरनुमतिं स्वीकृत्य अवशिष्टं भोजनं भोक्तव्यम्। भोजनानन्तरं दिनशेषस्य आयव्ययविचारः करणीय आसीत्। समनन्तरं भर्तुः परिचर्या करणीया। भर्तुः शयनानन्तरं सावधाना कामरहिता इन्द्रियजेत्री

भर्तीरिमनः प्रसार्य तस्य पार्श्वे शयिता च स्यात्। उच्चैर्नोच्यात्। परुषवचांसि नोक्तव्यानि तया। अप्रियं नोक्तव्यम्। पत्या सह अप्रलापिनी नकेनापि विवदेत्। अतिव्ययशीला धर्मार्थविशेधिनी च न स्यात। प्रमादोन्मादवञ्चनादिरहिता स्यात। पैशुन्यहिंसाहङ्कार धूर्तभावादिरहिता। स्यात। एवंरीत्या स्थिता सा कालं याप्यमाना आसीत।

IV आनुलोम्यप्रातिलोम्य जातिसम्बद्धानां पुरुषाणां कर्तव्यानि

अनु क्रमाङ्कः	सम्बद्धकन्या /स्त्री	सम्बद्धः पुरुषः	अनयोरुत्पन्नः पुरुषः	समुत्पन्नस्य पुरुषस्य कर्तव्यानि	विशेषांशः
१	२	३	४	५	६
१.	ब्राह्मणकन्या	नृपः	सूतः	रथचालनम्	
२.	ब्राह्मणकन्या	सूतः	वेणुकः		
३.	ब्राह्मणकन्या	क्षत्रियः	रथकारः	कटवयनम्, सुवर्णकर्म	चौर्यात्
४.	ब्राह्मणी	क्षत्रियः	मागधः	ब्राह्मणक्षत्रिययो धर्मः वैश्यस्य दासत्वस्, स्तुतिपाठकः	
५.	ब्राह्मणी	शूद्रः	चण्डालः	शवदहनादिकम्	
६.	वैश्यकन्या	चण्डालः	स्वपचः	शुनकबलविशिष्टः	
७.	क्षत्रियकन्या	वैश्यः	आयोगवः	तन्तुवयनम्	
८.	ब्राह्मणकन्या	आयोगवः	ताम्रोपजीवी	ताम्रलोहविक्रयनम्	
९.	नृपकन्या	आयोगवः	सूनिकः		
१०.	क्षत्रियकन्या	सूनिकः	उद्बन्धकः	वस्त्रधावनम्	
११.	क्षत्रियकन्या	वैश्यः	पुलिन्दः	पशुमांसभक्षणम्	चौर्यात्
१२.	क्षत्रियकन्या	शूद्रः	पुलकसः	सुरावत्ति, मधुविक्रयनम्, सुरानिर्माणम् विक्रयणञ्च	
१३.	वैश्यकन्या	पुलकसः	रजकः		
१४.	क्षत्रियकन्या	शूद्रः	रंजकः		चौर्यात्
१५.	वैश्यकन्या	रंजकः	नर्तकाः, गायकाः	नर्तनम्, गायनम्	

contd.....

अनु क्रमाङ्कः	सम्बद्धकन्या /स्त्री	सम्बद्धः पुरुषः	अनयोरुत्पन्नः पुरुषः	समुत्पन्नस्य पुरुषस्य कर्तव्यानि	विशेषांशः
१	२	३	४	५	६
१६.	वैश्यकन्या	शूद्रः	वैदेहिकः	अजमहिष गवां पालनम् दधिक्षीराज्य विक्रयनाज्जीवनम्	
१७.	ब्रह्मणी	वैदेहिकः	चर्मोपजीवी	चर्मव्यापारः	
१८.	क्षत्रियकन्या	वैदेहिकः	सूचिकः		
१९.	वैश्यकन्या	शूद्रः	चक्री	तिलेभ्यः तैलानयनम् लवण विक्रयणम्, व्यवसाय करणम्	चौर्यात्
२०.	क्षत्रियकन्या	ब्राह्मणः	अनुलोम सवर्णद्विजः	सन्ध्यावन्दनादि नैमित्तिककरणम्, राजाज्ञया अश्वरथ- गजादीनां चालनम् सेनापति उत्तर- दायित्व स्वीकरणम्, भैषज्यकर्म	विधिपूर्व केन
२१.	क्षत्रियकन्या	विप्रः	भिषक्	चिकित्साकरणम् ज्यौतिष अथवा गणितविद्यया जीवन निर्वहणम्	चौर्यात्
२२.	क्षत्रियकन्या	विप्रः	नृप		विधिपूर्वकेन
२३.	क्षत्रियकन्या	नृप	गोलः	क्षत्रियधर्म	
२४.	वैश्यकन्या	विप्रः	अम्बष्ठः	कृषिकर्मनिरतः आग्नेयवृतिकः, शस्त्रोपजीवी	विधिपूर्वकेन
२५.	वैश्यकन्या	विप्रः	कुम्भकारः	कुलालवृत्तिः	चौर्यात्
२६.		कुम्भकारः	नापितः (कायस्थः)	जन्मसूतकेमण— सूतके मन्त्रोपदेश- दीक्षायां केश-	

contd.....

अनु क्रमाङ्कः	सम्बद्धकन्या /स्त्री	सम्बद्धः पुरुषः	अनयोरुत्पन्नः पुरुषः	समुत्पन्नस्य पुरुषस्य कर्तव्यानि	विशेषांशः
१	२	३	४	५	६
				कर्तनेन आजीविका-निर्वहणम्	
२७.	शूद्रकन्या	विप्रः	पारशवः	श्रेष्ठ पर्वतिषु- स्थित्वा जीविको- पार्जनम्	विधिपूर्वकेन
२८.	पारशवा	पारशवः	निषादः	वनेदुष्टमृगान् हत्वा जीवनयापनं, मांसविक्रयणम्	
२९.	वैश्यकन्या	क्षत्रियः	मणिकारः	मणीनां रञ्जनम्, मौक्तिकानां भेदनम्	चौर्यात्
३०.	शूद्रकन्या	विप्रः	उग्रः	राजः दण्डधारकः अपराधिनां दण्डनम्	
३१.	शूद्रकन्या	विप्रः	शुण्डिकः		
३२.	शूद्रकन्या	वैश्यः	सूचकः		विधिपूर्वकेन
३३.	ब्राह्मणकन्या	सूचकः	तक्षकः	शिल्पकर्म, भवन निर्माणम्	
३४.	क्षत्रियकन्या	सूचकः	मन्स्यबन्धकः		
३५.	शूद्रकन्या	वैश्यः	कटकारः		चौर्यात्
३६.	शूद्रकन्या	शूद्रः	शूद्रः	सेवाकरणम्	
३७.	क्षत्रियकन्या	सूतः	चर्मकारः		

धर्मशास्त्रानुगुणं स्त्रीपुरुषाणां कर्तव्यानि विशदीकृतानि। इतः परं निष्कर्षाः प्रस्तूयन्ते।

निष्कर्षा

मानवजीवन सौलभ्याय क्रमविकासाय चतुर्णानां पुरुषार्थानां सम्पादनाय चत्वार आश्रमाः निर्दिष्टाः। चत्वार आश्रमाः ब्राह्मणानां कृतेऽवनिर्दिष्टाः ब्रह्मचर्यगृहस्थवान्

प्रस्थाश्चेति त्रय आश्रमाः क्षत्रविशोः निर्दिष्टाः। शूद्रस्य कोऽपि आश्रमः न निर्दिष्टः। आश्रमनिर्देशाभावेन कर्तव्यानि अपि न निर्दिष्टानि भवन्ति। एवमाश्रमविभजने तरतमभेदः निर्दिष्टः। तत्रापि चतुर्षु आश्रमेषु ब्राह्मणानामेव अधिकानिकर्तव्यानि निर्दिष्टानि। ब्राह्मणानां षट् कर्तव्यानि क्षत्रवैश्ययोः चत्वारि कर्तव्यानि, शूद्रस्य कर्मद्वयम् निर्दिष्टम्। स्त्रीणां शूद्रवत् कर्मद्वयं निर्दिष्टम्। अर्थात् वर्णेषु आश्रमेषु कर्तव्यानि समानतया न निर्दिष्टानीति ज्ञायते।

आपत्काले ब्रह्मणस्य कृषिः, वाणिज्यं, गोरक्षणम् वृद्धिव्यापार इत्यादीनि कर्तव्यानि निर्दिष्टानि। एष अवकाश इतरवर्णनां न प्रकल्पितः विवक्षात्र प्रकल्पिता। अध्यापनं ब्राह्मणानामेव कर्तव्यमासीत्। अध्ययनेऽपि गर्भाष्ट-मादारभ्यरताः भवन्तिस्म। ब्राह्मणानां कृते क्षत्रियैः वैश्यैः स्त्रीभिश्च सेवा करणीया आसीत्। नाम ब्राह्मणान् विहाय अवशिष्टाः सर्वे सेवका एव। सेवा भावनिरतानां कृते स्वातन्त्र्येण यत्किमपि कर्तुम् अवकाशः नोपलभ्यतेस्म। फलतः समाजे सर्वसमत्वं लुप्तमासीदिति तदर्थमेव आरक्षणम् (Reservation) मण्डलसमितिः (Mandal commission). इत्यादयः समागताः।

स्त्रीणां कर्तव्यविषयेऽपि कश्चनविमर्शअस्ति। स्त्रियः पूजनीया इति धर्मशास्त्रिणाम् अभिप्रायः। गृहस्थाश्रमे पुरुषाः विना स्त्रीभिः गार्हस्थ्यं धर्म निर्वोढुमसमर्था एव। शिक्षाध्ययनाधिकारः नांसीत्तासाम्। किन्तु गृहस्थाश्रमे प्रमुखं पात्रमासीत्तासाम्।

धर्मशास्त्रकाराणामपि मातर अग्रजा अनुजाश्च आसन्। शूद्रय आनुलोम्य प्रातिलोम्य स्त्रियः विहाय अवशिष्टास्सर्वाः स्त्रियः द्विजसम्बन्धिन्य एव। परंतासां शिक्षाधिकारः न प्रकल्पितः। स्त्रीणां कर्तव्याणि अल्पान्येव। गृहस्थाश्रमे स्त्रीणां भर्त्रा सह केचन अधिकाराः प्रदत्ताः। परिशीलनं क्रियते चेत् स्त्रियः शूद्रा इव परिगणिता इति ज्ञायते। यथा शूद्राणां सेवा, शिल्पकार्याणि निर्दिष्टानि तथैव स्त्रीणां कृते सेवा, शिल्पकार्याणि च निर्दिष्टानि। प्रथमदासाः शूद्राः द्वितीयदास्यः स्त्रियः। परं दास्यकरणे स्त्रीणां सीमा निर्दिष्टा, पतिसेवा तासां प्रधानतया निर्दिष्टा। इयानेव भेद आसीत्। स्त्रियः ताडनीया आसन्। शूद्राः न ताडनीया आसन्।

स्त्रियः गृहस्थाश्रमस्य कृते एव परिमिता आसन्। ब्रह्मचर्याश्रमः सर्वात्मना

तासां नासीत्। वानप्रस्थाश्रमः विकल्पतया परिकल्पितः सन्यासाश्रमः क्षत्रवैश्ययोरेव नासीत् किमुत स्त्रीशूद्रयोर्विषये। अर्भात् सन्यासाश्रमे स्त्रीणां प्रसक्तिरेव नासीत्। अतो वक्तुं शक्यते यत् स्त्रियः गृहस्याश्रमस्य कृते एव सीमिताः आसन्। सूक्ष्मेक्षिकया परिशीलितञ्चेत् कर्तव्यानि सर्वाणि पुरुषाणां कृते निर्दिष्टानि।

धर्मशास्त्रम् अद्यतनीयं शास्त्रं नास्ति। यदा धर्मशास्त्रविचार आगच्छति तदा तस्मिन् शास्त्रे विश्वासः प्रदर्शनीयः। तस्मिन् समये या संस्कृति रासीत्, ये आचारा आसन्, ये विचारा आसन् तान् उद्दिश्य सद्विमर्शः करणीयः। अस्मिन्नेव समये एतदपि मनसि स्थापनीयं यत् अस्माकीनैः पूर्वैरपि एतत् विरचितम् अस्माकं पितृपैतामहादारभ्य अङ्गीकृतम् सन्तुदोषा एतस्मिन् शास्त्रे, वयं धर्मशास्त्रकारान् विश्वसिमः। तानेवानुसराम इति नोक्तव्यम्। धर्मशास्त्रे ये केचन दोषाः सन्ति ते अवश्यं त्यक्तव्याः सन्तिकेचनगुणास्तस्मिन् ते आश्रयणीयाः। धर्मशास्त्रं पक्षपातयुतम्, तस्मिन् शास्त्रेविद्यमानं साहित्यं सर्वं भस्मसात्करणीयमिति न वक्तव्यम्। धर्मशास्त्रे विद्यमानानि कर्तव्यानि, आचाराः, विचाराः, प्रभूतं साहित्यञ्च अस्माकं देशस्यौरसतया समागतम्। तत्साहित्यमेकः कलाखण्ड इति ज्ञातव्यम्।

शेक्सपियर महोदयस्य रूपकानाम् अवगाहनाय पाठकैः वा विमर्शकैः वा एलिजबेत् काले विद्यमाना आचारविशेषाः मनसि स्थापनीयाः। एवमेव धर्मशास्त्र विचारेऽपि स्मृतिकर्तॄणां कालः य आसीत् सः कालः मनसि स्मर्तव्यः। विशेषतया वक्तुंशक्यतेयत् स्मृतय अथवा धर्मशास्त्रस्य विचारविषये संकुचितभावाः त्यक्तव्या आधुनिकः कालः मनसि निधाय स्मृतीनां विचारः नैव करणीयः।

बुद्धिमत्सुनराः श्रेष्ठाः नरेषु ब्राह्मणाः स्मृताः वर्णत्रयस्य शुश्रूषां
कुर्याच्छूद्रः प्रयत्नतः। –मनु. १–९६.
दासवत् ब्रह्मणानाञ्च विशेषेनसमाचरेत्।। ल.हा. ११.
शूद्रान्नं शूद्रसम्पर्कः शूद्रेणच सहासनम्।
शूद्राज्ज्ञानागमः कश्चिज्ज्वलन्तमपि पातयेत्।। अ.स्मृ. ४९.

वर्णाश्रम धर्मानुद्दिश्य अद्यतनेकाले ये भावास्सन्ति तान् मनसि निधाय पूर्वश्लोकाः परिशीलिताश्चेत् विपरीततया गोचरेयुः। किन्तु एते श्लोकाः सहस्रवत्सरेभ्यः पूर्वं भारतेविद्यमानान् आचारान् प्रतिबिम्बयन्ति इत्यनुमतञ्चेत् एतेषां श्लोकानामुपरि धर्मशास्त्रस्योपरि विद्यमानः क्रोधः उपशमितोभवेत्।

सन्दर्भेऽस्मिन् सहृदयता आवश्यकी, एवमेविमर्शना प्रौढिरप्यावश्यकः। गुणदोषनिरूपणं कुर्वन् गुणानां विषये एव दृष्टिप्रसारणं सद्विमर्शकस्य कर्तव्यम्।

अत्राावधेय अंश अन्यः कश्चन अस्ति। स्मृतीनां क्षयोत्पत्तौ ब्रह्मविष्णुमहेशाः करणभूताः भवन्तीति पराशरस्याभिप्रायः। प्रत्येककल्पे श्रुतिस्मृति सदाचारनिर्णयकरणे एतेएव अर्हाः। धर्मशास्त्रेषु धर्माः प्रतिपदिताः ते धर्माः युगानुरूपाः। चतुर्युगेषु चतुर्विधाः धर्माः निर्दिष्टाः। सत्ययुगे तपः, त्रेतायां ज्ञानम्, द्वापरे यज्ञः, कलौदानञ्च प्रधानाः। प्रत्येक युगस्य प्रत्येकस्मृतिकारेण धर्मः निर्दिष्टोऽस्ति। कृतयुगे मनुप्रोक्तः धर्मः, त्रेतायां गौतमप्रोक्तः धर्मः द्वापरे शङ्खलिखिताभ्यां प्रोक्तौ धर्मौ कलियुगे पराशरप्रोक्तः धर्मोऽस्ति। तेषु तेषु युगेषु ये मानवाः भवन्तिस्म भवन्ति तैः इतर युगेषु विद्यमानाः धर्माः न निन्दनीयाः यतो हि ते मानवा अपि युगरूपा एव।।

28

प्रायश्चित्तस्य स्वरूपं लोकमर्यादा च

व्रजकिशोर स्वाई

धर्मशास्त्रे आचारव्यवहारप्रायश्चित्ताख्येषु त्रिषु विषयेषु आचार-व्यवहारयोः प्रान्तभेदं व्याख्याभेदं च उपजीव्य विद्यमानेषु सांप्रदायिकमतेषु पार्थक्यं दृश्यते। किन्तु प्रायश्चित्ते न तथा। तत्र प्रान्तभेदमुररीकृत्य मतान्तराणि परस्परविरुद्धानि न सन्ति।

मनुस्मतेः एकादशाध्यायस्य/११-४४, ४५, ४६./
अकुर्वन् विहितं कर्म निन्दितं च समाचरन्।
प्रसक्तश्चेन्द्रियार्थेषु प्रायश्चित्तीयते नरः।।
अकामतः कृते पापे प्रायश्चित्तं विदुर्बुधाः।
कामकारकृतेप्याहुरेके श्रुतिनिदर्शनात्।।
अकामतः कृतं पापं वेदाभ्यासेन शुध्यति।
कामतस्तु कृतं मोहात् प्रायश्चित्तैः पृग्विधैः।।
इति त्रिषु वचनेषु, याज्ञवल्क्यस्मृतेः तृतीयाध्यायस्य-
विहितस्याननुष्ठानान्निन्दितस्य च सेवनात्।
अनिग्रहाच्चेन्द्रियाणां नरः पतनमृच्छति।।
तस्मात्तेनेह कर्त्तव्यं प्रायश्चित्तं विशुद्धये।
एवमस्यान्तरात्मा च लोकश्चैव प्रसीदति।। /३-२१९, २२०/
प्रायश्चित्तैरपैत्येनो यदज्ञानकृतं भवेत्।
कामतो व्यवहार्यस्तु वचनादिह जायते।। /३-२२६/

इति त्रिषु, गौतमधर्मसूत्रस्य च / ३.१. २-५/
अथ खल्वयं पुरुषो याप्येन कर्मणा लिप्यते।

यथैतदयाज्ययाजनमभक्ष्यभक्षणमवद्यवदनं शिष्टस्य अक्रियाप्रतिषिद्धसेवनमिति। तत्र प्रायश्चित्तं कुर्यान्न कुर्यादिति मीमांसन्ते। न कुर्यादित्याहुः। न हि कर्म क्षीयते इति। कुर्यादित्यपरम्।

इति वचनचतुष्टये सामान्येन प्रायश्चित्तस्य तत्त्वं लोकमर्यादा च प्रतिपादिता। एतेषां त्रयाणां धर्मशास्त्रकाराणामुपर्युक्तानि वचनानि आधृत्य सन्दर्भेऽस्मिन्–

क. संस्कारात् प्रायश्चित्तमन्यत्

ख. "न हि कर्म क्षीयते प्रारब्धस्य कर्मणो भोगादेव क्षयः" इति सिद्धान्तस्य प्रायश्चित्तं न विरोधि

ग. दण्डे प्रायश्चित्तस्य अन्तर्भावः, न प्रायश्चित्ते दण्डस्य भवति इति।

त्रयं विचार्यते।

१. प्रथमतया मनुः प्रायश्चित्तस्य त्रीणि कारणानि उद्घाटयति। यथा–विहितस्य कर्मणोऽननुष्ठानम्, निन्दितस्य कर्मणः अनुष्ठानम्, इन्द्रियार्थेषु प्रसक्तिश्चेति। मनोरेतादृशानि मन्तव्यानि उपजीव्य याज्ञवल्क्यः स्वीये वचने किंचित् विमर्शान्तरं दर्शयति। स कथयति यत् मनुष्यो यदा एतानि त्रीणि कारणानि अवलम्बते तदा असौ पतनं प्राप्नोति। यस्मिन् स्थले मनुः /११ᐣ४६/ प्रायश्चित्तीयते नरः" इति कथयति तस्मिन् स्थले याज्ञवल्क्यः "नरः पतनमृच्छति" इति कथयति। मनुयाज्ञवल्क्ययोरेतादृशं पदसंघटनमुपजीव्य व्याख्यातारः विवदन्ते भिद्यन्ते च। तत्र मनुप्रयुक्तशब्देन सह सामंजस्यमानेतुं विश्वरूपो याज्ञवल्क्यप्रयुक्तपतनपदे प्रायश्चित्तार्हत्वमभिप्रैति, दीपकलिकायां शूलपाणिः नरकमवगच्छति। गौतमस्तु विहितकर्मणोऽननुष्ठानं "शिष्टस्य अक्रिया" इत्यनेन निन्दितकर्माचरणं "प्रतिषिद्धसेवनम्" इत्यनेन च पदेन आचष्टे। इन्द्रियार्थे प्रसक्तिं स याप्यकर्मत्वेन निर्दिशति।

२. एतानि त्रीणि त्रिभिः स्तवकैः विवेचयितुं शक्यन्ते। तत्र पर्यायेण विचार्यते। मनुष्यः कदाचित् अज्ञात्वा विहितं कर्म च अनुष्ठापयति, कदाचित् प्रतिषिद्धमनुष्ठापयति। अनयोराद्यं विच्युतिरूपं द्वितीयं त्रुटिरूपम्। विहितकर्मणोऽननुष्ठानेन अभिलषितफलकामनया क्रियमाणस्य कर्मणोऽपूर्व नोत्पद्यते। नित्यकर्मणः त्यागेन च प्रत्यवायो जन्यते। अभिलषितफलधिया क्रियमाणस्य कर्मणः

सांगोपांगतासंपादनाय प्रायश्चित्ताख्यस्य कस्यचन अपरस्य अधिकस्य कर्मणोऽनुष्ठानेनैव विच्युतांशस्य अनुष्ठानं कर्त्तव्यं भवति। एतेन अत्र प्रायश्चित्तं क्रत्वर्थतामुपजनयति। नित्यकर्मत्यागजन्यप्रत्यवायध्वंसार्थकप्रायश्चित्तं तु पुरुषार्थतां सृजति। पक्षान्तरे अविहितस्य कर्मणोऽनुष्ठानार्थं पुरुषस्य प्रवृत्तिर्न जायते। तत्र फलेन सह कर्मणः संबन्धस्य प्रवर्त्तिष्यमाणस्य पुरुषस्य च तथाऽदर्शनात्। अविहितकर्मणः प्रतिषिद्धकर्म गुरुतरम्। अविहितकर्मणोऽनुष्ठानेन आकाङ्क्षितं फलं न जन्यते इति सत्यं, किन्तु प्रतिषिद्धस्य कर्मणोऽनुष्ठानेन पापापूर्वं जन्यते। उभयप्रकारकयोः कर्मणोः सकाशात् प्रतिषिद्धकर्मणः फले तात्पर्याधिक्यात् गौतमः "प्रतिषिद्धसेवनम्" इति पदं प्रयुङ्क्ते। गौतमवचनापेक्षया मनुयाज्ञवल्क्ययोः वचने कश्चन पृथक् स्वरसो विद्यते। विधेः विपरीतः प्रतिषेधः। विहितपदप्रयोगेण मनु-याज्ञवल्क्यौ विधिमाचक्षाते, एतद्विपरीततया तौ प्रतिषेधस्य वक्तव्यतां स्वीकुर्याताम्। किन्तु उभाभ्यां प्रतिषेधपदमदत्त्वा निन्दितपदप्रयोगः कृतः। अत्र इदमेव ध्येयं यत् निन्दा एकोऽर्थवादः। अर्थवादः विधिना निषेधेन वा सह एकवाक्यतां प्राप्यैव पुरुषं प्रवर्त्तयति निवर्त्तयति वा। किन्तु यया शक्त्या प्रशंसार्थवादः विधिवाक्यैकवाक्यतया पुरुषस्य प्रवृत्तिं जनयति, ततोऽधिकया शक्त्या निन्दार्थवादः पुरुषं निवर्त्तयति निषेधवाक्येन सह एकवाक्यतां प्राप्याऽपि निन्दार्थवादः निषेधवाक्यापेक्षया पुरुषमधितरं प्रभावयति। इति कृत्वा मनुप्रयुक्तनिन्दितपदस्वरसं गृहीत्वा याज्ञवल्क्यस्तथा आचष्टे। अस्माभिस्तु निषेधनिन्दयोः साकल्येन ग्रहणं कर्त्तव्यम्; इत्ययं भवति अज्ञानकृतकर्मणो विषये प्रायश्चित्तस्य तात्पर्ये हेतुः।

३. अथ इन्द्रियार्थप्रसक्तिर्विचार्यति। तत्र मनुः "प्रसक्तश्चेन्द्रियार्थेषु" इत्यादिना अन्वयमुख्न याज्ञवल्क्यश्च "अनिग्रहाच्चेन्द्रियाणामि" ति व्यतिरेकमुखेन इन्द्रियार्थप्रसक्तेः प्रायश्चित्तहेतुत्वमाहतुः। गौतमोऽमुं याप्यकर्मत्वेन उक्त्वा तत्फलस्य अनिर्वाप्यत्वमभिप्रैति। एतेन अवगम्यते यत् यस्य यस्मिन् प्रसक्तिः तस्य तस्मिन् अत्याग्रहः कामना वा। यस्य यस्मिन् अत्याग्रहः तस्य तस्मिन् मोहः स तस्य अन्याय्यत्वमवगत्याऽपि तस्मिन् प्रवर्त्तति। यो यस्मिन् प्रवर्त्तति तस्य तद्विषयिणी बुद्धिरवश्यंभाविनी। एतेन स ज्ञात्वैवाऽपराध्नुयात्। कामना सर्वथा ज्ञानपूर्वा। मनुः ज्ञानापेक्षया कामनायाः प्रायश्चित्तहेतुत्वं दर्शयति। याज्ञवल्क्यस्तु उभययोः। अन्द्रियाणामनिग्रहस्य प्रायश्चित्तहेतुत्वेन यन्मतं याज्ञवल्क्येन

प्रत्यपादि, तन्मतं व्याख्याय विश्वरूपेण प्रायश्चित्तस्य अकरणमिति यदुक्तं तदस्माभिः न सह्यते प्रायश्चित्ताकरणस्य ज्ञानकामनोपबृंहिताचारजन्यपापेन च सह अतुल्यार्थत्वात् अन्यथा अनवस्थापत्तेः। वस्तुगत्या अकामकृतस्य त्रुटिविच्युत्याख्यस्य कर्मणः उदर्कध्वंसाय क्रियमाणस्य प्रायश्चित्तस्य विषये न कस्यापि वैमत्यमस्ति। कामकारकृतस्य काऽपि विप्रतिपत्तिरस्त्येव। एतत् स्फुटयितुं मनुः "एके श्रुतिनिदर्शनात्" इत्यादिना तदितराणां मतानि स्मारयति यानि मतानि श्रुत्याधारेण प्रामाणिकानि भवन्ति। मनोः पन्थानमवलम्बमानो गौतमः "कुर्यादित्यपरम्" इत्यादिना तदितराणामेतद्विषयकं मतं स्वीकृत्य कामकृतपापस्य प्रायश्चित्तेन ध्वंसप्रसंगमवतारयति। एतेन अनुमीयते यत् प्रायश्चित्ततत्त्वस्य पर्यायक्रमेण विकाशो जातः। तत्र अज्ञानकृतपापस्य प्रायश्चित्तं प्रथमतया आकलितम्, अथ ज्ञानकृतस्य। अज्ञानकृतपापस्य विशुद्-ध्ये यो वेदाभ्यासो मनुना उपदर्शितः स पंचमहयज्ञेषु अन्यतमत्वेन ब्रह्मयज्ञाख्यां लभते। तत्र ब्रह्मयज्ञः प्रायश्चित्तरूप इति मन्तव्यम्। प्रायश्चित्तं सर्वथा नैमित्तिकं कर्म। कस्याऽपि कर्मणोऽबुद्धिपूर्वतया अननुष्ठाने एतत् कर्त्तव्यं भवति। बुद्धिपूर्वतया कृतस्य पापकर्मणः अपूर्वध्वंसार्थिन्या बुद्ध्या क्रियमाणस्य प्रायश्चित्तस्य नैमित्तिकत्वेन काम्यत्वम्। ज्ञानकृतस्य पापस्य विशुद्धये यत् प्रायश्चित्तं कर्त्तव्यं भवति तत् सर्वथा विकाशधारायां कालक्रमेण अवतारितम्।

४. मनुष्यस्य आचरणेन या अशुद्धिर्जन्यते सा द्विविधा, बाह्या आभ्यन्तरा च। बाह्यशुद्धिः कालस्नानादिना अपगच्छति स विषयो धर्मशास्त्रेऽशौचप्रकरणे विचार्यति। तत्र शारीरशुद्धिरवगम्यते। आभ्यन्तराशुद्धिस्तु मनः आत्मानं च कलुषीकरोति। तयोः विशुद्धये प्रायश्चित्तं क्रियते इति स्थितम् कलुषितमनसोऽन्तरात्मा पीड्यते। लोकश्च कृतापराधेन कलुषितात्मना पुरुषेण सह उषितुं न प्रवर्त्तति। तेन सह वर्षावधि संसर्गेण स तत्तुल्ययोगितामर्जयति। एतत्स्फुटयितुं याज्ञवल्क्येन "यश्च तैः सह संवसेति" त्युक्तम्। कृतप्रायश्चित्तस्य विशुद्ध्या तेन साकं लोक उषितुं प्रवर्त्तति विगलितकलुषत्वात्। अनेन प्रायश्चित्तस्य लोकसंबन्धो व्यक्तः। याज्ञवल्क्यः "एवमस्यान्तरात्मा च लोकश्चैव प्रसीदती" त्वुक्त्या प्रायश्चित्तस्य लोकमर्यादां दर्शयति। अत्र प्रायश्चित्तेन कर्मणा नाशिता लोकर्यादा कृतप्रायश्चित्तेन अवाप्यते इति नावितथम्, किन्तु नरकपातरूपमपूर्वं तिष्ठति। अज्ञानकृतस्य पापस्य केवलं लोकहानिर्भवति। तत्र पुरुषस्य अन्तरात्मनोऽशुद्धिः प्रातिस्विकी।

प्रायश्चित्तेन अन्तरात्मा शुद्ध्यति, लोकश्च प्राप्यते। ज्ञानकृतस्य तु केवलं नाशिता लोकमर्यादा लभ्यते पापापूर्वं तु तिष्ठत्येव। "एके श्रुतिनिदर्शनात्" इति मनुना यदुक्तं तत् लोकप्राप्तयर्थकविषयम् उपलक्ष्यैव संप्रवृत्तम्। विज्ञानेश्वरः एतादृशं पक्षं समर्थयति। अप्रकाशितपापाचरणस्य रहस्यप्रायश्चित्तेन अन्तरात्मा प्रसीदति प्रकाशितस्य च मुक्तप्रायश्चित्तेन लोकः प्रसीदति इति स्थितम्।

एवं विधया विवरणया अन्ततो गवा सन्दर्भेऽस्मिन् त्रिषु कोष्ठकेषु तात्पर्यमुपन्यसितुं शक्यते-तदित्यम्-

क. प्रायश्चित्तेन या विशुद्धिर्जायते सा मलापनयनमिति कदाचित् संज्ञान्तरं भजेत। संस्कारस्यापि मलापनयनाख्यं किंचित् विशिष्टमुद्देश्यमस्ति। न केवलं तथा, मलापनयनेन सह गुणाधानाख्यस्य उद्देश्यान्तरस्यापि संघटना विद्यते। न सर्वथा उभयप्रकारकयोः उद्देश्ययोः समुच्चयः संस्कारेऽभिप्रेतः, अपि तु कदाचित् केवलगुणाधानेन, कदाचिद्वा केवलमलापनयनेन संस्कारः फलवत्त्वमर्जयति। विशुद्धिरूपस्य मलापनयनस्य प्रायश्चित्ते उद्देश्यत्वेन वर्त्तमानत्वेऽपि अत्र सोऽयं मलः पापमेव, संस्कारे तु न पापम्। संस्कारेण मलस्य अपनयनं विधीयते। प्रायश्चित्ते कृतेऽपि ज्ञानकृतमहापातकादीनां पापस्य नरकदायिनी शक्तिस्तिष्ठति लोकसंसर्गमात्रमवाप्यते। अतः -

१. संस्कारेण अपसार्यमाणो मलः स्वाभाविकः।

२. प्रायश्चित्तेन अपसार्यमाणो मलो मनुष्यकर्त्तृ कक्रियाजन्यः।

३. संस्कारस्य वर्णधर्मे, आश्रमधर्मे, वर्णाश्रमधर्मे, गुणधर्मे च अन्तर्भावो विद्यते।

४. प्रायश्चित्तस्य च निमित्तधर्मत्वेन स्थितिरस्ति।

५. प्रायश्चित्तद्धारा कृत्रिमता अपसार्यते स्वाभाविकता अर्ज्यते इति।

ख. मनुष्येण कृतस्य कर्मणः फलमवश्यं भुज्यते। कृतं कर्म फलावाप्तिपर्यन्तं तिष्ठति। फलत्वेन परिणतिमप्राप्य कर्म न शाम्यति न च नश्यति। एवं स्थितौ "न हि कर्म क्षीयते" इति गौतमेन यः पक्ष उद्भाव्य समाहितः तस्य फलपरिणतेरनिवार्यता अभ्युपगता। पापकर्मणः फलं यत् दुःखमस्ति, तत्तु कालक्रमेण अवश्यं भुज्यते। किन्तु कालक्रमेण तस्य आगमनात्, पाक्र चेत् कर्त्ता प्रायश्चित्तं कुर्यात् पुनः स तत्फलं न प्राप्नुयात् यतः स स्वेच्छया तत्फलं ग्रहीतुं वांछति। अत्र यत् प्रायश्चित्तं क्रियते तदपि तपोरूपं वर्त्तति। तस्य

निश्चयात्मकबुद्ध्या क्रियमाणत्वे भविष्यति आगमिष्यतः पापस्य प्रायश्चित्तेन ध्वंसः। अत्र एतदेव मन्तव्यं यत्–

१. फलमदत्त्वाकर्म विनश्यतीति न। न हि कर्म क्षीयते इति सत्यम्। किन्तु कर्मणः फलं यत् स्वाभाविकरीत्या कर्त्तारमागमिष्यति तत्तु कर्त्ता प्रागेव तपोरूपेण प्रायश्चित्तेन स्वीकुरुते।

२. तात्पर्यं त्वेतत् यत् पापकर्मणः यत् स्वाभाविकं फलं, तदपेक्षया तन्निमित्तकप्रायश्चित्ते क्रियमाणस्य तपसः परिमाणं लघु।

३. यथा लोके कश्चन पुरुषः स्वयमपराधमाचर्य चेत् स्वयं राजपुरुषमागत्य स्वीयापराधप्रख्यापनपुरःसरं दण्डं ग्रहीतुं वांछेत् स राजपुरुषेण न निगडबन्धनादिना पीड्यते। अपि तु तस्मै ततः लघुतरो दण्डः दीयते कदाचित् लध्वपराधस्य अज्ञानकृतत्वे क्षमाऽपि दीयते। किन्तु राजपुरुषश्चेत् स्वयमपराधिनमाहिण्ड्य निश्चिनुयात् तदा अपराधी आत्मसमर्पणेन प्राप्यमाणदण्डापेक्षया अधिकं दण्डं प्राप्नुयात्। एतेन एतत् निश्चप्रचं यत् –

१. प्राप्यमाण–कृतकर्मफलापेक्षया प्रायश्चित्ते क्रियमाणस्य तपसः परिमाणं लघु। तस्य सहने आत्मप्रस्तुतिदर्शनात्।
२. स्वाभाविकतया प्राप्यमाणकृतकर्मफलमधिकं पीडाकरं तत्र संक्षोभस्य सत्वात् सहने आत्मप्रस्तुत्यभवात्।
३. कर्मफलभोगात् परं प्रायश्चित्तं नापेक्ष्यते फलभोगेन कर्मणः समाप्तिदर्शनात्।
४. प्रायश्चित्तेन कर्मणः फलं लघ्वीक्रियते, तस्मिन् आत्मनश्च सह्यत्वं साध्यते। इति कृत्वा प्रायश्चित्ती स्वयमिच्छेत् चेत् प्रायश्चित्तं क्र्युात्। अपि स न इच्छेत् तर्हि अपरेण बलात्कारं तदुपरि तत्करणभारः नोपस्थापयितुं शक्यते। अतः प्रायश्चित्तं क्रियते न तु कार्यते। प्रायश्चित्तेन इच्छया क्रियमाणत्वे प्रायश्चित्तमेकमवश्यकर्त्तव्यं न तु अनिवार्यकर्त्तव्यम्।

ग. शासनेन सहप्रायश्चित्तस्य संबन्धो विद्यते। शासनकर्त्ता अपराधिने अपराधाद्धेतोः दण्डं प्रयच्छति। तं दण्डं प्राप्य प्रायश्चित्तमकृत्वा च अपराधी पापान्मुच्यते न वेति प्रश्नः कदाचित् जागर्त्ति। आपस्तम्बेन उच्यते यत् यदि कश्चन अपराधी स्वयं मुसलमेकं धृत्वा आत्मनः आपराधं ख्यापयित्वा

दण्डलाभाय राज्ञे निवेदयति, राजा च अपराधिनो हस्तात् तं मुसलमादाय तस्मिन् निक्षिपति, तेन निक्षेपेण चेत् सोऽपराधी म्रियेत तर्हि स मुच्यते, जीवेच्चापि मुच्यते। एतस्मिन् स्थले वस्तुतः अपराधी अपराधात् पापाच्च मुच्यते। यदि स राजानमगत्वा केवलं प्रायश्चित्तं कुर्यात् तर्हि स पापान्मुच्यते किन्तु शासनकर्त्तृकदण्डप्रयोगात् न निवर्त्त्यति। अत्र मरणान्तिकप्रायश्चित्तस्य विकल्पत्वेन विधीयमानस्य एतादृशस्य कर्मणः दण्डत्वेन प्रायश्चित्तत्वेन च प्रतिपत्तिर्भवितुमर्हति। मुसलप्रयोगस्य दण्डत्वेन स्वयं दण्डमभीप्सन् राज्ञे निवेदनं च प्रायश्त्तिं भवति। यत्र आपराधी शासने न स्ठर्वीयापराधं व्यनक्ति, न च प्रायश्चित्तं करोति तत्र अपराधित्वात् तेन साकं मिलनाय लोका जुगुप्सन्ते, एतेन तस्य लोकहानिर्भवति एव। प्रायश्चित्तस्य अकरणात् पापस्य नरकदायिनी शक्तिस्तिष्ठत्येव। यदि राजपुरुषाः प्रायश्चित्तमकुर्वन्तं राज्ञे आत्मापराध-मख्यापयन्तं च अपराधिनं शासनपक्षतोऽन्विष्य आनीय दण्डयेयुः, तर्हि तेन दण्डप्रणयनेन तेन अपराधिना नष्टो लोकव्यवहारः पुनः प्राप्यते, किन्तु पापापूर्वस्य नरकदायिन्याः शक्तेः तस्य आत्मनि गुणत्वेन सत्त्वात् न नश्यति।

राजभिः कृतदण्डाश्च कृतदणश्च कृत्वा पापानि मानवाः।
निर्मलाः स्वर्गमायान्ति सन्तः सुकृतिनो यथा।।

मनु. ८.३१८, रामा. किस्कि. १८ / ३३.

इति यन्मनुना उक्तं तत्र निर्मलत्वमुभचविधव्यवस्थया संभाव्यते। अत्र इदमेव ध्येयं यत् –

१. यत्र मरणान्तिको दण्डस्तत्र दण्डे प्रायश्चित्तस्य अन्तर्भावः।
२. यत्र मरणान्तिकं प्रायश्चित्तं तत्र प्रायश्चित्ते दण्डस्य अन्तर्भावो भवितुं नार्हति। दण्डापेक्षया प्रायश्चित्तस्य सहने लाघवात् न गुरुणि लघुनोऽन्तर्भावः। प्रायश्चित्तात् दण्डस्य सहने अधिकपीडाकरत्वात् दण्डे प्रायश्चित्तस्य अन्तर्भावो भवेत्।
३. स्वीकृत्य प्रायश्चित्तस्य क्रियमाणत्वात् कृते प्रायश्चित्ते पुनस्तस्य पापस्य करणेच्छा नोत्पद्यते या लोकसचेतनतां वस्तुगत्या सृजति।

एवं प्रकारेण प्रायश्चित्तस्य स्वरूपगतं तत्त्वं लोकमर्यादाभ्यन्तरे एव तिष्ठति। लोकमर्यादां हात्वा प्रायश्चित्तस्य अभिनिवर्त्तनं दुःशकमिति स्थितम्।

29

कर्मविपाकस्य प्रायश्चित्तेन सह सम्बन्धः

जयकृष्ण मिश्र

मनुष्यः समाजे जीवननिर्वाहकाले शास्त्रविहितान् नियमान् कदाचिद् भ्रमवशात् कदाचिज्ज्ञानवशाद् वा उल्लंघयति तदानीं तस्य पापमुत्पद्यते। उत्पन्नस्य तस्य पापस्य क्षयार्थं तेन प्रायश्चित्तमवश्यं कर्त्तव्यम्। प्रायश्चित्ताचरणानन्तरं सः सर्वैः व्यवहार्यो भवेत्। यदि मनुष्यः प्रायश्चित्तं न आचरेत्, तर्हि पापस्य परिणामरूपं नरकभोगादिकमवश्यं कुर्यात्। तस्य कृतस्य कर्मणः विपाकः स्यात्, तदनुसारं सुकृतर्मणः परिणामरूमं स्वर्गादिफलं लभेत, दुष्कृतकर्मणः परिणामरूयं नरकभोगादिकं हीनयोनिं च प्राप्नुयात्।

कर्मविपाकविषये स्मृतिकारेण शातातपेन बहु चर्चतम्। अनन्तरं याज्ञवल्क्यादिभिः अन्यैः स्मृतिकारैरपि प्रायश्चित्ताध्याये विशेषेण वर्णितानि सन्ति। स्मृतिकाराग्रगण्यो मनुः एकादशाध्याये कर्मविपाकप्रसंगे पापिनां नरकफलभोगानन्तरं हीनयोनिप्राप्तिमपि उद्घाटयति। ते च पातकिनः महापातकजनितान् तामिस्रादिनरकान् स्वजनितदुष्कृतानुरुपान् अतितीव्रवेदना-पादकत्वेन अतिभयङ्करान् दुःखैकभोगनिलयान् प्राप्यकर्मजन्यनरक-दुःखोपभोगक्षयानन्तरं पुनः इह मर्त्त्यभूमौ दुःखबहुलश्वशृगालसूकारदियोनिषु भूयो भूयो जायन्ते। रौरवादिषु नरकेषु श्वसूकरादियोनिषु च दारुणं दुःखमनुभूय अनन्तरं दुरितशेषेण जननसमये एव क्षयरोगादिलक्षणयुक्ताः प्रचुरेषु मानवशरीरेषु संसरन्ति। ततः दुर्लक्षणमनुष्यजन्मानन्तरं नरकाद्युपभोगद्वारेण क्षीणपापः प्रागभवीयसुकृतशेषेण महाकुले भोगसम्पन्नाः विद्याधनधान्यसंपन्नाश्च जायन्ते। शास्त्रेषु सर्वविधानां पापिनां कर्मानुरूपाणि जन्मानि वार्णितानि सन्ति।

वेदः यत् यत् कर्त्तुमुपदिशति तत् सर्वं सर्वैरनुष्ठातव्यम्। तस्यानाचरणे च अधर्मः जायते। स्मृतिः नित्यनैमित्तिककाम्यरूपाणि कर्माणि कर्त्तुमुपदिशति।

यत् निन्यं कर्म सन्ध्यावन्दनादिकं तस्यानाचरणे प्रत्यवायः संजायते। अतः प्रत्यवायनाशर्थं मनुष्यः नित्यकर्मावश्यमनुतिष्ठेत्। स्मृतिकारैः पापोत्पत्तिनिमित्तं विहिताकरणं, निषिद्धचरणमिन्द्रियप्रसक्तिश्चेति प्रथमतः कारणत्रितयमुपन्यस्तम्। अस्मात् पापकर्मणः निवृत्तिरपि स्मृतिकारैः कल्पिता। यथोक्तं मनुना – शुभाशुभफलं कर्म मनोवाग् देहसम्भवम्।

कर्गजा गतयो नृणामुत्तमाधममध्यमाः।
मानसं मनसैवायमुपभुङ्क्ते शुभाशुभम्।
वाचा वाचाकृतं कर्म कायेनैव तु कायिकम्।। /१२-३, ८./

याज्ञवल्क्येनाऽपि यथा – अन्त्यपक्षिस्थावरतां मनोवाक्कायकर्मजैः।

दोषैः प्रयाति जीवोऽयं भवं योनिशतेषु च।।
अनन्ताश्च यथा भावाः शरीरेषु शरीरिणाम्।
रूपाण्यपि तथैवेह सर्वयोनिषु देहिनाम्।।
विपाकः कर्मणां प्रेत्य केषांचिदिह जायते।
इह वा मुत्र वैकेषां भावस्तत्र प्रयोजनम्।। /याज्ञ.स्मृ. ३/३१-१३३.

मनुष्यः पापोत्पत्तिप्रकारेषु किमपि कारणं संसेव्य अथवा अविद्यासमावेशवशान्मोहरागादिभावैरभिभूयमानो नानाहीनयोनिजननसाधनं मानसादि त्रिविधं कर्मनिचयमाचरन् अन्त्यादिहीनयोनितामापद्यते। चण्डाल – पक्षि – स्थावरतां यथाक्रमेण मनोवाक्कायारब्धकर्मदोषैर्जन्मसहस्रेष्वयं जीवः प्राप्नोति। जीवानां शरीरेषु सत्त्वाद्युद्रेकतारतम्याद्यथा असंख्याः अभिप्रायविशेषा। भवन्ति तथैव तत्कार्यण्यपि कुब्जवामनत्वादीनि रूपाणि देहिनां सर्वयोनिषु भवन्ति।

केषांचित् ज्योतिष्टोमादिकर्मणां विपाकः फलं प्रेत्य देहान्तरे भवन्ति। केषांचित् कारीर्यादकर्मणां वृष्ट्यादि फलमिहैव भवति। अतः कर्मणां शुभाशुभफलजनकत्वे सत्त्वादिभावतारतम्यात् कर्मफलेषु तारतम्यं दृश्यत एव। परधनापहरणतत्परः सर्वथा अपहरणचिन्तां कृत्वा तथा ब्रह्महत्यादीनि हिंसात्मकानि सर्वथा चिन्तयन् श्ववचण्डालाद्यन्त्ययोनिषु जायन्ते। अनृतवदत शीलः पुरुषः, पिशुनः, परोद्वेगकरभाषणशीलः, प्रकृतासंगतार्थवादी बुद्धिपूर्वाबुद्धिपू- र्वादि तारतम्यादि हीनोत्कृष्टेषु मृगपक्षिषु जायते।

अदत्तपरधनापहरणप्रसक्तः परदारप्रसक्तश्च अविहितमार्गेण प्राणिनां घातकश्च दोषगुरुलघुभावतारतम्यात्तरुलताप्रतानादिस्थावरेषु जायन्ते। सत्त्वरजोतमोगुणानां विपाकात् जीवानां गतिः यथा - आत्मज्ञः शौचवान् दान्तः, तपस्वी विजितेन्द्रियः, धर्मानुष्ठाननिरतः, वेदार्थवेदी यः सात्त्विकः सत्त्वोद्रेकतारतम्यवशादुत्कृष्टोत्कृष्टतरसुरयोनितां प्राप्नोति। तूर्यवादित्रनृत्यादिष्वभिरतो, व्यग्रचित्तः, सदा कार्याकुलः, विषयेष्वतिप्रसक्तश्च यः रजोगुणयुक्तः दद्गुणतारतम्याद्धीनोत्कृष्टमनुष्यजातिषु मरणानन्तरमुत्पत्तिं प्राप्नोति। निद्राशीलः, प्राणिपीडाकरः, लोभयुक्तः नास्तिकः, याचनशीलः, कर्याकार्यविवेकशून्यः, विरुद्धाचारः असौ तमोगुणतारतम्याद्धीन-हीनतरपश्वादियोनिषु जायन्ते।

एवमयं मनुष्यः अज्ञानाविष्टः सन् इह संसारे पर्यटन् नानाविध-दुःखप्रदैर्भावैरभिभूतः पुनः पुनः संसारं देहग्रहणं, वारं वारं नरकं, नरकानन्तरं च संसारे तिर्यगादिषु योनिषु जायते।

पापस्य शक्तिद्वयं शास्त्रकारैः प्रपिादितम्। व्यवहारनिरोधिका, नरकोत्पादिका च। व्यवहारनिरोधिका शक्तिः प्रायश्चित्तेंन क्षीयते। नरकोत्पादिका शक्तिरपि द्विगुणप्रायश्चित्ताचरणेन क्षीयते। तत्र प्रायश्चित्तेन पापं क्षीयते इति गौतमोक्तवचनमेव प्रमाणम्। पुनश्च मिताक्षरोक्तं मतमपि यथा पापोत्पत्तिः शास्त्रगम्या तथैव पापक्षयोऽपि। अतः पापमुत्पद्यते इति यथा स्वीक्रियते प्रायश्चित्तेन पापं क्षीयते इति तथैव स्वीक्रियते। पुरुषाणामधोगमनं येन कर्मणा सम्भवति तदेव पापमिति। पुनश्च नरकादिषु घोरेषु पतनात् पापमुच्यते इति अपि पापस्वरूपं भविष्योत्तरे धर्माधर्मयोः नामान्तरमात्रम्। पापफलं नरकप्रदायकं दुःसाध्यक्लेशकररोगादिप्रदायकं च। तस्य पापं मनुष्यस्यानिष्टं साधयति। अतः मनुष्यः पापाचरणे प्रवृत्तः न स्यात्।

केनापि अनुष्ठितेन कर्मणा यदि मनुष्यः आमानं संकीर्णं मन्येत तर्हि पापमुत्पन्नमिति कृत्वा तदर्थं प्रायश्चित्तमवश्यमनुतिष्ठेत्। प्रायश्चित्तं च पापक्षयार्थेरूढः। यथा वैखानसश्रौतसूत्रे /२०-१/ - विध्यपराधे प्रायश्चित्तं दोषनिर्घातार्थं विधीयते। हारीतोऽपि /प्रा.वि.पृ. ४/ - प्रयतत्वात् उपचितमशुभं कर्म नाशयति इति प्रायश्चित्तमिति। यथा क्षारोपस्वेदचण्डनिर्णोदन-प्रक्षालनादिभिर्वासांसि शुद्ध्यन्ति एवं तपोदानयज्ञैः पापकृतः शुद्धिमुपयन्ति।

पापी पापाचरणानन्तरं प्रायश्चित्तज्ञानार्थं शुद्धभावनया स्नातः क्लिन्नवासाः समाहितश्च सन् पर्षदि उपस्थितो भवेत्। तत्र च स्वकृतं कर्म निवेद्य प्रायश्चित्तमभिलषेत्। पर्षत्सदस्याः प्रायश्चित्तं निश्चयं कृत्वा पापिनं श्रावयेयुः। पापी पापमाचरन् कदाचिन्न गूहेत। गूहमानं पापमवश्यं वर्धेत। पर्षत्सदस्याः पापकृतां वैद्याः। पाप्मनां च हर्त्तारः। अतः पापमाचरितं मयेति सः यदा निश्चयं कुर्यात् तन्निमित्तं प्रायश्चित्तं कृत्वा पुनः तत्कर्म न कदाचिदाचरेत्। पापी तत्प्रायश्चित्तं सर्वेभ्यः विज्ञाप्य प्रायश्चित्ताचरणे प्रवृत्तः स्यात्। प्रायश्चित्ताचरणानन्तरं यदि सः आत्मानं संकीर्णं मन्येत तर्हि पुनः कृच्छ्रादीनाचरेत् दानं वा कुर्यात् ब्राह्मणभोजनं वा कारयेत्। प्रायश्चित्तं समाप्य सः वृषभाय ग्रासादिकं दद्यात्।

तत्र पापक्षयार्थं केचन उपायाः शास्त्रकारैः परिकल्पिताः। ते च आत्मापराधस्वीकृति-पश्चात्ताप-प्राणायाम-तपो-होम-जप-दान-उपवास-तीर्थयात्रा-अध्ययन-ख्यापन-स्नान-नारायणस्मरणादयश्चा अतः केनाऽपि एकेन उपायेन पापं क्षालयितुं शक्यते इति शास्त्रकाराणां निर्यासः।

इदानीं कृत्याकृत्यनिर्णयविवेकवर्जिते विषमे काले धर्मविषयमुपजीव्य प्रतिपादितेऽस्मिन् विगतश्रद्धानामाधुनिकानामन्तिके श्रुतिमूलकस्यापि धर्मशास्त्रस्य तत्र च प्रायश्चित्तस्य प्रशस्तिवाचनं नितान्तदुःखजनकम्। अधुना समाजे मनुष्यमारण - मद्यपान - परधनापहरण - अगम्यागमनं , एतैः सह सम्बन्धस्थापनमनुदिनं च वर्धते। शासनं मद्यपाननिमित्तमनुमतिं प्रदाय /रेजिष्ट्रेसन/, गर्भपातं वैधरूपेण उद्घोष्य, अपहर्त्तारं च यथोचितं दण्डमप्रदाय, विचारे अयथा कालक्षेपं च कृत्वा पापचरणं सर्वानुत्साहयति। अतः समाजस्य अवस्था दयनीया वर्त्तते। यदि शास्त्रोक्तेन प्रकारेण शासनं प्रचलेत्, पापी च सर्वैरव्यवहर्यो भवेत्, निन्दितो भवेच्च, तर्हि अवश्यं पापी प्रायश्चित्ताचरणे प्रवृत्तः स्यात्। पुनश्च तत्कर्माचरणे मतिं न दद्यात्। समाजस्य अभ्युन्नतये, सुस्थित्यै, सुसंगठनाय च जनानां भूमिका गुरूत्वपूर्णा। वर्त्तते। सामाजिकानामाकांक्षा विधि /संविधाने प्रतिफलिता भवति। अतः सामाजिकः पापी सर्वथा निन्दनीया भवेच्चेत् प्रायश्चित्तस्य आत्यन्तिकः प्रयोगः साम्भवेत्। समाजे विशृंखला न दरीदृश्येत। तीर्थयात्रा-स्नान-दान-जप-होम-पश्चात्तापादिभिः पापक्षालने मनुष्यः प्रवर्त्तेत। अयथा पुत्रताडनादौ भार्याताडनादौ, भृत्यताडनादौ, अज्ञानात्

निष्ठुरभाषणे, अश्लीशब्दोच्चारणे, मिथ्यावदने, अभक्ष्यभक्षणे च यथा परस्मिन् काले अनुतापः क्रियते तथैव सर्वेषु कर्मसु यदि प्रायश्चित्तमनुष्ठीयेत, तर्हि मनुष्यः दुःखरोगादिकं, दारिद्रयं, च न प्राप्नुयात्। अयमेव परमः मार्गः मनुष्यस्य सुखप्राप्त्यर्थम्। नान्येन केनापि प्रकारेण मनुष्यः दुर्गतिं तर्तुं शक्नुयात् इति।

30

The Number and the Sequential Order of *Āśramas*

Kashi Nath Hota

Āśramadharma is one of the six *dharmas*[1] prescribed in Dharmaśāstra. The word *āśrama* means a place where one rests upon or haults; and the meaning of *āśramadharma* is the duties or norms of different stages of human life through which one has to undergo. Our ancient scriptures declare such stages of life as of four kinds. They are : (1) *Brahmacārī* 'the stage of staying in teacher's house, (2) *Gṛhastha* 'the stage of householder', (3) *Vānaprastha* 'the stage of being a forest dweller', (4) *Sanyāsa* 'the stage of ascetic'. Here, we come across some controversy regarding the sequential order of the four *āśramas*. The present paper highlights the issues related to the number of *āśramas* and their sequential order.

Regarding the number of *āśramas*, though there is not much controversy, still we find some views on this issue. Some of the scholars attempted to interpret the Upaniṣadic statement and their conclusion is : the number of *āśramas* is three. *Trayo dharmaskaṁdhā yajño 'dhyayanaṁ dānaṁ iti prathamaḥ tapaḥ eva dvitīyo brahmacāryācāryakulavāsī tṛtīyo' tyantaṁ ātmānaṁ ācāryakule' vasādayan sarve ete puṇyalokāḥ bhavanti brahmasaṁstho' mṛtatvam eti*. This passage has been quoted from *Chāndogya Upaniṣad* II.3.1. P.M. Modi[2] tried to interpret this passage and what appears to him from this passage is that in the beginning there were only three *āśramas*. Originally there was no such distinction between *Vānaprastha* and *Sanyāsa*, and both the *āśramas* had formed a single order of life. Those three stages of life are : (1) the household where one is expected to perform sacrifices, study and charity; (2) the stage where one performs the penance (*tapas*) and (3) the stage where one runs the student life throughout his life staying at the teacher's house. All these three receive the meritorious form of life after death, but any of the three who is established in Brahman alone attains the immortality (*amṛtatva*). To substantiate his stand, Modi has cited some verses from Manusmṛti :

Ta eva hi trayo lokās ta eva traya āśramāḥ /
Ta eva hi trayo vedās ta evoktās trayo ' gnayaḥ / /

(There are three worlds, three *āśramas*, three Vedas, as also there are fires). *Manusmṛti* (*Man.*) II : 230.

—The other verse that he quotes from the same source is :

yasmāt trayopyāśramiṇo jñānenānnena cānvaham /
Gṛhasthenaiva dhāryante tasmāj jyeṣṭhāśramo gṛhī / /

—(Because those who belong to the (other) three orders of life are daily supported by the householder with sacred knowledge and food, and therefore, the order of householders is the most excellent one). *Man.* III : 68. On the basis of *'ta eva traya āśramāḥ'* in the first verse and *'trayopyāśramiṇaḥ'* in the second, he concludes that there must be three *āśramas* in the beginning. As a matter of fact, when we go through the *Śāṅkarabhāṣya* of the passage quoted above from *Chāndogya Upaniṣad*, it seems that Śaṅkara had a clear opinion of enumerating the *āśramas* as four, though the fourth one is not enlisted along with the first three. It may be the reason that the purpose of the first three stages is different from that of the fourth. All of them who belong to the first three stages, attain the meritorious form of life (*puṇyaloka*), whereas those who belong to the fourth, attain the immortality (*amṛtatva*). Śaṅkara names the fourth stage of life as the ascetic (*sarva ete trayo 'pyāśramiṇo yathoktairdharmaiḥ puṇyalokā bhavanti. Puṇyaloko āśramiṇo bhavanti. Avaśiṣṭastv anuktaḥḥ parivrāt turīyo brahmasaṁstho brahmaṇi samyak sthitiḥ. So' mṛtatvaṁ puṇyalokavilakṣaṇaṁ amaraṇabhāvaṁ ātyantikam eti nāpekṣikaṁ devādy amṛtatvavat. Puṇyalokāt pṛthak amṛtatvasya vibhāgakaraṇāt*).[3] Śaṅkara himself quotes some other view where it is said that by the word *tapas*, both *tapas* and *parivrāt* are acceptable (*tapa eva dvitiya ity atra tapaḥ śabdena parivrāttāpasau gṛhītau*).[4]

From the above discussion it appears that Modi seems to be not correct to conclude that there were three *āśramas* in the beginning. To say so, *Śāṅkarabhāṣya* is the clear evidence where we find a mention of fourth *āśrama*. Moreover, it is also not correct to establish the three *āśramas* on the basis of the verses quoted from *Manusmṛti*. Because Manu himself has declared the *āśramas* are four (*Brahmacārī gṛhasthaśca vānaprastho yatistathā/Ete gṛhasthaprabhavāś catvāraḥ pṛthag āśramāḥ//* (*Man.* VI : 87). Not only that, the commentator of *Manusmṛti*, interprets *ta eva traya āśramāḥ* in the first verse (*Man.* II : 230) quoted above as the three *āśramas* other than the first *āśrama*, i.e., *Brahmacarya* (*ta eva ca trayaḥ prathamād brahmacaryād anye traya āśramāḥ*). *'Trayo' py āśramiṇaḥ'* in the second verse (*Man.* III : 68) has also been explained by Kulluka, a commentator of *Manusmṛti*, and according to him, this phrase *'Trayo'py ...'*will refer to those who resort to three *āśramas* other than those who belong to *gṛhasthāśrama* (*Gṛhasthavyatiriktāstrayo' pyāśramiṇaḥ*). Baudhāyana gives an interesting information regarding the number of *āśramas*. For him, it was the asura Kapila, son of Prahlāda, who ns his rivalry with Gods, devised the scheme of four *āśramas*, though there really existed only one *āśrama*, i.e., the *Gṛhastha*. The purpose behind this scheme is to make Gods less powerful. Out of the four *āśramas*, those who belong to *Vānaprastha* and *Sanyāsa* are denied to perform sacrifices and thereby the Gods would lose their offerings they receive from human beings and as a result they become less powerful (*Aikāśramyaṁ tvācāryā aprajananatvād itareṣām. Tatrodāharanti Prāhlādir vai kapilo nāmāsura āsa sa etān bhedāścakāra devaiḥ spardhamānas tān manīṣīm nādrieta, Baudhāyana Dharmasūtra* II. 6.29-31).

In Dharma-sūtras or in Smṛti literature, it is seen that most of them are of a common opinion of enumerating the *āśramas* as four. This can be observed from the following lines propounded by different authorities :

1. *Brahmacāri gṛhastho bhikṣu vaikhānasaḥ*, (*Gautamasūtra* (*Gau Sū*) III. 1.2)
2. *Catvāra āśramāḥ brahmacāri-gṛhastha-vānaprastha-parivrājakāḥ, Vāśiṣṭha-Dharmaśāstra* (*Vā Dh Sū*) VII. 1.2.
3. *Catvāra āśramā gārhasthyam ācāryakulaṁ maunaṁ vānaprasthyam iti, Āpastambīya Dharmasūtra* (*Āpa Dh Sū*) II. 9.21.
4. *Brahmacāri-gṛhasthaśca vānaprastho yatis tathā /*
   Ete gṛhasthaprabhavās catvāraḥ pṛthag āśramāḥ / / (*Man.* VI : 87)

From the lines above quoted it is clear that all are of the opinion of holding the *āśramas* as four. While quoting other's view in the commentary of *Manusmṛti* (VI.87), Medhātithi says, according to some *Śāstrakāras*, the stage of ascetic is not a distinct one, since it comes under some other stages of life, particularly it is the household.[5] Gautama has used the word *Vaikhānasa* for *Vānaprastha*, and except him all of them had a common word *Vānaprastha* for this *āśrama*. For the stage of ascetic we find different names employed by different authorities. Gautama says it is the *Bhikṣu*, while for Vaśiṣṭha, it is the *Parivrājaka* and *Yati* also (*Vā Dh Sū* XI. 34). For the same Āpastamba says of using the word *Parivrājaka* and *Mauna* (*Apa Dh Sū*. II. 9.21). Manu employs the word *Yati* and also *Sanyāsa* (*Man.* VI. 96) to indicate the fourth stage of life. It would thus be seen that a person who belongs to the last stage of life i.e., *Sanyāsa* called as *Parivrāj* or *Parivrāt* 'one who does not stay in one place, but moves from place to place', *Bhikṣu* 'one who begs for livelihood', *yati* 'one who controls his senses' and *Muni* 'one who ponders over the mysteries of life and death.

Now, the next question that arises is : Of the four *āśramas* whether one is allowed to jump to the second or to the third or to the fourth leaving the earlier order, or he has to resort to those *aśramas* one after another in the order. On this issue, different answers have been given. When we look into *Jābālopaniṣad*, what is found is that it is left with some options. Thus, after completing the student life, one proceeds for resorting to household life; after that he goes for the stages of being a forest dweller and then lastly he adopts the stages of ascetic life. It also finds some option that one can go for accepting ascetic life directly even either from student life or from the household life or from the hermit life.[6] Yājñvalkya supports the said option partially. According to him, one may resort to the ascetic life either after hermit life or after household life. Of course, he is silent whether one goes forward for ascetic life after the student life (*Yājñyavalkya Smṛti*-IV.56). While enlisting the *āśramas*, Gautama has placed the ascetic in the third order and the hermit in the fourth. Āpastamba follows the same order as Gautama does. However, Gautama and his commentator appear to be justifying why the hermit has been placed at the end. Thus, in order to perform a *pariṣad* or committee, there is a need of ten members who are the experts in different branches of knowledge. Of those members, four are the experts in four different Vedas; the other three, each from one *āśrama*, are chosen from the first three *āśramas* leaving the last one, i.e., *Vānaprastha*; and the remaining three are expected to be skill enough on three different *Dharmaśāstras*.[7] From this it is clearly evident that Gautama had in his mind to exclude the hermit from the *pariṣad*, and therefore, the hermit has been put in the fourth stage. Vaśiṣṭha places those *āśramas* in the following order : (1) *Brahmacārī*, (2) *Gṛhastha*, (3) *Vānaprastha* and (4) *Parivrājaka* (*Vā Dh Sū*. VII. 1.2). Manu follows the same order as *Vaśiṣṭha* gives.

Vaśiṣṭha recommends some option in this regard and accordingly one is allowed to accept any of the orders of life after the completion of *Brahmacarya* (*Vā Dh Sū*. 7.3.).

As regards the four *āśramas*, we find three different views. They are : (1) *Samuccaya* (orderly co-ordination), (2) *Vikalpa* (option) and (3) *Bādha* (contradiction). The first view is that a person is allowed to resort to the *āśramas* one after another in order and he is not supposed to accept any other *āśrama* without the completion of the previous one. This is of the opinion of Āpastamba (*Āp Dh Sū* II. 9.21). The second view is *Vikalpa* in which one is allowed to accept any of the stages of life after the completion of student life (*Vā Dh Sū* VII. 3). This is also found in *Yājñavalkya Smṛti* (IV. 56) where it prescribes an option : one may resort to the ascetic life either after the household life or after the hermit life. The last view is *Bādha* which gives an impression that there is only one *āśrama*, i.e., the *gṛhastha* and rest of the *āśramas* are inferior to this (*Gau. Sū*. III. 1.35).

To conclude, I have tried to establish that there were always four *āśramas* in ancient time, for which the evidence has already been shown. The second point that I have tried to make is that there was perhaps, not sequential regidity. However, I feel, Manu seems to be more correct for putting those *āśramas* in sequences. Because without completing the earlier stage of life, if one goes for accepting the next one, there is a chance of diversity of mind and as a consequence, he may lose to achieve his goal. So, to me, the sequential order as Manu has given, appears to be more justifiable.

Notes and References

1. There lies a controversy about the classification of *Dharma*. From the *Puranic* source (like *Matsyapurāṇa* 144. 30, 31; *Vāyupurāṇa* 59. 31-32, 39), there is an evidence that *Dharma* is of two types : (1) *Śrauta* and *Smārta*. *Mahābhārata* (*Anuśāsanaparva* 141.65; *Vanaparva* 207.87) gives an impression of classifying it into three : (1) *Śrauta*, (2) *Smārta* and (3) *Śiṣṭācāra*. Medhātithi held it as five: (1) *Varṇadharma*, (2) *Āśramadharma*, (3) *Varṇāśramadharma*, (4) *Naimittikadharma* and (5) *Guṇadharma* (Medhātithi's *Bāṣya* on *Man*. II. 25). *Mitākṣarā* finds it as six with an addition of *Sādhāraṇadharma* to the above mentioned five (*Mitākṣarā* on *Yājñavalkya Smṛti* 1.1).
2. Modi, P.M., "Development of the system of *āśramas*", *Proceedings and Transactions of Seventh All India Oriental Conference*, Baroda, 1935, pp. 315-16.
3. *Śāṅkarabhāṣya* on *Chāndogya Upaniṣad* II. 3.1.

4. *Ibid.*
5. *Kecid āhur na sanyāsa āśramāntaram atraivāntarbhāvo ' syeti darśayitum. Sa ca kasmin. Gṛhasthe ' ntarbhāvitaḥ. Gṛhe hi vāsastasya,* Medhātithi's *Bhāṣya* on *Man.* VI. 87.
6. *Brahmacaryaṁ parisamāpya gṛhī bhavet, gṛhī bhūtvā vanī bhavet, vanī bhūtvā pravrajet. Yadi vetarathā brahmacaryād eva pravrajet gṛhād vā vanād veti,* *Jāvālopaniṣad* - IV.
7. *Catvārś caturṇām pāragā vedānāṃ prāg uttamāt traya āśramiṇaḥ. Pṛthagdharmavidas traya etān daśāvarān pariṣad ity ācakṣate. Gau Sū.* 7. 47.